NEW PRODUCT DEVELOPMENT

The Portable MBA Series

The Portable MBA Series provides managers, executives, professionals, and students with a "hands-on," easy-to-access overview of the ideas and information covered in a typical Masters of Business Administration program. The published and forthcoming books in the program are:

Published

The Portable MBA (0-471-61997-3, cloth; 0-471-54895-2, paper) Eliza G.C. Collins and Mary Anne Devanna

The Portable MBA Desk Reference (0-471-57681-6) Paul A. Argenti

The Portable MBA in Finance and Accounting (0-471-53226-6) John Leslie Livingstone

The Portable MBA in Management (0-471-57379-5) Allan R. Cohen

The Portable MBA in Marketing (0-471-54728-X) Alexander Hiam and Charles Schewe

New Product Development: Managing and Forecasting for Strategic Success (0-471-57226-8) Robert J. Thomas

Real-Time Strategy: Improving Team-Based Planning for a Fast-Changing World (0-471-58564-5) Lee Tom Perry, Randall G. Stott, and W. Norman Smallwood

Forthcoming

The Portable MBA in Economics (0-471-59526-8) Philip K.Y. Young and John McCauley

The Portable MBA in Entrepreneurship (0-471-57780-4) William Bygrave

The Portable MBA in Global Business Leadership (0-471-30410-7) Noel Tichy, Michael Brimm, and Hiro Takeuchi

The Portable MBA in Strategy (0-471-58498-3) Liam Fahey and Robert Randall

Analyzing the Balance Sheet (0-471-59191-2) John Leslie Livingstone

Information Technology and Business Strategy (0-471-59659-0) N. Venkatraman and James E. Short

Negotiating Strategically (0-471-1321-8) Roy Lewicki and Alexander Hiam

The New Marketing Concept (0-471-59576-4) Frederick E. Webster

Psychology for Leaders (0-471-59755-4) Dean Tjosvold and Mary Tjosvold

Total Quality Management: Strategies and Techniques Proven at Today's Most Successful Companies (0-471-59538-1) Arnold Weimerskirch and Stephen George

NEW PRODUCT DEVELOPMENT

Managing and Forecasting for Strategic Success

Robert J. Thomas

John Wiley & Sons, Inc.

New York • Chichester • Brisbane • Toronto • Singapore

Copyright © 1993 by Robert J. Thomas
Published by John Wiley & Sons, Inc.

Library of Congress Cataloging-in-Publication Data

Thomas, Robert J.
    New product development : managing and forecasting for strategic
success / Robert J. Thomas.
        p.   cm. – (The Portable MBA series)
    Includes bibliographical references and indexes.
    ISBN 0-471-57226-8
    1. New products–Management.   2. New products–Marketing–
–Forecasting.   I. Title.   II. Series.
HF5415. 153. T48   1993
658.5'75–dc20

                                                                93-15395

*This book is dedicated to my parents,
Joseph H. and Mary M. Thomas,
who taught me the value of learning.*

Preface

Intense global competition, rapid technological change, and shifting patterns of world market opportunities compel firms to continually develop new products and services—if not for profit, at least for survival. However, the high risk of failure in new product development is legendary. Organizations often cling to their past successes to reduce their chance of failing. For these organizations, *new product development* means launching limited extensions of their own successful products, imitating successful competitors, or acquiring firms with new products. They often regard truly innovative products as serendipitous.

The ironic consequence of an organization's entrenchment in the face of turbulent market environments may be a string of ill-fated "me-too" products that fail to provide the needed long-term strategic advantage that more innovative firms enjoy. The business press constantly reports stories of firms that fail to respond to market changes in a timely fashion with truly new products. It should be apparent that new product development is an inherently *unstable* activity in most organizations—when market conditions pressure a new product response, the change necessary to bring about the new product interferes with the organization's natural tendency to maintain stability. How an organization chooses to respond to this state of tension defines the problem of new product development.

Naturally, numerous prescriptions have been offered to meet the challenges of new product development. Some books advise reducing the cycle time required to develop a new product so as to meet competition more quickly. Others recommend embracing project management, designating a product champion, or forming cross-functional teams. Still others suggest following the best practices in an industry, becoming customer driven, or employing total quality management. At best, these prescriptions are partial formulas for success; more realistically, they are tools that may work in some situations, but not others. At worst, these prescriptions can further restrict an organization's ability to respond to a market, thereby closing out opportunities to develop truly innovative products.

NEW PRODUCT DEVELOPMENT REQUIRES
INTELLECTUAL DISCIPLINE

How then can organizational resistance be overcome and new products developed that are responsive to turbulent environments and uncertain markets? The major thesis of this book is that successful new product development is a continual process of organizational renewal that requires an intellectual discipline to drive four major activities: *conceptualizing* the strategic factors in new product development, *managing* the process dictated by these factors, *forecasting* the value of the new product, and *implementing* the new product marketing program with proper attention to detail. This intellectual discipline must be shared among an organization's members, and it must be flexible enough to provide the acuity to respond to opportunities and threats, yet rigorous enough to maintain strategic focus for long-run success.

Because of the highly situational nature of business, every organization may define the intellectual approach to new product development differently. In fact, how an organization defines it becomes a source of competitive advantage. Further, whatever perspective is adopted, it must be *learned* by all organization members, especially those empowered to participate in new product development, so that they can respond to rapid environmental, market, and organizational shifts from the same cognitive orientation.

Although this thesis may appear intuitively obvious, the new product development tradition remains prescription-oriented, often ignoring the highly situational and strategic nature of the process. For example, reducing cycle time is often presumed to be absolutely essential for new product success. Yet, the benefits of cycle time reduction may not outweigh the costs; and if they do, how should the development process be designed and implemented? To answer such questions, a host of strategic issues relating cycle time changes to the organization's current practices, its environment, its customers, its competitors, and other stakeholders must be evaluated. To launch a cycle time reduction program without thinking through strategic implications may only increase the risk of failure.

EMPHASIS ON MANAGING AND FORECASTING

As developed in this book, the intellectually driven activities of *managing* and *forecasting* are central to implementing a shared conceptual approach to new product development. Managing and forecasting new product development are viewed as parallel, interactive processes that connect an organization with its environment. Managerial processes involve decisions about developing the new product, whereas forecasting processes provide relevant information about the *value* of a new product project from inception to implementation; both link the organization with its market environment.

Managerial decisions in new product development connect resource allocations with strategic outcomes. How does one determine which of several new product projects to develop for greatest return? How does one evaluate which of numerous alternative product concepts to pursue? How does one decide when to enter a market with a new product or when to terminate a product without regret during its development? Or decide when to institute a program to reduce cycle time of development? These types of questions require reliable information on how major stakeholders in the organization and the environment might respond to the new product—hence the need for a reliable forecasting process.

Continuous output from a new product forecasting process—a set of *new product forecasts*—ought to be available at any time during the course of a new product development project to enhance its management. The size and growth rate of the market opportunity over a reasonable planning period; expected sales response from one or more new product concepts (given different levels of marketing effort); estimates of organizational costs, risks, and time to develop the new product over the planning period; and profit estimates that can guide market entry and timing decisions are major forecasts needed to analyze the numerous strategic issues that might arise during new product development.

The absence of any historical record of sales data for the new product often makes it difficult to obtain new product forecasts. Further, performance estimates (often arrived at by judgment) vary considerably throughout the development of the new product. This variation is due in part to the learning that takes place during new product development—especially learning about the many factors, internal and external to the firm, that will affect the new product's performance. In this book, numerous sets of factors—organized into a conceptual framework that facilitates learning—provide the foundation for developing the critical measures of new product performance. In effect, the best way to improve new product development and forecasting is to focus on the *processes* that generate them, not the products or forecasts themselves.

MAJOR FEATURES OF THE BOOK

The 12 chapters of this book make up a set of guidelines that reflect major aspects of new product development. They are organized into four major parts according to the conceptualizing, managing, forecasting, and implementing activities of new product development. The first four chapters, Part 1, conceptualize the *strategic, environmental, market,* and *organizational* factors in new product development. The next two chapters, Part 2, emphasize the *management* and *decision support* activities necessary for new product development and forecasting. The next three chapters, Part 3, focus on the interaction of new product development and forecasting processes to estimate market opportunity, assess market response with sales forecasts, and establish financial control. The last three chapters of the book, Part 4, pertain to implementing a new product development plan. Test marketing, market entry decisions, and launching and tracking the new product and its marketing program are major activities essential for success.

Three levels of modeling implement the logic of the book. The first level is conceptual modeling of major sets of critical factors that stimulate a comprehensive view of new product development. The second level is the development of managerial spreadsheet models that operationalize relevant aspects of the conceptual model—usually in terms of variables and formulas that are comfortable to managers. The third level extends major variables of the spreadsheet models into more comprehensive response function modeling; that is, models that establish relationships between managerial decision variables and market response. These models are discussed in a nontechnical way, but with technical references where necessary. The three levels of modeling enhance managerial decisions and provide an intellectual discipline that drives the development of successful new products and achievement of forecasts.

Other features of the book's structure are summarized in the following list.

- The approach is sufficiently generic to cover new consumer and industrial products, as well as new services and major new technologies.

- To illustrate the various factors and modeling approaches, numerous examples and case studies are compiled from a wide variety of industries and situations, including products and services marketed to individuals, households, and organizations.

- The orientation is pragmatic, designed for managers—however, citations from the academic literature provide references for reader convenience.

- The writing style is intended to be highly readable in order to reach a variety of audiences. This is not a technical book, but the logic of the most important techniques (for example, diffusion models, conjoint analysis) is presented.

- In the presentation of the material, text is preferred to exhibits, though the latter are used to clarify complex issues. For example, the conceptual approach used in the book is presented in a boxed diagram in the first chapter and used as a reference point for diagrams in subsequent chapters.

- *Diagnostic* lists help to demonstrate the application of certain concepts and approaches.

THE READER

Anyone engaged in the problems of developing new products and achieving their forecasts will find this book of interest. Such individuals might include top-level executives in organizations developing new products, and managers involved in planning, developing, and forecasting new products. Although analysts and marketing research specialists will not find all possible methodologies useful to new product development and forecasting in this book, they will find that it provides a coherent logic within which to consider their industry-specific approaches and methodological preferences.

Consultants involved in framing new product problems for their clients, as well as entrepreneurs and venture capitalists involved in startup businesses relying on one or more new products, will also find the book of interest. Last, but not least, faculty members and students in the academic community who study problems of new product development and forecasting will find that the book complements more traditional product management textbooks on the subject. A class-tested syllabus for an MBA or executive education course on new product development, using this book and recommended cases, is available from the author.

ACKNOWLEDGMENTS

I am indebted to a number of people who have been instrumental in the development of this book, both directly and indirectly. Most importantly, I have been very fortunate to have known two individuals over the years who have been my professors, advisors, colleagues, and friends. I am especially indebted to Professor John B. Stewart, who shaped my early thinking about business, marketing, and new product development, and stimulated me to investigate complex problems in pragmatic ways. Professor Jerry Wind has had an enormous influence on my approach to the field of marketing, never failing to share with me his enthusiasm, energy, and intellectual approach on a spectrum of ideas and methods. His book, *Product Policy*, was a valuable source of information and inspiration on the problems of new product development.

I am very grateful to Dean Robert S. Parker of the Georgetown University School of Business, who has provided a climate in the Business School that continually supports faculty scholarship. His encouragement and advice have guided me through important stages of my career at Georgetown and I continue to value his friendship. I am also grateful to Associate Dean and Professor William G. Droms who greatly contributed to my understanding of key financial aspects of new product development as an investment project. He has also been a wise counselor on matters relating to book publishing and numerous other facets of faculty life.

I would like to sincerely thank Professor Vijay Mahajan, who read the entire manuscript and provided numerous comments and ideas that enhanced the overall quality of the book. Professor William B. Gartner made valuable contributions to many parts of the book, including reviews and comments on the material and, as coauthor on a study about accuracy in new product forecasting, some findings that are cited in this book. Professor James J. Angel carefully reviewed the chapter on financial forecasting and provided valuable comments. Professor George S. Yip has been an extremely supportive colleague throughout the writing of this book.

Over the years, I have benefited immeasurably from working on a variety of business projects with outstanding people. Since we met in 1981, Dr. Steven L. Diamond has been most influential in helping me bridge the gap between business and academia. His mastery of both worlds represents an unusual combination of talent and expertise from which I continue to learn and benefit.

The process of writing this book was greatly enhanced by the opportunity to present selected material and models to Georgetown MBA students who have taken my New Product Development course over the past three years. I am especially appreciative to those students in the MBA Class of 1993 who took the course and from whom I learned a great deal.

I would like to thank John Mahaney for his patience and guidance in the development of this book—a *new product development* project unto itself. He was particularly helpful in shaping the *core concept* of the book. I would also like to convey a special *thank you* to Emily P. McNamara who was instrumental in "fine tuning" the book.

Finally, and most importantly, I would like to thank my wife Bettee-Aynn, who gave up countless hours of our being together while I was buried in this project, and yet who could always be counted on to provide the necessary working environment to complete it. Her role as a sounding board, a catalyst, and the world's greatest *organizer* has kept this project on track right up to its launch.

Contents

Structuring New Product Development

1 Why New Product Development?

New products often glow with such promise, and their forecasts ring with such authentic precision, that entire business strategies defining an organization's future are built upon them. Consider the following examples:

- Predicted rapid market acceptance of a new computer work station promises to lift a manufacturer's technological reputation to new heights.
- Projected profits from a new line of health beverages suggest that a food company and its stock price will be raised out of the doldrums.
- Anticipated broad adoption of an innovative user-friendly computer telephone by customers makes a large financial services firm confident that it can implement its customer relationship strategy.
- Expected sales of a breakthrough enzyme described in the prospectus of a new biotechnology venture indicate substantial financial return to investors.

Unfortunately, the rosy expectations for business strategies based on new products don't always match the reality after product launch.

Ideas for new products arrive from any number of sources—the scientist in the laboratory, the inventor who walks through the door, the irritated customer, or a competitor's innovation. Key managers think the idea looks good and, with their best judgment and other data sources, generate forecasts for their planning documents that predict impressive market and financial performance for the new product opportunity. Top-line sales and bottom-line profits over the next five years appear great, and the heady atmosphere of promised success motivates a *go* decision to organize a team to develop the new product.

But soon after top management approves the project on paper, things seem to bog down. Weeks go by before the *right people* can be brought together in a team to discuss the next steps to proceed. Different parts of the organization

3

assemble to discuss plans for the new product, but there are disagreements about responsibilities. Some individuals even argue openly against the need for a new product, especially when current products are successful and everyone is busy with them.

In time, people from marketing, research and development (R&D), and manufacturing—who initially cannot resolve their differences about design features and how best to ensure quality—finally reach a compromise. Time seems to be of the essence, so outsiders are brought in to figure ways to speed up the development process. Other outsiders are brought in to conduct market research that might be useful in defining and positioning the new product and helping to forecast demand.

Eventually a prototype of the new product idea, perhaps favorably received at a trade show, becomes the design for the final product. While heated discussions about the best marketing approach for the new product are going on, recent research is brought in that suggests adding some previously omitted features to improve market acceptance. This input kindles a controversy over whether to ignore the new features and launch on schedule or postpone market entry.

Shortly after a delayed new product launch, cracks in the crystal ball used to forecast success begin to surface. At first they appear as hairline cracks. The sales force meets resistance from key members in the channels of distribution. Potential customers buy the new product with the improved features, but more slowly than anticipated. The ads do not run as scheduled, but with luck they can be rescheduled. Production problems occur with the first full run. Shipments arrive late. Sales recorded in the first three months are not nearly as high as hoped.

Unexpectedly, the business environment becomes turbulent. Rumors of an even newer technology threaten to make the just-launched product obsolete. Reports of higher interest rates circulate in the business community, causing consumer uncertainty. A few competitors respond more aggressively than ever before, almost desperately. Sales still do not materialize as forecast. The hairline cracks in the crystal ball now look like deep fissures.

Near the end of the first year of the new product's life, the gap between actual and predicted sales threatens the viability of the entire project. Stockholders hear about the poor performance of the new product from the business press. They begin to exert pressure on management to cut losses. The once precise and rosy forecast is now revised downward. Blame and acrimony are rife among the people involved with the project. The excitement of the new program drains from the organization.

Upon reflection, would anticipating factors that influence a new product's development and forecasts have resulted in different decisions, more realistic expectations, and improved market performance? For example, could the product have been designed differently? Could the severity of competitive reaction have been foreseen? Could slower acceptance of the new product have been expected? Could manufacturing and marketing have been better coordinated to avoid delays? Should the product launch have been delayed to include the additional features? These questions and others raise important issues about managing and forecasting new product development for strategic success—and they are not hypothetical questions.

THE REALITY OF NEW PRODUCT DEVELOPMENT

Compaq Computer Corporation, founded in 1982, rose to success by producing IBM-compatible personal computers.[1] Sales grew from $111 million in 1983, the first full year of operation, to over $3 billion by 1991! Compaq became the first company to be placed on the *Fortune* 500 list in less than four years. In the new and dynamic personal computer market, its strategy relied on being first to offer a continual stream of premium quality new products with the latest technology. Throughout the 1980s it achieved many new product triumphs, including the first practical transportable personal computer and the first really successful notebook-sized computer. Its personal computers included state-of-the-art technology, and it prided itself in maintaining the leading edge ahead of IBM during the period of rapid market growth of the 1980s. In all measures of performance, Compaq could be described as an organization that achieved success through new product development.

In a 1990 interview article in the *Harvard Business Review*, the CEO of Compaq, Rod Canion, provided insights into the new product development process within the organization. Much of the success emanated from the company's corporate culture, which stressed *teamwork* and *consensus*—concepts deemed important, and validated with stories and experiences from the so-called "Japanese style" of management. Mr. Canion's own words best describe the role of new product development within the firm:[2]

> The whole new-product cycle from the concept definition, research phase, design, testing, and into manufacturing has been the heart of the company's success. It's the foundation of everything else.... The reason for it, I believe, is our use of a process that doesn't rely on luck or the vision of just one or two people.
>
> Our process involves a team that deals with new product ideas.... But it's not just a matter of focusing on a specific product. The team also deals with long range strategic issues....

The process certainly carried Compaq to a preeminent position in the industry.

But intensive competition and the economic slowdown beginning in the 1990s brought a new reality to Compaq's success story. Sales and profits declined dramatically in 1991. As Mr. Canion remarked, almost prophetically, about new product development under conditions of rapid market growth in his 1990 interview:[3]

> I would say that growth *hides* all ills.... But depending on growth as the antibiotic for whatever ails you will eventually get you into serious trouble. In fact, growth can be a disease rather than a cure. We're trying to manage growth, and whether or not it's fatal, by managing the culture.

Unfortunately, the impatience of Compaq's directors prevented Mr. Canion from continuing his approach to managing the business. In a reported management change by the board of directors that was said to resemble a palace coup, Mr. Canion was replaced by a new CEO who moved the business in a different strategic direction.

The new strategic direction was also driven by new product development; however, it was not at the premium end of the market—Compaq's bastion of success—but rather at the low-price end. Intense pressure from competitors that built good quality personal computers from largely off-the-shelf components and sold them directly to buyers through mail order stimulated rapid price erosion in the market. Even large corporate buyers found it hard to justify the price differentials between a computer from Dell Computer Corporation and one from Compaq or IBM. Compaq's share began to decline.

Although Mr. Canion had prepared a plan to turn the business around, the chairman of the board and certain organizational members were impatient to develop a new line of less expensive Compaq models. However, to do so ran counter to the Compaq culture, which was based on very high-quality components and assembly. Reportedly, Compaq's chairman recruited two of the firm's mid-level managers to attend, incognito, the computer industry trade show. There they discovered they could source components for a personal computer that could be developed and launched quickly, be price competitive with the clones, and yet still retain a reasonably good level of quality. Nonetheless, a decision to develop a low-priced line of computers could risk jeopardizing the Compaq brand image of high quality.

At the board meeting in which Mr. Canion was ousted and a new president appointed, the new low-priced line was ultimately approved and assigned to an independent business unit for development. The decision to use an off-site independent group was motivated by the belief that Compaq's existing new product development process and consensual decision-making style could not adapt to the speed and quality requirements of the new project. The new group broke with traditional product design rules and supplier relations to build the lowest-cost unit possible. They sought to meet levels of quality that were not as stringent as traditional Compaq requirements, yet satisfactory for market needs.

The existing Compaq organization bristled at the new project, especially when they recognized that bids for components and assembly were being sought outside the company. With their jobs apparently at risk, current Compaq managers requested the opportunity to bid on the new line, and discovered they could be price competitive internally if they made the necessary quality compromises. They did, and the new production line turned out a new computer in a minute—about one-eighth the time of the old line!

Launched in mid-June 1992, the Compaq ProLinea line quickly achieved success. Sales and market share for Compaq rebounded. Reportedly, even sales of its traditional line of computers were not cannibalized, partly because of price cuts in those lines. Demand was so great that new production lines had to be quickly established. The new strategy appeared to bring immediate success. But could the old strategy have been so wrong, and the new one so right?

Couldn't price reductions on the existing lines of products have achieved the same outcome? Why then choose new product development to change strategic direction?

STRATEGIC REASONS FOR NEW PRODUCT DEVELOPMENT

As revealed in the Compaq situation, an organization's products and services are among its most visible assets (or liabilities). Products link a firm with its *stakeholders*—organizations and individuals that include its customers, suppliers, owners, employees, regulators, and others interested in the firm's performance. How an organization interacts with the stakeholders in its business environment through its current and planned portfolio of products in large part defines its *business strategy*. New products are therefore the basis for a variety of strategic reasons that define an organization's direction.

New Products Can Be a Source of Competitive Advantage

Business strategy entails the development of a sustainable competitive advantage in selected market segments.[4] A sustainable advantage generates value from invested resources to facilitate future investment—in theory, a time-based process of continual renewal. The essence of strategy combines decisions about *ends* (goals or directions to pursue) and *means* (how to achieve the goals through resource allocation). Because an organization defines itself by the products it offers to the markets it chooses to serve over a planning horizon, *new* products provide a means to achieve its goals.

In the Compaq case, five founders developed within eight years a world-class organization with sales of over $3 billion and a reputation as a premier manufacturer of personal computers. The business sustained itself through launching innovative, high-quality products. The ability to charge premium prices generated high margins that could be reinvested into other new products in a constant cycle of revitalization.

A *new product* is a multidimensional concept with need-satisfying capabilities not previously experienced by the stakeholders interested in it.[5] The concept offers some form of *value* to all relevant stakeholders. The degree to which something has not been previously experienced—or its *innovativeness*—can range from incremental improvements (*extension* products) to significant advances (*breakthrough* products). Extension products, which often require fewer resources and entail lower risk than breakthrough products, tend to constitute the bulk of a firm's portfolio of new product development projects. They run the gamut from simple renovations (cosmetic changes) to a strategy of incremental innovation that might eventually lead to a major breakthrough. Whether a new product is an extension or a breakthrough, the implied promise that it will lead to a sustainable competitive advantage lures firms to use the path of new product development as a means to strategically manage a business.

New Products Can Provide Opportunities for Reinforcing or Changing Strategic Direction

New products can be used to *reinforce* a firm's strategic direction by enhancing its competitive advantage in the market. New products developed for this purpose are typically *extensions* or *me-too* versions of existing products that introduce additional features to accommodate changing buyer or market needs. Such products emerge from new product development processes that emphasize incremental innovations and constant improvement. For example, Compaq's earlier strategy of continually incorporating the most advanced microchip technology to rapidly process data and video enabled it to be first-to-market with the next generation *new and improved* personal computers. These new products could be used to keep customers from moving to a competitor—a defensive move—or to attract new potential buyers from competitors—an offensive move.[6]

Me-too products that copy successful competitors are typically new for the firm, but not new to the market. For example, the development of the ProLinea line of personal computers was new for Compaq, but not necessarily for the market. Clearly this new product offering could have been viewed as a defensive move to keep Dell from taking market share from corporate customers. Alternatively, the company's decision to launch a new line of printers may be viewed as an offensive move to capitalize on the current base of Compaq computer users. Not all me-too products are straight copies—they often provide marginally improved features, and in some cases leap-frog to a new generation of products that reinforce the firm's competitive advantage in a targeted market.

New products can also be used to *change* an organization's competitive advantage. Although this sometimes happens by chance, more often than not it is the result of a process of continually listening to the market and its major stakeholders. Recognizing when new market segments emerge can create the opportunity for a new product. Working closely with *lead users* and listening to their problems and concerns can give an early indication of a shift in the needs and problems of potential buyers.[7] The resulting new product(s) can lead to a fundamental change in the way the market is viewed and subsequently change the organization's entire basis for competitive advantage.

For example, considering each new entry alone, it may be tempting to view Compaq's new products as extensions to reinforce a basic business strategy. However, in response to a changing market environment, Compaq appeared to be engineering a major change in strategic direction—from one that depended on high unit margins with highly innovative, premium-quality products to one that depended on higher-volume, lower-profit-margin competitive products. When a competitive strategy is based on lower price, and the resulting lower unit margins, continued total profit growth depends on an expanded procession of new products and markets willing to buy them. In fact, Compaq's launch of its ProLinea line was accompanied by some 41 new product announcements, and promises of more to come.

In effect, Compaq's strategic change was broad, pervading all aspects of the business. Its performance depended on the new low-priced ProLinea line, lower prices for existing models (through cost reductions), and the continual launch of a broader portfolio of related new products. With this strategy lower unit margins are traded for larger volume and total profit. Although price, expanded distribution, extensive promotion, and publicity all contributed, new products played a pivotal role in implementing Compaq's major strategic change.

New Products Can Enhance Corporate Image

The launch of a new product or family of products can enhance or detract from a firm's corporate image among its stakeholders. As illustrated in the Compaq case, the business press does not hesitate to build articles around performance-related issues that can affect stakeholder perceptions. The potential effects of these articles on stock price, managerial morale, and future decisions for a product can be substantial. For example, the business press pointed to Xerox's 1990 launch of its Docutech line of products as a vehicle for helping to refurbish the company's image.[8] They reported that after developing many computer industry innovations, Xerox had difficulty capitalizing on them. Further, over the years the firm reportedly lost market share to more efficient Japanese producers in its main business, stand-alone copiers.

The new Docutech products could deliver the capability to receive all types of input (paper documents, mail, graphics, computer information, and so on) and transform and redistribute it according to need. The extent to which the Xerox image benefits from the new products depends, of course, on market response. The purchase process for such machines by organizations is complex, because it involves many different functions—copying, fax, local area networks of personal computers, laser printing, and so on. Further, competitive reactions, implementation of the new product through the current sales force, and other factors also potentially affect market response. Therefore, ensuring the successful development of such units and anticipating their demand represented a challenge to Xerox. The forecasts and results (which were favorable) were not only tied to critical decisions about the future of the product line, but affected corporate image as well.

New Products Can Provide Long-Term
Financial Return on Investment

Part of Compaq's reason for launching the new ProLinea line of personal computers was concern for long-term return on investment, especially to stockholders. Similarly, business conditions in the late 1980s compelled the Marriott Corporation to restructure its business strategy in support of its long-term financial situation. The corporation decided to concentrate on the hotel business and exit the in-flight catering and restaurant businesses. In addition, it decided to invest an estimated $1 billion (over time) to launch a new line of "life-care" facilities as a source of future revenue and returns.

Life-care facilities, targeted to senior citizens, provide an apartment, meals, varying levels of nursing care, and other services for a monthly rent or alternative payment methods.[9] The decision to enter this market, however, was not made lightly, and required substantial research to forecast critical financial values for a new service concept yet to be constructed.[10] The idea for a life-care facility had to be translated into working concepts, for which segments of consumers could express preferences. In addition to the numerous amenities that would accompany such a service, the concepts were defined to include trade-offs of these amenities for various payment and pricing plans that would lead to estimates of revenue response.[11] To obtain profit and return estimates, the company also needed cost and cash outlay forecasts.

The research ultimately produced estimates of market size, sales response, costs, profitability, and cash flow over a time horizon. Consequently, the critical strategic decision to enter the life-care market depended in large part on the forecasted financials for the new service over a multi-year planning horizon. Of course, the substantial importance of this new project to the firm's future, as well as the sizable financial stake, compelled executives to invest in making sure the forecasts were solid. Since the decision to *go* with the project, Marriott has developed several successful life-care units; however, time will tell how good the long-term forecasts and investment decisions were.

New Products Can Capitalize on R&D

Organizations vary in the amount of resources they allocate to research and development (R&D), as well as in their actual R&D source(s). Some maintain their own R&D capability to support new products, some "borrow" from others who precede them in the market, some engage in strategic alliances or research consortia, and some do all of the above. Maintaining an R&D capability does not guarantee success, but coupling it with a strong new product development proficiency can benefit the organization in numerous ways. For example, from its R&D capability, Upjohn Co. developed minoxidil, a drug for treating high blood pressure. During the 1970s, researchers accidentally discovered that minoxidil grew hair. Upjohn then applied to the Food and Drug Administration (FDA) for use of the drug in topical applications and received approval in August 1988.[12]

Supported by a comprehensive new product development process, Upjohn launched Rogaine in September 1988 as the nation's first prescribed treatment for hair loss. Market potential for the product included 30 million men and 20 million women in the United States. The product proved most successful in clinical trials among young men just balding. Like other prescription drugs, Rogaine is sold only through physicians. The product does not necessarily work for all who use it, and when it does, application of Rogaine must be continuous. Although the market for Rogaine will be slow to develop because consumers must gain education and experience before using it on a regular basis, it nevertheless shows the potential to capitalize on an existing base of technology with new products.

New Products Can Utilize Production and Operations Resources

An organization not operating at capacity may be able to improve its utilization in a number of ways, but one common approach is to develop new products. This technique is obvious for manufacturing firms with fixed plant and equipment (such as automobile firms), but it applies to service operations as well. For example, delivery service firms like Federal Express and United Parcel Service have been able to leverage their operations by adding new products to their original lines. In addition to its original "priority overnight" letter delivery service (next business morning), Federal Express now has a "standard overnight" service (next business afternoon), an "economy two-day" service (second business day), a "freight service" for extra-large packages, and customized delivery services for government and other organizations that use the company frequently (for such things as overnight delivery of flowers, computer parts, and so on).

New Products Can Leverage Marketing/Brand Equity

Organizations that have used their marketing programs to build equity in a brand name can use new products to further capitalize on their investment. Marketing programs are typically defined by selected market segments, each with a positioning strategy, specific product features to meet segment needs, pricing, advertising, sales promotion, sales force, distribution, and customer service decisions. If the marketing program fits market segment needs better than the competition and (over time) attracts a loyal base of customers who perceive value in the brand's name, then an opportunity exists to extend new products under that name.

For example, much of the success of the new ProLinea line of lower-priced personal computers derived from Compaq's high-quality brand name. Ocean Spray used its quality name in cranberry products to launch grapefruit and other juice beverages. The success of the Toyota Motor Corp.'s Lexus LS-400 automobile provided an umbrella of opportunity to apply the Lexus name to subsequent models. One was a two-door sports car model, and the other a less expensive four-door sedan that was launched as "the next Lexus," an obvious play on the success of the LS-400.

Hewlett-Packard, which has achieved considerable success with its line of highly reliable laser printers (and earlier, calculators), has not only extended its name to fax machines, but has launched an innovative service agreement called the "HP SupportPack."[13] The new service agreement is packaged in a shrink-wrapped box that consumers can pick up from a shelf, thereby providing tangibility to an intangible. The agreement is spelled out in easy-to-read language and promises that if the printer breaks within its first three years, and can't be fixed over the phone, Hewlett-Packard will send a new printer overnight. The buyer then sends the broken printer back at Hewlett-Packard's expense. The cost of the service varies by product, but is estimated at about 10 to 15 percent of the original purchase price of the printer. The brand equity in the Hewlett-Packard name provided immediate credibility to this new service concept. Of course, because new products can also strain the credibility of the existing brand and jeopardize the entire business, the practice of using established brand names on new products must be carefully managed.[14]

New Products Can Affect Human Resources

Successful new products can create jobs and provide opportunities for career development. Compaq's success with the ProLinea line not only created jobs, but also reinvigorated the current work force. Although the need to add personnel throughout the development process and after launch can be positive, the consequences of new product forecasts that are not achieved—or even ones that are overachieved—can be costly in both dollar and human terms.

Clearly, the jobs of all personnel added for a new product project are at risk if it does not achieve its forecast. However, Apple Computer, Inc. provides an example that reveals a more profound and perverse set of risks—one that is a result of selling more than expected. In October 1990 Apple launched a new line of lower-priced MacIntosh computers. Customers responded enthusiastically to the new machines. Apple markedly increased its overall share of the personal computer market. The consequence of this success, though, was a significant erosion in Apple's profitability because the new computers had lower prices and profit margins.

From September 1990 to May 1991, Apple added 1,000 new workers to its payroll, primarily in product development and manufacturing to support the new computers. However, in mid-May, Apple announced plans to cut back its entire workforce by 10 percent, or about 1,500 personnel. What happened? Reportedly, Apple disclosed on May 1 "the shift to lower-priced computers occurred more quickly than it expected."[15] Apparently, the forecast of growth rate for the new line was low; the unexpectedly rapid profit erosion led to the employee cutback. In this case, the undesired consequence of a successful new product (albeit with poor forecasting) was not only lost jobs, but also potential morale problems among remaining employees.

Summarizing the Strategic Role of New Product Development

The eight strategic reasons or *bases* for new product development briefly reviewed in the preceding sections provide an indication of its potential role in an organization's long-run performance and survival. Further, they reveal that new product development cuts across critical organizational functions. Although those eight are not the only reasons to engage in new product development, the list should be kept in mind throughout the book because (1) it helps define the importance of new product development to the organization (and/or of a specific new product development project), (2) it is the basis for defining clear goals for new product development, and (3) it provides a preliminary set of criteria against which new product decisions can be made.

The table below illustrates how to begin clarifying the role of new product development in an organization. For example, in each cell of the table, the role that a new product development function might play in a specific organization can be written down. It should be consistent with an organization's overall mission, objectives, and goals. Note that the eight strategic reasons merely symbolize possible bases for defining importance, goals, and decision criteria. A related subset of financial goals, marketing goals, R&D goals, and so on can be specified to further clarify the role of new product development for each strategic reason. Other strategic bases not listed might include, for example, an organization's commitment to social responsibility or its industry role.

Strategic Bases for Evaluating New Product Development	Clarifying the Role of New Product Development		
	Impor-tance	Goals	Decision Criteria
Establishing competitive advantage			
Changing strategic direction			
Enhancing corporate image			
Improving financial return			
Increasing R&D effectiveness			
Improving utilization of production/operations			
Leveraging marketing effectiveness			
Effectively utilizing human resources			
Other			

PRINCIPLES OF MANAGING NEW PRODUCT DEVELOPMENT

The Compaq situation, discussed previously, raises several questions about managing new product development. How did factors in the market environment affect the new product development effort? Did an organizational culture that produced record-breaking good fortune really become imprisoned by its own success? Could modes of behavior in new product development have been so ingrained that responses to competitors would be too little too late without significant intervention? Or if the organization had been allowed to pursue its strategic course, would it be in a stronger future position? Would it have launched the next generation of premium-quality innovative personal computers with the newest technologies, thus catching the next economic upswing and thereby returning to profitability? The answers to these questions can never be known, but they do point to the need for some guiding principles for managing product development. Like most management processes, new product development is an intellectual process that provides ground rules for determining and allocating resources to achieve success.

New Product Development Should Be *Strategic*

Every business opportunity or problem in which new products play a role will be unique to the situation at hand. The timing, business environment, consumers, competitors, other major stakeholders, and organizational resources represent sets of factors that may be so idiosyncratic to a new product situation that relying on general prescriptions for success can be fatal for the new product. Managing under situational circumstances requires a kind of *strategic* intellectual scope and agility that facilitates response to *uncertain and unexpected* conditions—yet does not stray from the core business strategy without sufficient analysis. Building this strategic intellectual capability into an organization's daily life should become a guiding principle in managing new product development.

Building the necessary intellectual resources depends largely on education and accumulated experience. Although a book about new product development cannot provide direct experience, it can encourage and facilitate a managerial learning process to enhance responsiveness in thinking about new product situations that arise. If a conceptual view of new product development that includes numerous strategic factors defining new product situations is constructed, and if that view is communicated within the organization, the chances of succeeding with a new product in a turbulent business environment are significantly enhanced.

New Product Development Should Be *Flexible*

A key task of managing new product development is linking it to an organization's strategy. This linkage occurs through the typical *situation analyses* that provide the basis for developing strategic options (for example, assessing strengths, weaknesses, opportunities, and problems).[16] As is discussed in Chapter 2, such analyses begin with recognizing major global forces with pervasive trends (such as economic systems, demographics, or technology) that lead to complexity and rapid change, a major source of uncertainty. The improved technology and declining prices of microprocessor chips certainly had dramatic effects on Compaq's business environment. To manage new product development effectively under rapidly changing circumstances requires a development process that has *flexibility* to cope with them. Such flexibility is ensured by a *resource commitment* commensurate with the importance of new product development to the organization. The more resources are available, the greater the flexibility in handling turbulence.

To further clarify flexibility, it is important to distinguish between an organization's new product development *process* and a specific *project* within it. The process consists of the intellectual aspects of new product development that should permeate all aspects of an organization. The project pertains to a specific market opportunity for which a new product is being targeted. For smaller, newer organizations this could be a single product project; for larger organizations it could be multiple product projects carried on simultaneously or over time. Flexibility makes multiple projects possible and facilitates change within a specific project.

New Product Development Should Be *Interactive*

As environments change, so do the needs of various stakeholders within them. Thus, to keep up with these changes, establishing and maintaining an *interactive* relationship with major stakeholders throughout the development process is necessary (to identify and capitalize on market opportunities). In the Compaq case, potential buyers (personal and organizational) found it increasingly difficult to differentiate between more expensive personal computers, like Compaq, and the less expensive clones. Staying close to the customer to discover such changes quickly should be more than a cliché in new product development. Topics for better understanding and interacting with markets are considered in Chapter 3.

New Product Development Should Be *Integrative*

The way in which an organization responds to opportunities for new products determines the success of the development process. Unfortunately, although organizations recognize the need to develop new products, they also tend to resist change—a *new product development paradox* that is discussed further in Chapter 4. This resistance can often be traced to differences in functional departments within an organization, and differences in political coalitions that emerge over time. Motivating the organization to respond to opportunities (and problems) requires an *integration* to occur that overcomes the resistance to change. The most popular vehicle for achieving such integration is building new product development *teams* with strong leaders (or *new product champions*), strong followers, and adequate incentives. For these teams to bring about the needed integration, they should be cross-functional in composition.

New Product Development Should Be *Ongoing*

There is little that is static about new product development. Because environments, markets, and organizations are always changing, so too are their effects on new products. Even for a specific product, constant evolutionary changes occur—up to and beyond the moment of launch. It is therefore important to have a clear view of new product development as an intellectual process shared among organizational members so that program implementation and necessary adjustments (which are so often essential for success) can be made quickly. It is also important to maintain a data base of historical and current information along with a decision support system to facilitate relatively quick analyses and decisions and to resolve differences of opinion that frequently arise. Commitment to this "ongoing" principle recognizes the importance of *learning* throughout new product development and emphasizes the central role of new products in an organization's continual process of *renewal*.

Thus, managing new product development means crafting an intellectual process for the organization that (1) is strategic in its view of business situations (consistent with building a long-term competitive advantage), (2) has adequate resource commitments to sustain flexibility in response to rapidly changing environments, (3) interacts with major market stakeholders (whether personally or through market research) to continuously monitor market opportunities and problems, (4) builds integration within the organization through effectively designed and motivated cross-functional new product teams to bring about the change needed to capitalize on opportunities, and (5) is ongoing in its drive to achieve organizational renewal through successful new products. In effect, managing new product development involves mobilizing critical functions in the organization to respond to the *uncertainties* of complex and rapidly changing markets and environments. An important source of uncertainty reduction is the function of *new product forecasting*—a process that provides critical information.

NEW PRODUCT FORECASTING

New product development tends to be strongly associated with the activities of making the new product or operationalizing the new service. The role of new product forecasting, whenever considered, tends to be a back-burner issue—that is, until a few months or so after launch! The Compaq case reveals the importance of new product forecasting in the performance of an organization relying on new products to carry out strategy. As noted, demand for the new product was strong—the dream of every new product team! However, it was so strong that originally optimistic sales forecasts severely *underestimated* volume. Compaq could not produce enough personal computers to sell to all who wanted to buy them.

Consider the following item at the top of *The Wall Street Journal* front page column, "What's News—Business and Finance," on July 10, 1992, less than one month after the ProLinea launch:

> Compaq is struggling to meet demand for its new ProLinea line of low-cost personal computers. Company officials concede they misread the market, leading to a shortage that has upset many big customers and could jeopardize Compaq's bid to rebound from a disastrous 1991.

Unfortunately, the order backlog persisted. On September 1, 1992, as reported in *The Wall Street Journal*, "Compaq Remains Unable to Meet Demand for New ProLinea Line." Moving into 1993, six months after launch, Compaq still struggled to meet demand for the new product and was vulnerable to new competitive entries. During this time IBM launched its Value Point line of low-priced personal computers and Hewlett-Packard adopted a new, highly competitive pricing strategy for its Vectra line of personal computers. Further, both new and established Compaq dealer relationships strained under the pressure of scarcity. Propitiously, Compaq owned resources to increase production and meet demand; however, it still incurred both direct and opportunity costs (for example, sales lost to competitors). The Compaq product line survives, but for firms that forecast new-product sales volume significantly exceeding actual market demand, the threat of failure looms large.[17]

The Risk of Failing

Because new products can account for as much as one-fourth to one-third of a firm's annual revenues, reliance on the performance of new product forecasts can be critical—especially with the risk of new product failure. A summary of studies reports new product failure rates ranging from 24 percent to 98 percent, with an overall average of 38 percent. The wide variation in estimates may be due to the type of product and other situational factors. For example, average failure rates for consumer versus industrial products were reported at 55 percent and 31 percent, respectively.[18]

As the risks of failure inherent in every new product situation vary, so too do the returns. Balancing investments, risks, and returns is a major criterion in deciding whether or not to proceed with a new product project—the crucial *go/no-go* decision. New product forecasting provides important quantitative information for these types of decisions. Estimates of future sales, costs, investments, market growth, cycle time to develop the new product, and related market response factors contribute to deciding whether or not to continue with a new product project. However, new product forecasting and related marketing research techniques can be expensive, both in time and money; hence the decision to employ them requires careful consideration.

A New Product Barometer

A *new product forecast* defines a set of measures (market share, sales, cost, profit, return on investment, cycle time of development, and so on) that assigns *expected value* to the entire development effort. This value, largely an abstraction until the new product launch, depends on a host of factors, and may fluctuate as a firm proceeds from a new product idea to a full-scale launch program and post-launch sales results. These measures should be obtained from a forecasting process that parallels the new product's development and readily provides estimates for key decisions. In this sense, the forecasts become a *barometer* for a new product at any point in its development. They are measures that distill all that is known about the product's potential for success in the market over a planning horizon, measures that help estimate the sales that draw from competitors, cannibalize an organization's existing products, or attract altogether new potential buyers.

It follows that new product forecasts should be viewed with great care and concern according to the importance of the product to the firm's future. Generally, the more important a new product, service, or technology is to the firm and its future, (1) the greater should be the investment in developing and achieving better quality, more accurate forecasts and (2) the higher the level of corporate executive who should be involved. CEOs might expect that for more important projects, new product forecasts will eventually find their way into the corporate boardroom—if not to show the bright future for the business, then to show achieved results or to explain why expectations were not met.

Although the importance of a new product to a firm's future is a major reason for paying attention to its development and the accuracy of its forecasts, it is not the only one. Another is the uncertainty and turbulence created by an increasingly complex and rapidly changing business environment. Increased complexity and reduced stability of the business environment greatly increase the difficulty of making projections about future market response for new products. For example, the increasing globalization of business has had a profound effect on the behavior of a firm's customers, competitors, and suppliers—who may emerge from any part of the world. The result is a complex array of opportunities and problems that can affect the future performance of a proposed new product.

Although turbulent business environments can wreak havoc on the development of important new products and make forecasting difficult, other major factors also affect the preparation and accuracy of new product forecasts. In particular, *market forces* often slow the acceptance of new products. Consumers may not be ready to change their current patterns of behavior, or competitors may take actions to delay acceptance of the new product. For example, reducing price on an existing technology can slow consumer acceptance of a new one and create uncertainties in realizing demand. In cases where consumer acceptance will be slow, efforts to shorten development time may incur costs without significant benefit.

Finally, conditions within an *organization* can affect the quality and timeliness of a new product's development process. Understanding these conditions can determine if, when, and with what features the new product will enter the market, all of which have a major influence on whether or not the product is purchased. Estimating the uncertain effects of environmental turbulence, market acceptance, and organizational conditions on new products helps shape their final form and performance.

Such is the challenge of new product forecasting. Whatever the difficulty of making new product forecasts—whether they are buried in a business plan or broken out separately—it will be difficult to ignore large gaps between expectation and reality once the new product is launched.

INTEGRATING NEW PRODUCT DEVELOPMENT AND FORECASTING PROCESSES

Thus far it is apparent that new product development can play a vital role in a firm's business strategy and performance. It is also apparent that new products can fail in the face of uncertain business environments. Although new product forecasting processes have the potential to provide continuous information on the expected value of a new product development effort and reduce uncertainty, these processes are not foolproof and can be expensive. Because new product development takes on different roles for different organizations (and even different roles for different products in the same organization), and because different organizations operate in business environments with different levels of uncertainty, a framework for visualizing the integration of new product development and forecasting is needed to put these processes in perspective.

The following table depicts a framework for beginning to think about the integration of new product development and forecasting for an organization, and for allocating resources between these two critical functions. The rows of the table represent a summary indicator of the role of new product development in the organization. More specifically, this indicator can be estimated by the importance of the process (or a specific project) to the organization—for example, an importance ratings scale based on the eight strategic reasons for new product development discussed previously can be used. The columns of the table represent a summary indicator of the uncertainty facing the organization and its new product development process. This indicator can be estimated with a consideration of the organization's business environment, market, and organizational factors (discussed in Chapters 2–4). For purposes of illustration, consider the high versus low dimensions of each of these factors in the following table.

Degree of New Product Importance to Organization	Degree of Environmental, Market, and Organization Uncertainty	
	High Uncertainty	**Low Uncertainty**
High Stakes		
Low Stakes		

High stakes/high uncertainty situations may call for heavy investment of resources in both development and forecasting activities to make sure adequate information is obtained to better fit the new product to the market. Development expenditures are largely for R&D, design, engineering, and related resources, whereas forecasting expenditures are largely for marketing research and related resources. These situations may also call for a very prudent market entry strategy, with careful assessment of any apparent pressures to accelerate development efforts that may compromise quality.

Implications for new products in the other situations are also apparent. High stakes/low uncertainty situations call for greater relative emphasis on development rather than forecasting efforts; low stakes/high uncertainty situations call for information to reduce uncertainty rather than emphasis on development. Clearly, in low stakes/low uncertainty situations (for example, line extensions in mature markets), minimal investment in development and forecasting resources may be required—to the point that it may be smarter to launch the next-generation product without significant up-front investment and study market response after the fact, modifying the product and marketing program accordingly.

Although this classification is referred to throughout the book, and revisited in Chapter 10, its major purpose is to raise the level of awareness of new product forecasting activities with respect to those of new product development. New product *forecasting* is often seen as the domain of marketing and the concern of finance and accounting. New product *development* is often seen as the domain of R&D and manufacturing. A new product development *team* must not only integrate thinking on development issues, but also integrate thinking on forecasting issues. Gathering information that reduces uncertainty about the environment, the market, and the organization is as fundamentally important in the development of strategy and allocation of resources as the magnitude of potential investment in a new technology, process, product, or service.

Traditional Views of Forecasting

Part of the difficulty of integrating new product forecasting with development is the historic attitude toward forecasts. A forecast is often viewed as the result of a one-shot estimation procedure—a number that connotes a real value that is static and can be used as a basis for planning. In the case of new products, however, the number is at best an *abstraction*, and anything but static. The values defining a new product's forecasts may change throughout its development and are highly *dynamic*. New product forecasts should be the consequence of an evolutionary *forecasting process* that requires consideration of numerous factors affecting the new product's development, as well as of the multiple methods and data sources that integrate information into practical estimates of the project's value.

To aid decision making, a sequence of forecasts may be necessary at key points in the new product development project. By consideration of the numerous factors involved, the forecasts can be successively refined so that (1) critical *go/no-go* decisions can be made prior to launching and (2) if the product is launched, the forecasts are reasonably achievable. The importance of viewing new product forecasting as a process rather than an outcome becomes evident when one recognizes that regular feedback leads to modifications in new product development. Information about competitive response may alter product design, speed the development process, or generate a different launch strategy. Thus new product development and forecasting processes are interactive and must be integrated for success.

Overview of Factors Affecting New Product Development and Forecasting

Perhaps the best way to view the link of strategic factors with new product development and forecasting is through an organizing diagram (see Figure 1.1). The factors considered in the diagram also help to explain the organization of this book into its four major parts.

Part 1: Structuring New Product Development (Chapters 1–4)

The largest frame in Figure 1.1 represents the *business environment,* which by definition includes all relevant forces that might affect an organization's achievement of its new product objectives and goals. At the broadest level, six pervasive global forces (natural resources, population, cultural values, technology, economic systems, and laws and regulations) potentially influence new products and their forecasts directly or indirectly through other factors within the environment. These forces are monitored and influenced by *environmental mediators* whose actions can generate laws, regulations, and other norms of behavior that alter relationships among major stakeholders and affect new product development. These forces in the business environment, and their mediators, are discussed in Chapter 2.

Nested within the environment are factors that define the *market* for the new product or service. The market includes its major stakeholders, each presented as a separate frame. Stakeholders include the *industry,* whose *competitors* and their *suppliers* offer goods and services to *potential buyers* (and segments of buyers), sometimes directly, but often through *trade intermediaries* (for example, wholesalers, retailers). In Chapter 3, the influences of potential buyers, market segments, competitors, and trade intermediaries on market acceptance of new products are discussed.

The frame defining the *organization* (singled out as one of the competitors within the industry) is where new product development and forecasting occur. At one level, the organization and its forecasts are affected by the more encompassing business environment, market, and industry forces. At another level within the organization, four interacting subsets of factors help to characterize the new product situation. The first subset, labeled *organizational factors,* includes the conditions that lead to expediting or resisting new product development. These conditions emerge from the structure and processes of an organization. Factors such as an organization's identity, the flexibility of its resources, and processes of influence, communication, decision making, and implementation can lead to conditions that foster or impede the change necessary to develop new products in a timely and high-quality manner.

FIGURE 1.1   Factors affecting new product development.

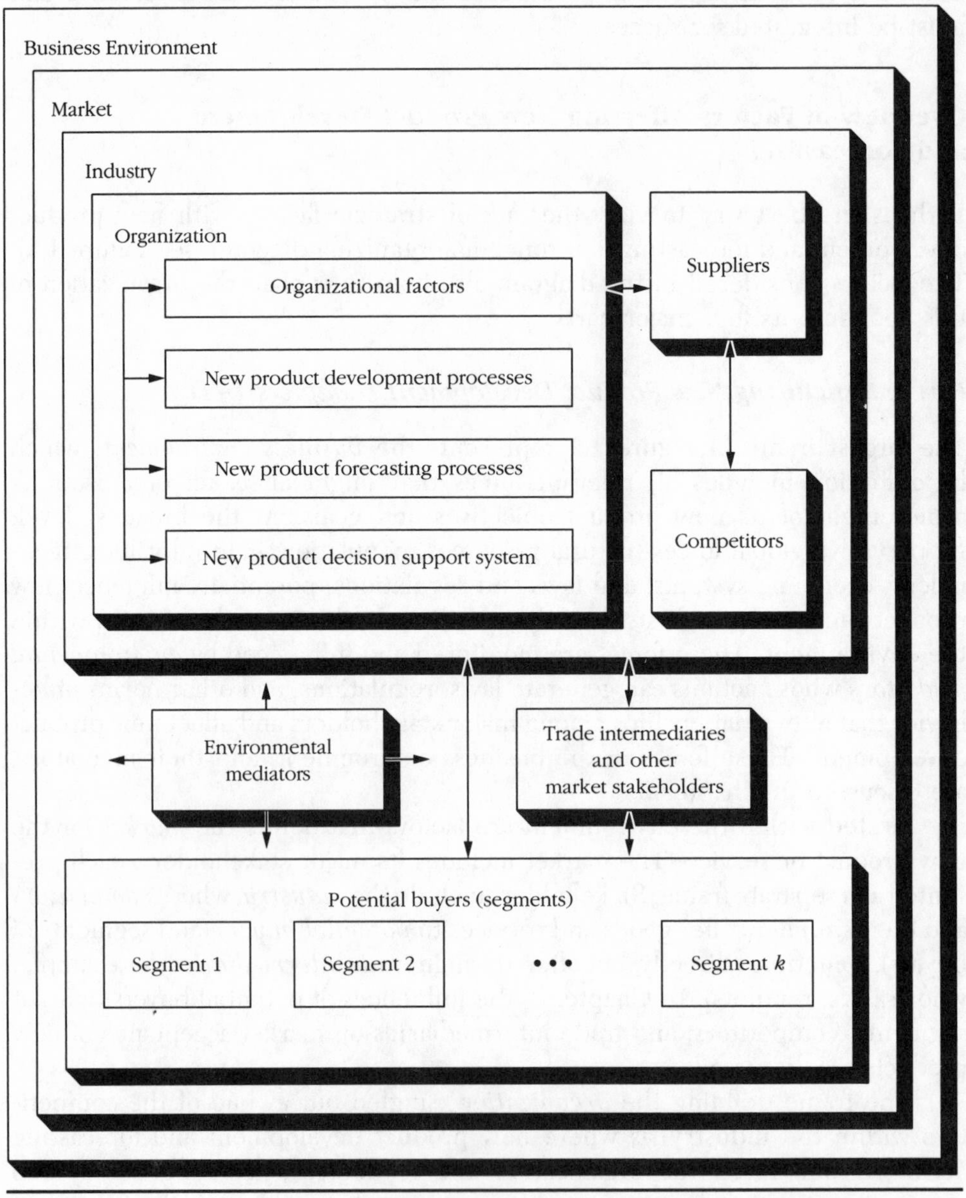

The role of leadership and management in influencing these conditions is also a central factor. Organizational factors are discussed in Chapter 4 and set the stage for managing new product development processes.

Part 2: Managing New Product Development (Chapters 5–6)

Part 2 of the book emphasizes the management aspects of new product development—primarily process and decision support issues. The second subset listed in the organization frame of Figure 1.1—labeled *new product development processes*—focuses on the operationalization of a process of new product development based on the level of a new product's definitional refinement (idea, concept, prototype, product, marketing program) and on the major managerial activities needed to decide whether and when to proceed. This process is discussed in Chapter 5. In Chapter 6, the design of a *new product decision support system* (the fourth subset listed in the organization frame of Figure 1.1) complements the managerial activities required in the new product development process. It recognizes the problem that new products generally have no historical data on which to base forecasts. Models, research methods, creative data sources, and optimization procedures are defined as major components of the system.

Part 3: New Product Development and Forecasting (Chapters 7–9)

The third subset listed in the organization frame of Figure 1.1 includes *new product forecasting processes* as an integral activity for new product development. In Part 3 of the book, three types of forecasting processes are deemed critical for new product development: *marketing opportunity, sales,* and *financial* forecasting. A more detailed relationship between new product forecasting processes and their resulting forecasts is depicted in Figure 1.2. The general approach to new product development and forecasting in Part 3 of the book emphasizes multiple methods (to reduce error in uncertain situations) and their reconciliation and combination. A three-level approach to modeling new product forecasts is recommended. The factors discussed in Part 1 of the book can be used to structure *conceptual models* of a specific new product situation. From these, key factors are selected for inclusion in *spreadsheet models* of the market opportunity, sales, and financial values related to market response to the new product. By design, spreadsheet models should be accessible and interpretable to managers and support their decision making. In addition, more specific *submodels* for selected variables included in the spreadsheet model may be needed to refine the estimation process.

Market opportunity forecasting (Chapter 7) involves estimating market potential and penetration (not all potential can be realized immediately) for new product concepts. Sales forecasting (Chapter 8) involves estimating year-to-year sales for the new product as its marketing program and competitive situation are defined. Financial forecasting (Chapter 9) involves estimating costs, investments, and the launch date (and corresponding financial measures of interest). Taken together, all of the forecasts provide a *new product control chart* that can guide the new product team throughout development and launch.

Part 4: Implementing New Product Development (Chapters 10–12)

Once a new product has passed selected development and forecasting hurdles, implementing it with a successful launch marketing program becomes the primary goal. As discussed in Chapter 10, various forms of *test marketing*

FIGURE 1.2   New product forecasting.

New Product Forecasting Processes

New Product Forecasts

Market opportunity forecasting

Market opportunity forecast

Sales forecasting

Sales forecast

Financial forecasting

Financial forecast

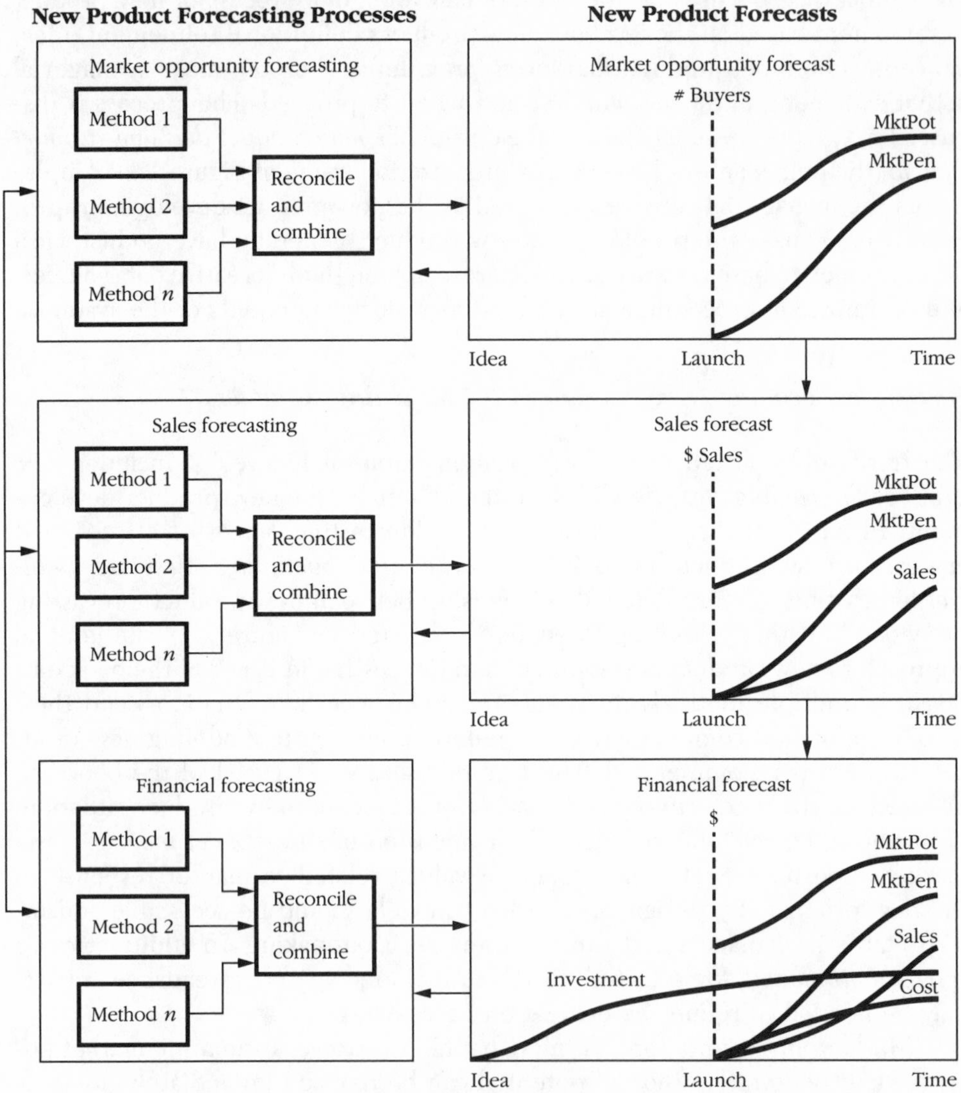

(simulated, controlled, and conventional) are available to experimentally refine the product and its marketing program. In Chapter 11, approaches to achieve *market entry* are discussed, with emphasis on the timing, scale, and resonance of the new product launch. Once the market entry launch program commences, tracking market response (Chapter 12) with appropriate measures provides a basis for modifying the new product and its program. Occasionally it may be advantageous to bypass all test marketing and move immediately to launch the new product; in these cases, careful tracking can help make the necessary modifications to ensure success.

Positioning This Book

The extent to which new products are developed and their forecasts achieved therefore depend upon a host of factors as depicted in Figure 1.1. Numerous books are available on new product planning that include concern for many of the factors in Figure 1.1.[19] However, within these books, the subject of new product forecasting is often relegated to a single chapter. This book elevates concern for new product forecasting as a critical organizational process parallel to new product development. This process represents an essential control function for the high risks of new product development, and provides input to strategic business decisions. Without a control capability, few organizations will have the confidence to take chances on potential breakthrough products that can make a difference for the organization and society.

In an era of *global* business, new product development obviously plays a crucial role for strategic success. Although this book does not explicitly address what might be called "global new product development," to do so would be redundant. It should be clear that consumers, competitors, regulators, and other key players in new product development can originate from anywhere in the world. The concepts and tools addressed throughout the book are intended to be basic to the *process* of new product development across a variety of cultural values. Thus culture (and cultural values) is simply another important construct in defining new products and their development, rather than the basis for a different set of concepts and tools to manage "global" new product development.

Finally, a few words about motivation. This book—in a spirit of *self-determination*—presumes that steps can be taken in the planning stages to improve the design and quality of new products and to achieve forecasts of them in the face of numerous and complicating factors. The philosophy is to control the environment by interacting with it—and what can't be controlled can be managed.[20] This idea of self-determination is best illustrated in a study showing that the more important new product forecast accuracy was to executives in software firms, the more accurate were their first-year forecasts![21] The proposition that plans and forecasts can be achieved through human will and effort cannot be overlooked.

The other aspect of motivation assumed throughout the book is the ethical responsibility associated with new product development.[22] Because new products affect the well-being of individuals at all levels of society, decisions throughout the development process should be made in a spirit of *fairness* to all stakeholders involved. In fact, sensitivity to the needs and concerns of major stakeholders, and the demand to make difficult tradeoffs among them, are cornerstones for strategic success in new product development.

SUMMARY

New product development is identified as a critical activity vitally linked to an organization's competitive strategy. It affects an organization's competitive advantage, corporate image, financial value, R&D, marketing, production and operations, and human resources. The relative importance of new product development to an organization's strategy and the uncertainty of its outcome should energize a commensurate allocation of resources to increase the likelihood of success. Consequently, new product development requires an intellectual discipline that pervades all parts of an organization, and is committed to a process that is *strategic* in scope, *flexible* in response to environmental turbulence, *interactive* with market stakeholders to find and measure opportunities, *integrative* within the organization to respond with the necessary teamwork to get the job done, and *ongoing* in its continued commitment to develop new products for organizational learning and renewal.

The reality of managing new product development and forecasting is complex and requires consideration of numerous factors. A summary of the major sets of factors involved is presented in Figure 1.1 as a conceptual model. At the core of Figure 1.1 are parallel interactive processes of new product development and forecasting that support the planning and launch of new products or services. Forecasts derived from the process at critical stages in the product's development cycle provide input to the decision of whether or not to go ahead with the product. The *control* imparted by systematically pursuing these development and forecasting processes can help organizations reduce the risks and uncertainties of new product development.

2 Mediating Turbulent Business Environments

Electric-powered cars have existed for over 100 years, yet few have been widely available for consumers to purchase for general transportation. Currently, electrical battery-powered vehicles succeed mainly as golf carts and in other selected off-road utility applications. In 1985, Sir Clive Sinclair (pioneer of the pocket calculator) introduced to England the C5, his version of an electric-powered vehicle. It was intended as a mass market product with breakeven estimated at about 100,000 units. The three-wheeled, single-seat vehicle resembled a battery-assisted tricycle. Designed to operate at a maximum of 15 miles per hour, it could climb an incline of up to 20 degrees. It came equipped with pedals in case the motor failed or the grade was too steep. Pushing a button accelerated the vehicle on demand. Riders pedaled or coasted between motorized accelerations. Some 5,000 cars reportedly sold during the C5's first few months, but production halted shortly thereafter. Apparently sales were insufficient to reach breakeven.[1]

Meanwhile, pressed by threatening environmental legislation in California, several large automobile manufacturers began research on improving battery systems and on developing electric vehicle prototypes:[2]

- In 1991, Ford, General Motors (GM), Chrysler, the Department of Energy, and the Electric Power Research Institute formed the U.S. Advanced Battery Consortium to develop improved battery power. The size, weight, and charge of a battery strongly affect vehicle performance.

- Tokyo Electric Power Co. developed a prototype vehicle powered by nickel-cadmium batteries that reportedly reaches 111 miles per hour and covers a range of 310 miles.

- In addition to U.S. and Japanese firms, Fiat, BMW, Volkswagen, and Peugeot developed electric car prototypes around various battery technologies.

Among the more publicized electric vehicle development programs was GM's Impact. In 1988 GM commissioned AeroVironment, Inc. to develop the concept and prototype of an all-electric vehicle with the same performance, comfort, and safety as a conventional gasoline-powered sports car. After a secret developmental process, the prototype emerged at the 1990 Los Angeles Auto Show. In April 1991 General Motors designated its Lansing, Michigan plant as the production site for their new electric car. It expected to roll the Impact off the assembly line in 1993 for a 1994 launch. Plans called for a sleek aerodynamic two-seater car that weighed about 2,200 pounds. Using 32 standard 10-volt lead-acid batteries, it accelerated to 60 miles per hour in 8 seconds and reached a top speed of about 100 miles per hour. It ranged up to 120 miles on an eight hour charge. Speed, terrain, load, and other factors determine range in use.

Certainly, several key questions loomed in GM's planning for the Impact. For example, among alternative vehicle power plant and fuel technologies, which will dominate in the year 2000, the year 2010, and so on—internal combustion (gasoline, methanol, ethanol), electric (lead-acid, nickel-cadmium, nickel-iron, sodium-sulfur, solar), or a hybrid approach? To answer this question, assumptions about the direction of energy resources, alternate technologies, economic conditions, cultural values about internal auto-emission pollution, public policies, and other factors would have to be studied. The answers would drive estimates of future market share for each type of power plant and fuel system, providing input to forecast market size for electric vehicles in general.

Unfortunately, the causes and effects of major environmental forces on any business or new product are complex and clouded in uncertainty, which makes them difficult to describe and measure. Further, as a project develops, assumptions about the forces can change and lead to different design features, demand estimates, resource requirements, and *go/no-go* decisions for the new product. For example, in December 1992, GM decided to shelve the Impact electric car project—perhaps because of market-driven uncertainties, increasing costs, and GM's financial problems at the time.

To cope with complexity and uncertainty in the business environment, the first step is to identify and conceptualize major global forces that affect a specific new product situation. Conceptually, (1) forces from the *business environment* can permeate all aspects of new product development and (2) various *mediators* in the business environment can alter the effects of those forces. The second step, where possible, is to interact with the mediators of major forces for the new product. Once these forces and mediators are recognized, an organization may be able to develop strategies that favorably affect the business environment for the new product. The third step involves estimating the effects of the forces that cannot be influenced and adjusting the product in response to them.

Understanding forces in a business environment and the potential effects of mediators helps define the size and trend of a market opportunity for a new product, and in many cases helps to redefine the new product idea. In any case, it is the degree of *uncertainty* of these forces that complicates new product development and forecasting. Generally, *the greater the turbulence in a business environment surrounding a new product, the more uncertain its development and forecasts.* Although this conclusion is intuitively obvious, it is all too easy to assume stability or overlook forces in the market environment, only to later discover their undesirable effects. Failing to identify, define, and measure the impact of key factors in the market environment on a new product only increases the risk of development.

In this chapter, components of turbulence in a business environment are conceptualized; in Chapter 7, more specific methods to estimate the size and growth of a market opportunity in uncertain market environments are considered. Throughout the discussion in this chapter, the electric vehicle case study provides useful examples to illustrate the complexity and uncertainty of various environmental forces as well as demonstrate their importance in new product development. Where useful, examples from other industries are also included.

GLOBAL FORCES IN BUSINESS ENVIRONMENTS

In Chapter 1, the groundwork for developing and forecasting new products for strategic success recognizes that turbulent business environments create both problems and opportunities for organizations. For example, the development of electric vehicles by auto firms may be interpreted as an opportunity to respond to growing consumer interest in a cleaner ecological environment. Alternatively, the vehicles may have been a defensive reaction to regulatory threats against pollution from traditional internal combustion vehicles. In any case, new product development and forecasting for electric vehicles must be considered in the context of selected global forces that interact with and affect the development of a market opportunity for them.

A conceptualization of global forces in a business environment is highlighted in Figure 2.1. These forces are global in the sense of their interaction and pervasiveness through all levels of society and market structure, as well as in their geographic scope. A new seafood restaurant launched locally in Denver, Colorado depends on the demand and supply of fish, lobster, and shrimp around the world. The effects of air pollution in one region of the world may derive from sources in another region.

Forces in a business environment surround and influence an organization in different ways and with different levels of intensity. As such, they must be identified and evaluated for every new product situation from different organizational perspectives. A CEO's view, for example, might include forces associated with economic conditions, government regulations, stockholders, institutional investors, and labor unions. Alternatively, an R&D manager's view might be dominated by forces related to the development of various technologies.

Because perceived demand for a new product depends on a variety of organizational perspectives, a broad and holistic set of global forces relevant to the situation must be included in any analysis. Further, whereas some forces can

FIGURE 2.1 Factors affecting new product development: focus on the business environment and its mediators.

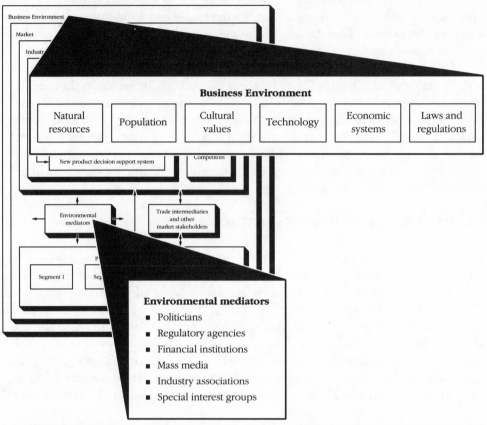

immediately affect a specific new product concept—for example, the approval or disapproval of a new pharmaceutical product by the U.S. Food and Drug Administration—global forces tend to be pervasive and often undetectable on a day-to-day operational basis in an organization. Consequently, a process of data collection among key members of the organization to obtain perceptions of relevant global forces may be required. Nevertheless, the analysis can start with some generic forces.

Six sets of generic global forces that might help an organization to conceptualize a new product business environment are *natural resources, population, cultural values, technology, economic systems*, and *laws and regulations*. Although discussed independently in the following sections, these forces link together at critical points as parts of larger systems. For example, an ecological systems view of natural resources includes at some point the study of human populations; the study of human populations links to the cultural values and technologies employed to accomplish work; technologies affect economic exchange and the supply of natural resources; and so on.

Natural Resources

The development of most new products and services relies in some way on the availability of certain natural resources from the physical environment. Natural resources provide the energy and raw material base for manufactured products. The *ecology* of natural resources clarifies their key role as an important set of forces for new products. A three-tier classification of natural resources is presented in the Appendix of this chapter: *primary, secondary,* and *tertiary.*[3]

When human labor and energy are applied to primary natural resources (for example, oceans, land, and the climate), secondary resources emerge. For example, fish can be harvested from the sea, vegetables grown on land, and minerals extracted from the ground. These activities represent basic agricultural and extractive industries. Similarly, human labor and energy applied to secondary resources result in tertiary resources, and so on to various kinds of manufactured products. At the secondary resource level, processing and refining industries emerge; at the tertiary level, manufacturing and construction industries emerge; and ultimately the service industries emerge, with the implication that they are dependent on the other industries.

The dynamic of this process defines a *resource cycle*, similar to the more familiar food cycle or *food chain* (that is, the sun transforms soil ingredients into plants, which are in turn consumed by animals and humans and subsequently returned as waste). In this cycle, high-quality, concentrated resources are fed back to upgrade low-quality or dispersed resources. For example, with labor, extracted ores can be converted to functional metals, which in turn can be transformed to machinery (such as trucks and bulldozers) that is then used to extract still more metal ores. Because the feedback in this cycle is positive (more metals can be used for more applications), the use of resources can grow at exponential rates.

To achieve the kinds of resource transformations that are central to modern economies, significant amounts of fossil fuel energy are required. Because of the inefficiencies of energy transformations when resources are transformed from one type to another, there are unrecoverable losses of energy, or *entropy*. Much of the energy lost from the combustion of fossil fuel escapes into the atmosphere as pollution with a potential global impact.[4]

The exponential growth of the resource cycle foreshadows eventual resource depletion rates that affect new products and technologies and must be incorporated into their development and forecasting. These rates can influence the cost of the resource, its availability, and psychological reactions to information about its depletion—all of which influence the size of a market opportunity and the cost structure of a new product.

For example, the volatile (and generally increasing) price and decreasing supply of oil represent trends that are favorable to the development of an electric car that does not rely on gasoline (developed from fossil fuel). Whether or not and when the new electric vehicles can be priced competitively with current combustion-powered vehicles for consumers remains an issue. Additional resource concerns might include the materials necessary to produce batteries or other aspects of the vehicle. For example, lead-acid and nickel-cadmium batteries may require resources whose supply has been declining rapidly, or they may create waste problems if they are not reusable. Further, high-strength, lightweight vehicle components may be required that are higher in cost or shorter in supply than more traditional materials and components (such as thermoplastics versus steel). The effects of increased electric power production necessary to recharge batteries may be another concern.

Clearly, natural resource trends for all materials defining a new product or service should be estimated. The extent to which key resources are limited in supply may affect manufacturing costs, which in turn may affect the prices that consumers pay, and hence the volume of demand for the new product. Also to be noted are the interactive effects of natural resource trends with other factors in the business environment (population shifts, economic conditions, and so on).

Population

The size, composition, distribution, location, and change in human populations and, importantly, the connections between population phenomena and societal conditions constitute a fundamental force central to understanding markets and the emergence of new products within them.[5] At a global level, the demographic patterns of population by geographic location influence the availability and cost of labor, and hence are a driving force in determining product cost and the development of competitors in various parts of the world. These patterns also determine market structure and preferences for new products. The heterogeneity of populations throughout the world necessitates continual analysis and segmentation of labor and consumers to assess market opportunities and threats to new products.

For example, in the case of the GM Impact electric car, if its primary concept is planned as a sporty two-seater, it may appeal to people who are ecologically sensitive, yet do not want to give up stylish transportation. Further, suppose this segment encompasses consumers in a particular age and income group, say 21–35 years of age and earning over $35,000. If the research and planning began in 1988 for a car to be launched in 1994, GM would be concerned with the 15–29 age group at the equivalent of $35,000 income in 1988 dollars. It would therefore be important for GM to understand how changes in this age and income group will evolve over the six years (1988–94) on a variety of demographic factors. How many people will be in this group? What will be the composition of the group in terms of gender, education, occupation, marital status, geographic concentration, and so on?

The Appendix lists typical demographic factors that are commonly used to study populations. Nevertheless, more in-depth analyses are often necessary to understand the link between the population changes and possible behaviors related to any new product. A study of the market "fragmentation" brought on by changes in household demographics reveals implications for traditional grocery marketing in the United States.[6] The 1980 Census disclosed that only 13 percent of the households typified the "traditional American family:" working father, homemaker mother, and children. Dual-career couples, single individuals, single parents, and non-family households composed the rest of the population of households.

The study suggests that supermarket shopping might be less important to several of these emerging demographic segments than to the traditional female-housewife-mother segment. Marketers of new grocery products need to consider the shopping behaviors of men, working women, singles, and senior shoppers. The demographic changes provide both opportunities and problems for supermarkets and firms introducing new products into them. For example, because customers have less time for shopping and food preparation, supermarkets now offer in-store salad bars and takeout food that enable shoppers to take home prepared meals. Because the salads and food selections can be made in any size or quantity desired, various household segments can be accommodated. However, these salad and food bars compete with a variety of current and new convenience foods (frozen, dried, and so on) offered by manufacturers and sold in other parts of the store.

Cultural Values

Cultural values permeate populations. Culture includes the learned values that shape human behavior in the direction of satisfying human needs.[7] These values are handed down from generation to generation through family, religious, and other social institutions and constitute powerful forces that influence response to new products. The importance of understanding culture for new products is evident when market segments are defined across cultures and sub-cultures and when the features of the new product may challenge values within a culture.

For example, when developing new refrigerators for a pan-European market, Electrolux considered a common design. However, it discovered that some Europeans shopped once a week and needed large units, whereas others shopped more frequently and preferred smaller units. Some preferred freezers on the top; others preferred them on the bottom. Although Electrolux would like to benefit from economies of scale—fewer products that have larger volumes and lower unit production costs—the presence of market segments, partly driven by cultural differences, may preclude them.[8]

The emergence of world markets for products and services compels every firm to consider the opportunity for launching new and existing products across cultures—but with care. Federal Express Corp. was attracted to markets outside the United States. It wanted to take its highly successful and innovative overnight package delivery service from this country to the European continent and beyond. However, after six years and about $2 billion in invest-ment, market share in Europe was reportedly about 10 percent (compared to 50 percent in the United States), and the operation ran at a loss. Although numerous reasons might explain the company's market position (late entry, international regulatory issues, and so on), failing to respond to cultural dif-ferences could be included among them. For example, through 1990, shipping bills and promotional materials were reportedly printed in the English lan-guage only. Further, pickup time for packages was maintained at 5:00 P.M., even though executives in some countries (for example, Spain) worked later.[9]

What is valued in one culture may or may not be valued in another. Con-sequently, demand for new products may vary from culture to culture. Looked at as a global marketing opportunity, GM's Impact electric vehicle may hold promise outside the United States. Many large cities in Europe, Asia, and Latin America suffer the difficulties of pollution by internal combustion engines. As-suming that technical differences can be overcome (for example, availability of electrical power sources to recharge batteries), the cultural values of potential buyers in these cities must be examined. Will cultures that value tradition over change be more likely to resist the innovation of an electric car? Will cultures that embrace fatalism resign themselves to the consequences of a polluted en-vironment and pay scant attention to such cars? Will cultures that value nature (for example, clean air) be less resistant to electric vehicles?

The social values that emerge within a culture (or subculture) are often viewed as stable and pervasive. Although this may be true for a small number of basic values (such as freedom in the United States), the increasing pace of change brought about through telecommunication and other technologies challenges more traditional values and gives rise to social trends that must be examined for their long-term implications. In effect, are today's cultural values a function of the latest scientific studies or media reports that alter long-term values—or simply short-term behaviors that extinguish over time? For example, concern for personal health in the United States appears to be a stable and emerging value, yet it is subject to question. For years cigarette smoking declined because of health concerns, but reports in 1992 revealed increasing rates of smoking among young women.

Consequently, in assessing the effects of a culture on new products, basic values must be examined for their degree of permanence and contrasted with social trends, especially those associated with the increasing pace of scientific and technological change. The Appendix lists selected factors that character-ize human values within and across cultures and provides a starting point to help define differences for new products. Although the effects of cultural forces on potential buyers for a new product are important, so too are their effects on competitors, suppliers, intermediaries, and regulators, whether directly or through potential buyers. For example, popular demands to clean the environ-ment may compel governments or regulators to mandate changes and develop pollution standards that are difficult for internal combustion engines to meet (as in the California case).

Technology

Within an organization, technology is defined by the tools, techniques, processes, and procedures—or "know-how"—used to provide the products and services that satisfy human needs.[10] Ongoing technological development by thousands of organizations located around the globe creates a broad technological force that contributes to rapid change in other environmental forces as well as in markets for new products. The benefits of both new-to-the-world technologies (for example, fiber optics) and enhancements to existing technologies are rushed into the next-generation product to better meet consumer needs and gain competitive advantage.

Biotechnology, microprocessors, fiber optics, material composites, digital electronics, non-woven fibers, imaging, and other technologies have propagated new products and services to meet consumer needs. For example, the pulp form of DuPont's Kevlar aramid fiber molds into tennis racket frames, boat hulls, and a variety of products where added strength and lightness are valued.

The emergence of new technologies and the increased rate of change in existing technologies tend to shorten the life cycle of products. As new products emerge more rapidly to satisfy similar consumer needs, existing ones decline more quickly. Shortened life cycles put time pressure on the organization to plan and launch the next-generation product. In addition, for purposes of forecasting, shorter life cycles make it difficult to apply the growth rates of analogous products to the current technological environment. Shortened product life cycles also create a variety of pressures and uncertainties on major market stakeholders—especially consumers and competitors.

The broad effects of technological forces on consumers may be subtle, complex, and situational. Whereas some potential buyers rush to adopt the next generation of a new product, others quietly alter their prospective purchase decisions because of the effects of rapidly changing technologies. Perhaps the most obvious example is potential buyers' confusion, which often results in delayed purchasing. To illustrate, developments in personal computer software are often so dramatic that some buyers immediately purchase the new version, but others wait on the sidelines for the state of the art to settle down. Those who buy later cling to major existing brands, rejecting even improved products. This helps them to cope with the uncertainty raised by prolific technology improvements.

For example, numerous competitive spreadsheet programs have been introduced since Lotus 1-2-3, and many have advanced features. Sensitized by the rapid changes in software technology, potential buyers were slow to consider many of these new, improved competitors. Even after a several-year delay in launching its own improved version, Lotus still managed to maintain its market dominance. Thus, the effects of rapid technology change and shorter product life cycles can stimulate buyer confusion and uncertainty and slow the acceptance of new products—a topic considered further in the next chapter.

Technology introduces new and sometimes unexpected competitors. As technological improvements were made in the capabilities and quality of fax machines, and prices declined, their use increased dramatically and the U.S. Postal Service gained a new competitor for First-Class mail. To take the cascading competitive effect of a new technology one step further, consider the effects of fax machines on business practices of firms in certain industries.

For example, with the widespread adoption of fax machines, National Fisheries, a seafood wholesaler in Miami, Florida, went from having a few local competitors to having a large number of international competitors. With fax machines and overnight delivery, independent seafood brokers could enter the business quickly, give potential buyers immediate price quotes, and drop-ship products directly from suppliers. Buyers used the speed and availability of faxed price quotations to secure lower bids from other competitors, thereby driving the price down and dramatically changing the structure of the industry in a short period of time.[11]

The development of digital electronics technology has clouded the competitive distinctions among the computer, communications, entertainment, and consumer electronic industries.[12] Developments in digitized sound, text, and pictures span all these industries and will create not only unexpected competitors, but also unexpected strategic alliances to speed up product development and meet competition. For example, Apple Computer, Inc.'s entry into the electronic games market pits it directly against Nintendo and Sega, established manufacturers of electronic games.

The potential appearance of competitors with new technologies in their products creates uncertainty in the planning process for new and existing products. For example, in 1991, Nissan Motor Co. announced the development of a new quick-charge nickel-cadmium battery that can be used for electric cars.[13] The battery recharges in just 15 minutes, compared to an hour or more for lead-acid batteries. Although the new battery has problems (for example, it can't easily be charged on standard home electric outlets), it represented a new pressure in the planning process for GM's Impact car. Further, a 15-minute charge may favorably influence market response: Potential buyers may perceive less risk of being stranded without power if they are able to recharge in less time.

Finally, one of the many ironies of broad technological forces is that even though they appear to be changing rapidly, sometimes specific technologies don't materialize as quickly as they are conceptualized. For example, in 1985, Ford, General Motors, and Chrysler were actively working on navigation systems for use in automobiles.[14] The product design depended on NAVSTAR, the U.S. government's system of satellites that can pinpoint the location of any object on the Earth's surface. The system requires an on-board computer to locate the car on a mapped videoscreen, and the technology is still expensive for the average family car. Meanwhile, using a different technology, Blaupunkt, a unit of Robert Bosch, G.m.b.H., of Germany, launched the first mass-market automotive navigation system (TravelPilot) for $3,495 in the California market during 1991.[15] At that price, the systems will most likely be used in commercial applications and for niche markets. Until the price falls within the range of $500–$1,000—considered a reasonable expenditure for an automobile accessory—the product may not draw broad sales response.

The effects of new technologies are frequent and pervasive in society. Their impact creates uncertainties for new products. Consequently, care is warranted in assessing the consequences of relevant technology trends for a new product's design and market opportunity. The Appendix lists a number of factors to stimulate thinking about the consequences of technological forces on new products and services.

Economic Systems

Within a country, an economic system is the mechanism by which labor, resources, and skills are brought together to produce and distribute goods and services to satisfy human needs. Central to this mechanism is the concept of a market. The way in which the participants in a market organize to exchange goods and services to satisfy their needs is the basis for the allocation of society's resources. The aggregate effect of several markets in operation throughout the world satisfying varieties of human needs defines global economic forces that must be considered for any specific new product situation under study.

Traditionally, markets for some products and services have been global— especially markets for commodities like gold, silver, copper, or coffee. However, improved communication technologies and distribution systems have globalized markets for a variety of other products and services. Markets for products as divergent as fast food, motor vehicles, weapon systems, aircraft, computers, cameras, banking, beer, processed foods, entertainment, and consulting services are global. A potential consequence of this ongoing globalizing process is a global economic system linking the economies of individual countries and multi-country regions.

Numerous variables can be used to characterize the overall level of economic activity. Estimates of the magnitude and direction of these variables over a planning period can alter the market opportunity for a new product. Such variables include a country's gross national product (GNP), gross domestic product (GDP), interest rates, inflation, unemployment, personal savings, business inventories, housing starts, exchange rates, and export/import balances. Of course, these economic variables can also be examined at state, regional, and local levels; however, they will all be intertwined with effects at national and global levels. Although tracking these variables over time may help to forecast the economic conditions during the planning period for the new product, it is also important to look at the underlying market factors and other global forces that drive these variables.

For example, the actions of the Federal Reserve System (an important U.S. regulator in major money markets) should be observed carefully to evaluate its effect on interest rates and inflation. The size of the federal deficit is also a key determinant of interest rates and inflation. The planned purchases of raw materials and plant and equipment by business firms are major determinants of their expected employment and production. More importantly, the planned purchases and savings of household consumers are major determinants of the production output sold versus that maintained in inventory.

Though it is important to examine these variables and activities for an overall economy, it is particularly important to assess economic activity in a specific market within which the new product will be introduced. For example, launching a new electric vehicle during a recessionary or expansionary period will make a difference in the sales performance of the new car. The trend in interest rates will also affect a potential buyer's ability to purchase a new electric vehicle. The Appendix includes items that can be considered when beginning to assess the effects of economic forces on new products.

Laws and Regulations

The laws and regulations that permeate all countries, states, cities, and communities around the world represent tremendous forces that both constrain and free the people and organizations under their authority. Of all the global forces, these may have the most immediate impact on new products because they are primarily rules and guidelines that must be met. They represent both problems and opportunities for designers of new products. Laws and regulations can be considered at two levels: those that are already in place and those expected during the planning horizon and life of the new product.

The number of existing laws and regulations to consider for a particular new product could be large. It depends on the nature of the product, the geographic locale of the organization, and importantly, the market served by the new product. For example, new products for children will generally encounter numerous regulations in most countries of the world. Regulations for new pharmaceutical, tobacco, alcohol, food, and other health- and safety-related products can also be expected in most countries, as well as in the United States.

In the United States, a myriad of laws and regulations might affect the launch of new products. Beginning with the establishment of the Interstate Commerce Commission (ICC) in 1877 to regulate the nation's railroad system (and later trucking), the U.S. government has been increasingly "regulatory." Numerous acts and commissions first regulated industries (Civil Aeronautics Board, Food and Drug Administration, Bureau of Alcohol, Tobacco, and Firearms), then more general societal problems (Federal Trade Commission, Occupational Safety and Health Administration, Environmental Protection Agency, International Trade Commission, Consumer Product Safety Commission, the Clean Air Act).[16]

Under U.S. President Ronald Reagan (1980–1988), attempts were made to reduce national regulation and shift the burden of government to state and local levels. Hence, new product developers in the United States must be sensitive to laws and regulations at those levels. For example, in 1991 California adopted auto emission standards more stringent than the U.S. 1990 Clean Air Act. Besides substantial reductions in emissions, the state called for 2 to 10 percent of new car production from 1998 to 2003 to be zero-emission vehicles—most likely electric cars. California's passage of this regulation stimulated at least nine other states to follow suit.

At the global level, scores of regulations confront developers of new products—from the mundane paperwork of import and export processes to trade quotas and other restrictions that may reflect protectionist motivations. Perhaps most relevant to new product development are intellectual property rights that vary from country to country. The role of patent, trademark, copyright, and other forms of intellectual property protection often determines a firm's ability to enter markets, not to mention its competitiveness within a market.

The view of patent rights in the United States differs from that in most other countries. In the United States, the inventor owns the right, whereas in most other countries the first to file the invention owns the right. Although there are proposals to alter the U.S. patent system, other concerns among countries must be resolved, including protecting and enforcing any agreements reached. The state of international patent law for new products is therefore often complex for firms venturing abroad. To accommodate such ventures, numerous reciprocal agreements have arisen over the years that sometimes facilitate the protection of patent and other intellectual property rights. (Publications of the World International Property Organization summarize the patent situation for most countries of the world.) Nevertheless, sufficient problems remain to create uncertainties for international new product development and forecasting.

Like other environmental forces, the patent laws and numerous other regulations affecting new product development and launch are dynamic. The laws and regulations 5 and 10 years in the future may be more important for a specific new product than those in existence today. The Appendix provides a list of factors helpful for monitoring laws and regulations. However, tracking the historical patterns of laws and regulations helps identify trends that will be most important during a product's planned launch and future. Tracking such trends requires monitoring the people and institutions that are most involved in their creation and change—*environmental mediators.*

MEDIATORS IN A BUSINESS ENVIRONMENT

The pervasive effects of the business environment on new product development appear to be largely uncontrollable from the perspective of an individual firm. However, their direction and intensity can be influenced through people who have been elected, appointed, or self-designated to *mediate* them. For example, political leaders are often elected because of their promises to correct certain perceived societal problems—economic conditions, education, health, and so on. The direct control that these mediators have over global forces varies considerably. Some influences can be fairly direct—for example, the lowering of interest rates—whereas others can be less direct and slow to emerge, such as legislation to reduce the emissions of pollutants into the air.

Environmental mediators are individuals or groups of individuals who make decisions that influence some aspect of the broader business environment. Like most individuals, they can be lobbied or otherwise persuaded to act in a particular way. Defining their possible effect on new products therefore entails understanding and anticipating their role in society, as well as the role of persons who might influence them. Further, a firm can develop a program as a part of the new product development process to interact with mediators to better understand their decisions and actions. In this sense, an organization can influence forces in the business environment shaping its future.

The mediators identified and briefly discussed in the following sections— *politicians, regulatory agencies, financial institutions, mass media, industry associations*, and *special interest groups*—are generic and illustrative. For specific new products deemed important to a firm's performance, environmental mediators should be identified and studied for their direct and indirect influence.

Politicians

Politicians use the power of their offices to make or influence a variety of decisions that affect numerous environmental forces and other mediators. In his 1992 State of the Union message, U.S. President George Bush announced a 90-day moratorium on regulations in hopes of reducing interference with business activity and stimulating a sluggish domestic economy—in a presidential election year. An immediate consequence of the decision was a slowdown in enforcement of EPA standards. The White House mounted an effort to prevent the Environmental Protection Agency (EPA) from issuing rules that implemented a more comprehensive system of reporting on the release of air pollutants.[17] These rules required a wide variety of manufacturing firms, oil refineries, bakers, and dry cleaners to get permits from state pollution authorities certifying that their emissions are within the limits set by the U.S. Clean Air Act.

The immediate impact of this 90-day moratorium may have been negligible on firms planning the development of new electric vehicles. However, if the moratorium signaled a longer-term relaxed attitude toward regulatory constraints on pollution, especially for auto emissions, then the urgency of developing new electric cars would be reduced. Although the effect on demand may be muted by strong consumer preference in a target segment of the population, firms developing the new product may slow their own processes in hopes of extending the life of the internal combustion engine. The election of Bill Clinton to the U.S. presidency of course eliminated the impact of the moratorium, but nevertheless created additional uncertainty while his new environmental policy was formulated. In any case, the consequences of such announcements and political office changes must be factored into the potential effects of broad environmental forces and various mediators on new product development.

The effects of politicians and their influence emanate from all levels of government—local, regional, and national. Further, effects ripple from international politicians as well. When Russian President Boris Yeltsin announced in January 1992 that Russian missiles would no longer be pointed at the United States, repercussions were felt in every firm that provided products and services to the defense industry. One possible consequence is transformation of military technologies to consumer markets, with attendant new products, as these firms seek to replace military business with nonmilitary opportunities. One area to which the Westinghouse Corporation has turned its "nonmilitary" attention is the electric vehicle—supplying the electrical power systems for Chrysler's launch of 50 electric vans in 1993. In the Appendix, a list of political offices that might mediate environmental forces for new products is presented.

Legal/Regulatory Agencies

Legal and regulatory agencies perform a monitoring role in a market. National, state, and local courts and governments are primary regulators in many markets. National agencies such as the Federal Trade Commission, the Consumer Product Safety Commission, the International Trade Commission, the Securities and Exchange Commission, the Food and Drug Administration, and the Federal Communications Commission are not only responsible for specific legal regulations, but also hold prevailing attitudes or sentiments toward regulation in various markets that could affect new product demand.

Regulatory groups are beginning to emerge at a global level. A study conducted by the United Nations proposed the development of a global environmental protection agency. The agency would issue pollution allowances that turn air and water into commodities. An allowance would enable a firm to pollute at the rate of one ton of carbon dioxide annually. Firms with high rates of pollution would have to purchase adequate allowances to continue operation; clearly the motivation to reduce pollution would also reduce a firm's operating costs.[18]

The performance of the U.S. International Trade Commission (ITC) illustrates the potential monitoring role a regulator plays in the regulation of foreign competition in the domestic market. On March 9, 1983, when Apple Computer Company was launching its new line of Apple IIe personal computers, it filed a complaint with the ITC against foreign firms in Taiwan, Hong Kong, Singapore, and Switzerland that manufactured some 15 different knock-offs. These machines looked like the Apple IIe, sold at much lower prices, and contained duplicate operating systems. The ITC investigated the matter and found violation of Apple's valid U.S. patents. Twelve months later, the ITC issued a general exclusion order to the infringing firms, barring them from competing in the United States.[19]

Although not all cases end the way Apple's did, the ITC provides an opportunity to defend companies from unfair foreign competition. The ITC has broad powers to investigate all factors relating to the effect of U.S. foreign trade on domestic production, employment, and consumption. Threats of patent infringement by foreign firms strongly interest innovators with patented new products. The ITC, through Section 337 of the Tariff Act of 1930, can offer relief to the complaining U.S. firm, although trends in the development of ITC cases over time should be reviewed before a complaint is filed. A study of 195 Section 337 cases over a 14-year period revealed that 12 firms lost their patent rights as a result of the proceedings. Nevertheless, an analysis of the cases showed that overall, the ITC has been effective in carrying out its role.[20] The Appendix lists illustrative legal and regulatory agencies whose actions might affect new products.

Financial Institutions

Actions by leaders of financial institutions influence economic systems. For example, the leader of the Fed (the U.S. Federal Reserve Board) sets discount rates and reserves for banks that influence interest rates and money supply. These factors determine the flow of money into and through the United States and the world economies. Lower discount rates lead to lower interest rates, which affect consumer buying and corporate borrowing. Though it may be tempting to view financial institutions as domestic organizations with consequences for domestic economies, their decisions also have global impact in the world economic system. For example, higher interest rates in one country can attract investors from other countries.

More explicit global effects are associated with major international institutions. The International Monetary Fund (IMF) and its leaders decide which countries receive loans from its funds and which don't. The World Bank and its leaders decide which developing countries should receive financial and other assistance for major projects that might enhance their economies. The actions of the leaders of these global financial institutions affect the flow of capital, exchange rates, development assistance, and other factors among countries.

Besides their impact on organizations and potential new products, the actions of domestic and global financial institutions can affect a variety of environmental forces and mediators. They can change the amount of money available for investment in technology, economic conditions (recessionary versus expansionary periods), and population flows (for example, from less to more developed countries). They can also influence (or be influenced by) politicians, regulatory agencies, mass media, industry associations, and other mediators. To the extent that new product opportunities exist locally or in countries throughout the world, and that these markets are affected by local and global financial transactions, then financial institutions must be considered in terms of their current decisions and what their decisions might be during the life of the new product, with or without intervention. The Appendix includes selected financial institutions.

Mass Media

Organizations that control mass media influence a variety of environmental forces. Social and cultural values can, over time, be influenced by the communication and diffusion of ideas through the informational, editorial, and commercial content of media.[21] Media are, of course, conscious of this power and generally exercise it responsibly. For example, in 1991, Capital Cities/ABC issued new guidelines that loosened the standards for competitive advertising claims, endorsements by doctors, and diet products. These revisions updated rules established in the early 1960s and may have been due to the pressure of some advertisers. However, months later ABC backed off from these changes under pressure from other advertisers and special interest groups.[22] ABC's actions illustrate how pressures from firms can affect environmental mediators, which in turn can influence broader environmental forces. In this case, the messages delivered to consumers on network television can eventually influence their values.

Because the purchase of advertising by organizations is the primary revenue source for media, there is a natural tendency for each to be sensitive to the other for reasons that are not duplicitous. For example, the public may be truly interested in progress in the development of electric cars, and mass media may accept publicity releases from auto firms to build their journalistic reports. On the other hand, advertisers will be very conscientious about monitoring what the media allow competitors to advertise and report in the form of publicity. Nevertheless, occasional examples of influence on the editorial content of media are found in the business press:[23]

- A letter from *Healthline* magazine to Weight Watchers proposed to feature two Weight Watchers products in separate articles for a sponsorship fee of $25,000. Weight Watchers didn't accept the offer, though a competitor did and its products were rated number one in a subsequent survey by the magazine.

- Reportedly, for between $26,500 and $35,500, the magazine *Electronic Gaming Monthly* offered advertisers a 16-page "advertorial" that looked like articles, with graphics and layout that were identical to the rest of the magazine. It would be difficult for readers to discern differences between the advertising and the articles with editorial content.

- In the automobile magazine field, writers customarily accepted fees of several thousands of dollars a year for providing consulting and other services. This practice became apparent when, on January 10, 1991, *Car and Driver* magazine sent a letter to the auto industry announcing that its employees would no longer accept gifts or fees for work.

Some of the susceptibility to influence may be due to increasing fragmentation and competitiveness in mass media. The success of cable TV, in particular, has drained audiences from major broadcast TV networks and given advertisers alternative media vehicles. The desire to be competitive may pressure people involved in media to base editorial and other decisions on the need to build audience share.

Perhaps one of the more important aspects of mass media has been the emergence of global media. The use of satellites to broadcast global television signals (for example, those of MTV—music television) facilitates the communication of tastes, lifestyles, and other information across diverse cultures. This cross-pollination of ideas may, over time, influence values within cultures. Although an advertiser's ability to send a single message globally has been piecemeal (program-by-program), Cable News Network (CNN) has been developing a single media buy that will result in the delivery of messages to a variety of world markets.[24] The Appendix provides a list of factors to consider in examining media trends and their possible effects on new product development.

Industry Associations

Industry associations take a variety of forms. The traditional ones encompass organizations in the same industry with a common set of goals—usually to assist development and protection of the industry. In the United States alone, hundreds of such associations exist to further the goals of their members. These associations perform a variety of lobbying functions to influence governmental and political mediators, to secure favorable publicity through the mass media, and to influence technology.

An emerging industry association and organizational form, especially related to new product development, is the R&D consortium.[25] When Congress passed the National Cooperative Research Act (NCRA) in 1984 to foster precompetitive R&D among competitors, it did so to maintain U.S. competitiveness with Asian and European countries. Models for these types of consortia existed prior to 1984, but only among hospitals, universities, and certain regulated industries—not among competitors. For example, the Electric Power Research Institute (EPRI), also part of the U.S. Advanced Battery Consortium, conducts studies related to the electric vehicle.

The NCRA encourages precompetitive R&D, including such activities as data collection, experimentation, and development of testing techniques and prototypes. The 137 R&D consortia (filed by 1989) range in size from 2 to 92 and include organizations that conduct basic research as well as those that simply coordinate research across consortium members. The U.S. Advanced Battery Consortium illustrates an alliance among major competitors to improve battery technology for electric-powered cars.

Consortia and industry associations can directly affect the technology available for a new product under development. They may also be the source of strategic alliances for new product development. When GM decided to shelve the Impact electric car, an alliance between Ford, Chrysler, and GM to undertake cooperative development of a line of electric cars became a possibility.

Monitoring and participating in these consortia ensure prompt and reliable information for the new product development and forecasting process. In the Appendix, factors to help evaluate consortia and industry associations are listed.

Special Interest Groups

A variety of other special interest groups can become important mediators of global forces that affect the market environment of a firm's new product development situation. Labor unions, lobbying groups, religious groups, and other special interest groups monitor the behavior of selected market participants. For example, Mothers Against Drunk Drivers (MADD) focuses on the alcoholic beverages market and can potentially affect legislation and social values about drinking. Consumerist groups such as Ralph Nader's Public Citizen regularly monitor selected markets. The Coalition for Better Advertising monitors television broadcasts and tries to bring pressure against media firms and their advertisers.

Consider the case of Vindicator of Florida, Inc., a firm launching the first food irradiation processing plant in the United States with an investment of $6.8 million.[26] Food and Water, Inc., a U.S.-based consumer action group, led a coalition of international consumer groups in opposition to the irradiation of food. The U.S. Department of Agriculture considers food irradiation an important weapon in fighting food-related illnesses and the U.S. Food and Drug Administration has approved the process for several foods. Nevertheless, the International Organization of Consumer Groups promised a global boycott of Florida citrus products. Food and Water, Inc. allocated $30,000 for a Florida campaign and $300,000 for a national campaign to broadcast the message that eating irradiated food "might kill you."

Although debate continues about the potential effects of food irradiation despite the efforts of special interest groups, groups that target a new product or service can have a significant impact. G. Heileman Brewing Co. learned this lesson when it attempted to launch Colt 45 PowerMaster, a malt liquor brew with a 5.9 percent alcohol content.[27] Although the liquor was approved by the U.S. Bureau of Alcohol, Tobacco, and Firearms (BATF), that decision was later reversed and Heileman agreed not to launch the product as scheduled. The reversal came from pressure by several special interest groups, not to mention competitors. In particular, the belief by several clergymen that PowerMaster was targeted to the black community motivated them to threaten to encourage a boycott of the product when launched. The BATF reversed its decision in apparent agreement that the brand name—PowerMaster—constituted marketing on the basis of alcoholic content and therefore violated the Federal Alcohol Administration Act.

Knowledge of such groups and their potential effects on new product development and forecasting is crucial. In the case of electric-powered vehicles, the American Automobile Association (AAA), the American Council for an Energy Efficient Economy, and the University of Michigan's Center for the Study of Automotive Transportation illustrate the kinds of special interest groups that might have an effect on legislation, regulation, competitiveness, or other aspects of the market for electric vehicles. A generic list of possible special interest groups is presented in the Appendix.

FORECASTING ENVIRONMENTAL FORCES AND INFLUENCING MEDIATORS

The major environmental forces that affect organizations and their new products and services are generally thought to be uncontrollable. Typically, relevant factors are identified and measured, their trends estimated, and possible effects on the new product assessed.[28] However, the preceding consideration of environmental mediators suggests that within a certain time horizon, some of these forces can be controlled—or *influenced*—to some degree.

Clearly, some forces will remain uncontrollable, but others can be altered. The supply of crude oil is finite and little can be done to increase its size; however, its flow rate may be influenced. The 1991 Persian Gulf War was fought in part to preserve the flow rate of oil resources, which in turn affects international economic exchanges. At one time, birth rates were believed to be uncontrollable. However, efforts at population control provide evidence that birth rates can be influenced.

The organization developing a new product may therefore be able to take planned action during both the development cycle of the new product and the period after launch to transform aspects of the environment. Even aspects that cannot be changed should be studied to identify current situations and trends as they affect the new product. However, aspects of the environment that are susceptible to change and affect the new product should be targeted with special programs. Such programs can be furthered through selected mediators identified for their potential influence on environmental factors that might be changed. The matrix of influence suggested in Figure 2.2 illustrates a way to conceptualize and estimate possible effects that developers of new products might have on environmental forces.

In the top matrix in Figure 2.2, the effects of mediators on the market environment for the new product can be organized. The basic question driving this matrix is: *What direct effects do each of the various mediators have on various forces defining a business environment?* In the second matrix of Figure 2.2, the basic question is: *What are the interactions among major forces in the business environment?* In the third matrix of Figure 2.2, the basic question is: *What are the interactions among specific environmental mediators?* Through data collection and experience, the critical relationships and patterns of influence can be mapped, and estimates developed that assess the patterns and trend for the relationships. The general approach consists of the following steps:

1. For each category of global environmental force, identify the more specific factors that potentially affect the new product. The Appendix lists such factors for the various forces and mediators.

FIGURE 2.2   Effects of forces and mediators in a market environment.

A. What effects do mediators have on the forces defining a business environment for new products?

Environmental forces→ Mediators ↓	Natural resources	Population	Cultural values	Tech- nology	Economic systems	Laws and regulations
Politicians						
Legal/Regulatory agencies						
Financial institutions						
Mass media						
Industry associations						
Special interest groups						

B. What are the interactions among forces in the business environment?

Environmental forces	Natural resources	Population	Cultural values	Tech- nology	Economic systems	Laws and regulations
Natural resources						
Population						
Cultural values						
Technology						
Economic systems						
Laws and regulations						

C. What are the interactions among environmental mediators?

Environmental mediators	Politicians	Legal/ Regulatory agencies	Financial institu- tions	Mass media	Industry associa- tions	Special interest groups
Politicians						
Legal/Regulatory agencies						
Financial institutions						
Mass media						
Industry associations						
Special interest groups						

2. For each category of mediator, list the specific players that have a role in influencing other mediators and specific environmental factors.

3. Gather information about the current and past behavior of environmental forces and mediators and estimate trends over the development and early life cycle of the new product.

4. Specify the patterns of linkages between and among forces and mediators in the market environment, noting which may or may not be influenced.

5. For mediators and forces that can be influenced, develop a plan of action to achieve desired outcomes.

6. For mediators and forces that cannot be influenced, develop scenarios that characterize major trends, then estimate the impact of each scenario on new product development.

Specific data collection sources and methods for developing scenarios are discussed in greater detail in Chapter 7.

The outlined approach and the conceptual factors suggested in this chapter afford an integrated and dynamic view of a new product's market environment. By beginning broadly and considering numerous factors, then focusing on those that are most important to the new product, the environmental analysis is very thorough. It avoids the problem of environmental selectivity—letting one or two of the most popular environmental factors dominate planning. In the case of electric vehicles, this problem might be an overly narrow focus on battery technology and state regulators, to the neglect of such a factor as economic conditions or changing cultural values about the ecology of natural resources. Also, although the approach may involve significant data collection, it is focused and interactive with the environment rather than random and reactive. Following the patterns of inquiry suggested in Figure 2.2 ensures a more productive allocation of data collection resources than is possible without a pattern to follow.

SUMMARY

The greater the turbulence of business environments for a new product, the greater the uncertainty associated with its development and forecasting. Business environments are often viewed as relentless forces to which products must adapt, either to reduce uncertainty or for survival. However, though many environmental forces are inexorable and must be accommodated through planning, other environmental forces can be influenced through individuals, organizations, and institutions that mediate their effects. In this chapter, a conceptual approach facilitates assessment of the effects of environmental mediators on major environmental forces that affect new product development and forecasting.

Natural resources, population, cultural values, technology, economic systems, and laws and regulations are generic categories of environmental forces that may bear on new products. Possible mediators of these forces include politicians, legal and regulatory agencies, financial institutions, mass media, industry associations, and special interest groups. By identifying the mediators and forces that can or can't be changed, interacting with them where possible, and planning accordingly to accommodate or influence them, an organization paves the way for reducing uncertainty in new products to tolerable levels. This effort can enhance development of the new product and provide the foundation for market opportunity forecasting. It also sets the stage for understanding the *market* aspect of the environment, especially buyer, competitor, and trade responses to the new product.

APPENDIX: POTENTIAL FORCES AND MEDIATORS IN THE MARKET ENVIRONMENT FOR A NEW PRODUCT

Selected Global Forces (Size and Trends)

Natural Resources	Population	Cultural Values	Technology	Economic Systems	Laws/Regulations
PRIMARY	Size	Individuality	**TYPE**	Gross National Product	Patent status
Land	Birth/death rates	Status	Product	Gross Domestic Product	Trade secret status
Oceans	Life expectancy	Tradition	Components	Money supply	Copyright status
Water	Age distribution	Competitiveness	Package	Inflation rate	Trademark status
Sunlight	Households (number, size, formation)	Youth orientation	Process	Interest rates	Trade names
Atmosphere	Geography	Materialism	Labor related	Disposable income	Service marks
Wind	Education	Leisure	Distribution logistics	Sectoral growth	Warranties
Genetic heritage	Employment	Risk taking	Information	Exchange rates	Product liability
Other	Time budgets	Problem solving	Telecommunications	Transportation systems	Grading standards
		Fatalism	Marketing research	Employment rates	Licenses/permits
SECONDARY	Sex	Role of nature	Advertising	Stock markets	Exclusive dealing
Animals	Race	Family life	Direct mail	Commodity markets	Tying arrangements
Vegetables	Ethnic origin	Male/female roles	Other	Energy supplies	Boycotts
Minerals	Marital status	Gratification		Other	Price fixing
Other	Family life cycle stage	Humor	**CHANGE**		Price discrimination
	Religion	Romanticism	Rate of change		Dumping
TERTIARY	Social stratification	Cleanliness	Type of change		False advertising
Animal products	Other	Creativity	■ Continuous		False marking
Vegetable products		Institutional reliance	■ Discontinuous		False designation of origin
Mineral products		Lifestyle	Diffusion process		Other
Human health		Other	Substitutability		
Other			Other		

APPENDIX (continued): Selected Environmental Mediators (U.S. Examples)

Politicians	Legal/Regulatory Agencies	Financial Institutions	Mass Media	Industry Associations	Special Interest Groups
NATIONAL LEVEL	**LEGAL**	U.S.	**BROADCAST**	**ASSOCIATIONS AND RESEARCH CONSORTIA**	Consumer protection
President	Federal level courts	Commercial Banks	Network television	Management structure	Consumer activists
Vice President	Federal special courts	Savings and Loan Associations	Local television	Membership criteria	Cooperatives
Cabinet	State level courts	Mutual Savings Banks	Cable television	Number of members	User groups
Members of Congress	Arbitration	Credit Unions	Spot cable television	Size of members	Community associations
■ House	Other	Pension Funds	Network radio	Membership change patterns	Labor unions
■ Senate		Life Insurance Companies	Local radio (AM/FM)	Relative influence of members	Political action committees
Congressional staff	**REGULATORY**	Investment Companies	Other	Mission, objectives, goals	Retired persons organizations
Committee members	Departments of:			Location	Children's organizations
Subcommittee members	■ Agriculture	Federal Reserve System	**PRINT**	Budget and resources	Religious groups and organizations
Nonregulatory agencies	■ Commerce	■ Board of Governors	National, regional, local magazines	History of recent activities	Animal rights organizations
Executive branch offices	■ Energy	■ Federal Open Market Committee	National, regional, local newspapers	Other	Social rights organizations
Scientific and technical offices	■ Transportation	■ Federal Reserve Banks	Other		Health interest groups
Other	■ Treasury	■ Mortgage associations			Environmental interest groups
	Consumer Product Safety Commission	Federal Home Loan Bank System	**OTHER**		Other
STATE LEVEL	Environmental Protection Agency	Federal Land Banks	Direct mail		
Governor	Federal Trade Commission	Farm Credit Banks	Outdoor		
Other	Food and Drug Administration	Student Loan Marketing Association	Transit		
	International Trade Commission	Other	Point-of-purchase		
COUNTY LEVEL	Other		Other		
County manager					
Other			**MEASURES**		
			Audience composition		
CITY LEVEL			Coverage		
Mayor			Circulation		
Other			Costs		
			Other		

3 Anticipating Market Acceptance of New Products

Anticipating the needs of major market stakeholders for a new product can provide important information for its design, launch, and ultimate acceptance. It enables an organization to take actions that might influence a variety of market stakeholders, any one of which might stall or accelerate the product's performance. The interactions between an organization and the major stakeholders that define a market for a new product cannot be taken for granted. Goldman, Sachs & Co. learned this lesson through the 1990 launch of a new "vulture fund" called the Water Street Corporate Recovery Fund.[1]

Goldman raised some $783 million to invest in the bonds of troubled firms (hence the predatory term "vulture fund"). The fund depended on the purchase of high-yield bonds at low prices. This ownership was then leveraged to influence the firm's restructuring. A successful restructuring could keep a firm from bankruptcy and increase the value of the bonds. The fund was very successful. Reportedly, it nearly doubled the value of its first major investment and promised annual returns greater than 25 percent.

Unfortunately, the new Goldman Water Street Fund also had the potential for conflicts of interest. A reported 9 of the 21 firms in the fund were current or past clients. It might be reasonable for clients to perceive that Goldman could use information from current or past relationships to obtain outcomes not always in their best interests, but rather in Goldman's. Just the *perception* that difficulties could ensue among important Goldman clients and other stakeholders (including the financial media) threatened other aspects of Goldman's business. Consequently, about a year after the launch, Goldman announced plans to terminate the fund by the end of 1991—despite its profitability.

The Goldman situation highlights the need to anticipate the behavior of major stakeholders in the market of a firm's new offering. In this case, the reaction of *current* customers threatened other Goldman products and services. A firm developing a new product must—before product launch—incorporate into its actions (including product design) the prevailing and expected behaviors and responses of current and potential buyers, competitors, trade intermediaries, suppliers, and other market stakeholders. After launch, it must incorporate actual stakeholder response into the new product, making adjustments where necessary to enhance market acceptance—and, as in the case of Goldman—being prepared to terminate the new product if it risks other parts of the business.

The ideal market conditions for launching a new product among multiple stakeholders are, of course, those that are *friction-free*! Under such favorable conditions, potential buyers discover and adopt the new product without delay, current customers and competitors do not react against it, retailers and wholesalers make it readily available, suppliers cooperate in delivering components and services on time, and other stakeholders do not interfere with its launch or marketing—and all of this under stable business conditions!

Unfortunately, a friction-free new product launch is unlikely in rapidly changing and complex market situations. Key market stakeholders outside the organization represent sources of *market friction* that can delay (or accelerate) adoption of a new product. The continuing presence of major environmental trends in natural resources, population, culture, and technology, and actions by environmental mediators that moderate these forces, create additional uncertainties and turbulence that affect market friction. Generally, *the greater (less) the market friction between the new product and major stakeholders, the slower (faster) the rate of new product acceptance or adoption among potential buyers.*

Developing new products that achieve strategic success therefore requires an understanding and estimation of the degree of market friction in new product acceptance. The firm must (1) identify the sources of friction, (2) overcome those that can be changed (including modifying the firm's own new product development and launch program), and (3) develop an approach to estimate the rate at which potential buyers will adopt the new product from an analysis of the remaining sources of friction. The three major sections of this chapter cover these topics.

SOURCES OF MARKET FRICTION

In Japan, consumers enjoy canned liquid coffee as a beverage in much the same way that U.S. consumers enjoy cola drinks. In 1991 Kraft General Foods and Nestlé set out to answer the question of whether or not U.S. consumers would also enjoy a similar liquid coffee beverage.[2] Although the product was not "new" in terms of its global existence, it would be very new to American consumers, possibly requiring reformulation and a different marketing program. Kraft developed Cappio, a new cappucino-type bottled coffee drink in coffee, mocha, and cinnamon flavors. Nestlé, which successfully markets the beverage under the brand name of Georgia Coffee in Japan, developed two new drinks for the U.S. market: Mocha Cooler and Ice Breaker.

Consider some of the questions that each firm might have asked in developing their new coffee beverage for the U.S. market:

- Given the strong tradition of hot coffee in the United States, will *potential buyers* find it inconsistent to drink coffee from a can or bottle, chilled or at room temperature? Who will be in the market segment of U.S. potential buyers that respond favorably to the new drink, are there enough of them to support the product, and will they repeatedly purchase it?

- If purchased, will the new drink replace currently consumed beverages—for example, brewed coffee, juices, bottled water, sodas—or will it add to total beverage consumption? Will it be viewed as similar to iced coffee (that is, as a warm-weather beverage), or will it be viewed differently? How will various *competitors* react to this new entry?

- Why should supermarket *retailers* stock the new beverage, especially if it only takes away sales from existing products? If they stock it, where will they place it in the store—in the beverage section, in the coffee section, in the juice section? How receptive will other retailers be to the new beverage—convenience stores, vending machines, coffee specialty stores, fast food outlets, drug stores?

- Will *suppliers* of coffee, cocoa, sugar, sugar substitutes, flavor enhancers, and other ingredients be cooperative during new product formulation and in production ramp up? Are there potential conflicts of interest for advertising agencies between the new product and other products they are currently servicing?

- Will potential buyers be favorably or unfavorably affected by cultural, demographic, economic, natural resource, or other major global trends? Will the approval of certain regulators be required? Will other *stakeholder groups* express a special interest in the new product and affect potential buyer behavior?

Of course, numerous other questions can be raised, but these five reveal key sources of market friction for a new product: potential buyers, competitors, trade intermediaries, suppliers, and other market stakeholders in the business environment.

Potential Buyer Inertia and New Product Adoption

Managers immersed in their new products for months, or perhaps years, must often remind themselves that most of their potential buyers know little or nothing about their new product before launch. Therefore, at the minimum, organizations offering a new product want potential buyers to be *aware* of it. But awareness alone will not guarantee new product purchase. It is only a first step leading to new product acceptance or adoption—or its purchase and use on a regular basis.

Within their constraints, individual and organizational potential buyers have worked out ways of satisfying many of their needs and reaching their goals with existing products and services. Consequently, firms offering anything new may have to pry potential buyers loose from current preferences and learned patterns of behavior to convince them to purchase. In effect, firms offering new products will have to overcome some form of informational, attitudinal, and/or behavioral *buyer inertia* to achieve their sales forecasts.

Consider again the new liquid coffees by General Foods and Nestlé. Consumers currently satisfy their thirst needs with a variety of beverage options and may even feel inundated by the number of alternatives. Why should they be motivated to try yet another new beverage? How much and what kind of information will consumers need before they even contemplate trying the new product? How will prevailing attitudes toward coffee—as a beverage served hot at breakfast, as a stimulant, or as an after-meal complement—affect perceptions of a bottled coffee? What types of consumers might respond more favorably than others to the new product?

Answering difficult questions about response to any new product depends on understanding buying behavior for the product, whether by individuals, families, or organizations. The complexity of potential buyer behavior for a new product is illustrated in Figure 3.1, which elaborates the basic conceptual model of Figure 1.1 but focuses on key aspects of the market. The following brief overview and discussion of Figure 3.1 provide background for understanding the concepts and measures of expected buyer behavior and new product adoption rates as a source of market friction.[3]

Overview

Current marketing thought advocates that the *needs* of potential buyers and related market stakeholders drive the design of a new product offering, as well as the entire marketing program, so as to gain buyer purchase decisions and accomplish the organization's objectives. This concept is easy to state, but difficult to implement. The difficulty lies in clarifying the multidimensionality of human needs and recognizing that many needs are currently satisfied. Further, the new product may address a need that is only part of a broader, yet ever-changing need system. This dynamic aspect of needs creates gaps of unsatisfied needs that provide opportunity for new products. The identified and unsatisfied needs of potential buyers in targeted market segments largely define the nature of the subsequent buying process to satisfy them. Needs that generate longer, more complex buying processes increase the opportunity for market friction and may confound new product development efforts as well as estimation of market demand.

Needs can stimulate a person to commence buying processes for new products and, in turn, buying processes affect the shape of needs. For example, if consumers respond to the possible need for a new sensation in beverage taste, information about the new liquid coffee concept may provoke search for and trial of the product. However, if trial reveals an unexpected taste (too bitter, too sweet) or the contents include unexpected ingredients (preservatives, taste enhancers, artificial sweeteners), other concerns may be flagged and the buyer's interest wanes or escalates. In effect, the interaction between the identification of a need and the processes through which consumers resolve it may alter the need and further complicate a potential buyer's purchase process, if not accelerate, terminate, or postpone it.

FIGURE 3.1   Factors affecting new product development: focus on potential buyers.

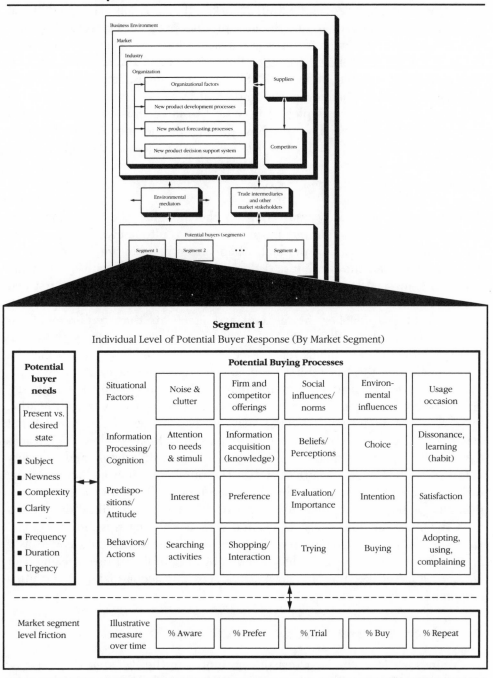

Segment 1

Individual Level of Potential Buyer Response (By Market Segment)

Potential buyer needs	Potential Buying Processes					
Present vs. desired state	Situational Factors	Noise & clutter	Firm and competitor offerings	Social influences/ norms	Environ- mental influences	Usage occasion
■ Subject	Information Processing/ Cognition	Attention to needs & stimuli	Information acquisition (knowledge)	Beliefs/ Perceptions	Choice	Dissonance, learning (habit)
■ Newness ■ Complexity ■ Clarity	Predispo- sitions/ Attitude	Interest	Preference	Evaluation/ Importance	Intention	Satisfaction
■ Frequency ■ Duration ■ Urgency	Behaviors/ Actions	Searching activities	Shopping/ Interaction	Trying	Buying	Adopting, using, complaining
Market segment level friction	Illustrative measure over time	% Aware	% Prefer	% Trial	% Buy	% Repeat

Buying process complexity at the *individual buyer level* is a major source of buyer inertia, and may explain delays in purchasing a new product. When aggregated to a market or a segment within a market, the variation among individual buyers in their propensity to buy the new product presents a picture of the degree of *market-level* friction to anticipate in achieving new product forecasts. In Figure 3.1, the boxes labeled *Potential Buyer Needs* and *Potential Buying Processes* represent possible interactions of these important aspects of new product adoption at the individual level. The important lesson of Figure 3.1 is that because buyer behavior is complex, it is critical to include as much information as possible about it throughout the new product development cycle. Methods for obtaining information about buyer behavior are reviewed in Chapter 6.

Understanding Potential Buyer Needs

Buyer needs are a primary motivation for the thoughts, predispositions, and actions that define potential buying processes and, ultimately, the decision of whether or not to buy a new product. At any given point in time, a need is the difference between the present and desired state of some focal aspect of the human organism. After eating salty food, a person may experience thirst and desire to quench the thirst. To the extent that a potential satisfier (or product, such as a thirst quencher) fits a need and meets its time requirements, it may be consumed. At the basic biological level, water may satisfy the need. However, other related needs (effervescence, sweetness, smoothness) may be superimposed on the basic thirst need, and thereby complicate it.

Beyond the motivational requirements of the body's biological or physiological system, needs can be cultural, social, psychological, or a combination thereof. For example, bottled coffee may satisfy a biological thirst, but thirst may not be the primary motivation for its purchase. Related physiological motivations for trying or using it might include physical stimulation and a variety of taste sensations. Social motivations for the purchase might include drinking with or serving to friends in order to be accepted or liked. Psychological motivations for buying bottled coffee might be the personal gratification derived from the status or uniqueness associated with consuming this new beverage. However, cultural motivations—such as the tradition of drinking coffee as a brewed hot beverage—may induce friction against trial and use of canned or bottled liquid coffee, thereby slowing and possibly jeopardizing its eventual acceptance.

Defining the Shape and Temporal Aspects of Need

The framework of need characteristics presented in the *Potential Buyer Needs* box of Figure 3.1 provides a language to help describe the nature of human needs and to assess how they might affect buying processes and new product adoption.[4] The seven aspects of needs identified fit into two categories: the first four relate to the *shape* of the need and the last three relate to the *temporal* aspects of individual needs.

1. **Subject of need.** The *subject* of a need is an individual's perception of the topic defining the need. In the consumer's language, the subject may be defined at very general levels (such as thirst) or at very specific levels (such as thirst to reduce body temperature, thirst to replenish lost fluids, or thirst to sip something effervescent).[5]

2. **Newness of need.** The *newness* of a need defines the potential buyer's experience with it and helps to shape the buying process for a new product. New needs generally require more learning on the part of the buyer as a basis for the purchase decision and may delay new product adoption. For example, the first time the need for purchasing a new automobile arises, significant amounts of shopping and information acquisition may be necessary. The next time the need occurs, learned experiences may result in a different buying process—such as less information acquisition.

3. **Complexity of need.** The *complexity* (or number of facets) of a need perceived by the potential buyer determines the extent of features or attributes a new product must have to meet the need. More complex needs will generally require more complex products and services, which in turn require more information for the consumer to learn. Need complexity tends to involve longer buying processes and often invites consultation with others and consideration of competing alternatives to satisfy the need, thereby further delaying purchase. A thirst need based on salty food may be relatively simple in comparison with a thirst need that involves social and ego motivations (for example, serving beverages at a dinner party). An organization's need to replenish the supply of paper for its fax machines is much less complex than its need to purchase a new computer system to support increased transaction processing with its clients.

4. **Clarity of need.** The *clarity* of a need is the precision with which a consumer perceives the need (or some facet of it). In many situations potential buyers may not think, or care to think, about their need beyond its very fuzzy initial concept, whereas in others they may have very specific ideas about their need. Buyers whose needs are fuzzy may engage in a search for a significant amount of information, including an evaluation and a trial of the product if possible, to better define their need and alternatives to satisfy it. As a result, their buying process is longer than that of buyers whose needs are more clearly perceived.

5. **Frequency of need.** The frequency of a need is defined by how often the same need occurs during a time period. Hunger may occur several times in a day, depending on how often it is satisfied. An organization's need for a new telephone switching system may occur once every 10 years.

6. **Duration of need.** The duration of a need is how long the state of tension associated with it lasts. Hunger or thirst may last for a few minutes and then pass. The need for a new car may last for two or three years (unless the old car finally breaks down).

7. **Urgency of need.** The urgency of a need is the perceived amount of time within which the consumer believes the need must be resolved. Some

individuals may get severe headaches if they do not eat when they perceive a hunger need; they would clearly perceive such a need as urgent. An organization that depends on reliable response to customer telephone calls may deem a new switching system urgent when the old one reaches a certain calling capacity.

Generally, the newer, more complex, and less clear the shape of a particular need, the longer the buying process. The needs that might be satisfied by a new bottled coffee may not be readily apparent to a potential consumer because the more basic thirst needs are most likely satisfied by current alternatives. Its taste, how and when it should be used, and its relationship to other needs make bottled coffee somewhat more complex and fuzzy than carbonated or juice drinks. The time consumers must spend to learn about the need and how it may fit into their overall system of needs may, of course, slow the adoption process. To enhance learning and speed the process of adoption, the firms offering bottled coffee must reach potential consumers with timely, informative, and persuasive communication about the new product, its taste, and/or its use.

As a rule, the less frequent, less urgent, and shorter the duration of a need, the greater the likelihood a buyer can postpone satisfying it. The more frequent, more urgent, and longer the duration of a need, the less it can be postponed. In the bottled coffee example, the need related to the beverage is not urgent, so it will most likely be of short duration. Further, the need's frequency of occurrence may not be clear to potential buyers. Therefore, they could be expected to postpone satisfying it unless substantial inducements to try the product are established (such as free samples or coupons).

Although speculation about the needs for a bottled coffee beverage begs for market research, it should be apparent that needs and buying behavior involve dynamic processes that make them a difficult target for firms developing and forecasting new products. Nevertheless, bringing structure and understanding to these complex processes is possible and aids new product decision making. The role of market research in understanding market needs, product development, and the rate of adoption are considered in Chapter 6.

Clarifying Potential Buying Processes

The complexity and dynamic nature of buyer behavior for new products make their development and forecasting highly situational. Therefore, the conceptualization and measurement of buyer behavior for a new offering require flexibility. The need satisfied by a new home sound system might define a buying process that is very different from one used for a new frozen food entree. The former product might require extensive information processing and evaluation, whereas the latter can be tried with minimal information processing and directly evaluated in use. Nevertheless, even a new frozen food entree may involve more extensive information processing and evaluation for someone who is a first time potential buyer of a particular brand than for someone who is already familiar with the brand.

To accommodate a flexible view of buyer behavior, the set of 20 smaller boxes in Figure 3.1 (within the larger box labeled *Potential Buying Processes*) identifies numerous factors that characterize new product purchasing. No specific theory of how or why consumers buy prevails in this diagram; rather, several conventional concepts are identified to organize thinking and market research on buyer behavior.[6] Although the 20 smaller boxes reflect a logic, no specific interconnections are hypothesized. Further, the diagram represents buyer behavior for an individual, but can also be modified to include family and organizational buying behavior. Organizational buying processes involve multiple persons in a *buying center*, where the role of social processes and interpersonal influence become central.[7]

Four categories of buyer behavior factors define processes at the individual level: situational factors, informational or cognitive factors, predispositional or attitudinal factors, and behavioral factors. Within each of these categories, at least five activities can be thought of as proceeding from earlier to later stages of buying. For example, in the behavioral category, *search* activities may precede *shopping, trying, buying/adopting*, and *using* the new product. Conceptually this may be a logical time-dimensioned process; however, in reality consumers are not necessarily expected to follow this exact sequence. For example, they might buy and use a product without appreciable search, shopping, or trial. They may be motivated not by a product-specific need, but perhaps by some other human need—for example, the desire to satisfy curiosity, to be surprised, or to try something novel. Each of the four categories of buyer behavior factors is briefly reviewed.

1. Situational Factors   The noise and clutter of an information-rich environment (brought about largely by increasingly ubiquitous information technologies), the commercial offerings by numerous competitors, social and interpersonal influences from other people (such as family and friends), environmental influences (such as regulatory action or technology change), and special occasions that bias product usage (such as holidays, social outings, vacation) are potential *situational* factors that may stimulate needs or moderate various buying processes. For example, entertaining friends at home may be an occasion to serve something new—such as a new liquid coffee beverage.

2. Information Processing/Cognitive Factors   *Information processing* by potential buyers (the second row of smaller boxes in Figure 3.1) occurs at the cognitive or intellectual level.[8] Through *attention* processes, potential buyers selectively filter and *acquire* information from the situational aspects of their environment, as well as recall it from their memories (short- and long-term). Typically, buyers are responsive to information that may be relevant to solving a need or problem, or that may otherwise interest them. However, unless the need is particularly urgent or frequently recurring, information about a new product may not reach a potential buyer immediately. When (and if) the information is received may cause a delay in the potential buying process.

Once information has been acquired that better defines a need, it might be organized into *beliefs* and *perceptions* about how alternatives (products and their features) satisfy the need. Numerous conceptualizations characterize how potential buyers organize acquired information in order to choose among alternatives.[9] Many involve the formation of beliefs about each alternative along several attributes defining the need (and the product).[10] These beliefs about each multiattribute alternative become the basis for stronger predispositions to choose and buy one alternative instead of another. *Choice* can also be made on the "whole" alternative (new product) without respect to its features, it can be postponed to a later date, or a decision can be made not to purchase at all.

When viable alternatives (including the new product) are present, beliefs have been formed about each, and a purchase made, a state of *dissonance* may arise that requires additional information to quell. Dissonance arises because the alternatives rejected usually have some positive features that are forgone in the decision.[11] The classic practical proof of cognitive dissonance (often called "buyer's remorse") is based on evidence that advertising generates consistently higher effectiveness scores among recent buyers of a new product than among potential buyers—the recent buyers are seeking information to reduce their dissonance. Another consequence of information processing up to and after choice is the *learning* that takes place from the information collected and from using and experiencing the new product. This learning may register in short- and/or long-term memory for future use.

3. Predispositions/Attitudes   As potential buyers find themselves in various situations that stimulate needs, and acquire or recall information that might help them solve their problems, they engage in processes that lead to the formation of *predispositions or attitudes* toward various alternatives (the third layer of boxes within *Potential Buying Processes*). These processes may begin with an *interest* in one or more of the alternatives (possibly including a new product), followed by the formulation of a *preference* for each, and then possibly a more detailed *evaluation of the importance* of the multiple attributes defining each alternative.

An even stronger predisposition toward satisfying a need with a new product is the *intention to buy*,[12] and subsequently the degree of *satisfaction* with the product.[13] Although much of new product development and forecasting depends on measures of the intention-to-buy concept, estimates of expected satisfaction can be very important. Unfortunately, they are often overlooked. Satisfaction is especially important for products that depend on repeat purchases and/or interpersonal communications from early buyers to other potential buyers. Typically, customer satisfaction is measured after new product launch, but its estimation during the use-testing stages of new product development (prior to launch) can be informative—for example, in anticipating the design and implementation of customer service prior to launch.

4. Behaviors/Actions   The fourth category of small boxes in Figure 3.1 includes specific *behaviors and actions*. Potential buyers may engage in various overt *searching activities* that generate information useful to resolving their needs. For example, potential buyers can thumb through catalogs and magazines to get ideas for solving a particular problem. *Shopping* is an even more overt behavior, in which potential buyers visit retail stores to examine the product first-hand and get additional information from sales personnel.

The activity of *trying* the new product may be particularly helpful in evaluation. Test driving a new car, sampling a new perfume, trying a new piece of software demonstrated at a trade show, or buying a new beverage to try its taste are examples of trying behaviors.[14] *Buying* a new product involves activities necessary to facilitate ownership. For industrial products, buying may include a detailed set of behaviors that requires a purchasing department for execution. For consumer products, it may involve similarly detailed purchasing behaviors, including negotiation, obtaining credit, disposing of an existing product, and agreeing on terms of sale.

The ultimate goal of new product development is, of course, *adoption*, which involves continued *usage* and *experiencing* by potential buyers. For many new products, adoption differs from simply *buying*. Adoption means that the new product has taken a legitimate position in the life of the individual or organizational buyer. Adoption implies an acceptance of and commitment to the new product that represent a change in behavior from previous patterns. With commitment and ownership, many buyers will exercise rights to *complain* and otherwise voice their concerns about the new product if its performance fails to meet their needs in any particular way. Building in the service capability to respond to complaints may prevent *rejection* of the new product, even after purchase. (Rejection can take the form of switching to another brand or otherwise discontinuing purchase.)

The decisiveness of new product adoption behavior affects the other processes involved in buying. In addition to stimulating post-purchase dissonance, experience from using the new product becomes stored in memory and can be used as information for future purchases. Experience also translates into information communicated to others about the new product. Product adoption and usage therefore interact with situational factors—forming the basis for social interaction or the possible redefinition of usage occasions as more is learned about the new product. Moreover, adoption and usage influence attitudinal processes, especially intention to repeat purchase the new product (if necessary) and the degree of satisfaction. The degree of satisfaction can also affect the communication of information to others about the new product.

Summary of Individual-Level Sources of Buyer Friction

At this point, the complexity of potential buyer behavior should be apparent from the many possible interactions among buyer needs and among the 20 aspects of buying processes identified. However, it should also be apparent that this complexity is tractable. Not all variables are needed to develop predictions of response to new products. Further, simplified models from these concepts can be descriptive of a new product adoption process or predictive of ultimate purchase behavior.

Several examples in the marketing and innovation literatures describe adoption processes by using selected factors listed in Figure 3.1. A typical comprehensive eight-step summary *adoption process model* includes problem perception, awareness, comprehension, attitude, legitimation, trial, adoption, and dissonance.[15] The approach allows feedback processes at most stages, and cuts across the cognitive, attitudinal, and behavioral fields. Further, it recognizes that stages can be skipped—for example, impulse purchases move directly from awareness to the trial stages.

Other approaches focus on modeling selected aspects of potential buyer behavior for new products.[16] For example, measuring *perceptions* and *preferences* of current products (and their features) against new concepts helps to define positioning for the new product. Modeling choice for proposed multiattribute product concepts (using conjoint analysis) facilitates the estimation of market share (of choices) for new concepts against competing ones. Using measures of attention and information acquisition (comprehension) helps to determine potential buyer response to ads for the new product. Thus, the rich set of concepts and variables that characterize potential buyer response to new products can be used to facilitate a variety of new product design and marketing decisions, as well as forecasts of demand.

Aggregating to the Market-Segment Level

The preceding discussion of potential buyer behavior focuses on the individual buyer's likelihood of adopting a new product. However, an individual is part of a previously identified *market segment* of potential buyers. Within a segment, potential buyers can be classified according to various stages in their progress toward adoption (or nonadoption). The bottom set of boxes in the enlarged part of Figure 3.1 illustrates market-level measures that characterize selected aspects of buying behavior.

For example, the percentage of the market segment *aware* of a new product at a particular time helps to determine the level of information in the market. An S-shaped hypothetical awareness curve over time after new product launch is illustrated in Figure 3.2. In this case awareness is very low at launch, rises rapidly as a result of word-of-mouth communication among buyers and any external communication (such as advertising), and then levels off.

Because awareness is a precondition of any additional information processing, measuring awareness helps to estimate the percentage who might *prefer*, *try*, *intend to buy*, or *repeat purchase* the new product. Which of these measures to use in a particular new product situation, and how to develop estimates over time prior to launch, are essential questions in estimating response to new product designs. These types of measures, taken for a market segment, are considered in greater detail in Parts 2 and 3 of the book.

Continuously Evaluating Market Segmentation for a New Product

Markets for new products and services rarely include the total population of individuals, households, or organizations. Most successful new products are based on the identification of market segments and meeting the needs of poten-

FIGURE 3.2   Market awareness of new product over time.

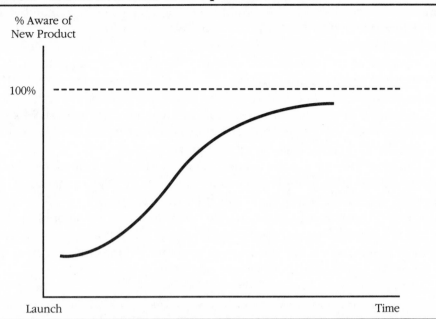

tial buyers and other stakeholders within them.[17] The preceding discussion on potential buyer behavior focuses on a single segment. The assumption is that a process of segmentation reveals somewhat homogeneous groups of potential buyers whose preferences can be targeted with alternative new products. However, just as markets are ever-changing, so too are segments within them.

Changes in market segments while new products are under development can have dire consequences for achieving new product forecasts. Consequently, segmentation, defined as a *dynamic decision process* that enables a firm to responsively allocate marketing resources to achieve business objectives, must become part of the analysis to understand market friction.

The segmentation decision process seeks to implement the *marketing concept*—to define an offering (products and services) that meets the needs of target buyers while recognizing the behaviors of competitors and other stakeholders that define the market. Although there are several decisions to be made in the process of segmentation, they revolve around the identification of groups of potential buyers or buying centers such that responses to a marketing program are similar within each group, but different between groups.

The concepts and variables identified in Figure 3.1 can be used as possible bases for partitioning a market into segments, depending on the decision problem. For example, the nature of the *need* for a new product can serve to define an important basis for segmentation that will drive new product design. By identifying the product features that are reflective of possible needs (through focus groups and other research methods), defining alternative concepts around them, and eliciting potential buyer choices for the concepts (preferences, intentions to buy), individual measures of need help to identify segments.

Suppose, for example, that after some exploratory research among consumers, the concept of a new liquid coffee beverage can be defined along its social dimension (family drink, after-dinner drink with guests), its taste dimension (full-bodied, lightly effervescent), its cultural origin (French, Italian, American), and its package (bottle, can). This definition suggests 24 possible new product concepts (a full-bodied French coffee that comes in a bottle and can be served after dinner with guests is one concept). Obtaining individual consumer preferences for these concepts (through conjoint analysis in a sample survey, for example) provides measures of how important the various features of bottled coffee are to each potential buyer.

Once preferences are obtained, segments can be formed by clustering together into various groupings persons who are more alike in their preferences than others (through a technique called *cluster analysis*). By inclusion of other measures of consumers from the sample survey (such as demographics, lifestyle, and media usage), the segments can be more fully described as a basis for developing a comprehensive marketing program.[18] From these segments, one or more can be selected as targets for new products.

Thus, segmenting markets on the basis of individual consumer needs and buying behavior (to identify the best new product concept and design to meet the need) provides an important link from the individual buyer to the market-segment and total-market level of analysis. Once decisions are made on target segments and their corresponding new products, estimates of market and sales demand can be forecast to help evaluate the financial viability of the project—keeping in mind the possibility that each segment is a dynamic concept and will change over time.

However, to constrain the product design and financial estimates to just potential buyers may limit understanding of the entire market structure for a new product. The response of competitors, the retail and wholesale trade, suppliers, and other market stakeholders must be incorporated into the development and forecasting processes.

Competitive Friction

The presence of competitors can have mixed effects on new product development and forecasting. In some cases, competitors create market friction that can slow the acceptance of new products. Shortly after Quantum Corporation introduced its Plus HardCard expansion disk drive for personal computers, competitors announced cards with twice the storage space and priced some $100 less than the HardCard. Retailers slowed their ordering until the performance of the promised competitive products could be evaluated.

In other cases, the presence of rivalry from competitors can accelerate acceptance and market development. Although VisiCalc was the first spreadsheet available for personal computers, market acceptance of spreadsheets did not grow rapidly until Lotus Development Corporation introduced Lotus 1-2-3, its competitive product. The presence of multiple competitors launching new products provides additional information and alternatives in a market, which can facilitate potential buyers' decision processes.

The process of estimating competitor effects on potential buyers' acceptance of a new product begins with a consideration of the factors that define competition. Factors that might be used to characterize competition are illustrated in the Appendix. They include both *industry-* and *firm-level* factors. Predicting how competitors, with certain combinations of factors and past behaviors, will react in a given situation (before and after launch) is critical to the development and forecasting of the new product. However, this task is not easy.[19]

Research on how competitors might respond to specific new product situations is scant.[20] The complexity of possible competitive reactions and their highly situational nature make it difficult to generalize about how and when a particular competitor might respond to a new product. Consequently, the following guidelines might be used to generate information to estimate the nature, strength, and probability of response by each of a number of competitors. These guidelines follow a logic based on data gathered from research, expertise, and historical patterns to estimate time delay, market development, and new product sales consequences from competitor response.

1. **Determine characteristics of industry structure.** The structure of an industry can influence competitive response. In a review of four industry groupings, the following four "lessons" about industry characteristics and competitive response are offered: (1) high fixed costs promote competitive response to share-gain attempts, (2) low storage costs reduce competitive reactions, (3) growing primary demand reduces competitive reaction, and (4) large firms avoid price competition.[21] Of course, these lessons can vary according to any given situation; thus, evaluating the general characteristics of an industry will add insight to individual competitor responses. In the Appendix, several characteristics of industry structure are identified.

2. **Identify potential competitors.** Competitors can be defined according to the extent to which they satisfy the need of a particular target segment of potential buyers. For example, the competitor set for a new liquid coffee beverage might be defined to include carbonated beverages, coffee, tea, juices, and other liquid drinks. However, the segment of consumers who may view a liquid coffee drink as an afternoon pick-me-up may consider a chocolate candy bar, a piece of fruit, or a stick of chewing gum as an alternative. A market segmentation analysis of potential buyers will help uncover relevant sets of competitors, and may lead to a redefinition of industry structure.

3. **Determine competitor strengths and weaknesses.** At the organization level, several factors identified in the Appendix can be used to profile a competitor's strengths and weaknesses. They include the organization's technologies, manufacturing, finance, management, marketing, and customer base. Although some of the firm's strengths and weaknesses will be apparent from market research on the structure of the market for the proposed

new product, other data about competitors, especially their historical reaction to competition, will be useful to collect and analyze.

4. **Assess new product threat to each competitor's current position.** Beginning with an assessment of potential buyer response to a new offering,
estimates of revised competitive market shares can be developed assuming
no competitive response. If a *pro forma* financial picture of each competitor's situation were hypothesized, and the effects of market share changes
estimated, the potential loss (and its timing) may be an important indicator of the nature and magnitude of the new product's threat to each
competitor, and hence their future reaction.

5. **Estimate probability of competitor response to threat.** The preceding step
helps to estimate the probability of a response. The more substantial the
threat, the greater the probability of a response. For example, other factors
held constant, a large and quick share loss to a new product may increase
the likelihood of a competitor's response. However, the historical pattern
of competitor response must also be reviewed. Some competitors (often
large, inflexible organizations) are notoriously slow in their response to
competition—if they respond at all. It's possible that significant share and
profit losses may not be enough to generate a response.

6. **If a competitor responds to threat of a new product, estimate type and
strength of response.** Assume that the new product is introduced into a
market situation with existing competitors and consider their likely reactions. Will they lower prices in response to a new product entry to avoid
losing market share? If they lower price, what effect will it have on demand for the new product? Will they increase their promotional efforts?
Change product features? If so, what effects will those strategies have on
new product demand? Alternatively, if a new product is introduced into
a new market with no direct competitors, can the entry of new competitors be expected? If so, when? In a study of two products, it was found
that firms retaliate against a new entrant when they have effective marketing weapons (elasticity of their marketing mix variables).[22] Firms will
retreat from new entrants when they lack effective marketing weapons.
Consequently, knowledge about competitors' marketing program effectiveness (and the other factors identified) helps a firm to anticipate actions
and reactions when planning the development and forecasts of the new
product.

7. **On the basis of expected competitor response, determine revisions in new
product development as well as the market and sales forecasts associated
with it.** Depending on specific expected responses, defensive moves can
be taken. Price can be lowered, more advanced features can be included
in the design process, heavier promotions can be planned, and possible
entry barriers can be erected. The effects of these actions can then be
weighed against future competitive response to those actions and factored
into development decisions and forecast estimates.

In most cases, the effects of competitors will be realized through potential buyers and their decisions about whether or not to adopt the new product. However, competitive reactions that affect the trade and other stakeholders might also be expected. For example, large competitors may make it difficult to obtain shelf space through major retailers. They may also bring lawsuits and stimulate regulatory agencies to investigate a new product in the hopes of delaying and possibly derailing its launch.

As an example of competitor retaliation to a new product, consider the 1991 launch by McNeil Consumer Products Co. (a division of Johnson & Johnson) of Tylenol PM to compete with Bristol-Meyers Squibb's Excedrin PM.[23] Tylenol PM, packaged in a blue box similar to that of Excedrin PM, combined painkilling and sleeping pill capabilities. The new product quickly gained share and volume (reportedly $60 million) and Bristol-Meyers brought suit against McNeil. A consequence of the Bristol-Meyers/McNeil legal battle was a temporary injunction on sales of the product; however, McNeil attorneys obtained a delay pending outcome of the court decision. Aside from the risk of lost sales due to an injunction, legal fees and lost management time are costs that, if anticipated, must be factored into the development and forecasting processes.

Trade Intermediary Friction

When organizations launch new products that require distribution through various channels, they are dependent on the cooperation and performance of trade intermediaries. Generally, the retail and wholesale trades provide *availability* of the new product to potential buyers. Depending on the nature of the product and market, an organization tries to orchestrate a selection of retail, wholesale, and other intermediaries to define its *channels of distribution*. Building an effective channel requires cooperation from each member. Numerous competing and noncompeting manufacturers besiege desirable channel members for often scarce shelf space. Placing a new coffee beverage on already crowded retail beverage shelves may be an exceedingly difficult challenge for all but the largest manufacturers that have clout with retailers.

The sought-after channel members make allocation decisions on whether or not to handle various products. Because new products represent high-risk situations, intermediaries are often reluctant to stock them without substantial proof of sales performance. Any reluctance to take on new products reduces availability to potential buyers and translates into increased market friction — or reduced opportunity to sell the new product. However, successful market acceptance of the new product among a small number of intermediaries can lead, through a diffusion process, to adoption of the new product by additional channel members. The result is an increasing availability. Figure 3.3 shows one possible pattern of growth in availability over time for a new product measured by the number of outlets stocking the product. Other measures include the depth of availability within each outlet, such as number of facings, displays, and depth of stock.

FIGURE 3.3   Distribution availability of new product over time.

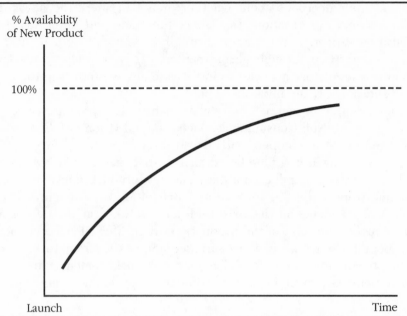

Wholesalers, agents, brokers, manufacturers' representatives, warehousing firms, and transportation firms are different types of intermediaries that may be involved with the distribution of a new product or service. Key factors to consider in assessing the behavior of such intermediaries for new product development and forecasting are listed in the Appendix.[24]

Holly Farms' experience with launching a new "roasted chicken" product provides an interesting case study that reveals the effects of distribution.[25] After a year of test marketing the fully cooked roasted chicken product, Holly Farms began national distribution in the fall of 1987 through the same system used for their fresh chickens. The new product targeted potential buyers with the need for convenient meal preparation: high proportions of working couples in major urban areas who have little time at home for cooking. Three flavors of roasted chicken were developed: Cajun, barbecue, and "original." In an Atlanta test market, 22 percent of women said they had tried the product and 90 percent said they would buy again. With these strong results, marketing success was expected. Financially, $20 million was committed to a new plant to produce the roasted chicken, and a reported $14 million in first-half marketing expenditures was committed to its launch. However, sales results did not meet expectations.

The test market revealed favorable response to Holly Farms' product, but poor reception among supermarkets sent the developers out to the trade to research the problem. Retailers expressed concern about the relatively short shelf life for the product and were slow to reorder the chicken. Although the product had a shelf life of 14 days, it took up to nine days after shipping to get to the retailer. So as not to be stuck with a backlog of outdated chickens, grocers didn't reorder until their stock had sold out. Thus, the chicken could be out-of-stock for up to another nine days until the next shipment arrived. Inconsistent availability of a new product can dampen consumer demand. Rather than ask for the product (in most supermarkets, consumers must ring a bell to bring someone out from behind the meat counter), potential buyers may select an alternative.

To resolve this difficulty, Holly Farms began to pay more attention to marketing the product to supermarkets as well as household consumers. Increased education among traditionally conservative meat departments in supermarkets promised to help lower resistance. Further, Holly Farms planned to lengthen the shelf life of the roasted chickens by packing them in nitrogen instead of air. In addition, they considered a new distribution system, separate from their fresh chicken system, to get the product to retailers sooner.

Although Holly Farms eventually straightened out its program, failure to anticipate the response of the trade not only affected the accuracy of sales and profit performance forecasts, but also had implications for product redesign. A more comprehensive study of major stakeholders for the new product may have enabled the company to anticipate these and related issues earlier in the new product's development process. For example, other concerns among retailers may have included the extent to which the new roasted chicken competes with other ready-to-eat items in their stores. Many supermarkets operate successful delicatessen departments that offer cooked meats, including roasted chicken. Unless the roasted chicken product offers financial and other benefits, chain grocers may see it as a threat to their profit margins.

The Holly Farms situation reveals that new product difficulties can emerge from behaviors among trade intermediaries. The new product effort included measures of market response by potential buyers through test marketing, but the company apparently misjudged reactions by retailers. Interacting with the trade ought to become part of the new product development process. Although it may be impossible to anticipate all relevant trade factors that may influence new product development and introduce friction in market response, taking a systematic approach that encourages consideration of multiple factors may take some of the surprise and disadvantage out of unexpected events.

Supplier Friction

Firms within a competitive industry may compete for suppliers as well as potential buyers. In some cases organizations engage in sole-source relationships to speed the process of development and improve product quality. To the extent that relevant suppliers are unavailable or limited in their ability to deliver needed components, services, and other resources for the new product, delays may occur in development and meeting early demand for sales.

Typically, suppliers are thought of in the narrow role of manufacturing or service delivery—raw materials, components, supplies, process technology, or equipment. However, a broader view of suppliers includes a variety of productive inputs to the organization developing the new product. For example, because of possible client conflicts of interest, the services and creativity of a desired advertising agency or business consultant for the new product may not be available. The need to launch a new product with a particular media schedule may require waiting until television time is available. The supply of a qualified work force may not be adequate to quickly ramp up production for the new product. Or the flow of funds from external sources of capital may slow at critical points during development. The Appendix lists possible suppliers to new product development processes, and factors related to their ability to meet supply needs for the new product.

Other Market Stakeholders

In Chapter 2, various forces and mediators in the business environment are identified. These forces can clearly affect markets, especially the potential buyers, competitors, trade intermediaries, and suppliers in them. Because changes in these forces are often pervasive and undetectable on a daily basis, an organization's interpretation of their real effects on the market for a new product is generally based on *information* about them. The interpretation of this information, and actions based on it, may be much more relevant to new product development and forecasting than the actual influences.

For example, the *perception* of economic conditions over the next year will guide the new product development decisions of organizations today, not to mention purchasing plans of potential buyers. Therefore, the quality of information about major trends and mediators that influence them is highly relevant to the nature of the market for a new product (hence its development and forecasting). If the media repeatedly report expected economic decline, buyer behavior may begin to reflect this expectation and, ultimately, bring the predicted decline.

In addition to environmental mediators, whose actions may influence major environmental forces, more specific *market stakeholders* should be monitored. These market stakeholders are individuals and organizations that have an interest in the outcome of the new product development process. They might include current or past customers, labor unions, local or regional media, industry regulators, industry trade and technology groups, and other special interest groups (such as consumerists, environmentalists, and religious groups). Their actions and reactions to the expected new product may impede or accelerate its market response.

MARKET DEVELOPMENT FOR A NEW PRODUCT

Anticipating and overcoming any one or a combination of the sources of market friction prior to and after new product launch present major challenges. For example, in the highly competitive disposable diaper market, the needs of several market stakeholders must be considered. In 1992, Kimberly-Clark developed a superabsorbent diaper that was half the thickness of current products and offered a snugger fit.[26] With this new Huggies UltraTrim product, priced the same as current products, Kimberly-Clark hoped to gain a competitive edge over Procter & Gamble Co.'s Ultra Pampers.

In addition to appealing to the absorbency and fit needs of diaper buyers, the product should respond to concerns of environmental interest groups. The new product consisted of 20 percent less material than the existing Huggies product, as well as 25 percent less plastic in the packaging. Further, the thinner product takes up less retail shelf space, a growing problem among retailers confronted with numerous brands and sizes and limited space. Finally, the thinner product also takes up less space in shipment and storage, reducing marketing costs. Such products, designed to anticipate and resolve the concerns of multiple stakeholders, can be the basis for competitive advantage.

First and foremost, however, because potential buyers are at the core of market development, the new product must meet their needs. By identifying the needs of potential buyers and translating them into viable products or services, a firm can expect a market to develop, albeit with varying degrees of growth. This growth will depend on the overall level of friction present among stakeholders in the market.

Even if a product is developed to meet the needs of a market segment, gaining awareness among potential buyers is a hurdle that must be overcome for the new product to even be considered for adoption—consumers can't buy it if they aren't aware of it! Communication about the new product will therefore be central to its adoption, closely followed by the formation of preference, trial, buying, repeat purchase, and other selected measures used to model buyer response to the new product.

In response to communication about a new product, usually from the organization that developed it, a relatively small number of potential buyers will enter the market, who will then be followed by others. The first buyers to enter, often called "innovators," do not guarantee success. Other potential buyers must be attracted to the new product. In some markets, the adoption of the new product by others may depend on the experience of the innovators, and subsequent word-of-mouth (interpersonal communication) about that experience to others. New restaurants are often the victim or beneficiary of word-of-mouth from early customers about their reactions to the dining experience.

In other product/market situations, potential buyers may be more independent, and their adoption of a product will depend largely on information from more impersonal sources of communication (such as advertising and promotion from the organization developing the new product and expert reviews published in the media), the product's availability, and its perceived value. For products of a highly personal nature, it is unlikely that people will talk about their consumption experience. Personal care products (for example, deodorants), certain magazines and videotaped movies, and cosmetic treatments are products and services that may not be discussed widely among potential buyers. For potential organizational buyers, supplies, certain components, and various services purchased may not be discussed much outside the organization.

Clearly, for any new product, both personal and impersonal sources of information can simultaneously stimulate the early growth rate of adoption, and hence market development. However, market friction from any of the market stakeholders can cause variation in patterns of market growth. Possible growth patterns in the number of buyers or adopters, over time, are depicted in Figure 3.4.

At one extreme are new products that, because of low levels of market friction across all possible sources, undergo rapid adoption and market growth (panel A). At the other extreme are new products that, because of high levels of market friction across all possible sources, undergo slow adoption and mar-

FIGURE 3.4   Potential market growth patterns in response to new products.

Panel A: Rapid market growth (low market friction)

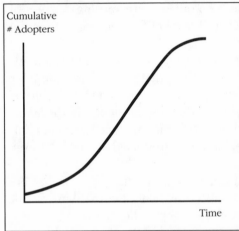

Panel B: Slow market growth (high market friction)

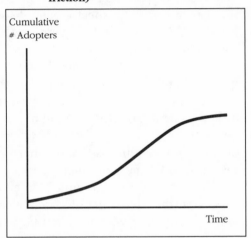

Panel C: Stepped market growth (removal of major source of friction at time *t*)

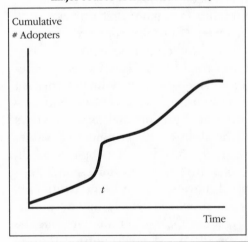

Panel D: Postponed market growth (appearance of specific source of friction at time *t*)

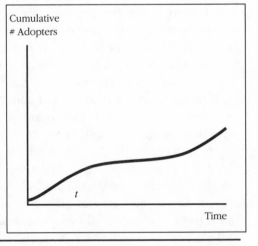

ket growth (panel B). Among other possible market development patterns is stepped market growth (panel C), which represents slow market growth until a particular source (or sources) of friction is removed. It could occur, for example, when weak initial consumer awareness and preference are overcome by broad publicity resulting from the new product's top ranking in a consumer rating poll. Market response and sales for the new Lexus luxury car shot up after its number one ranking in automotive ratings during 1990. In contrast, panel D in Figure 3.4 shows a situation of suspended market growth due to the appearance of a specific source of friction. Holly Farms' experience with its retailers' acceptance of roasted chickens (discussed previously) illustrates this type of growth pattern. Depending on actions taken by the organization, the product could either fail at this point or benefit from identification and removal of the source of resistance.

Although the shape of market development curves in response to new products will vary by situation, models are available that help to quantify and estimate possible growth patterns. New product diffusion models of market growth are introduced and illustrated in subsequent chapters.[27]

A problem in using the diffusion models is that actual sales data are needed to estimate the parameters—data not available for a new product yet to be launched. Nevertheless, the use of judgment, market research, and product analogies can help provide estimates for the parameters of market growth. In addition, variables can be included to represent sources of market friction that can slow (or speed) growth rates. Thus, once a base model of market growth is estimated, various assumptions about sources of friction can be introduced to generate more refined sales estimates.

DESIGNING PROGRAMS TO REDUCE MARKET FRICTION

It's not enough to recognize that the response of various stakeholders to a new product can increase market friction for the product. An aggressive approach must be taken to reduce the friction and speed favorable market response.[28] The variety of marketing strategies and tools that can be used to reduce market friction is limited only by an organization's creativity and resources. Actions built around product modifications, pricing, distribution, advertising, sales promotion, and public relations—before and after launch—can influence targeted stakeholders. In addition to product design and marketing actions, programs designed around social, legal, and political actions, as well as strategic alliances and other forms of organizational response, can be used to influence different market stakeholders.

Figure 3.5 illustrates the kind of planning that might take place during new product development to cope with various sources of market friction. Possible program factors that are the basis for actions are listed as rows in the matrix, and possible stakeholder sources of friction are listed as columns. The actions within each cell illustrate possible approaches to use to respond to

FIGURE 3.5 Illustrative actions to influence selected stakeholders to reduce market friction and accelerate new product acceptance.

Program Factors	Market Stakeholders				
	Potential Buyers	Competitors	Trade	Suppliers	Other Stakeholders
New product design	Determine optimal number of product options or features (e.g. colors, styles) to meet needs and speed consumer decision-making	Patent critical processes or features to defend competitive advantage; maintain trade secrets	Design product to easily be stocked, serviced, returned, etc.	Design product to take advantage of supplier strengths	Design product to meet environmental concerns (e.g. recovery of components, recycle capability)
Marketing program	Advertising to build awareness; price for value; promotions for trial; distribution for availability	Use to strengthen brand identity and positioning	Use price, advertising, sales force, and sales promotion to build cooperation	Use communication and promotion to build cooperation	Use communication to "hype" new product among targeted special interest stakeholders
Legal actions	Anticipate product liability	Protect patents, monitor unfair trade practices	Where possible maintain contractual relations	Where possible maintain contractual relations	Anticipate other liability
Political actions	Support "causes" of potential buyers	Support legislation to defend market position	Support trade "causes" and concerns	Support supplier "causes" and concerns	Use communication to "lobby" key stakeholders; offer grants to support related social "causes"
Strategic alliances	Develop new product design teams with customers	Cooperate through research consortia	Vertical integration if needed to control channels	Vertical integration if needed to control supply	Anticipate possible alliances with other stakeholders
Other program factors					

different stakeholders. Because every new product will be different according to the dynamics of each situation, the actions in Figure 3.5 should be used to stimulate possibilities rather than accepted as generic recommendations. There are numerous books to guide decisions on marketing and other business factors, but the approach in Figure 3.5 focuses the design and implementation of actions to reduce anticipated friction in response to the new product.

SUMMARY

The market for a new product is defined in terms of the exchanges among its potential stakeholders, including buyers, trade intermediaries, competitors, suppliers, and others. Among these various stakeholders in the market, potential buyers are deemed central to the ultimate success of a new product. However, their response to, and acceptance of, a new product is not without friction. Friction includes the inertia exhibited by potential buyers who may believe their current needs are satisfied, as well as the friction introduced by other stakeholders. Generally, the greater (less) this friction among market stakeholders, the slower (faster) the rate of new product adoption.

The various sources of market friction are reviewed, with special emphasis on identifying and satisfying the unmet needs of potential buyers. Although these needs drive successful new product development, the situational, informational, attitudinal, and behavioral aspects of potential buyer behavior also affect response to the new product, and possibly redefine buyer needs. Taking into account the complex behavior of individual buyers, and the segments into which they can be clustered, can suggest guidelines that represent the line of least resistance for a new product.

In addition to the needs and behaviors of potential buyers, those of various competitors, trade intermediaries, suppliers, and others must be understood in the context of market development for the new product. Different market growth patterns may occur depending on the response of various stakeholders. Consequently, both anticipating the range of responses among major stakeholders and taking actions that will reduce market friction define an interactive approach that an organization should take in managing and forecasting new product development.

APPENDIX

Selected Competitor Factors	Selected Trade Factors	Selected Supplier Factors

INDUSTRY LEVEL
Size
Growth
Number and size of competitors
Competitive intensity
Cost structure (fixed vs. other)
Mobility barriers
Reputation of industry
Technology standards
Frequency of innovations
R&D resources, etc.

ORGANIZATIONAL LEVEL
Technology
Technical/service superiority
New product capability
R&D
Patents, etc.

Manufacturing/Operations
Cost structure
Value added
Quality of suppliers
Production flexibility
Access to raw material
Inventory capability
Workforce attitude/motivation
Capacity, etc.

New Product Development
Average development cycle time
Prior experience
New product success rate
Product champion
Cross functional teams
Development process, etc.

Finance
From operations
From net short-term assets
Cash flow, etc.

Management
Quality of leadership
Quality of management
Organizational culture
Strategic goals and plans
Entrepreneurial thrust
Loyalty/turnover, etc.

Marketing
Market share
Product portfolio quality
Brand name
Segmentation
Distribution
Advertising/promotion skills
Sales force
Customer service, etc.

CHANNEL SYSTEM LEVEL
Degree of channel coordination
Degree of channel cooperation
Degree of channel conflict
Degree of channel leadership
Degree of channel innovativeness
Capacity to absorb new products
Attitude to absorb new products
Relations with media
Relations with trade associations
Relations with consumer groups
Relations with regulatory agencies
Relations with interest groups
Strength of channel brands
Management sophistication, etc.

WHOLESALE LEVEL
Extent of coverage
Number of accounts
Warehousing capability
Delivery capability
Margins
Services offered
Computer capabilities
Sales force coverage
Sales force size
Financial stability
Organizational stability
New product support, etc.

RETAIL LEVEL
Number of outlets
Location of outlets
Modernity of outlets
Number of facings
Type of exposure
Depth of inventory per outlet
Amount of slotting fees
Sales personnel support
Service support staff
Stock clerk support
Financial stability
Organizational stability, etc.

LOGISTICS LEVEL
Transportation
Warehousing
Material handling
Material packaging
Liability, insurance
Order and data processing
Inventory
Just-in-time capability
Scheduling, etc.

SUPPLIER GROUP LEVEL
Degree of competitiveness
Degree of cohesiveness
Relations with regulators, etc.

SUPPLIER LEVEL
Financial stability
Organizational stability
Willingness to sole source
R&D capability
Manufacturing capability
Quality procedures
Component testing
Prototyping capability
Inventory capability
Just-in-time capability
Conflicts of interest, etc.

SUPPLIER TYPES
Components
Raw materials
Process technology
Process equipment
Warehousing/inventory
Repair services
Maintenance services
Other services
Advertising
Business consultants
Capital sources
Lines of credit
Educational institutions
Employment agencies
Executive search firms, etc.

4 Preparing the Organization for New Product Development

Facing turbulent and uncertain business environments, organizations naturally seek order and stability to help people work together and achieve goals. However, when the demands of changing buyer needs, competitive threats, or other market transformations must be met, new products may be needed to meet the challenge. How an organization responds internally to the conditions stimulated by new product development will determine whether or not products reach the market in time and in a form to meet the needs of potential buyers and other market stakeholders. Consider the case of Motorola, Inc.

Motorola excels in manufacturing quality. It has won the U.S. Malcolm Baldrige National Quality Award and the Japanese Nikkei Prize for manufacturing. However, as reported in *The Wall Street Journal*, Motorola's "obsession with technological excellence" and "infighting" between champions of existing versus new microprocessor chip technologies may have delayed launch of one of its new products by about one year after major competitors had entered the market.[1] This delay occurred at a critical juncture in the market for work stations—when potential buying organizations were appraising and selecting new microprocessor chips for their work station designs.

Historically, Motorola's 68000 series chips have been used in personal computers, especially by Apple Computer Inc. Although a technically successful chip, the 68000 series trailed in personal computer market share behind Intel Corporation's chips. Intel microprocessors were used in IBM PCs and in IBM-compatible PCs, which dominated the PC market. The Motorola 68000 series also held a large share of the small but growing work station market. However, this share began to slip for two reasons. First, Motorola announced a new, more powerful 68040 chip in 1987, but did not ship it in volume until November of 1990. Driven by pursuit of technological excellence, the company sought to perfect the chip while its customers became impatient and some

77

selected other suppliers. Hewlett-Packard Co., which had announced its own work station based on the 68040, had to delay its entry by several months waiting for the chip. Second, the newer RISC (reduced instruction-set computing) microprocessor technology began to gain market acceptance as the chip of choice for the needs of more powerful work stations.

As early as 1983, Motorola had begun exploring the development of a new RISC chip to keep pace with emerging technology and in response to the needs of one of its customers (Sun Microsystems Inc.) for its work station computers. By 1986, a powerful RISC chip (the 88000 series) had begun to emerge from the planning stages as a viable contender for market needs. However, the continued development of the 68000 series of non-RISC chips absorbed most of the firm's resources. The major proponent of the 68000 series chip reportedly lobbied against the new chip and even vied for potential RISC customers with the promise of a more powerful 68040 chip. This organizational infighting led to reduced resource allocation to the 88000 series RISC chip. As a consequence, buyers sensed organizational uncertainty and lack of commitment to the new RISC chip by Motorola.

In 1987, Sun, which had all along asked Motorola to develop a more powerful chip to replace the 68000 series in its work stations, launched its own RISC chip (called Sparc) and proceeded to dominate the work station market with it. The eventual market growth of the RISC chip finally stimulated Motorola's introduction of the 88000 series chip in 1988. Unfortunately, though the chip was ready, software for it was not. Some companies planning to use the 88000 complained that Motorola had not spent enough to get software makers to modify programs for it. By 1991, few manufacturers had chosen to use the new 88000 RISC chip, opting instead for ones made by competitors (Sun, Mips Computer Systems, and Intel). Although the 88000 series chip may survive and undergo further development for future opportunities, its initial market advantage may be lost.

The Motorola case illustrates vividly the effect of *organizational* forces at work that wreak havoc with new product development and forecasting in general. These difficulties actually present a *new product development paradox*—although organizations are frequently motivated to launch a successful new product in response to buyer needs, competitive factors, and corporate goals, they also erect barriers and otherwise create difficulties that jeopardize the process. Motorola's ideology of manufacturing excellence and its infighting over resources appear to have delayed new RISC chip development. Moreover, any attempts to achieve new product forecasts, either with the 68040 or the 88000 RISC chip, would have been ill-fated because of the delays in market entry. This paradox often occurs despite the best of intentions, with some of the best-performing members of an organization, within some of the best organizations, and sometimes with positive as well as negative consequences. But why—and is it controllable?

Major organizational factors that underlie the new product development paradox are summarized in Figure 4.1 as part of the overall view of factors affecting new product development. The interaction of an organization with its market environment triggers potential forces that *motivate* new product development, such as recognizing a customer's changing needs or responding to competitive actions. Simultaneously, organizational forces that generate *resistance* to new product development may emerge.

The problem of these opposing forces is conceptualized as an *organization's propensity to innovate* in new product development. High organizational propensity to innovate implies the potential for rapid and responsive new product development, whereas low propensity to innovate implies resistance to new product development. Whatever an organization's propensity to innovate, knowledge of it (and the factors that drive it) will facilitate needed changes during development. In addition, it will contribute to an estimation of the critical schedule of development that determines market entry time.

This chapter is organized to consider first the new product development paradox, including forces motivating new product development and those stimulating resistance to it. Then selected factors that influence an organiza-

FIGURE 4.1   Factors affecting new product development: focus on the innovating organization.

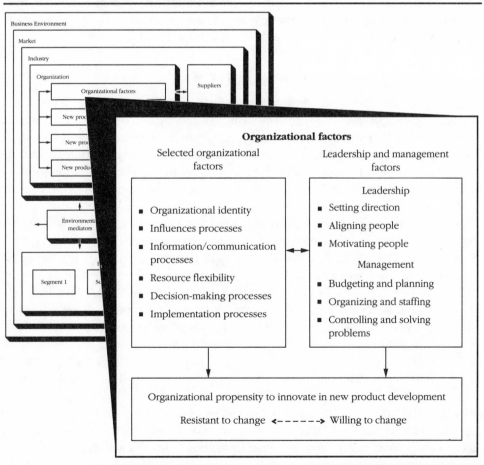

tion's propensity to innovate are reviewed. Ways in which leaders and managers can facilitate organizational change in new product development situations are next considered. Finally, an approach for estimating an organization's propensity to innovate in new product development provides insight into the amount of time needed to develop the new product and modify market-based forecasts.

THE NEW PRODUCT DEVELOPMENT PARADOX

By their nature, new product development processes require continuous *change* on the part of various members of the organization to achieve the goal of successful market introductions. As in the case of Motorola, these changes usually include revised resource allocations, the involvement of different personnel and departments, new behaviors, and the formation of new attitudes among involved parties, frequently from different departments in an organization. However, as noted, these changes do not always occur in the same direction.

The new product development paradox recognizes that strong motivating forces of change propel new product development, and that these motivating forces also often stimulate countervailing forces of resistance to change that may stifle the product's evolution. Outcomes include a product that is altered from its intended form and/or a delayed time to market entry, either of which can affect the quality of the product and the achievement of its forecasts.

Motivation for New Product Development

External market forces and internal organizational goals motivate decisions to invest in new products. Aside from the central underlying assumption that buyer needs drive the development of new products, research reveals two other frequently mentioned motivations: defending market share position and establishing a foothold in a new market.[2] For example, in the competitive market for athletic shoes, when Reebok International Ltd. introduced The Pump basketball shoe, Nike, Inc. responded with its own version of a basketball shoe that allowed wearers to pump air into the shoe for a snugger fit. Nike's hope for this "me-too" product was to defend market share against Reebok's innovation. Similarly, in 1991, IBM launched a new laptop computer in part for defensive reasons, but also to establish a foothold in a rapidly growing new market.

New products are also developed for *internal* motivations, including the desire to be an innovator and to capitalize on technology, distribution, or other strengths. Procter & Gamble Co. provides a good example of a firm that launches new products to maintain its position as an innovator.[3] Its successful Pert Plus shampoo, which grew from 2 percent in 1985 to 12 percent of a fragmented $1.4 billion market in 1990, was the result of commitment to innovation. By 1985, scientists at Procter & Gamble had developed a combination shampoo–conditioner for consumer use in a single application. This product brought a clear benefit of convenience to an otherwise two-step process of shampooing, then conditioning. Test market results with the new formula under the Pert brand name showed a favorable response and paved the way for market success.

Frito-Lay Inc. pursues a strategy of innovation, in part to capitalize on its distribution and process technology strengths.[4] Using its process technology to formulate snack chips, Frito-Lay spent the better part of a decade developing Sun Chips, its first major national new product launch since Tostitos in 1981. Its existing product line included potato and corn-based chips (for example, Lay's, Ruffles, Fritos, Doritos, Tostitos), but the new product contained whole wheat, corn, and other grains with the texture of a chip and the taste of a snack cracker. The chips proved viable in test markets and (with a $70 million dollar budget) were launched in 1991, achieving successful first-year results. A key ingredient in the success of any new snack item is, of course, availability to consumers—and Frito-Lay's extensive "store-door" distribution network (from supermarkets to vending machines) enables it to have drivers personally set up displays, put products on shelves, and keep them stocked.

Although a variety of motivations can generate new products, they all result in the need to engage in a process that portends change for the current organization. The prospect of change from current patterns of behavior may excite some members of the organization and heighten their desire to move ahead with a new product, but more often than not it generates resistance.

Resistance to New Product Development

The prospect of significant change within an organization stimulates uncertainty and doubt among persons most affected. Organizations and their members inherently recognize the need to engage in new product programs for future growth and survival, but they also resist it. They often strive to retain current patterns rather than accept new ones. The U.S. Navy's adoption of continuous-aim-firing guns for its ships illustrates organizational resistance very well.[5]

The major problem of firing a gun from one ship to hit a target ship at sea is that both ships are moving with sea swells and in various directions under their own power. Firing these guns created such a tremendous recoil effect that the gunnery crews could not use the gunsights. Naval shooting was at best haphazard under these conditions. Nevertheless, the crew that fired the guns on each ship were highly trained and followed orders from a captain.

Recognizing the difficulties of aiming, a young Naval officer developed a way to manage the effects of the recoil by separating the gunsight from the gun. His invention also included a new gear system to better control the movement of the gun for improved aiming. He tested his system and it worked, so he sought to get the Navy to adopt his new method. When they indicated they were not interested, the inventor persisted. After continued rejection within the organization, he presented his case to President Theodore Roosevelt, who ultimately forced the Navy to adopt the innovation!

The innovation was adopted and shooting accuracy was substantially improved. But why did the Navy resist? In short, the Navy was trying to protect the social system of the ship from the new technology. Introducing continuous-aim firing threatened a highly trained team. Any ordinary recruit could now fire more accurately than the specialized team! This type of resistance to change— or the tendency to fight to remain the same—has been given several labels, including "dynamic conservatism" and "structural inertia."[6]

There are numerous reasons why organizations resist change and maintain inertia even at the risk of not surviving—avoiding uncertainty, reluctance to deviate from plans or ideologies, past success of decisions or formulas that may no longer be relevant in the current environment, political infighting within the organization, the power structure, and the cost of change.

In the Motorola case, the reported organizational infighting over resources between the 68000 series chip and the 88000 RISC chip illustrates one possible reason for Motorola's apparent reluctance to respond to the market's need for the RISC chip. Further, the organization's strong commitment to manufacturing excellence, which was rewarded and reinforced with prizes, resulted in product delays that cost Motorola customers. In fact, Hewlett-Packard, a customer-in-waiting, went on to develop its own high-performance RISC chip for use in its work stations, thereby becoming yet another competitor for Motorola.

Thus, new product development processes, which by their very nature promote change, will surely raise resistance to it within the organization. In effect, the new product development paradox represents the forces for and against change. However, both forces are legitimate and functional: resistance to change helps maintain the stability and order necessary for the proper functioning of the organization, and the change needed to develop new products helps the organization and its members grow and otherwise achieve their goals. Because new product development includes processes that require change, understanding the forces that affect an organization's propensity to innovate, especially when resistance to change is anticipated, is essential.

FACTORS DEFINING AN ORGANIZATION'S PROPENSITY TO INNOVATE

The concept of an organization's *propensity to innovate*, which represents the *balance* of organizational forces that propel and resist change in new product development, helps identify factors that can influence change. It can be viewed as a variable that can range from *low* (or zero) to *high*. When an organization exhibits substantial resistance to change relative to the motivating forces to develop a new product idea, its propensity to innovate is low; however, if the resistance is low relative to the motivating forces to develop a new product idea, its propensity to innovate is high. Organizations differ in their propensity to change, and it may vary over time within an organization in response to a variety of pressures.

To illustrate the concept of propensity to innovate, consider again the Motorola case. From about 1983 to 1986, the organization's propensity to innovate in response to Sun Computer's need for a new RISC chip for its work station could be interpreted as low. Reportedly, its development team encountered resistance from others in the organization. Furthermore, resources were inadequate to sustain the product's development and to show the necessary commitment to develop the chip over the long term. However, when Sun introduced its own RISC chip (Sparc) in 1987 and the market for RISC chips grew more rapidly, Motorola began increasing its propensity to innovate. It invested more effort into the chip, launching it in 1988. Thus, propensity to innovate, as defined here, varied over time in response to a changing mix of internal and external forces.

To make the concept useful, factors must be identified that will facilitate estimation of an organization's propensity to innovate throughout new product development. This estimate will be instrumental in diagnosing needed organizational changes and in preparing new product forecasts. For example, if propensity to innovate is low, two major courses of action with respect to product development and forecasting are possible:

1. If the estimate is accepted and cannot be changed, it can be used as a basis for realistic approximations of the product's design and time to develop, which in turn affect forecasts of volume, costs, and profitability.

2. If the estimate is *not* accepted, leadership and management activities can be deployed to identify sources of organizational resistance and implement programs to accelerate change in the new product process. Revised time estimates and product improvements or compromises can then be factored into the forecasting.

To illustrate an approach for estimating propensity to innovate, six selected organizational factors that characterize the fundamental structure and processes of an organization are considered: *organizational identity, influence processes, information and communication processes, resource flexibility, decision-making processes,* and *implementation processes.* Differences in these factors can lead to different conclusions about an organization's propensity to innovate. Although the management and organizational literatures use a variety of characteristics to describe organizations (such as age, size, formalization, and centralization), few are consistently associated with successful (or failed) new products or innovations.[7] As the six selected factors are described in the sections that follow, it will become apparent that each provides a fundamental basis for assessment, and taken together they form a profile of an organization's propensity to innovate.

Organizational Identity

The metaphor of an organization as a *psychic prison* helps explain why some firms have difficulty coping with the shifting demands of their environment and resist change.[8] In this view, a particular aspect of an organization's structure or culture may, in an unconscious way, come to assume special significance and be preserved and retained even in the face of great pressure to change—hence the term "psychic prison." Motorola's strong adherence to "technological excellence" in the face of market pressures for the RISC chip illustrates the identity problem. Clearly, the pursuit of technological excellence, manufacturing quality, and other ideals was worthy—and reinforced by winning the Baldrige quality award. However, this aspect of the company's identity impeded other organizational processes that were attempting to respond to a changing environment.

Fear of losing organizational identity often generates a reaction that may be out of all proportion to the importance of the issue (relative to a more objective perspective). In the "psychic prison," old ways or even wrong ideas about things may be adhered to, even at the expense of hindering a new product's development. The presence of such a prison mentality, as well as the likelihood of getting out of it, must be considered in developing new products and preparing any forecasts of new product demand.

An organization's identity can have two consequences in response to change introduced by a new product. First, a strong and clear identity widely received in an organization will channel decision making and actions within its scope. Among business strategists, this is considered an ideal state of affairs; that is, letting the business mission (identity) drive day-to-day decisions. Thus, any possible new products within the context of the identity may be received with enthusiasm (high propensity to innovate). The other consequence, of course, is that new products outside the identity will not be received with enthusiasm, and are likely to be resisted (low propensity to innovate).

An organization's *history* and *culture* are at the root of its identity. Organizational history generates constraints on change.[9] Once standards of procedure and allocations of tasks and authority become norms, the costs of change increase greatly. Organization members wanting to oppose change can find legitimate justifications beyond their own self-interest. These norms also provide legitimate reasons to preclude certain options in the face of an environmental threat or opportunity. For example, "Pursuing a new product program at this time will only siphon resources from satisfying current customers."

The beliefs and values that define an organization's culture (and identity) also constrain new product change. In the mid-1960s and early 1970s, strong cultural beliefs prevented NCR management's acceptance of electronics over electromechanics as the technology to drive cash registers. Even while management openly recognized the emerging importance of electronic computers, NCR clung to past ways, refining further its electromechanical machines that were rapidly becoming obsolete. From 1972 to 1976 the market share of electromechanical over electronic machines dropped from 90 percent to 10 percent.[10]

The consequence of history and culture is that as environments change more rapidly and become more complex, comparisons with historical precedents often become less valid without a complete understanding of the environment and actions that produced them. Nevertheless, appraising an organization for historic, cultural, and other factors that define its identity is critical to assessing propensity to innovate in new product development situations.

Influence Processes

Few who have worked in organizations would deny the omnipresence of organizational politics.[11] Conflict and competition among departments and other factions for budgets, opportunities for promotion, and other resources may stimulate organizational units to use their power bases to influence others. Clearly, the possibility of a new product (or most other innovations) in the organization will raise any number of concerns from various members and coalitions. For example, certain new product formulations may be blackballed because their adoption would be unacceptable to one or more of the dominant coalitions.[12] Political devices that can stifle or champion innovation may be deployed, such as dummy task forces without real power or top-level commitment, complex control and checkoff systems, next-to-impossible hurdles to achieve approval, or inadequate incentives.[13]

Knowing that an organization's politics can influence new product development is one thing; trying to understand it in a specific situation is quite another. One clue for estimating the possible acceptance of a new product project depends on the current balance of power in an organization. When the power and influence processes of an organization's political units are in a state of balance, anything that threatens to upset them—such as a new product project—will stimulate strategies to maintain power bases and resist change.[14]

In the Motorola case, the successive generations of successful 68000 chip developments may have led to a balance of power within various subunits of the organization. The 88000 new chip project may have been a perceived (if not real) threat to the distribution of resources within the firm, thus raising resistance against its development. In such cases, political maneuvering may take place to preempt change and maintain the current power balance. Conversely, in an organization with an unsettled balance of power, a new product project may provide the focal point for resolving the imbalance. That is, the new product project may be adopted by a coalition as its way to maintain or regain power in the organization.

Information and Communication Processes

Organizations have long been known to have ways of "killing the messenger," or removing individuals who bring bad news![15] For various reasons (often of a political or self-interest nature) organization members selectively filter information to control the news that their superiors receive. In a study of a major new computer purchase by an organization, the head of the "management services" department put himself in the position of "gatekeeper" of information flows to the top management board of the organization.[16] In this position, he was able to bias the flow of information about a complex and uncertain matter in such a way that it was favorable to his own interests and disadvantageous to his opponents. For example, the numerous documents that this person forwarded to the management group about the four brands under consideration included statements that were 71.4 percent positive, 20.4 percent neutral, and only 8.2 percent negative with respect to his preferred brand. Positive statements about the three brands he did not prefer were under 15 percent of all statements!

The organizational filtering process also affects information relevant to new product development. One reported case study illustrates the problem well.[17] The new product being considered involved the development of a facial cleanser designed to meet the needs of two different market segments: consumers who responded to the cleansing property of facial creams and consumers who responded to moisturizing properties. The company implemented a comprehensive research procedure (a simulated test market). The findings suggested that a change in the ad agency's proposed advertising copy and a modest sampling program were necessary to achieve a successful market share. However, neither of these recommendations was accepted. The product was launched, and eventually withdrawn from the market for poor performance.

A post-mortem analysis of the failed product revealed that the marketing research director (for whom the market study was conducted) had little communication (or influence) with the president and chief decision maker on this new product. The advertising agency (which had a long relationship with the firm) believed it had created the right campaign for the product (different from the one recommended by research) and convinced the president that it was the best copy approach. Because the research director did not have a good communication link with the key decision maker, critical information about the product's performance under the proposed copy was either not received or not valued by the president.

Such information filtering is often fostered by the hierarchical and departmental structure of organizations, which allows for information to flow upstream (to higher level executives) and rewards and punishments to flow downstream. Thus, a manager, who might be concerned about career or organizational position, will tend to send positive (or consonant) information upstream in the hope of gaining rewards and avoiding punishment. If the research director in the preceding case study had recognized the relationship of the advertising agency with the president, he or she might not have been aggressive in promoting a finding that was at variance with the prevailing recommendation. The result of such filtering is that senior-level managers may not receive adequate information for new product decision making until resources for implementation of the solution are badly drained.

Studies of the effects of communication on technological innovation have found that greater frequency of communication affects a project's success, whether the communication is within a single organization or between organizations.[18] Communication facilitates problem solving, especially among marketing, R&D, and manufacturing departments, and stimulates other creative and operational processes that are instrumental to completing successful new product projects. Thus, one might expect that organizations with more frequent and open communication processes will have a greater propensity to innovate in new product development than those with less frequent and closed communication processes.

Though not absolutely essential, readily accessible management information systems (MIS), decision support systems (DSS), and other tools that facilitate data collection, analysis, and interpretation are useful indicators of an organization's ability to support frequent communication. Further, computer networks with electronic mail, voice mail, and the spatial architecture of an organization may be manifest indicators of interpersonal communication processes.

Organizational Resource Flexibility

Organizational resource flexibility, or *slack*, can be viewed as a cushion of resources that enables a firm to adapt successfully to internal and external demands.[19] This slack can be defined in terms of real or perceived resources. If slack exists, or managers believe it exists, they may engage more readily in the changes necessary to develop new products. Generally, the less resource slack (real or perceived) available in an organization, the lower its propensity to innovate in new product processes.

The role of slack in implementing an innovation within an organization is evident from a study of the development of NOW accounts (interest paying checking accounts) by financial institutions.[20] The study findings revealed that the use of slack resources to invest heavily in training and communication with personnel made possible a more ready response to the need for developing NOW accounts—a competitive necessity brought about through regulatory change.

Slack resources can exist in various forms. For example, an organization may have excess investments in plant, equipment, and specialized personnel, but if they are not easily transferable from existing to new product situations, there is little slack. Although financial resources may represent the most obvious and flexible of resources, personnel, equipment, and manufacturing capabilities are other important bases for resource flexibility in the organization. An organization's technological expertise provides a good example.

Every organization, whether industrial, consumer, or service, relies on technology as the means whereby inputs are transformed into outputs. Computer firms rely on microprocessor technology; diet beverage manufacturers rely on sweetener technology; travel agent services rely on information technology; marketing research firms rely on management science modeling technology; and so on. However, technological expertise too narrowly focused can interfere with successful product development.[21]

The S-curve phenomenon provides one explanation of how a narrow, inflexible view of technology can become a barrier to innovation.[22] The S-curve describes the general relationship between the effort and performance results of a particular technology. As low levels of effort increase, there is little or no gain in performance. As effort increases, at some point performance begins to increase at a significant rate. However, at another point, further increases in effort begin to yield diminishing performance returns. The key to this concept is knowing the shape of the S-curve. This requires expertise and study. When diminishing returns set in for a particular technology, it will be critical for an organization to be *flexible* and adopt a new, usually emerging, technology. For example, in the Motorola case, the 68000 series chip may represent a maturing technology, whereas the 88000 RISC chip may represent a newly emerging S-curve. Motorola did not initially exhibit flexibility in moving resources behind the new RISC technology, and thus may have jeopardized the company's position in the work station market.

Organizational Decision-Making Processes

There are a variety of ways to characterize organizational decision processes, but differences in the level of *participation* in decision making are especially relevant to new product development. Organizations with less participation among their members (often a hierarchy in structure) take more time to execute complex new product decisions. Information must travel to sequentially higher levels of the organizational hierarchy before decisions can be made. Alternatively, organizations with more participation among their members (often "flatter" in structure) take less time to execute complex new product decisions. Decisions can be made by a process involving numerous organizational members in a more participatory, consensus-building style, thereby reducing the need for continuous approvals at various levels of management.

The effects of empowering lower levels of an organization with decision-making capability in new product development can be dramatic. Traditionally, IBM Corporation was an organization in which numerous members were vested with decision-making authority at multiple levels of hierarchy.[23] Normally, disagreements about product development decisions were encouraged, taken up to the next level for resolution, and so on, requiring numerous meetings. To their credit, however, IBM executives recognized the benefits of more participatory decision making and began to dramatically decentralize operations. In addition, they set up project teams that cut across traditional IBM lines of business to tackle special new product development projects. Their launch of a competitive laptop personal computer in 14 months (compared to their usual two- to three-year time frame to introduce new projects) realized some of the benefits of more participatory decision making.

Implementation Processes

Implementation of new product decisions involves how an organization gets work done to develop and launch a new product. When faced with work to be accomplished, some managers may follow an internal line of least resistance; that is, one that minimizes the delay and difficulty of successfully implementing a program. The outcome of this line of least resistance may not necessarily be the best product for the external market. For example, in a commentary on the innovation practices of Xerox Corporation's Palo Alto Research Center (PARC) described by John Seely Brown, Arnold S. Wasserman reveals how—despite the best intentions—following the line of least resistance can have adverse consequences:[24]

> One detail in Brown's story about how Xerox redesigned its copiers deserves clarification. When PARC anthropologist Lucy Suchman began studying why users could not understand how to operate Xerox copiers, she was not looking at machines that had been blessed by our human-factors engineers. On the contrary, our human-factors people blew the whistle on the "lemon" copiers long before they were introduced to the market. We conducted extensive usability tests and delivered reports predicting every one of the difficulties users eventually had understanding these machines in the field. Our reports were ignored, rejected, and in some cases, deliberately suppressed by the product engineers and project managers rushing to get the machines into production!

In the Xerox case, the drive to begin production led to apparent shortcuts, resulting in a product not quite right to meet customer needs. This approach contrasts with Motorola's pursuit of manufacturing excellence, with the consequence of delays in the new product development process. Clearly tradeoffs must be made between the quality of the final product and the time spent getting it to market. Balancing this tradeoff is a difficult task. One part of the problem can be managed with the support of a forecasting process that provides estimates of the financial consequences of delaying market entry.

The other part of the problem of balancing the tradeoff between quality and speed of development requires estimation of how the organization might perform in implementing its new product development tasks. One approach to this estimation is to consider a continuum of organization work from *routine* to *nonroutine* activities.[25] Organizations with technologies or work processes at the routine end of the continuum are not very adaptable to change. Those with nonroutine work processes are much more adaptable to change. Thus, one would expect that generally, the more routine an organization's implementation processes, the more likely it will be to resist change throughout development.

In effect, when confronted with a new product development project, organizations used to more routine situations will be less willing to change their current behavior, and will follow the line of least resistance to get back to their routines. Frequently recurring nonroutine problems and projects attune people who perform implementation tasks to unusual patterns, and increase the likelihood that they will not take the line of least resistance. In addition, if problems are spotted during implementation, the "attuned" workers will be more likely to solve them before proceeding.

An Organizational Profile

The preceding discussion treats each organizational factor separately. In reality, the six factors run together to form patterns of organizations. For example, organizations with very rigid identities, balanced power structures and influence processes, infrequent communication, inflexible resources, low levels of participation in decision making, and highly routinized implementation processes may have a relatively low propensity to innovate in new product development situations. Alternatively, organizations can have a relatively high propensity to innovate based on high levels of the six factors or a modest propensity to innovate based on mixed levels of the six factors.

Using an "innovation audit" process (one will be illustrated later in the chapter), experienced executives applying their judgment to these factors should be able to ascertain a profile of their own organization's propensity to innovate in general and with respect to a particular new product situation. This assessment should lead to planned actions to facilitate and otherwise influence organizational conditions to overcome anticipated impediments to change.

FACILITATING ORGANIZATIONAL CHANGE
THROUGH LEADERSHIP AND MANAGEMENT

Facilitating organizational change to improve an organization's ongoing propensity to innovate requires *leadership* and *management*. Although numerous studies of new product development cite the critical role of new product *champions* in the ultimate success of a project, other leaders and managers in the organization must provide support on a continual basis. The key activities of leadership and management determine how an organization interacts with its environment and how it operates internally. Importantly, leadership and management activities influence the less-controllable factors defining an organization's structure and processes discussed previously.

Management involves coping with complexity; by contrast, leadership involves coping with change.[26] Both are integral to the performance of an organization and, in particular, to the performance of new product activities, but strong leadership is absolutely essential to cope with the resistance to change—to break out of the "psychic prison"—inherent in the structure of organizations. Leadership requires using power to influence the thoughts and actions of other people—in effect, to overcome strong patterns of conservatism in organizations.[27] Once the resistance is broken for new product development, the complexity of the situation becomes apparent and strong management is necessary to ensure that goals are set and the critical work gets done in a timely and high-quality fashion.

The problems posed by an organization's resistance to change can be addressed by a host of leadership and management activities, many of which have been described in the literature on organization change.[28] Each of the

TABLE 4.1   Examples of overcoming organizational resistance through leadership and management processes.

Potential sources of organizational resistance to new product development	Leadership and management processes to overcome organizational resistance
Narrow and strong organizational identity based on culture and history; new product outside its boundaries	Define the core new product concept in a way that is consistent with the firm's identity, yet sufficiently unique to capitalize on market opportunity and reset organizational direction
Well-balanced bases of power and influence processes within subunits of the organization	Assign new product champion and empower other leaders from key subunits to support new project and overcome existing patterns of power
Constricted information and communication processes that prevent critical information from reaching key decision-makers	Leader (especially the new product champion) must energize and motivate people to the point of interacting more often and with proper information to achieve goals
Insufficient resource flexibility to supply new product project requests	Develop careful plans to support additional budget request and creatively plan and budget existing resources
Low level of participation in decision-making processes requires longer time to approve decisions	Organize and staff new product project to stimulate and support greater participation in decision making
Organization supports highly routinized tasks to get work done	Institute feedback and control processes to closely monitor new product project and identify obstacles to implementation

six leadership and management activities described hereafter is directed, respectively, at the six less-controllable organization factors that may generate resistance to change. In Table 4.1, ways to overcome organizational resistance through leadership and management activities are illustrated. Although they are presented here one at a time, in practice the various activities may interact to create more (or less) effective performance.

Leadership Factors

To cope with change, especially rapid change from external environments, leaders must (1) set a direction or vision for the firm, (2) align people through communication and coalition building to understand the vision, and (3) motivate and inspire people to achieve the vision.[29]

Setting Direction—Define the Core Product Concept

Direction setting by leaders generates visions and strategies that describe a business and/or a new product in terms of what it should become over the long run. It also involves articulating a feasible way of achieving this goal. In part creative, it is the result of a process that depends largely on gathering and analyzing information. In particular, the organization's cultural history and present identity must be considered in setting any new directions. In a study of strategic change, a *new* strategy was more readily supported by persons believing that the firm was continuing to pursue distinctive behaviors associated with success in the past.[30] Defining a future direction different from that of the past requires careful study and a recognition that the other leadership and management activities will be critical to success.

In the case of a new product, setting direction means defining the *core product concept*, or the central meaning of the new product that is communicable among members of the organization who have different backgrounds and orientations. Ideally, a core product concept should be linked with an organization's identity. For example, an office furniture manufacturer that views its mission as delivering comfortable working conditions might describe the core concept for a new office desk chair for executives as "powerful comfort in style." This concept certainly would be embellished further, but it is consistent with the general business mission and clearly signals to the organization the need for engineering, design, manufacturing, and other functions to coordinate electromechanical controls, materials, and aesthetics to realize the concept.

However, if a core product concept strongly differs from the organization's direction, it not only may be difficult to communicate, but also may meet resistance. This situation could necessitate changing the concept, changing the strategic definition of the business, and/or changing aspects of the organization. The important task of defining the core product concept is discussed in greater detail in Chapter 5.

Aligning People—Build a New Product Development Team

As the new product concept becomes clear, it provides the basis for a leader to align people to achieve the new product vision—in effect, to create the new product development team. This alignment is necessary to overcome the organizational inertia that might prevail among traditional coalitions. Clearly, an understanding of current organizational power bases and influence processes will be essential to properly align people. Identifying and assigning a new product champion or team leader early in the process is a critical first step. The need for strong leadership in new product development efforts has been well recognized in the new product literature.[31]

For important projects, the champion, in conjunction with the CEO and/or top-level executives, must identify key personnel linking critical parts of the organization that are necessary for the new product's success. For example, leaders from design, engineering, marketing, manufacturing, or finance departments might be designated to the team for their ability to bring about change from traditional patterns of behavior. These people must be able to create and/or energize coalitions that understand the vision of the core product concept and are committed to achieving it. Successfully communicating the vision through key people also helps to empower people at all organizational levels. This empowering brings them into the project and encourages (rather than discourages) participation. Participation occurs because individuals at lower levels can initiate actions without fear of reprisal when their actions are consistent with the vision.

Motivating People—Constantly Infuse Vitality into the Process

Once a vision is articulated and key people aligned to achieve it, leaders must continually motivate and inspire everyone in the right direction despite obstacles to change. Motivation and inspiration can work by "satisfying basic human needs for achievement, a sense of belonging, recognition, self-esteem, a feeling of control over one's life, and the ability to live up to one's ideals."[32] Ways to accomplish this type of motivation include:

- Articulating the organization's vision in a way that taps the values of the audience being addressed.
- Involving people in deciding how to achieve the vision in order to give them a sense of control.
- Providing coaching, feedback, and role modeling to help people grow professionally and enhance their self-esteem.
- Recognizing and rewarding success with appropriate incentives to make people feel that they belong to an organization that cares for them.

The more a business environment is characterized by change, the more leaders must motivate others to provide leadership.[33] As leadership multiplies across the organization, individuals are prepared to initiate change when necessary. However, multiple leaders sincere in carrying out the vision can often create conflict. To handle it, strong networks of *informal* relationships are necessary to help coordinate leadership activities in the same way that formal structure coordinates managerial activities. Communication and trust fostered by the informal network can lead to ongoing processes of accommodation and adaptation that help to resolve emergent conflicts. In effect, the use of information and communication processes, especially through informal channels, is central to motivating and inspiring people in new product development.

Management Factors

Leadership obliges organizations to change, and change often raises complex problems. To cope with complexity, managers bring a degree of order and consistency to the organization through (1) planning and budgeting, (2) achieving the plan by organizing and staffing, and (3) controlling and problem solving to ensure the plan is accomplished. These management activities must interact with leadership activities for effectiveness, and are critical to new product development.

Planning and Budgeting—Harness Complexity

Whereas leadership provides direction through vision and strategies to achieve that vision, management engages in planning and budgeting to cope with the complexity of the organization and its environment and thus bring logic and consistency to its performance. Goals (linked to the vision) are set, steps to achieve the goals are established (action plans), and resources are allocated (budgets) to achieve the goals. Clearly, the more flexible and available resources are for new products, the easier planning and budgeting will be. Conditions of scarce, inflexible resources, however, necessitate creative planning and budgeting or redefinition of the new product project.

Organizing and Staffing—Draft the Team

Whereas leaders align people to achieve the vision, management develops the capacity to achieve its plan through organizing and staffing. Numerous decisions must be made to achieve the plan. Consequently, management must work within existing organizational decision-making processes (or else design new approaches) to facilitate these decisions. This involves creating an organizational structure and a set of jobs and tasks to accomplish elements of the action plan, staffing the jobs with qualified personnel, communicating the plan, delegating responsibility for carrying out the plan, and devising systems to monitor implementation.

In the context of new products, organizing and staffing are especially critical to the development process. Research on various organizational structures for new product development reveals that certain structures are more effective than others. In a study of five organizational structures for project management (see Table 4.2), the functional matrix and functional organization structures were less effective than others.[34] For complex new product projects, project teams were more effective; however, the project matrix approach performed equally well on both more and less complex projects. Project structures that provided strong leadership were greatly preferred, and the leadership dimension of the project matrix approach was most preferred among the various structures.

Controlling and Solving Problems—Tracking and Troubleshooting

In the drive to implement plans, managers pursue control and problem-solving activities. They use reports, information systems, decision support systems,

TABLE 4.2   Organizational structures for new product development projects.

Structure	Description
Functional	The project is divided into segments and assigned to relevant functional areas and/or groups within functional areas. The project is coordinated by functional and upper levels of management.
Functional matrix	A project manager with limited authority is designated to coordinate the project across different functional areas and/or groups. The functional managers retain responsibility and authority for their specific segments of the project.
Balanced matrix	A project manager is assigned to oversee the project and shares the responsibility and authority for completing the project with the functional managers. Project and functional managers jointly direct many work-flow segments and jointly approve many decisions.
Project matrix	A project manager is assigned to oversee the project and has primary responsibility and authority for completing the project. Functional managers assign personnel as needed and provide technical expertise.
Project team	A project manager is put in charge of a project team composed of a core group of personnel from several functional areas and/or groups, assigned on a full-time basis. The functional managers have no formal involvement.

Source: Erik W. Larson and David H. Gobeli, "Organizing for Product Development Projects," *Journal of Product Innovation Management,* 5 (September 1988), pp. 180–190. Reprinted by permission of Elsevier Science Publishing Co., Inc.

meetings, and other tools to identify differences between results and planned outcomes, and then take steps to solve these problems. In a sense, this is the "nitty-gritty" of implementation—once steps to achieve goals are set, they are implemented and monitored. This effort is critical throughout the new product development process, especially after the product's launch. In organizations where new product development occurs frequently, managers and staff may be expected to readily implement plans. However, where new product development is infrequent and the organization uses more routine activities, special managerial effort will be required to monitor implementation activities.

ESTIMATING AN ORGANIZATION'S PROPENSITY TO INNOVATE: THE INNOVATION AUDIT

As noted before, new product development is highly situational to the firm. Consideration of factors *within* the organization is necessary to facilitate the process and help achieve new product forecasts. Estimates of an organization's propensity to innovate in a new product development situation help determine whether actions should be taken to speed the process of development internally and whether to incorporate the estimates into demand forecasts.

An illustration of an auditing procedure for measuring an organization's propensity to innovate is presented in Figure 4.2. It includes the six major factors discussed previously, along with more specific indicators of those factors. Using judgment, one can rate each of these indicators on the extent to which it would be present in the organization for a particular new product development situation. The wording of each indicator and the accompanying scales in Figure 4.2 are such that low values correspond to a low propensity to innovate and high values correspond to a high propensity to innovate. Although any measurement scale can be employed, a zero-to-one scale with one-tenth of a point intervals is used here for illustration. A benefit of this scale is that the simple average of all items yields an index number ranging from zero (low propensity to innovate) to one (high propensity to innovate).

In the simplest form of the procedure, all indicators can be assumed equal in their effect on propensity to innovate, and the average for all indicators reveals an index number for the total propensity to innovate. If one believes the indicators should be given different weights, estimates of each indicator's relative contribution can be made. This can be accomplished with a similar zero-to-one rating scale, where zero indicates no contribution at all to propensity to innovate and one indicates maximum contribution. Multiplying the weighting of each indicator by the rating yields a revised value for each indicator. The average of these weighted ratings then produces an overall index of organizational propensity to innovate. Mathematically, these simple relationships can be expressed as follows:

$$\text{OPI} = \left(\sum_{i=1}^{n} w_i r_i \right) / n \qquad [4.1]$$

where   OPI = composite measure of organization's propensity to innovate for a new product development situation,

w_i = judgmentally estimated weight of each indicator, with $i = 1$ to n indicators (drop if ratings are equal in weight), and

r_i = judgmentally estimated rating of the extent to which each indicator is believed to be present in the organization's new product development process.

Thus, the sum of the checked ($\checkmark$) rating (r) values across the 18 illustrative indicators in Figure 4.2 is 5.1. If equal weights (w) of importance are assumed for all indicators, dividing 5.1 by 18 (the value of n) yields an OPI estimate of .283. Based simply on the perceptions of the rater (or a composite of several raters), this estimate might be interpreted as relatively low.

FIGURE 4.2 Estimating organizational propensity to innovate in new product development.

Illustrative indicators	Characterizes the organization — Strongly ... Not at all										
	.0	.1	.2	.3	.4	.5	.6	.7	.8	.9	1.0
The organization's identity											
The organization has a long and valued history, including profiles of the founders and other historic documentation.			✔								
The organization is steeped in tradition; what it stands for is very well known in the industry.			✔								
The organization has numerous written policies and procedures that prescribe how things should be done.						✔					
Organizational influence processes											
The organization has a power structure that is very balanced; there are few struggles for power among the leaders.		✔									
It is not easy to influence someone else informally in this organization; things pretty much go by the rules.		✔									
No particular group dominates the direction of this organization; not the engineers, the financiers, nor the marketers.				✔							
Information and communication processes											
The organization does not capture information from the environment in a timely or effective way.									✔		
The organization does capture valuable information from the market, but it seldom gets to the right person.							✔				
Generally, communication among departments in this organization is rather poor; departments rarely talk to each other.								✔			
Resource flexibility											
Human resources in this organization are fully allocated; there are no personnel available for new projects.			✔								
Financial resources in this organization are fully allocated; there is no capital available for new projects.	✔										
Technological expertise in this organization is relatively focused; it will be difficult to adopt a new technology.			✔								
Decision-making processes											
There is very little participation in decision-making processes in this organization; certain executives make all decisions.	✔										
There are numerous levels of approval required in this organization for any decisions related to new products.		✔									
This organization does not even attempt to reach consensus or agreement on important new product decisions.	✔										
Implementation processes											
This organization works well on routine projects; an out of the ordinary new product project creates problems.			✔								
When confronted with a new problem, this organization follows a path of least resistance to solve it.						✔					
When confronted with a new problem, this organization brings in outside consultants rather than disrupt current operations.					✔						

Illustrative computation of composite Index of OPI: $OPI = 5.1/18 = .283$

Recall that an organization's propensity to innovate can vary over time. This is illustrated graphically in Figure 4.3 as a possible path of propensity to innovate over the time of new product development. Note the assumed "normal operating OPI" (which could be based on an estimate such as the one developed in Figure 4.2). Also note the assumed "desired OPI." It recognizes that a certain level of propensity to innovate may be desirable or necessary to complete the project in a certain time frame. When there is a substantial difference between the two levels, interventions may be necessary to reach the desired level of change.

The interventions will depend on leadership and management actions, because the underlying organizational factors are difficult to change in the short run. For example, in Figure 4.3 a "leadership intervention" illustrates initiation of a gradual increase in OPI. In the Motorola case, this intervention could represent launching of the RISC computer chip project in 1983. However, because of other factors (for example, competitive action, a consumer shift in preferences, or a regulator's action), several additional leadership and management interventions may be necessary to accelerate the rate of OPI. In the

FIGURE 4.3   Illustrative dynamic path of organizational propensity to innovate (OPI).

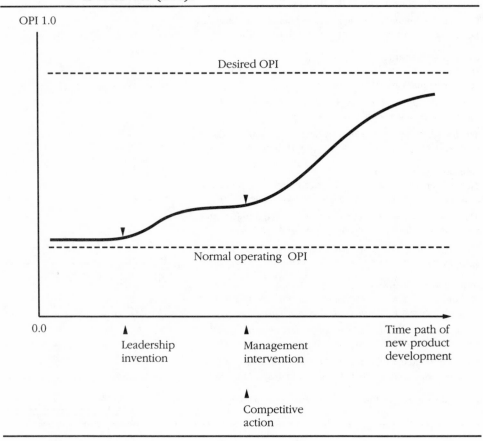

Motorola case, management's decision to intensify development of the RISC chip in 1987 could have been strongly motivated by Sun's decision to launch the competitive Sparc chip.

Incorporating the effects of leadership and management actions in the new product project helps in estimation of the time path of an organization's propensity to innovate function. It represents a type of organizational diagnosis that is central to new product forecasting. If new product development time goals or milestones were established on Figure 4.3, and the OPI was not at the desired level for these goals, major time delays could be predicted. Specific time estimates of these delays could then be incorporated into the schedule to help set (or reset) the approximate launch date. Alternatively, the cost and product design compromises to overcome these delays with a crash program can be estimated—although all delays may not necessarily be possible to overcome.

Clearly, the preceding type of analysis can be performed for the organization's ongoing new product development process and/or for specific projects. Additional organizational factors can be included, different approaches to quantifying judgment can be used, and multiple organization members can get involved in the estimation process. The primary benefit of the auditing approach as described is to provide a diagnostic capability. Reviewing and evaluating numerous organizational factors can reveal sticking points or opportunities for change and thus lead to more focused leadership and management actions.

For example, the sum of the three indicators for communication processes in Figure 4.2 reveals an organization with higher scores on this factor than on others; activities that take advantage of these communication patterns may provide a basis for change. On the other hand, participation and consensus in decision making are perceived to be low; to speed change in the development process, it may be necessary to organize and staff the project to support greater participation in decision making (for example, using a project team organizing approach).

The importance of conducting an innovation audit and estimating an organization's propensity to innovate is related to the strategic importance of new product development for the business. Organizations that rely on successful new products for their future need an organizational structure that continuously supports a high propensity to innovate. Such structure minimizes the time and dollar costs of intervening and raising OPI when efficient and effective new product development is required. In this sense, an organization can acquire, over time, the history and culture of innovating that it needs to interact with the market environment to capitalize on opportunity.

SUMMARY

Organizations bring new products to life. However, the process by which they do so is not an easy one. It is often the victim of the new product development paradox, which occurs when the organization and its members recognize the need for and importance of a new product, yet forces within the organization emerge that resist development and create impediments to progress. An organization's propensity to innovate in new product development, defined as the balance of forces that propel and resist innovations, is a conceptual tool for estimating the impact of organizational factors on new product development.

Six fundamental, and not readily controllable, organizational factors are identified that underlie an organization's propensity to innovate: an organization's identity, the influence processes among its members and departments, its information and communication processes, its resource flexibility, its decision-making processes, and its implementation processes. Six leadership and management factors are also identified that are the basis for actions that can facilitate new product development by overcoming various organizational impediments. An innovation audit approach for identifying and measuring organizational propensity to innovate is suggested as a diagnostic tool for assessing the impact of selected organizational factors on new product development.

Organizational factors are seldom built into new product development and forecasting processes. Product designs and forecasts tend to be developed with an eye to market forces alone. However, at least part of the equation for success depends on what happens inside the organization. Conceptualizing the impact of organizational factors on new products provides a foundation for estimating new product development time and costs, and subsequently for deciding whether and how to prepare the organization for needed changes.

PART TWO

Managing New Product Development

5 The Ongoing Process of New Product Development

Challenges to strategic success in new product development include the uncertainty of increasingly turbulent business environments, market friction from potential buyers and other stakeholders, and varying degrees of organizational propensity to innovate when faced with a new product project. Consequently, the need for leadership and management intervention to define and guide an ongoing *process of development* for new products is paramount in trying to achieve reasonable and predictable performance. The case of Gavilan Computer Corp., an entrepreneurial organization, provides a useful starting point to illustrate this need.[1]

In early 1983, Gavilan introduced the first full-function laptop portable personal computer, anticipating in many ways the concept and design of the successful Compaq and Toshiba lines of portable computers in the late 1980s. The machine weighed nine pounds and was targeted to the "mobile professional." The computer had an eight-line liquid crystal display, a three-inch disk drive, and a touchpad for cursor movement. It was based on the Intel 8088 microprocessor, the same foundation used for the successful IBM PC.

To create a uniquely competitive machine, the firm's president and key engineers decided to develop a proprietary operating system instead of adopting DOS, the operating system IBM used for its PC. The DOS system allowed many independent software firms to develop a variety of applications for users. However, Gavilan decided to avoid IBM/DOS compatibility because it was the path followed by most IBM clone competitors. Instead, Gavilan chose to offer users an integrated set of applications based on its unique operating software.

Gavilan took 12 working prototypes of its new portable computer to the spring 1983 computer industry meeting and generated considerable excitement. Subsequently, some $6 million in advertising and promotion generated 80,000 inquiries and $85 million in orders over the next few months. This backlog of orders buoyed the spirits of the young management team.

Unfortunately, Gavilan did not meet the promised fall 1983 shipping date to fill these orders. The programming for a new operating system that provided an integrated software applications environment proved to be more difficult than anticipated. The shipping date for the new machine slipped to a year after the planned introduction. Subsequently, engineers and early customers began to find a chain of technical problems. Ultimately, only a few thousand units were sold and the firm filed for bankruptcy in October 1984. Gavilan was barely two years old, and had spent some $50 million in venture capital.

Several issues are raised by this case:

- Why didn't Gavilan let current market behavior (use of the DOS standard and the software developed for it) drive its product design decisions rather than generating its own operating system? The requirement to clearly *define and communicate a core new product concept* that responds to market needs and creates value is central to the new product development process.

- Why did Gavilan generate $85 million in orders when the product was unproven? What happened during its new product development process that led marketing to be out of sync with manufacturing? To realize a new product from a core product concept, managers must decide how to bring an intellectual discipline to an organization's *new product development process*.

- Although Gavilan's initial volume of orders suggested no need for a new product forecast, had the company developed one, the outcome may have been very different. For example, if investors had been given a reliable forecast of the core product concept that revealed slow but substantial growth over time (assuming certain adjustments in the new computer), they may have been willing to continue investing to support the product's development. Providing critical input for decision making and control requires management to implement a *new product forecasting process* that is in sync with the new product development process.

These issues suggest that to operationalize a new product development process that will lead to strategic success, managers must intervene in its design and implementation, paying attention to three critical requirements: (1) the new product idea must be formulated into a core product concept that is clear and communicable among everyone involved with it; (2) the concept must be operationalized through a process that copes with turbulent business environments, varying degrees of market friction, and organizational resistance; and (3) the process must be accompanied by a measurement and control system that provides critical feedback to support ongoing new product decisions. Each of these major requirements is discussed in this chapter.

The major topics of new product development and forecasting addressed in this chapter are summarized in Figure 5.1. The new product development process is divided into two time segments: pre- and post-launch. The pre-launch segment consists of the evolutionary stages of a new product concept, the managerial activities necessary to support new product development, and the major types of new product forecasting that provide needed measurement and control. The post-launch segment consists of the new product's marketing program and the comparison of results with forecasts to define measures of achievement. It sets the stage for tracking the performance of the new product after launch in order to make necessary adjustments.

FIGURE 5.1   New product development and forecasting processes.

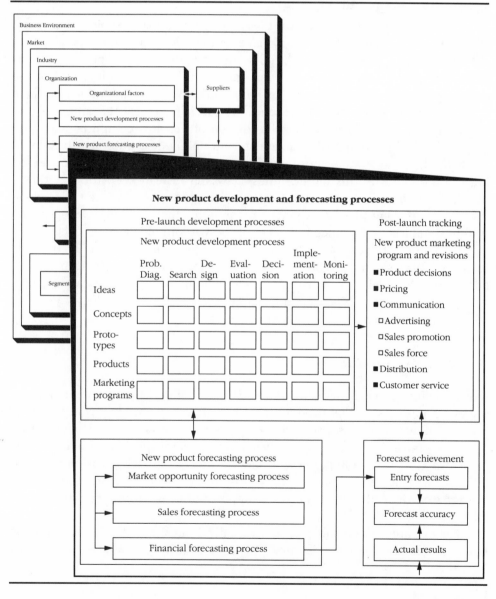

DEFINING A CORE NEW PRODUCT CONCEPT

It is deceptively simple to believe that one has completely defined a new product when what one has is at best only a partial definition. This is especially true when the definition includes concrete aspects of the new product. In the case of Gavilan Computer Corp., defining the uniqueness of the new portable computer in terms of the operating system presaged subsequent problems. As noted, the computer was based on the Intel 8088 microprocessor, the same foundation used in the successful IBM PC personal computer. Although there was some internal disagreement, the firm's president and key engineers decided not to adopt the same operating system as was used in the IBM PC (DOS). With this strategic design decision, Gavilan believed it would be unique and not just another IBM "clone."

In retrospect, it is always easy to second-guess a firm's choice of strategy. However, in this case, Gavilan may have had ample opportunity to select an alternative approach rather than build a unique operating system into its computer. First, operating systems are generally invisible and unimportant to the potential buyer. Buyers' concerns have more to do with getting their jobs done than with the operating system. Second, the specialized market segment of mobile users and the innovative portable design of the new computer may have provided sufficient competitive advantage and uniqueness upon which to build a new product and strategic position. The nature of the operating system added little to the needs of this target, unless it was critical to keep the size down. Third, the earlier 1983 success of Compaq Computer Corp. with an IBM clone strategy for its "luggable" size personal computer that used a DOS operating system should have convinced Gavilan of the wisdom of this approach.

Gavilan's subsequent switch to a DOS operating system in the late spring of 1984 seems to confirm the importance of working within market behaviors. Developing an early and clear definition and understanding of a new product concept based on the market rather than technology can affect the success of the entire development program.

What Is a *New Product*?

A clear definition of a firm's *new product* is essential for its development and for achieving a forecast of that product. However, defining a product is not a trivial task. In an absolute sense, something that is *new* has not existed before. In a relativistic sense, something that is *new* has not been experienced before—it is *perceived* as new. In defining new products, the relativistic view is more useful because, whether or not something is absolutely new, stakeholders who have not yet experienced it may represent opportunities (or problems) for consideration.

For example, shelf-stable or aseptic milk (sold without refrigeration) has been consumed for years in Europe, yet it is a relatively new concept for most consumers in the U.S. market. Consumers who drink refrigerated milk may be very uncertain about milk sold from a non-refrigerated shelf. Further, the newness of the concept to retailers may also create difficulties—should the product be placed in the dairy section, the beverage section, the dried and condensed milk section, or some other section of the store? This relative newness to potential buyers and retailers, perhaps compounded by any newness of the manufacturing process to the firm, would create some difficult marketing problems—the least of which might be the education of consumers about any apparent health concerns over drinking non-refrigerated milk.

Just as the concept of something new is relativistic, so too is the concept of a product. A *product* is a multidimensional concept that has need-satisfying capabilities for the stakeholders interested in it. It represents a major opportunity for an organization to create *value*. It can be defined differently by each stakeholder, and can potentially take a variety of forms. Some dimensions will be tangible product features and others intangible. Some dimensions will endure over time, whereas others will be short lived. Although each stakeholder may have a different perspective, and therefore a different definition, a successfully defined product will have a *core product concept* (on which all agree) that holds the promise of a sustainable competitive advantage to the organization creating it.[2]

Thus, a *new product* is a multidimensional concept—with need-satisfying capabilities—that has not been experienced by a significant number of stakeholders potentially interested in it and is capable of offering a strategic competitive advantage. Because the views of potential buyers, trade intermediaries, and key parts of the organization are instrumental in defining a product, clear definition presumes research among these market stakeholders—a topic addressed in the next chapter. Although there are numerous perspectives from which one could define a new product, the ones reviewed in the next section (in the context of a "portable computer") are central to most new products and services and help to reveal some of the difficulties that may have confronted Gavilan.

The Potential Buyer's View

To the potential buyer, a new product should represent possible benefits that might satisfy needs in ways not previously experienced. As discussed in Chapter 3, human needs are complex and exist at multiple levels. In one sense, the central idea of a portable computer promises the ability to move one's work from place to place, presumably to be more productive. Thus, the core product concept attracting buyers may have been based on the need to be free to move about, productivity, and, at least to early buyers, the intangible symbolic status associated with the product. Hypothetically, a central concept such as "power notebook" may convey these core benefits of the portable computer. The word "notebook" conveys portability and a place where work can be done, and "power" connotes potential energy that can deliver computing power, along with the psychological interpretation of power (wielding force, status, and so on).

Because potential buyers do not all have identical needs (especially simultaneously), it is possible that other core new product concepts could emerge from the definitional process. For example, a "portable office" concept may appeal to the traveling salesperson, who must keep records, communicate, and perform other functions while on the road. Alternatively, an "executive slate" concept may tap the needs of managers with ambitions for executive status.

Clearly, from among alternative core product concepts, just one should be selected as the focal point of development for a targeted market segment; but multiple concepts could be developed for a portfolio of segments. Because different concepts may have different market and sales potential, and tap different segments, care should be used in the evaluation and selection of core product concepts. Identifying and matching the nuances of a core product concept and potential segments of buyers requires a combination of experienced judgment and creatively designed marketing research—topics covered further in Chapter 6.

Of course, beyond the core product concept, which is defined and selected to meet a fundamental market need with a competitive advantage, other features of the product are relevant to the potential buyer (such as ease of use, software that performs needed tasks to be productive, and reliability), but they often play a supporting and/or complementary role in defining the central meaning of a product. The importance of clarifying the meaning of a core product concept is to provide a linkage, for purposes of communication, to all the relevant stakeholders involved in the product's development. The concept should be understood by all, and maintain its integrity throughout the new product development process.

Consider development of the core product concept for the successful Honda Accord.[3] The third-generation Accord, designed in the early 1980s and launched in 1986, was based on the concept of "man maximum, machine minimum." This core concept captured the way the firm wanted consumers to feel about the car. However, as the market changed in the mid to late 1980s, Honda decided it needed to revise this concept for its 1990 model launch. After considerable review, discussion, and analysis, the company decided on a new concept of the Accord as "a rugby player in a business suit." Through this core concept, it wanted to communicate ideas of "rugged physical contact, sportsmanship, and gentlemanly behavior."

Honda's core concept of the rugby player was further broken down so as to translate into specific attributes of the new Accord: "open-minded," "friendly communication," "tough spirit," "stress-free," and "love forever." To illustrate, "tough spirit" translates into the attributes of maneuverability, power, and sure handling in extreme driving conditions; "love forever" translates into long-term reliability and customer satisfaction. This translation facilitated communication of the core concept to functional groups within the firm, especially design engineers, as well as to other key stakeholders.

The Trade Intermediary View

To a trade intermediary—for example, a wholesaler or retailer—a new product represents new opportunities for adding value in delivering the product concept to potential buyers. This value can be delivered in terms of low prices, highly educated sales personnel, buyer training, high levels of installation and repair services, broad selection, or some combination of these and other factors. The value is usually delivered to potential buyers.

For example, faced with several computer alternatives, a potential buyer may need technical and other information about different machines and their capabilities. The extent to which retailers are educated and motivated about the new product concept (for example, a "power notebook") will in part determine how well potential buyers perceive that the product meets their need. Thus, when designing service features for a new portable computer product concept, the firm must consider the information and training needs of retailers and their sales personnel in doing their job. Otherwise, the concept may not be properly communicated and market acceptance may be slowed.

The Organization's View

Different functional areas within an organization may view a new product differently. Key functional areas in which differences are important are marketing, research and development (R&D), and production.

Marketing

To an organization's marketing function, a new product represents the bundles of related *features* that define a core product concept and deliver the need-satisfying *benefits* sought by consumers. Using market research, people involved in the marketing function seek to identify the benefits desired by potential buyers to solve their needs and problems (not currently being met by competitors). Once identified, these buyer benefits not only help to reshape the core product concept, but can also be translated into more specific product features to better communicate the product's meaning to all involved. In this sense, the marketing group often views itself as representing the voice of the customer within the organization.

In the context of the portable computer, important buyer benefits such as portability, ease of use, reliability, status, and price can be translated into specific features, including size, shape, weight, computing power, processing speed, battery life, keyboard, and so on. The translation process is not easy because buyer benefits are often perceptual (style, status, touch and feel, color, and so on). Consequently, various research methods and analytical techniques (for example, conjoint analysis—discussed in Part 3) are useful to identify features and to quantify the "psychophysical" relationship between a buyer's psychological perceptions of a product and its more tangible features. This quantification is instrumental to new product design, and also provides valuable input to forecasting market acceptance.

Research and Development

To a firm's R&D group, the product represents a compilation of basic *elements* that provides a foundation to derive and explain its structure and operation. With an understanding of these foundational elements, the product can be shaped in many ways by engineers, designers, scientists, or others involved in giving it structure. In the portable computer example, key technology elements to design a "power notebook" include silicon computer chips, circuit boards, disk drives, the power supply, and display screen. A firm's ability to engineer and/or extend the existing technology of these and other elements into the features that can deliver need satisfaction is a critical link to the product's development, consumer acceptance of the product, and expected sales response.

For example, progress in display screens affects viewing clarity, which in turn affects potential buyers' attraction to the computer and ability to use it regularly without fatigue. The R&D group must therefore have an accurate assessment of the technology curve for screen displays. This includes knowledge of the current status of major display technologies (such as liquid crystal display and gas plasma) and when major technical features will be ready during the product's definition and development. Resolution, contrast, brightness, screen refresh rate, and availability of color are critical technical attributes of a display screen that define users' perceptions of screen clarity. Errors in estimating the delivery of new technology jeopardize the time and quality estimates of new product development and the achievement of forecasts.

Production and Operations

To a firm's production and operations group, the product represents *components* that must be assembled into the final product or service. The process and operations by which the power supply, the display screen, the disk drive, the main circuit board, the case, and other parts are assembled may define the portable computer product from a production perspective. Because production parameters can actually influence the design characteristics of a product, an organization may want to consider an approach called *design for manufacturability*.[4] For example, certain designs may be easier to assemble and disassemble than others, and therefore less costly and more time efficient.

Design for assembly may not only reduce production costs and manufacturing time, but increase overall quality (fewer parts that fit better are less subject to breakage). *Design for disassembly* may be especially important to customer service personnel and retailers who may be required to repair a unit. Design for disassembly also facilitates the recovery and recycling of components for ecological purposes. As a consequence, production must be involved with R&D (and/or engineering and design) to produce the best design possible—according to the core product concept and marketing's interpretation of it. Design and production flaws can delay, if not destroy, market acceptance of new products.

Finally, *design for market segmentation* should be considered. In markets where buyer needs are changing, segments may emerge more rapidly than the new products to fit those needs. This may be especially true for high technology markets where potential buyers are taught to expect more. The design issue then becomes how to conceptualize the new product to anticipate a rapidly segmenting market. A product *platform* or base may be required from which to generate alternative new products to meet emerging segment needs. For example, designers might leave space for expansion components that, with little change in the manufacturing process, would yield different versions of a new laptop computer to serve emerging segments. The expansion space could be used for a miniature modem that would provide communication on the go and appeal to a "portable office" segment of buyers. Clearly, design for market segmentation requires a strategic view of market evolution based on research and experience.

Merging the Different Views

A *new product* is many things to many people—a need-satisfying concept with benefits for buyers, bundles of need-satisfying features for marketing, a way for trade intermediaries to add value, design elements for R&D, and assembly and processing components for production—yet all must work together to bring about the desired final result. These different perspectives also lead to divergent opinions that frequently emerge during development and can threaten the viability of the project. All of the stakeholder viewpoints may be valid to some extent, as responsible individuals seek to accomplish their goals through the product.

For example, marketing would like to satisfy potential buyers by offering a very easy-to-read display screen, but that may conflict with R&D capabilities (given current technology). Careful decisions must be made in balancing the time to develop improved displays and the time to reach the market. Manufacturing's desire for a keyboard that is easy to assemble may conflict with marketing's desire for one that is easy to use and has the right touch and feel for consumers. Again, a careful decision must be made to balance design for low cost assembly and design for keyboard touch. These decisions directly affect consumer response to the product and the new product forecast.

Sorting out the complex tradeoff issues that emerge in new product development teams requires considerable internal discussion, consensus-building, and an agreed-upon decision process when consensus can't be reached. This decision process should be driven by prioritized criteria defined by the new product development team at the outset of the project. The criteria should reflect the major objectives for new product development, based on a situation analysis and proposed strategic direction for the organization. The following list of criteria for which objectives can be set is typical:

- **Meeting potential buyer needs.** Perhaps highest priority for decisions on features, elements, and components of a new product concept should be reserved for their ability to meet buyer needs.

- **Meeting needs of other stakeholders.** The role of other stakeholders must be recognized when new product success depends on meeting their needs (with special distribution arrangements, regulatory approval, and so on).

- **Financial resources.** Capital and budget availability will certainly influence new product concept design decisions.

- **Timing resources.** The competitive environment may impose time-based needs on the new product concept that will influence tradeoffs made during the design process.

- **Human resources.** Certain new product concept decisions will be altered by the availability of specific human resources, especially when their services are critical to new product design.

- **Other capabilities.** An organization's current business strategy, corporate positioning, customer base, product quality, plant and equipment, information technology, and other capabilities are additional criteria that may shape decisions for a new product concept.

The specific criteria selected and their relative importance should be incorporated into a group decision-making process that can be invoked when differences of opinion arise about a clear definition for the new product concept. Applying these criteria will not only expedite the process, but will also be essential to crucial *go/no-go* decisions at critical phases of new product development.

In summary, defining a viable product concept is a difficult task. Research, expertise, creativity, analysis, astute decision making, and many other factors are key ingredients for progress. Despite the difficulty, a clear core product concept definition is essential as the basis for communication among everyone involved in the product's development. Figure 5.2 illustrates some of the definitional considerations stemming from different points of view about the core product concept for a portable computer. The core product concept of a "power notebook" reflects benefits to potential buyers, which in turn are translated into a variety of features. These features are further refined into design elements, which become the basis for components that, when assembled, represent the finished product. A marketing program complementing the finished product then helps to ensure that buyer needs are satisfied. The translation of an idea for a core product concept into a final product is operationalized through an organization's new product development processes.

FIGURE 5.2   Formulating core new product concepts from different stakeholder views.

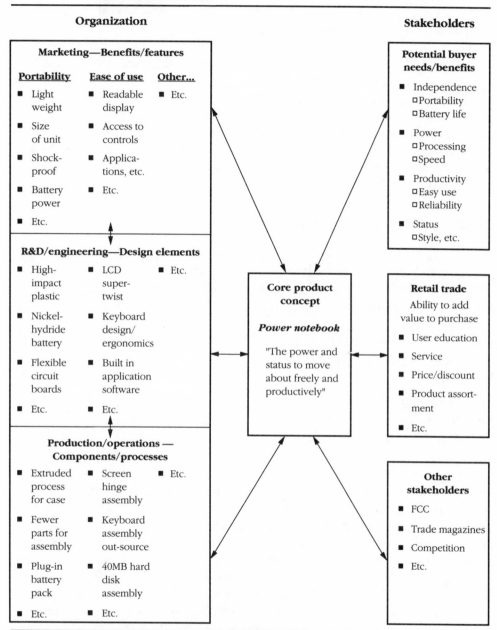

NEW PRODUCT DEVELOPMENT PROCESSES

New products begin as ideas that evolve into comprehensive marketing programs designed to meet the needs of potential buyers and other market stakeholders. Throughout this evolutionary process, the definition of the core product concept will be challenged by people both within and outside the organization.

As the needs of buyers and other market stakeholders are considered, changes to the core concept may be necessary or the original concept may be reinforced. In any case, an explicit *new product development process* to evaluate and cope with such changes is critical to maintain the integrity of any core new product concept.

An outsider looking in on the new product development processes of several organizations may describe them in a variety of ways. In one firm new product development may appear to be a very *sequential* step-by-step approach, with occasional looping back to previous steps. In another it may seem *overlapping* or *holistic*, with interacting and parallel processes that carry out its multiple aspects. In still others new product development may be seen simply as *chaotic* activity. These four views of new product development processes are briefly considered in the following sections.

Sequential New Product Development

Perhaps the most cited and enduring view of new product development is the six-step process described by the consulting firm Booz-Allen & Hamilton, Inc.[5] After the firm's new product strategy has been determined, the process proceeds through the following steps:

1. Idea generation
2. Screening and evaluation
3. Business analysis
4. Development
5. Testing
6. Commercialization

Because the mortality of new product ideas is often high, organizations need to generate a sufficient flow of them to achieve their growth objectives. After screening and evaluation, the ideas are submitted to a business analysis that evaluates the remaining product concepts for estimated sales, costs, profitability, and other financial indicators. If a new product idea meets business analysis criteria, it enters development. This step may include R&D, engineering, and other activities to develop prototypes and operational products. Because these activities often require heavy financial commitment, the business analysis step is all the more important. Ultimately, the product is submitted to testing, such as use testing, various forms of market testing, and other procedures that will facilitate measuring market response to the new product. Finally, commercialization involves the launch strategy for the new product, as defined by the target market segment, the marketing program, and launch timing.

At specific steps in the process (such as screening, business analysis, and testing), decisions can be made on whether or not to go ahead with the project. These *go/no-go* decisions fulfill management's role of imparting some sort of discipline to the process. Further, although these stepwise processes appear sequential, they are often iterative or looping. That is, the steps of generating and screening ideas may be repeated often before an idea is selected for business evaluation. If none of the ideas pass business analysis, the organization may return to idea generation, and so on. In any case, the presence and integrity of each step are crucial to provide the necessary discipline to manage a successful process.

At Gavilan, some steps in new product development may have been overlooked. For example, Gavilan apparently decided to pursue an early product launch without adequate product testing. When Gavilan took 12 working prototypes to the spring 1983 computer industry meeting, they generated considerable interest and orders. However, Gavilan did not meet the fall 1983 shipping date to fill these orders because of programming problems with the new operating system. This delay put considerable pressure on the development process.

Gavilan engineers also found other design and technical problems: The power supply, located too close to the floppy drive, functioned improperly; hinges on the pull-up screen kept breaking; keyboard keys stuck when used; and the batteries that provided portability leaked. The first Gavilan computers shipped in early 1984 broke in the hands of buyers after a few days' use—because of problems that might have been identified and resolved with comprehensive product use testing. The lessons learned here include the consequences of the decision to launch a technical product prematurely without adequate product testing under use conditions.

Following a sequential approach to new product development ensures that each step will be executed. It is therefore a desirable process when there is a high degree of uncertainty about an organization's ability to carry out a new project. Such is often the case with newly formed organizations that may lack the necessary discipline to adequately meet market needs. Sequential product development may also be useful when time is available for development, when the market is stable and no surprises are anticipated, when major product quality improvements are not essential, or when the organizational structure is hopelessly departmentalized (that is, when a cross-departmental team will not work and the new product must be handed off from one department to another to complete necessary tasks). However, when time and responsiveness become critical, the sequential approach may have drawbacks.

Overlapping New Product Development: Quality Function Deployment (QFD)

One of the major limitations of sequential new product development is the "disconnect" in the handoff of the product from one department or functional team to another. Accumulated learning is lost as each group tries to interpret the requirements set by the previous one. If the design and engineering group is handed a list of potential buyers' needs and benefits from marketing, it will spend considerable time and effort translating those requirements into design elements. The problem is compounded when the design and engineering group hands off the design elements to manufacturing, and so on.

To resolve these handoff difficulties, many Japanese firms use an overlapping development process known as *quality function deployment* or QFD.[6] Originated by Mitsubishi in their Kobe, Japan shipyards during 1972, and extended by Toyota, this approach to new product development involves the use of a series of *interaction matrices* that specify the relationship between one phase of development and the next. Teams from different functions must meet to agree on the specifications in the matrix to ensure clear communication and translation of potential buyer needs into an operational product or service. In effect, this approach eliminates the "wall" between organizational functions by overlapping them in the matrix and defines and records the rules for their interactions.

A simplified version of an interaction matrix between potential buyer needs and engineering design elements is illustrated in Figure 5.3; it has been called the *house of quality*. The major steps in building a house of quality interaction matrix are:

1. Identify the needs of potential buyers and other stakeholders and measure their importance (the left side of the house). From market research, these needs can be expressed as bundles of benefits; for example, the need for portability in a personal computer may be described by consumers in terms of the benefits of "lightweight" and "fits in a briefcase."

2. Identify potential buyer perceptions, or *positioning*, of competing brands relative to the new product (the right side of the house). This step indicates opportunities for competitive advantage along the benefits, according to their relative importance. The measures can be obtained as ratings of competing brands among potential buyers.

3. Identify the engineering and design elements that affect the various potential buyer benefits (the ceiling of the house). Each element should link in some way to one or more benefits.

4. Complete the interaction matrix, which indicates the degree to which engineering and design elements affect benefits (the interior of the house). Through a rating system, the team estimates the potential impact of each design element on buyer benefits. These evaluations can be based on research and/or judgment and summarized at the base of each element with an objective measure to indicate the new product's expected performance against competitors.

5. Evaluate the interactions among the engineering and design elements (the roof of the house). Because a new product requires overall performance integrity, the design elements must be engineered to work together in

FIGURE 5.3   "House of quality" for new portable laptop computer: partially completed.*

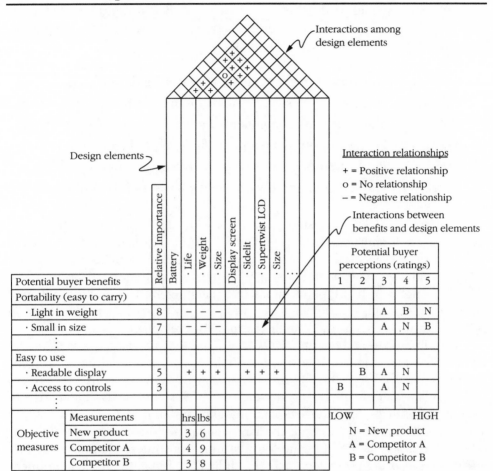

*For a more detailed description of building a "house of quality," see John R. Hauser and Don Clausing, "The House of Quality," *Harvard Business Review*, 66 (May–June 1988), pp. 63–73.

synchronization. Changing one element may necessitate changes in others, or whole new elements may need to be designed lest the performance of the entire system suffer. For example, a lighter battery may improve the weight of the computer, but it may shorten the length of operating time. Resolving such critical design tradeoffs requires creative engineering and use of the latest technologies and processes.

At minimum, a cross-functional team from marketing and engineering should determine the structure of the house of quality. Ideally, a cross-functional team from all major areas of new product development (manufacturing, purchasing, process engineering, cost accounting, and so on) should be involved in constructing the house.

It should be apparent that the development process is not complete when design elements are specified. Additional interaction matrices should be constructed until the final product features clearly satisfy consumer benefits. Consider the following sets of interacting matrices, noticing that the dimension determined in each is carried to the next:

Matrix I: Potential buyer benefits *by* engineering/design elements;

Matrix II: Engineering/design elements *by* manufacturing components;

Matrix III: Manufacturing components *by* process assembly operations;

Matrix IV: Process assembly operations *by* final product output features;

Matrix V: Product output features *by* marketing program variables;

Matrix VI: Marketing program variables *by* buyer satisfaction of benefits.

The six matrices suggested here come full circle, starting with potential buyer needs and benefits and ending with their satisfaction. The matrices encompass the major functions of an organization, including R&D, new product design, production and operations, marketing, and customer satisfaction. The primary benefits of this type of interactive planning are the *quality* built into the product through the detailed execution of process tasks and the focus on potential buyer needs as the source of product development.

Despite apparent benefits of QFD, its use has not fared as well in the United States as in Japan. In a study of 35 new product development projects, short-term performance results did not match the development process improvements experienced by Japanese users.[7] This finding is due partly to cultural differences, but the tremendous efforts required to launch a QFD initiative within an organization, the large amounts of marketing research and other information needed to complete the numerous interaction matrices that might define an entire project, and the difficulty of maintaining commitment and ongoing participation of a cross-functional team from project start to finish are also areas of concern. Nevertheless, reports from 29 of the 35 projects indicated the belief that using QFD offered the potential for long-run efforts. Cross-functional decision making, highly motivated teams, and the efficient utilization of information hold the promise of improving ongoing new product development processes.

Holistic New Product Development

As business and market environments became more turbulent and competitive throughout the 1980s, response in terms of new product development speed and flexibility became a hallmark of success.[8] These factors created skepticism about the wisdom of following a traditional sequential approach to new product development. The sequential approach, and to some extent the overlapping approach, were compared to a "relay race," in which the baton is handed off from one phase (and often organizational unit or department) of development to another—from marketing to engineering to production and so on. This linear approach takes time and can be rigid, especially when the baton passes from one department to another. Time delays occur when one department must hand the baton back to another for refinement and/or change—otherwise errors become frozen into the process. It is the passing of the "bear" back and forth over departmental walls that can bog the process down. Even the QFD approach to development can get bogged down in the details of the interaction matrices and their sequential nature.

A new approach was the "rugby" style of product development, in which a new product *team* moves through all phases of development together, passing the ball back and forth as they move down the field. Under this holistic approach, improved speed and flexibility of development are possible. One study of six firms believed to use this approach identified the following characteristics of holistic new product development:[9]

- **Built-in instability.** Top management creates tension for the new product team by giving it substantial leeway on an important project, but only within the context of stringent corporate requirements.

- **Self-organizing project teams.** Beginning with "zero knowledge," the project team begins to exhibit autonomy, self-transcendence (pursuing higher order goals to stimulate discovery), and cross-fertilization among team members from different functions within the organization.

- **Overlapping development phases.** As the project team works together, it eventually gains its own cohesiveness and "rhythm" to absorb development problems more rapidly than separate groups working through sequential phases of development.

- **"Multilearning."** As the project team acquires knowledge about the environment, the market, the organization, and the product, learning occurs across different levels of the organization (individuals, groups, departments, and so on) and across different business functions (marketing, production, engineering, and so on); this learning creates a team that can solve problems fast and obtain speed benefits.

- **Subtle control.** The built-in instability and autonomy of the project teams may lead to chaos; however, it should not engender strict controls. Instead, more subtle control by management is required, including such approaches as recruiting the right people for the job, fostering an open work environment, basing the incentive system on group performance, visiting customers, and learning from mistakes.

- **Organizational transfer of learning.** The benefits of learning at multiple organizational levels and functions transfer to other new product projects, as well as other parts of the organization.

Examples from the six Japanese and American organizations used in the study were given to prove the value of this approach. Products included cars, copiers, cameras, and computers from firms such as Fuji-Xerox, Canon, Honda, NEC, Epson, Brother, 3M, Xerox, and Hewlett-Packard. These new products appear to be primarily durable goods, and it is not clear that the holistic process works as well for consumer packaged goods (foods, beverages, cosmetics, etc.), industrial products and processes, or services. Further, the holistic new product development approach requires extraordinary time commitment from team members and an early cushion of financial and other resources to support the up-front learning that must occur. Also, the process may be more appropriate for continuously evolving new products than for breakthrough innovations, and for larger organizations that must overcome resistance to change than for smaller firms with zealous founders and entrepreneurs.

Chaotic New Product Development

For many organizations, a structured process to discipline new product development is an afterthought. First there is an idea—then there is action. Everyone energizes to get the work done to make the idea a reality. Although chaos and disorder appear to reign, somehow a product is launched, and in some cases it succeeds. The very successful software firm Autodesk Inc. is a case in point.[10]

Autodesk began in 1982 with a strong founder/leader and a group of computer programmers who wrote software for the IBM PC. While the new firm was working on a variety of new products, an outside programmer walked in the door with a new idea—a program that provided computer-aided design (CAD) for the PC at substantially lower costs than existing systems. The excitement over the apparent potential for the new product resulted in termination of all other programming work. The product was developed and became a major success, carrying the company through several years of growth.

Other new products began to emerge from Autodesk, but with no evident strategic consistency. For example, a family of products based on intelligent computer games was developed because of the founder's interests. Despite the other products, the basic AutoCad product propelled the firm's success. Organizationally, the firm was dominated by its founder and a group of elite programmers called the "Core."

In 1986, the founder appointed a president and unofficially exited the firm. However, considerable conflict characterized operations. Through the use of so-called "flame mail" (electronic mail messages), various factions of the organization argued frequently over numerous issues, especially the technical direction of the firm. The firm's marketing managers and the Core programmers disagreed often about how and when to respond to customer needs. Despite the conflicts, progress was made and growth continued from 1986 to 1991. The various factions somehow balanced each other out to the point of making operational gains.

However, during 1991, Autodesk profits were 25 percent below expectations and the stock dropped 22 percent in one day. After publishing a 44-page internal electronic mail memo about the state of the firm, the founder returned for several months. The memo stung everyone into action. A new president of the firm was appointed in late 1991. To get the next version of the software product completed, a list of some 7,000 items to be accomplished was developed—a list previously kept in the programmers' heads. Completion deadlines and responsibilities were agreed upon. Several new products were also launched during the fiscal year 1992.

The first 10 years of Autodesk's new product development may best be described as *chaos*.[11] Great disorder and conflict appeared to characterize the process. However, as in most chaotic situations, an underlying pattern drove new product development. The many conflicts, which gave the process its apparent disorder and complexity, may in fact have counterbalanced conflicting forces within the firm. Or it may have been the role of the founder as a *significant attractor* (a concept in chaos theory). All of the oscillation in the organization came to rest when he issued a call for strategic direction and a changed course (in effect, "attracting" everyone's attention). Directions were changed and development continued, albeit with a different focus to developmental activities. Over time, however, unless the new president makes substantial organizational changes, the strong presence of the Core and the distant but still involved founder (living in Switzerland) foretell a return to what appears to have been a new product development process based on chaos.

Chaotic new product development is not necessarily a bad process. The greater freedom to move about in such situations may yield creative solutions to problems or breakthrough ideas. Further, for many startup companies that have new ideas but are oblivious to their environment, it may be the path of least resistance. Most chaotic situations have simple underlying patterns, although they are not necessarily evident. The programmers at Autodesk knew the 7,000 tasks that had to be completed for the product; the details were simply not recorded. They would have eventually completed the jobs, but perhaps not in the most efficient way according to the time and development goals imposed by market needs and the competitive environment. However, market needs were not the same in 1992 as in 1982. Autodesk therefore may impose more discipline in new product development—as indicated by its willingness to make lists—in order to maintain its market position.

What becomes evident from reviewing various approaches to new product development—sequential, overlapping, holistic, and chaotic—is that each specific new product situation may require a different new product development process. The sequential approach may not work in some cases, but it may work well in others. A holistic approach that affords speed and flexibility may be the most effective process to follow in specific situations. Or chaos may be desired under certain circumstances in which breakthrough ideas are sought.

Crafting an Ongoing New Product Development Process

Confronted with the challenge of developing a core new product concept, an organization's leaders and managers should use their talents to craft an ongoing product development process built on five fundamental intellectual principles. The first four principles suggested here are based on the first four chapters of the book. More specifically, the process should be *strategic, flexible, interactive,* and *integrative* with respect to the environment, the market, and the organization. The fifth principle, espoused in this chapter, is the *ongoing* aspect of new product development.

Strive for Consistency with an Organization's Strategic Objectives

As discussed in Chapter 1, determining an organization's business strategy helps to clarify the major long-run objectives for new product development. Objectives may include improving product quality to better satisfy consumer needs, speeding the development process to respond to competitive actions, reducing costs to improve market share or financial performance, maintaining employment, or some combination of these objectives and others. Effectively building and managing the new product development process requires consistency with prioritized objectives. For example, if a primary objective is to develop quantum improvements in product quality over time, a QFD-type process may be an appropriate one to follow in new product development. If a primary objective is the development of a breakthrough project in a reasonably short period of time, a more chaotic development process, located offsite (so as not to interfere with current organizational processes), may be advisable. In short, well-reasoned strategic direction should drive the design of an ongoing new product development process.

Build Flexibility with Adequate Resource Commitment

An organization's new product development process should be flexible in order to respond to rapidly changing and turbulent environmental conditions. It should be prepared to cope with unexpected events as well as an increasing intensity of ongoing observable trends—as discussed in Chapter 2. It should also be capable of coping with different types of new product projects, whether they are incremental improvements or major breakthroughs. Generally, the greater the resources available, the greater the opportunity for flexibility. Thus, flexibility can be achieved with adequate commitment of financial, time, human, and other resources. Underfunding a new product process can choke its ability to respond to varying conditions.

Become Interactive with a Stakeholder Orientation

An organization's new product development process should be interactive with its major stakeholders, especially potential buyers. Because environments change, so too will buyer and other stakeholder needs. Therefore, establishing and maintaining relationships with major stakeholders throughout the development process is necessary to capitalize on new product opportunities and solve problems. Such relationships are particularly important when selected mediators are identified who will influence portions of the environment that affect the product. For example, pharmaceutical firms make a habit of carefully monitoring the U.S. Food and Drug Administration's approval processes and regulatory decision making, insofar as they might affect a new pharmaceutical product. Maintaining an ongoing, interactive relationship with such key stakeholders to address their activities, needs, and problems is clearly beneficial. Depending on the market in question, the same logic holds for other key stakeholders (such as competitors, the trade, and suppliers) as identified in Chapter 3.

Build Integration with Organizational Teams

More than most organizational activities, new product development requires significant integration among many parts of an organization for success. However, as discussed in Chapter 4, an organization will tend to resist change in the face of a new product project within the very parts of the organization that should be working together. Consequently, a team approach is necessary to overcome the differences and resistance to change among organizational participants.[12] Typically, as a project proceeds, a lead team will give way to several interrelated teams to carry out various functions.

The team approach proves effective because overall goals and objectives guide new product development, yet the contribution of each player on the team is recognizable. The *new product champion*, a leader/coach with the support of top management, is instrumental in sheltering the team when necessary and otherwise managing resources to maintain its flexibility and interaction with its market environment.

Pursue New Product Development as an Ongoing Process

Traditional views of new product development processes are project oriented: They begin with an idea and end with a launch program. The limitation of this view is that the organization may return to a state of complacency between projects, meaning that the next new project will inevitably face the usual resistance to change. To break this cycle, organizations must view new product development as an ongoing process of learning and renewal that becomes part of the organizational culture. *Ongoing* entails continual attention to the needs of important market segments, with constant product improvements, new product extensions, and occasional breakthrough products that satisfy emerging needs better than competitors.

A strategic commitment to a market segment demands dedicated new product attentiveness to achieve long-run success. The benefits of this commitment go beyond the traditional financial criteria for success. Organization members who experience the ups and downs that accompany ongoing new product processes gain a rewarding sense of accomplishment and renewal.

Thus, crafting a new product development process requires a consistency with strategic objectives, a flexibility to cope with varying degrees of environmental turbulence, interaction with the market to anticipate and/or overcome friction in formulating the new product, an integration of organizational efforts to energize cross-functional new product teams, and a commitment to pursue new product development as an ongoing process of organizational renewal. Implementation of these principles operationalizes the new product development process.

OPERATIONALIZING NEW PRODUCT DEVELOPMENT PROCESSES

Operationalizing a new product development process should begin with a clear understanding of an organization's current development process (if one exists) and an audit of its *propensity to innovate* (as discussed in Chapter 4). The intellectual principles of new product development suggested in the preceding section (strategic, flexible, interactive, integrative, and ongoing) can be used to assess an organization's current and desired propensity to innovate. The difference between the two indices (recall Figure 4.3) largely defines the magnitude of change required, as well as the process factors that drive the differences. Building a *new* new product development process thus compels the exercise of leadership and management activities to bring about the desired change.

Two central dimensions to operationalizing new product development are (1) the level of new product concept refinement (from the idea to the launch of a marketing program) and (2) the managerial activities necessary to implement each level of concept development. After a brief review of each dimension, they are taken together to illustrate how a variety of possible processes might be pursued to realize a new product or a continual stream of new products.

Level of New Product Concept Refinement

A core new product concept can be viewed as proceeding from an abstract to a specific level. Five arbitrary but useful levels of concept development help define managerial checkpoints during development. A new product originates as an *idea*. Subsequently it is shaped into a *concept*, a *prototype*, the actual *product*, and ultimately a comprehensive *marketing program* that augments the product.

Idea

An idea is the highest form of abstraction a new product can take. It is usually represented as a descriptive statement, written or verbalized. Generally, the more ideas the better; however, improved management of the product development process may reduce the number of ideas needed to ensure success. In a 1982 study, seven new ideas were needed to generate a successful new product, compared to 58 in a similar 1968 study.[13] Although this reduction varied by industry, it was attributed to organizations better understanding their markets and market segmentation, as well as applying existing (rather than new) technology to develop the product.

Figure 5.4 suggests that a variety of procedures and sources can be used to generate new product ideas. Research findings show major market stakeholders to be important sources of successful ideas. In a study of nine types of industrial

FIGURE 5.4   Generating new product ideas.

Idea generating procedures	New Product Stakeholders						
	Potential buyers	Users of similar products	Retailers	Competitors	Suppliers	Organizational members	Other
Procedures based on the context of the new product situation							
Historical analysis							
Scenario analysis							
Consumption systems analysis							
Patent search							
Competitive product analysis							
Technology tracking							
Other							
Procedures based on individual response							
In-depth interviews							
Complaints analysis							
Requests analysis							
Suggestions analysis							
Inventors							
Design/creative consultants							
Creativity							
Surveys w/open-ended questions							
Other							
Procedures based on group response							
Focus group interviews							
Brainstorming groups							
Synectics problem solving							
Other							
Procedures based on structural analysis of the new product and potential buyer needs							
Listing							
Attribute stretching							
Heuristic ideation technique							
Morphological forced connections							
Product analogies							
Creativity software							
Other							

innovations, the primary sources were distributed among users, manufacturers, and suppliers.[14] Differences were due to the economic benefits gained by the respective innovators. For example, of 111 scientific instrument innovations studied, 77 percent came from users. Of 16 tractor shovel-related innovations, 94 percent came from manufacturers. Of 20 wire termination equipment innovations, 56 percent came from suppliers. Clearly, manufacturers will benefit from all of the innovations, whatever their source. The practical implication of this research is that an organization seeking new, profitable ideas must actively and systematically seek ideas from all of its market stakeholders.

Although numerous new product ideas may be generated, they must be evaluated and screened to reduce the number to a viable set for further development and evaluation. In particular, the size of a market opportunity represented by an idea or set of ideas will be a valuable input to its evaluation and decision process. Approaches for assessing market opportunities are considered in Chapter 7.

Concept

A new product concept, more specific in description than an idea, should include the major consumer benefits and features defining the new product. It can be a verbal or written description, an artist's rendering, a model, or appear in another suitable presentation format that depicts the idea. An illustration of a new product concept is provided in Chapter 8.

In practice, ideas and concepts are often combined and considered to be part of one creative process. The value in separating them is that concepts can be made more operational for closer scrutiny and evaluation by different stakeholders. For example, engineering needs to visualize how existing technology might be applied to implement the concept, and marketing needs to identify the relevant features of the concept to define its broader marketing program (information needs, customer service needs). Finally, before the selection of one or more concepts with which to proceed, several iterations of concept development may be necessary.

Through concept evaluation procedures (illustrated in Chapter 8), the outcome of the concept development stage ought to be a fairly clear definition of the core product concept in terms of the features that drive the product's continued development. Because the decision to move beyond the concept stage can involve substantial dollar costs, the concept evaluation procedures should also include financial implications. For example, the resources required to develop a new type of automated test equipment for electronic circuit boards would be significant enough to warrant investment in concept evaluation research to provide sales and financial forecasts.

Prototype

A prototype is a working model or preliminary version of the final product, achieved through an implementation of the product concept. Several iterations may be necessary before a final prototype is perfected. For many products, the prototype is the first full-scale likeness of the product; for others, it is a scaled-down model. For some products a prototype is not possible without at least a small-scale product launch (for example, a new retail store or a new cable channel dedicated to a specific theme). In these cases, prototyping and product development proceed simultaneously in-market.

Scientists, engineers, designers, marketers, and others responsible for product design and creativity will be heavily involved in prototype development. Some prototypes may be relatively easy to develop, especially for organizations already in the business—for example, a new bar soap, a new insurance policy, or a new credit card. Others may be more difficult, if not impossible—a new industrial robot, a new aircraft, or a new lifecare community. The prototype development process can be facilitated and shortened by the development of special tools. For example, computer-aided design (CAD) coupled with stereolithography equipment enables prototyping of plastic molds of designs in a relatively short period of time (in hours for smaller parts). *Virtual reality* (discussed briefly in Chapter 7 in the context of new product scenarios) can also be used to facilitate the prototyping process.

Product

A *product* is the realization of the core product concept and the means by which stakeholders can experience true benefits. For example, in the case of a new high-strength carbon fiber for lightweight structural applications, prototypes may be generated with a pilot machine to set specifications; however, the development of the final fibers that can be used in applications by potential buyers may require a full-scale plant operation. A product's final definition may be the result of several iterations of development and refinement and may involve the satisfaction of all relevant stakeholders, especially potential buyers. The use of various product and prototype testing procedures is briefly discussed in Chapter 6.

Marketing Program

The most refined form of development for the new product is the *marketing program*. It includes the product's price, the degree of availability to the market through channels of distribution, the kind and amount of information to be communicated to potential buyers, and the level of service to support the product. Although these decisions are tentatively made as early as the concept definition, they can only be simulated and pretested until decisions are made to launch the actual marketing program. Like earlier stages in the product's evolution, the marketing program can go through various iterations and adjustments before launch decisions are made. In fact, throughout a product's development process, iterations may occur within any particular stage, and returning to prior stages may also be necessary. The mechanism for monitoring these iterations involves understanding the major managerial activities of new product development.

New Product Managerial Activities

For each checkpoint on the levels of new product refinement, major sets of activities must be performed to manage the development of the new product. These activities are *problem diagnosis, search, design, evaluation, decision, implementation* and *monitoring*.

Problem Diagnosis

Problem diagnosis activities include finding and defining the factors that drive the problems and opportunities at various levels of concept refinement. They begin with a strategic situation analysis (strengths, weaknesses, opportunities, problems/threats) associated with the development of business strategy and include a variety of research procedures to generate data and information on complex situations. The diagnosis process continues with each level of new product refinement as problems and opportunities are encountered. The search for causal factors can be time-consuming and expensive, but rewarding when solutions are discovered.

Search

Search activities involve the generation of options at each new product checkpoint. Basic texts on new product development review the various techniques that can be used to search for and generate creative new product ideas and concepts (see the summary of techniques in Figure 5.4). These approaches (for example, motivation research, brainstorming, synectics, gap analysis, morphological analysis, and patent searches) can also be used to find creative solutions to problems throughout the process.

Design

New product design involves the translation of abstractions into observable realities, as well as creativity. Design is based on four integrated requirements: *usability, technical/economic viability, aesthetic sensibility,* and *image congruity*.[15] Usability is the extent to which a new product will meet the multiple levels of needs of potential buyers. A portable computer may be small, but will its use over time become very uncomfortable? Technical and economic viability depends on recognition of the underlying technology of the new product in addition to the costs. Do the materials used yield a durable and reliable design; is the design energy efficient; are unit, operational, and maintenance costs reasonable? The aesthetic sensibility of a design is conveyed by its style and the impression it gives to various market stakeholders. Finally, image congruity requires that the design fit the corporate image, the image of a division or product family, and an image consistent with the self-concept of consumers and the retailers that might sell the product.

Managing the design process, including the creativity that produces a good design, is a challenge to many organizations, and can be generated internally and/or out-sourced.[16] NCR Corporation provides an example of pursuing design excellence through an entire business, not merely its products. It seeks to develop products that incorporate six identified principles of design—usability, aesthetics, reliability, functionality, innovation, and appropriateness—from the inside to the outside to provide customer satisfaction. The company cites five characteristics of its products that typify design excellence, in order of importance:[17]

1. **Fit and finish.** Attention to detail in overall design and the way parts fit together.

2. **Environmental fit.** The relationship of the machine to its immediate environment of use.

3. **Visual continuity.** The use of a recurring theme throughout a product or product line.

4. **Innovation.** The introduction of something new.

5. **Price/value.** A fair price for a well-designed machine.

Every organization can develop its own design principles, but consciously linking new product design to other products and organizational assets seems to provide synergies that enhance strategic advantage.

Evaluation

Evaluation activities require setting new product performance criteria, clarifying procedures to eliminate or keep (screen) various options, and collecting data to use as a basis for decisions. In addition to the general classes of criteria applied in synthesizing different views on the core product concept, more specific criteria, including ones relating to technical, financial, marketing, production, and organizational aspects of product development, are a major concern. Estimated sales, market share, sales growth, cost, return on investment, technological fit, operational fit, and organizational fit are illustrative of criteria that might be used to evaluate ideas, concepts, prototypes, products, and marketing programs. Clearly, forecasting is central to evaluation activities. It provides estimates on certain criteria, especially those involving market response. In particular, financial estimates provide key input to the important *go/no-go* decisions.

Decision

Decision activities involve key actions to confirm the direction of the development project for the new product. The most obvious decisions, based on the evaluation of several relevant criteria, are the *timing*, the *modify*, and the *go/no-go* decisions at critical phases of the project. Timing decisions determine *when* to execute and with what speed. For example, a *go* decision on a particular concept implies that the project will move forward to prototype development. However, incorporating timing parameters into the decision may enable certain opportunities to be capitalized upon, or problems to be circumvented, if the project is accelerated, delayed, or held. A *hold* decision suspends all activities on the project. The project would be subject to further evaluation and decision at a future date.

The timing decision for the launch of the final marketing program is especially critical for turbulent market environments in which the response of potential buyers and/or competitors depends on the product's availability. Decisions to accelerate or delay the new product development process to better synchronize the launch date with the market environment are considered in subsequent chapters.

A *no-go* decision terminates the current project. It implies that a particular phase of product development did not meet the essential criteria established for it. A *modify* decision means the product will undergo more development. Typically, evaluation would have revealed some opportunity (such as a large, attractive market) to proceed, but also difficulties in designing a product to meet the opportunity. Project teams, as well as key leaders and managers, ought to be involved in these major new product decisions.

Implementation

Implementation involves the *execution* of all planned and unplanned tasks necessary to operationalize the process. Defining who will perform what tasks (assigning responsibilities) and on what schedule is the major planning activity. However, as for any project, unanticipated circumstances require flexibility. How does one respond when beta-test users report that the personal computer is unstable in their laps when they use it, when the external plastic case for the computer has a minor flaw after the first production run, or when the printing on the final package for the new product is blurred? It is at this point that the value of an ongoing intellectual discipline for new product development can be realized. Broad understanding and experience with the new product processes enable a company to cope with unanticipated circumstances.

Monitoring

Monitoring activities focus on tracking and controlling major new product decisions. The various planned paths and performance measures of the new product development project are monitored to inform the team and key managers about exceptions that are identified (and can be used to take corrective steps). An effective monitoring capability is one that supports rapid modification of the new product throughout development, but especially after formal launch. More practically, it represents a continuation of the new product development process into the market.

Planning a New Product Development Process

In Figure 5.5, the managerial activities involved in planning and establishing new product development are arrayed with the various levels of product concept refinement. The top part of Figure 5.5 illustrates a *comprehensive full-term* new product development process. This exhaustive and in a sense *ideal* process,

FIGURE 5.5   Illustrative new product development processes.

Comprehensive Full-term Development

Levels of Core New Product Concept Refinement	Major Managerial Activities						
	Problem Diagnosis	Search	Design	Evaluation	Decision	Implementation	Monitoring
Ideas	□	►	►	►	►	►	▼
Concepts	►	►	►	►	►	►	▼
Prototypes	►	►	►	►	►	►	▼
Products	►	►	►	►	►	►	▼
Marketing programs	►	►	►	►	►	►	■

Parallel Speed-up Development

Levels of Core New Product Concept Refinement	Major Managerial Activities						
	Problem Diagnosis	Search	Design	Evaluation	Decision	Implementation	Monitoring
Ideas	□	►	►	►	►	►	▼
Concepts	□	►	►	►	►	►	▼
Prototypes	□	►	►	►	►	►	▼
Products	□	►	►	►	►	►	▼
Marketing programs	□	►	►	►	►	►	■

Crash Development

Levels of Core New Product Concept Refinement	Major Managerial Activities						
	Problem Diagnosis	Search	Design	Evaluation	Decision	Implementation	Monitoring
Ideas	□	►	►	►	▼		
Concepts	□	►	►	►	▼		
Prototypes					▼		
Products			□	►	►	►	▼
Marketing programs			□	►	►	►	■

Note: □ = start activity; ► = continue activity; ▼ = GO decision to next level; ■ = launch decision.

in a stable world, consists of systematically following managerial activities sequentially for each level of product refinement. Feedback loops from any level to another are possible according to managerial needs for revisions. The comprehensive nature of this process implies that, upon analysis, the environment, market, and organizational conditions require an approach that affords time and other resources to develop the new product. The development of Frito-Lay's Sun Chips (see Chapter 2) over a 10-year period illustrates a comprehensive process.

However, if environmental or market conditions require quicker response, and organizational resources are available, a more streamlined process can be planned that includes parallel activities to reduce development time. Through deliberate tradeoffs, selected phases of development or managerial activities can be omitted. As illustrated in the middle part of Figure 5.5, once a concept has been approved, parallel development of the prototype and marketing program can commence. Thus, when the prototype is complete, the product can move directly to launch with the planned program. The risk of eliminating product testing among users and other stakeholders is traded off against the time gained.

In some situations, it may be defensible to go into a "crash" development mode for competitive reasons. Deciding to launch from concept evaluation moves the process directly to marketing program development. For example, when MCI developed its Friends and Family service, once it had the idea and checked the feasibility of the concept from an internal technology perspective, it was able to launch the service successfully within six weeks—with minimal market testing and with the service and marketing program unfolding simultaneously.[18]

Rapid development processes obviously require a clear understanding of strategic objectives and tradeoffs among them, maximum flexibility, high levels of responsive interaction with potential buyers, and an integrated organizational capability that allows rapid processing of all managerial activities. For example, close interaction with potential buyers can substantially speed the managerial activities of problem identification, search, and design.

In other situations, a new product may emerge by chance from ongoing product development work in the laboratory (for example, a new fragrance or a new pharmaceutical drug). However, rather than proceeding to evaluate and develop a marketing program for the product, the company may take the "product" back to the idea and/or concept levels of refinement and work through all levels of the process to provide a more rigorous test of the new product opportunity.

The summary point of this discussion is that establishing a new product development process for a particular organization can begin with the ideal of comprehensive full-term development as shown in Figure 5.5. However, as organizational objectives, the degree of uncertainty in the business environment, the level of anticipated market friction, and the organization's propensity to innovate become evident from analysis, alternative forms for the development process must be considered:

- Situations with greater uncertainty will require greater flexibility in the development process—most likely dictating more resources to develop parallel activities and respond to changes.

- Situations with lower market friction will require greater interaction with stakeholders to quickly spot market opportunities and problems—most likely shortening the managerial activities of problem identification, search, and design.

- Situations with low organizational propensity to innovate will require greater management intervention and typically more time to carry out managerial activities—forming teams (as in the QFD process) and overcoming traditional patterns of resistance in evaluation and decision activities will occupy more time than for organizations with higher propensity to innovate.

Once an organization clarifies its business strategy and profiles the sets of factors critical to new products, its goal should be to plan and establish an ongoing development process that is clear to all participants. The process, which must be communicated and learned by all, in effect becomes a learning process unto itself. This learning occurs among everyone involved in the process, including stakeholders, and should be recorded in an organizational data base to facilitate learning among an ever-shifting set of participants.

As argued in the first chapter, the increasing relevance of new product development to organizational performance compels firms to consider establishing a lasting process rather than a separate one for each new project. Nevertheless, every new project will have its own characteristics and demands. Whatever the defined process in Figure 5.5, a continual stream of modifications and tradeoffs will be made to accommodate each new product. Analysis of the situational factors for each new product development project will help determine the difficult tradeoff decisions of when and whether or not to omit managerial activities or stages of the product concept. Information that is central to making these tradeoff decisions will be obtained from ongoing forecasting processes.

INTEGRATING FORECASTING WITH NEW PRODUCT DEVELOPMENT

Recall that the expectation for and realization of a strong initial demand for Gavilan's computer was stimulated by the company's marketing hype. This early market response surely made any kind of market or sales forecasting appear useless. After all, if sales materialize, why forecast them? "Let's just get the product out the door as fast as we can!" may have been the battle cry. However, if Gavilan, and its investors, had thought carefully about the way in which markets respond to innovations, their time perspective on the development process—and their ultimate payoff—may have been entirely different.

As discussed in Chapter 3, major innovations tend to bring *innovators* into the market early—that is, those who must have the new product immediately, regardless of cost or other factors. Those who *follow* the innovators into the market may not enter as quickly. Quantifying these concepts into measures of growth and sales estimates for the market and the firm could have put Gavilan's early sales response into perspective and assured its managers and investors of the value of taking a longer-term approach to development. That is, the early orders were most likely from innovators at the tip of the iceberg for a market with tremendous potential, but slow growth.

Patiently waiting to get the product and production "right" and pacing sales with market growth may have ultimately paid off for Gavilan. In fact, rapid growth for the portable computer market did not begin until the late 1980s, and it increased dramatically into the early 1990s. The attempt to accelerate the development process to realize early orders clearly backfired for Gavilan—as evidenced by the numerous technical difficulties it experienced and the ultimate program demise.

To minimize problems and lost opportunities due to faulty new product forecasts, or none at all, a forecasting process is needed that parallels and interacts with the process of new product development. At least three major interrelated questions emerge throughout most new product development processes:

1. What is the estimated size and growth rate of the market or market segment—that is, market opportunity—for the new product concept?
2. What are estimated sales and market share for the new product concept in the selected market or market segment?
3. What is the value of the new product program in terms of its expected financial performance?

These questions imply three types of new product forecasting: *market opportunity forecasting, sales forecasting*, and *financial forecasting*. Each of these forecasting processes addresses a different set of problems, and they should be conducted simultaneously throughout the development process. Most importantly, all three forecasting processes and their forecasts must be integrated to provide a complete picture of the commercial viability of the new product.

Market opportunity forecasting assesses market size and growth for a new product in a potential market under various assumptions. It is essential for evaluating new product ideas and early concept formulations. For example, how many portable computers might potentially be sold under conditions of an ideal business environment, how might that market potential grow over a 5- to 10-year planning horizon, and how would those estimates change with different assumptions about the business environment and variations in the product idea? That is, how would the estimates vary if targeted to a market segment of managers versus senior-level executives? The answers to such questions are essential in deciding to continue pursuit and development of particular ideas. A variety of methods and techniques to facilitate market opportunity forecasting are discussed and illustrated in Chapter 7.

Sales forecasting assesses the response of key stakeholders, especially potential buyers, to new products under assumptions about proposed marketing programs. Specific marketing research and modeling techniques are employed to measure sales response to alternative product concepts, prototypes, and products, as well as price, distribution, promotion, and so on. This effort ensures that key product design decisions are made interactively with the market. For example, through choice simulations, measures of incremental volume and/or market share provide estimates of the response to various features that might be included in alternative product concepts. In Chapter 8, the methods and procedures for new product sales forecasting are developed further.

Financial forecasting addresses the important question about the value of the new product and its launch program. It is an attempt to focus all relevant information on the *go/no-go* decision as it arises throughout product development. This forecast reconciles market potential, market penetration, sales costs, and investment forecasts to support decision making. Estimates of profitability, cash flow, and other pro forma financial measures over a planning period can be established. The approach to financial forecasting is presented in Chapter 9.

In summary, the three types of new product forecasting address major decision problems, and provide an integrated system of forecasting that facilitates a reasonable amount of monitoring for the new product project before and after launch. By basing forecasts on market response, as moderated by marketing decision variables (product features, price, advertising, promotion, and distribution), a company can track results after launch against the forecast and adjust decisions accordingly. In effect, the forecasting processes provide a framework for a control system to track new product launch and make necessary revisions and modifications to achieve desired results—or at least to explain why those results were not achieved.

SUMMARY

When business strategy dictates the development of new products to gain competitive advantage, an ongoing organizational process should support the needed capability to provide those products. In its operationalization, a new product development process should be *strategic* in terms of organizational objectives, *flexible* in response to environmental turbulence, *interactive* with market stakeholders to quickly identify problems and opportunities that might slow or accelerate product acceptance, *integrative* across business functions to enhance an organization's propensity to innovate, and *ongoing* in its commitment to the organization and stakeholders it can serve. Generally, flexibility requires sufficient resources, market interaction requires a stakeholder orientation (that is, sensitivity to their needs), and integration requires team building. In any case, these activities must be managed for success.

A prerequisite for any specific new product development process is a clear definition of the *core new product concept*. It originates from and sustains the interactive link with the market, and provides a communication link among other stakeholders, especially within organizational functions. General approaches to new product development are discussed—sequential, overlapping, holistic, and chaotic—but establishing and planning a particular approach ought to reflect the organization's strategic and environmental situation.

Planning a new product development process involves a series of managerial activities (problem diagnosis, search, design, evaluation, decision, implementation, and monitoring) applied to various levels of new product concept refinement (from idea to launch marketing program). The specific path chosen to move through all possible checkpoints and activities depends on the situation at hand as defined by selected criteria. To impart the necessary degree of control, new product forecasting processes that are parallel to the new product development process are recommended. They include market opportunity forecasting, sales forecasting, and financial forecasting. Before each is considered in subsequent chapters, the problems of data and methods to support new product decisions are discussed next.

6 Building a New Product Decision Support System

In 1982, Beecham Products eyed the $103 million cold-water detergent market as an attractive opportunity.[1] Managers believed they could achieve reasonable returns at the expense of one major competitor that held a 90 percent market share—American Home Products Corp.'s Woolite. After two years of development, Beecham prepared to launch its new offering under the Delicare brand name. This preparation included purchasing a $75,000 market research service from Yankelovich, Skelly & White. The service involved implementation of a *pre–test-market* model, using simulated test market data, that in May 1985 estimated a 45 to 52 percent market share for the new Delicare product, assuming an $18 million advertising expenditure.

Armed with the market share estimate, Beecham launched Delicare in early 1986. Unfortunately, sales did not materialize as estimated. By September of that year, Beecham was apparently displeased with the results; market share reportedly did not break the 25 percent mark. Beecham asked the research firm to re-examine its estimate. Yankelovich returned a revised share estimate of 24 percent. Then, in 1987, Beecham brought suit against Yankelovich for $24 million in damages. Beecham charged negligence, negligent misrepresentation, professional malpractice, and breach of contract on the basis of Yankelovich's behavior and the model's earlier predictions. Apparently, Beecham required more than 25 percent market share to meet its goals. It discontinued the product.

On the other side, Yankelovich disputed the charges. The case eventually was settled out of court, but it nevertheless raises numerous questions about the use of basic marketing research methods and more sophisticated modeling approaches in new product development and forecasting. Importantly, can these methods and models make a difference in new product performance? If, for example, pre–test-market modeling in simulated test markets can be accurately used to leapfrog traditional test marketing and shorten market entry time, they can make a difference. However, to achieve this outcome, every attempt should be made to ensure the quality of the research methods, the data collected from them, and the variables and assumptions in the model that drive key new product decisions.

In the model for Delicare, the quality of the number used to estimate market potential (total number of households using detergent for finer fabrics) apparently made a difference in the share predictions. In the lawsuit, Beecham claimed that Yankelovich had used a 75 percent market potential estimate whereas it (Beecham) had recommended a 30 percent estimate. Further, the model was reportedly adjusted by a subjective *clout* factor, which contributed to overstated forecasts.

Whether or not unique, the Delicare case signals the clear possibility that even the most sophisticated models and methods to support decision making are subject to problems. Carelessness, misuse, faulty logic, and the natural biases that influence decision-maker judgment introduce error into the decision process and diminish the value of market research data, methods, and models in the development of new products and their forecasts. These errors and problems can't be eliminated but, through knowledge about possible research and modeling approaches and attention to detail in implementing them, the quality of information for new product decision making and forecasting can be improved.

The purpose of this chapter is to provide a managerial overview of the major data sources, methods, and models useful to new product development and forecasting. Taken together, they form the basic components of a *decision support system* for new products. Many of these components—briefly described next—are applied and illustrated in the context of new product situations in subsequent chapters.

NEW PRODUCT DECISION SUPPORT SYSTEMS

High quality decision making on new product development requires information that incorporates market stakeholder *response* to new product decisions. For example, specific product features can be engineered and styled to introduce new dimensions to the market; however, obtaining the response of key market stakeholders, especially potential buyers, will add insight to decide whether these features are acceptable and/or whether they should be redesigned. The same holds true for setting the new product's price, creating advertising themes, selecting channels of distribution, and deciding to accelerate the development process. Decisions without stakeholder response information run the risk of reflecting the judgment of the decision makers involved and their inherent biases.

Information that incorporates stakeholder response into new product development decisions has the added value of contributing to the formation of new product forecasts. Clearly, the size of a market opportunity, sales and share estimates, and financial projections depend on the decisive shape of the product and marketing program offered, as well as expected market response to it. The inclusion of stakeholder response splices together the new product development and forecasting processes.

The organizational mechanism of a *decision support system* provides a framework for incorporating stakeholder response, along with other information, into the new product decision-making process.[2] The diagram in Figure 6.1 illustrates a rudimentary new product decision support system. Key elements of a new product decision support capability for managers are identifying new product *decision problems, modeling* those problems, establishing a *data base* of the important variables and relations in the model, collecting and analyzing the data through *marketing research methods*, and using *optimization procedures* to make better decisions. A brief overview of each decision support element follows in the next five sections of this chapter.

FIGURE 6.1   New product decision support system.

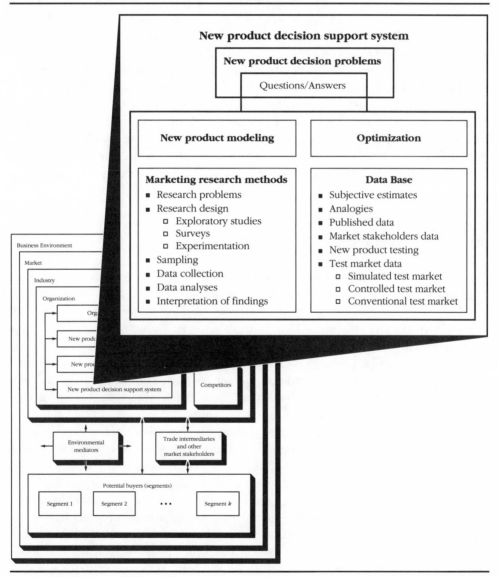

NEW PRODUCT DECISION PROBLEMS

As shown in Figure 6.1, the logic of a new product decision support system begins with decision problems facing managers of new products. The process of modeling these decision problems leads to the development of research questions, which, when answered through collected data, help determine the major new product decisions. Figure 6.2 sets forth a generic set of major new product decision problems, along with illustrative research questions. Because every new product situation is unique, managers involved must develop their own definitions of relevant decision problems and research questions in sufficient detail (beyond Figure 6.2) to support decision making.

The generic new product *decisions* in Figure 6.2 (third column) characterize the types of decisions made (implicitly or explicitly) at each checkpoint in the levels of new product refinement—from the idea to the program launch. The traditional *go/no-go* decisions are amplified to include *modify* and *timing* decisions. A *modify* decision means that additional search, design, and evaluation may be necessary to achieve satisfactory market response. A *timing* decision involves whether to *accelerate*, *slow*, or *hold* a project's development.

Typically, a major change in the market environment or within the organization triggers new product decision problems throughout the development process. Consequently, structuring new product decision problems as illustrated in Figure 6.2, but in as much detail as possible, helps to direct modeling of the decisions, determining the data required, and selecting the market research methods necessary to collect data to improve decision making.

MODELING NEW PRODUCT DECISIONS

Academic researchers are often surprised when they discover that the business community seldom uses sophisticated models and procedures to solve new product development and forecasting problems. In a study of 69 *Fortune* 500 firms (78 respondents), researchers found that even though new products represented about 25 percent of total sales, the use of new product models was not widespread.[3] The focus group is clearly the dominant method used by the sample, followed by limited rollout and concept testing. The more analytical new product models receive only a footnote. Nevertheless, firms that used models reported medium to high levels of satisfaction!

The use of *formal* modeling may appear low, but managers engage in some form of intuitive modeling through their judgment whenever they make decisions. They focus on key factors that appear to be involved in the decision (such as size of market and presence of competitors); they make assumptions about certain relationships (for example, the larger the market, the greater the opportunity); and they decide whether or not to proceed with a project. In a study of new product forecasting methods and accuracy among 103 new software firms, managerial judgment was by far the most frequently used method—however, its use made little or no difference in the accuracy of first-year sales

FIGURE 6.2 Structuring new product decision problems.

Illustrative new product decision problems	Illustrative research questions	New product decisions
■ Should a new product be developed?	■ Is there a strategic need for a new product in the portfolio? ■ What are the criteria that will define a successful new product? ■ What are market opportunities for new products (segments, size, growth, etc.)?	☺ **Go:** launch new product development process ☞ **Modify:** continue identifying/evaluating opportunities ◷ **Timing:** accelerate/slow/hold ⊗ **No-go:** terminate
■ Which new product ideas should be developed?	■ What are alternative creative ideas for new products to meet opportunities identified? ■ How do market stakeholders respond to new ideas? ■ How do ideas evaluate on the relevant criteria?	☺ **Go:** select set of promising new ideas ☞ **Modify:** continue to generate/evaluate new ideas ◷ **Timing:** accelerate/slow/hold ⊗ **No-go:** re-examine steps/terminate
■ Which new product concepts should be developed?	■ What are alternative new product concepts that implement ideas? ■ How do market and other stakeholders respond to new concepts? ■ How do concepts evaluate on the relevant criteria?	☺ **Go:** select set of promising new concepts ☞ **Modify:** continue to generate/evaluate new concepts ◷ **Timing:** accelerate/slow/hold ⊗ **No-go:** re-examine steps/terminate
■ What features should be designed into a new product prototype?	■ What are alternative design features to operationalize selected new product concepts into prototype(s)? ■ How do market and other stakeholders respond to new prototype(s)? ■ How do prototype(s) evaluate on the relevant criteria?	☺ **Go:** select major design features from prototypes ☞ **Modify:** continue refining prototypes ◷ **Timing:** accelerate/slow/hold ⊗ **No-go:** re-examine steps/terminate
■ What should be the new product's final design?	■ What are alternative product designs that operationalize new product concept? ■ How do market and other stakeholders respond to product? ■ How do product(s) evaluate on relevant criteria?	☺ **Go:** select final new product design ☞ **Modify:** continue refining product designs ◷ **Timing:** accelerate/slow/hold ⊗ **No-go:** re-examine steps/terminate
■ What should be the new product's marketing program decisions (pricing, advertising, etc.)?	■ What are alternative marketing program(s) decisions? ■ How do market and other stakeholders respond to new marketing program(s)? ■ How do marketing program(s) evaluate on relevant criteria?	☺ **Go:** select final new product marketing program ☞ **Modify:** continue refining marketing program ◷ **Timing:** accelerate/slow/hold ⊗ **No-go:** re-examine steps/terminate
■ When should the new product be launched?	■ What are relevant environmental circumstances affecting timing? ■ What are anticipated competitive reactions to new product entry? ■ What is expected market/sales growth pattern for new product?	☺ **Go:** launch at time t ☞ **Modify:** continue refining marketing program ◷ **Timing:** accelerate/slow/hold ⊗ **No-go:** market opportunity has changed substantially—re-examine steps/terminate
■ What post-launch changes should be made in the new product program, if any?	■ How have market and other stakeholders responded to the new product? ■ How should the new product and its marketing program be modified (if at all) to improve market response? ■ How is the new product marketing program tracking on relevant criteria?	☺ **Go:** continue new product launch as planned ☞ **Modify:** change and refine relevant aspects of marketing program ⊗ **No-go:** market opportunity has changed substantially—re-examine steps/terminate

forecasts.[4] Although ubiquitous, judgment alone offers little hope to improve decision making about uncertain futures.

Using Managerial Decision Models

That models are less frequently used than judgment for new product decisions does not mean formal modeling procedures should be abandoned. To the contrary, available evidence supports the notion that formal modeling can improve decision making. However, the models should have a *managerial* orientation. The so-called *decision calculus* approach to modeling exemplifies a managerial orientation.[5] It is a model-based set of procedures for processing data and judgments to assist managers in decision making.

A model in the decision calculus approach should meet the following criteria:[6] (1) *simplicity*, for ease of understanding by managers; (2) *robustness*, so that bad answers are difficult to obtain; (3) *ease of control*, so that users can understand the relationships between inputs and outputs of the model; (4) *adaptability* to incorporate new data; (5) *completeness* on important issues, even to the inclusion of subjective estimates on variables for which data might not be available within the decision time horizon; and (6) *ease of communication* so managers can quickly obtain outputs in relation to inputs.

Reported applications of the decision calculus approach suggest it has considerable merit. Variables in a decision model can be estimated subjectively, as well as obtained from other data sources. For example, in the absence of data about the relationship between advertising and new product sales, managerial judgment can be used to estimate the response function. Further, once the pattern of estimation is understood by the managers involved, the model can be made more sophisticated as needed. In a model of sales response to advertising estimates, sales response can be broken down further into awareness, preference, trial, and repeat purchase. Also, advertising expenditures can be broken down by media, creative message, and scheduling.

Three Levels of New Product Modeling

Implementing managerially oriented new product decision models according to the six criteria noted above is not always easy. The simplest approaches often belie more complex understanding of the phenomena under study. Consequently, the new product decision modeling recommended here embraces three related levels: (1) *conceptual models*—rich in their description of new product development to stimulate identification of appropriate variables and understand important relationships, (2) *spreadsheet models*—easy for managers to understand and related to recognizable financial measures to enhance use, and (3) *specialized submodels*—usually quantitative expressions and analyses to stimulate more robust estimates of important relationships to enhance decision making.

Conceptual Modeling

The first level of modeling is developed in Part 1 of this book. Beginning with the integrated conceptual model in Figure 1.1, and continuing with subsequent *highlighted* components of the model presented in greater detail, general sets of key factors affecting new product development and forecasting are identified. The goal of conceptual modeling is to provide a framework to stimulate a sense of *completeness* of the phenomena studied. Numerous factors and relationships are explored as possible descriptions of a particular new product situation. Managers are encouraged to use this approach to formulate decision problems and develop their own conceptualizations based on the situations they face in practice. Hypotheses about the variables and relationships to include in subsequent modeling levels can be identified.

Spreadsheet Modeling

The second level of modeling is done at a managerial, or *spreadsheet*, level. From the first-level conceptualizations, relatively simple, understandable, and intuitive models of the phenomena under study can be organized in a spreadsheet framework to enable a manager to easily connect with, and control, the process. For example, the size of a market opportunity may be modeled as the product of population size in the target market and the proportion of the population in that target market who express a specified level of intention to buy a new product concept. Growth in market potential (over time) may be modeled as the product of the proportion of the population estimated to enter the market each year and the market potential estimate. Data for these variables can be collected through marketing research procedures, and the size of the market opportunity can be computed in a straightforward spreadsheet model (for example, multiplying measures taken on the variables). Further, multiplying the number of potential buyers by the average price (assumed in the intention-to-buy measure) yields a dollar estimate of the market opportunity.

Although it appears simplistic at first glance, the spreadsheet approach makes modeling accessible to managers and introduces them to a procedure that can be made successively more comprehensive according to need and motivation. This aspect is illustrated further in Chapter 7.

Specialized Submodeling

A third level of modeling involves somewhat more specialized submodels of specific processes that provide insight to the managerial spreadsheet models. In particular, these models attempt to incorporate the effects of controllable marketing variables, often in the form of response functions. For example, what is the relationship between levels of firm or industry promotion and new product awareness? What is the relationship between changes in the new product concept, including its price, and intention to buy it? Such modeling approaches tend to be somewhat quantitative and have been developed by marketing academics and practitioners to address new product decision problems. Pre–test-market modeling, mentioned in the Delicare case, is an example. These specialized submodels can either link directly to the spreadsheet models or be used as a source of independent estimates to corroborate the spreadsheet models. Specific examples are provided in Part 3.

In summary, the three-level modeling approach links directly to managers at both the conceptual and spreadsheet levels, and opens doors to more specialized modeling procedures. The conceptual level of modeling helps to meet the *completeness* criterion. The spreadsheet level helps to meet the criteria of *simplicity*, *ease of control*, *adaptability*, and *ease of communication*. All three levels of modeling help to achieve *robustness*, but the use of more specialized submodels for particular variables in the spreadsheet helps to provide checks and balances to ensure that the results make sense—that is, making it hard to get bad answers. The real benefit of using more specialized submodels is often to provide *multiple* modeling approaches, which tend to reduce errors in estimates.

In the next three chapters, several types of new product modeling useful for new product development and forecasting are introduced and illustrated.[7] The modeling approach selected, or the modeling procedure formulated, depends on the managerial decision problems of interest. Both, however, drive the nature of data to be collected—in terms of questions to be answered and data for the variables to be used in a particular modeling approach.

DATA BASE: DATA SOURCES FOR NEW PRODUCTS

Properly collected and analyzed, historic data for existing products provide a valuable source of information for marketing and other decisions. Trends can be studied, various correlations can be estimated, and ongoing tracking of sales and consumer response to program changes (for example, through scanner data for certain products) provides useful decision support. However, decisions for *new* products in their planning stages do not have the benefit of historic data.

New technologies—such as high definition television (HDTV), fiber optics, video discs, cellular radio, microprocessors, and quadraphonic sound—often embody new ideas and engender a vast number of decision problems that must be addressed to manage their successful development and forecast their market demand. For new technologies to be realized, a series of new products and services must be developed that enable potential buyers to enjoy their benefits. The numerous decision problems raised in Figure 6.2 must be multiplied by the variety of potential stakeholders, market responses, and decisions. For example, part of the true market potential and benefits of microprocessor technology could not be realized until personal computers were developed, which in turn depended on operating system and application software, video displays, keyboards, and printers, as well as sales, maintenance, and repair services. The responses of stakeholders that develop, distribute, regulate, and buy such products must be factored into the equation of determining market opportunity.[8]

New products extending existing technologies or existing brand names may have some historical data on which decisions can be based, but it does not eliminate the uncertainty of new product acceptance. For example, in 1989, Stouffer Foods Corp. launched Right Course, a new frozen entree line. Building on successes with the Stouffer name on the company's traditional "red box" line and the Lean Cuisine frozen entree line, as well as a growing market opportunity and a sizable marketing budget, the line nevertheless was withdrawn from the U.S. national market after 17 months of effort.[9] Whatever the market experience and historical data base on the existing lines, market response to the new line failed to measure up (reportedly achieving only a 2 percent market share). Clearly, market uncertainties required data beyond the history of even Stouffer's own similar line of products (Lean Cuisine), not to mention management experience.

Consequently, whether the product or technology is really new to the world, is an extension of an existing technology or brand, or simply represents a change in the process or technology used to create the original, the potential uncertainty of market stakeholder response compels the development of a data base that delivers information to facilitate key decisions. Six major sources of data that will contribute to building a new product data base, or complement an existing one for new product decisions, are *subjective estimates*, *analogies*, *published data*, *market stakeholder data*, *new product testing data*, and *test market data*.

Subjective Estimates

The background, expertise, and related experience of decision makers and selected experts represent a potential source of data to help estimate market response for new product decisions. For a new product with absolutely no information, the mind of the manager or expert can generate hypotheses, make assumptions, and provide subjective estimates to test the hypotheses. In a practical sense, a subjective estimate is a person's quantification of a particular phenomenon—usually one that is not readily or directly measurable—and is the approach used most frequently to quantify future events or outcomes associated with new products. "I think we can sell 10,000 units of the new product during the first year" represents a typical *global* estimate of new product sales.

Alternatively, the phenomenon can be *decomposed* into parts and estimates can be obtained for each, then aggregated to a total estimate. Not surprisingly, *decompositional* subjective estimates improve judgmental predictions in forecasting, especially when uncertainty is high.[10]

- Estimates of the components of the problem may have errors that cancel each other out to improve overall accuracy.

- Recognizing components of the problem may help identify other sources of data and information, such as members of the new product team and others both within and outside the organization who have expertise germane to the problem.

- By considering *time* as an important component, especially in forecasting market and organizational behavior, estimating change over time provides a different dimension to the problem.

Several decompositional approaches to subjective estimation are briefly reviewed next.

Decision Analysis

Decision analysis recognizes that a decision needs to be made (for example, a *go/no-go* launch decision or whether or not to conduct a test market), then decomposes the decision problem into its parts.[11] A decision tree diagram helps to understand this approach by setting forth four pieces of information: (1) courses of action, (2) events following from those courses of action, (3) the likelihood of each event, and (4) the utility or value of each event to the decision maker. After courses of action and subsequent events for each are identified, the decision maker subjectively estimates the probability of each event occurring and the value ("What's it worth to me?") of each event. The courses of action can then be compared by calculating a *subjective expected utility* for each outcome as a product of the probability of each event and its value to the decision maker. The expected utility of some outcomes will dominate that of others and, if the decision maker's estimates are accepted, suggests the best course of action. When alternatives are close, a sensitivity or "what if" analysis of modifications to the probabilities and values may confirm the decision or suggest additional study of the alternatives. Though this type of decision analysis is simple enough to create and compute by hand, personal computer software is readily available to facilitate it.

Decision Calculus

As reviewed previously, a *decision calculus* approach to modeling involves procedures for processing data and judgments to assist managers in decision making.[12] Of most interest in the decision calculus approach is the procedure for eliciting subjective estimates about response functions. For example, to estimate sales response to advertising expenditures, a manager can be asked to estimate what sales level might be achieved with zero-level advertising and then what might be considered maximum- or saturation-level advertising. The manager can next be asked to estimate the sales level that might be achieved with, say, 50 percent of the maximum advertising level; subsequently, the manager can be asked to estimate the sales level if this value were halved (25 percent of maximum). The four answers can then be used to define a response curve for which an equation can be developed. Once the relationship (and equation) has been established, "what if" questions can be asked about advertising decision levels for the new product and expected sales response. Despite criticisms, numerous reported applications of the decision calculus approach suggest it has considerable merit, especially to provide a more disciplined approach with which to use subjective managerial estimates.[13]

Delphi Method

The Delphi method of collecting data for new product situations helps minimize some of the problems of having a group of managers (often from different parts of the organization) cooperatively develop subjective estimates. These problems include the tendency toward "group-think," interpersonal influence and political processes, and the "noise" and distractions of group meetings. Essentially, Delphi is a method for effectively structuring a group communication process to address complex problems.[14] Delphi succeeds over traditional group methods by obtaining independent and anonymous responses from selected participants, then feeding them back for additional rounds of responses. Although highly useful for forecasting applications, Delphi also facilitates numerous types of planning and decision-making activities that involve multiple persons.

Key aspects of the Delphi approach are (1) careful definition of the problem(s) studied, (2) selection of participants, usually on the basis of their expertise or involvement in the problem, (3) anonymity of participants via electronic or print questionnaires, (4) assessment of anonymous "group" response with feedback (often statistical summaries) to original participants, and (5) opportunity for participants to revise their views through second, third, and subsequent rounds of questionnaires or computer processing.

The Delphi method for obtaining subjective estimates lends itself to the new product development and forecasting problem. New product decisions often bring together organizational members whose personalities aren't always compatible. Time-consuming differences may arise as to the best solution for the problem. The anonymous and iterative aspects of the method may facilitate the development of collective judgment to break disagreements and thereby speed the development process. Also, as the pressure on the new product development process increases, inclusion of multiple stakeholders (retailers, regulators, and others) is sometimes forgotten. The Delphi approach can help define a process to ensure other stakeholder representation on key new product issues, thereby giving them a formal voice in the problems at hand.

Although the Delphi method has its weaknesses (conformity to the group average can still occur as multiple rounds proceed, participants drop out, disagreements are not properly studied, the moderator intimidates participants or poorly specifies the problems, or poor group summarizing techniques are used), its careful application to a wide range of new product development and forecasting problems can prove beneficial.

Analytic Hierarchy Process

The analytic hierarchy process (AHP) is a measurement approach based on subjective estimates of components of a problem formulated hierarchically.[15] The approach consists of three major steps. First, a complex problem is decomposed into a hierarchy of elements at multiple levels. At each level, the component is broken into a subset of elements, each of which is subsequently decomposed until the most basic units of action are identified. Elements at each level are potentially related to each element at the next higher level and the next lower level.

Second, subjective evaluations of each pair of elements are obtained from managers or other participants in the process. The evaluation includes an estimate of the extent to which one element in a pair dominates the other (with respect to an element at the next higher level). The estimates can be obtained from an individual or a group, depending on the problem. Third, the subjective estimates collected are organized into data matrices from which the relative weight of each element in the hierarchy is computed.

Illustrative results of AHP applied to a new product opportunity are presented in Figure 6.3. The application involved new concepts for a frequently

FIGURE 6.3 Illustration of the analytic hierarchy process applied to the evaluation of new product concepts.

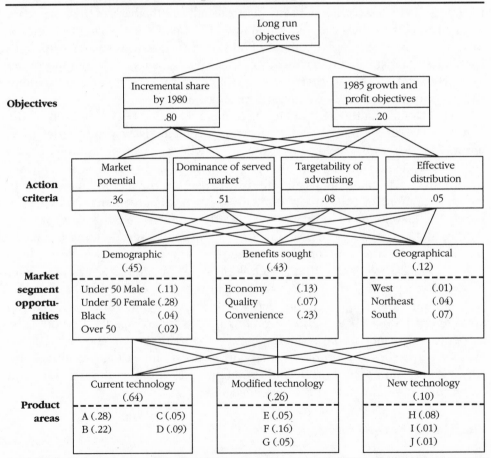

Source: Yoram Wind and Thomas L. Saaty, "Marketing Applications of the Analytical Hierarchy Process," *Management Science*, 26 (July 1980), pp. 641–658. Reprinted by permission of The Institute of Management Sciences, 290 Westminster Street, Providence, RI 02903.

purchased packaged good. Subjective estimates were obtained from seven executives in different functional areas within the firm. The relative weights in
this example illustrate possible resource allocations based on the judgment of
the executives involved. For example, the relative weight of current technology
(.64) suggests it should receive the most resources in satisfying market segment
opportunities. Within current technology, new product concepts should be developed in product areas A and B, which have the highest weights (.28 and .22)
among the 10 product areas. Within modified technologies, product area F has
a reasonably attractive weight (.16) and may warrant resource consideration.

In summary, the AHP helps managers quantify their opinions about complex hierarchical problems through comparison processes. It provides a useful
source of data to help make decisions and resource allocations that will achieve
higher levels of objectives and goals. The ready availability of software to help
collect these data from participants in the decision process make the computa-
tional aspects of AHP relatively easy.

Biases in Subjective Estimates

Despite the relative attractiveness and ubiquity of subjective estimation in practice, human decision makers exhibit a wide variety of biases in the way they
process information to formulate quantitative estimates of certain outcomes or
events. The list in Figure 6.4 describes several such biases uncovered from
numerous academic studies of human judgment and decision making. This
list should raise cautionary flags about the use of subjective estimates as the
sole source of data for new product development and forecasting. Nevertheless,
knowing some of the biases may suggest ways to overcome them.[16]

In new product situations, estimates of future market response to various
decisions can be high or low with respect to some potential "true" value. However, the "true" value for many new product decisions may never be known;
only the response associated with the decision implemented may be known.
If either grey or black can be chosen as the color of the case for a new palm-
size computer (but not both), and black is chosen because it is estimated to
generate a higher response, it will never be known (through subjective estimation alone) whether grey would have generated an even higher response.
Therefore, not only the direction of the error, but also the sources that might
explain it, will be difficult to pinpoint in practice.

Four major recommendations can be considered to help counter expected
error in subjectively estimated data for new product decisions:

1. Anticipate the most likely errors presented in Figure 6.4 and take convenient steps to reduce them. For example, *optimism* biases inevitably occur in most new product decisions and forecasts. A conservative approach
   would be to call for three estimates on each issue—optimistic, pessimistic,
   and most likely—and then use the more pessimistic estimate.

2. Use multiple and, to the extent possible, independent participants. The
   many possible sources of error may average out with different participants.

FIGURE 6.4   Sources of bias in managerial subjective estimation.

Source of Bias	New Product Example
Availability of information is limited to recent memory or current environment	Current fads or short-lived trends might affect new product design
Selective perception, in which the problem structure follows one's experience and anticipations, seeking information to support views and avoiding conflicting data	The classic marketing versus R&D perspective on the new product may be very different and produce different subjective estimates from each organizational function
When *frequency* of observed relationships dominates judgment, rather than relative frequency in which both occurrences and nonoccurrences of behavior are considered	Subjective estimates may be driven by experiences from primarily successful product launches, rather than a balanced consideration of successes and failures
Illusory correlation, in which two variables that are thought to vary together do not	Associating a particular event with a new product's success when other factors may explain the success
A tendency for *linear extrapolation* in estimating growth	New product forecasts often look like positive sloping straight lines, when curvilinear may be more realistic
Simplification of information processing by *anchoring*, or focusing on a fixed cue or value and making future estimates based on adjustments to that fixed value	Estimating that potential buyers will only respond favorably to a new high definition television if it is priced at $500, the average cost of current high quality TV sets
Simplification of processing through *representativeness*, or estimates based upon characteristics of an object that are similar to another based on the characteristics	Selecting analogies to the new product (e.g., to establish market growth rates) for their similarities on selected attributes rather than understanding the whole situation
Simplification of processing through the *law of small numbers*, or the reliance on small samples as representative of a larger population	Results of new product focus groups are used to formulate estimates, rather than waiting for the results of a large sample survey
Simplification of processing through the *regression bias*, or using extreme values of a variable to predict extreme values of the next observation, neglecting average values	Estimating response to a new product advertising program based on a recent very successful campaign, rather than on average response over a number of campaigns
Simplification of processing through the *best-guess strategy*, or ignoring multiple sources of uncertainty and focusing on the most likely	Ignoring potential uncertain environmental and competitive responses and focusing only on consumer response from marketing research
Complex, stressful, and multi-person *decision environments* reduce quality and consistency of judgment	Time pressures brought about in accelerated new product development processes induce complexity, emotional stress, and social pressure to conform to make decisions
The *response mode*, or how subjective estimates are collected, can induce bias	Wishful thinking and the illusion of control can affect new product subjective estimates
Hindsight bias, or past occurrences, offer few surprises that cannot be explained in some logical way	When "surprising" new product ideas are encountered, they may be explained away and not used in planning

Source: Adapted from Robin M. Hogarth and Spyros Makridakis, "Forecasting and Planning: An Evaluation," *Management Science,* 27 (February 1981), pp. 115–138. Parts reprinted by permission of The Institute of Management Sciences, 290 Westminster Street, Providence, RI 02903.

3. Use multiple and independent data sources and research methods. Again, errors from the different data sources and methods may offset each other.

4. Model the problem by using a decompositional approach. With decomposition, multiple errors on estimates of each component of the problem may cancel each other.

Although these steps will not produce error-free estimates, they will reduce the chance for *wild* estimates that could lead decision making astray.

Analogies

Managers use analogies as a natural part of their reasoning, subjective estimation, and decision making. In the context of new product decisions, an analogy is the mapping of knowledge from one domain (the *base*—for example, an existing product) to another domain (the *target*—for example, a new product) in such a way that the system of relations for the base product also holds with the target new product.[17] Data from existing product analogies may be useful in some ways to the new product.

Because the basis of analogy is the inference that if things are alike in one or more respects, they may be alike in other respects, the new product does not have to be exactly like the existing product. That is, the products need not have a one-to-one correspondence. Rather, they can be alike in terms of their roles in a common relational structure. For example, a new product that might be launched in a poor economic environment might be compared to an existing product that was launched previously in a poor economic environment. A new product that requires significant retailer cooperation might be compared to an existing product that also required retailer cooperation when newly launched.

Though popular (and often implicit in managerial thinking), analogies as data sources should be used with care. First, potential judgmental biases (see Figure 6.4) might invoke new product analogies that are not truly appropriate. Comparing a new product with an existing one in terms of launch into a poor economic environment must be qualified by other factors (such as relative market price of each product and perceived value). Each candidate analogy should be qualified in a *systematic* way. Second, even though the two products might be evaluated as similar in numerous attributes, there is no reason to believe that a one-to-one mapping from the existing product(s) to the new product is defensible. Potential analogies must be based on a theoretical or conceptual link between the new product and the existing product.

The conceptual structure of new product development in Part 1 of this book provides a useful point of departure for identifying criteria that might be used to find candidate new product analogies. In Figure 6.5 a matrix structure compares the target new product with existing products on several criteria. The criteria should be recognizable from concepts presented in preceding chapters. Through secondary studies, primary marketing research, and/or expert judgment, measures for the new product and those of the candidate products can

FIGURE 6.5   Factors for comparing product/market situations and identifying candidate product analogies.

Comparative criteria	New product	Candidate product 1	Candidate product 2	...	Candidate product N
Environmental factors					
Natural resources					
Population					
Cultural values					
Technology					
Economic systems					
Laws and regulations, etc.					
Potential buyer factors					
Buyer needs					
Buying processes					
Situational factors					
Information processing					
Predispositions/attitudes					
Behaviors/actions					
Segmentation, etc.					
Organizational factors					
Organizational identity					
Influence processes					
Information/communication					
Resource flexibility					
Decision making					
Implementation, etc.					
Marketing program					
Competitive strategy					
Product features, including: 　Relative advantage 　Compatibility 　Complexity 　Divisibility 　Communicability					
Pricing					
Communication program					
Distribution					
Customer service, etc.					
Other stakeholder and situational factors					
Environmental mediator actions					
Competitive actions, etc.					

be developed. By comparing the profile of the new product with those of the candidate products, a basis for ranking the candidates on overall similarity can be obtained.

For example, if the values in the cells of the matrix of Figure 6.5 are based on different measurement scales, they can first be standardized; then absolute differences between each candidate and the new product can be computed. If the bases of similarity are assumed to be equally important, summing the absolute differences provides an overall similarity score for each candidate. Alternatively, an importance measure of each factor might be used to provide a weighted summation score. The analytical hierarchy process, a decision calculus approach, or any of the subjective estimation procedures discussed before can also be used to assist in the evaluation of candidate analogies. The use of data from analogies is illustrated in Chapter 7.

Data from Published Sources

When new product decision problems and modeling call for data on environmental trends (technology, economy, demographics, political actions, and so on), competitive activities, potential buyer lifestyles, and other factors for which some historical data may exist, it is useful to conduct a literature search of published data. The increasing availability of electronic information networks greatly facilitates this activity. Using key words or phrases, one can search an electronic data base in a relatively short period of time. Summaries of citations, abstracts, and even full documents are usually available.

For published data not included on electronic data bases, more traditional sources for literature searches are libraries, government documents, industry associations, brokerage firm reports, organizational files, and firms that specialize in such data collection. Searching published data sources almost always yields information of some value to a new product project, but usually doesn't quite fulfill one's expectations. Published data is historical, and therefore out of sync with current events. Further, it is rarely designed to solve an organization's specific decision problems, but someone else's problem. Consequently, the recommended approach is to *start* exploring a decision problem with a search of published data, especially to amplify the historical data base, but to be prepared to include other data sources as well.

Data from Market Stakeholders

Motivated by specific decision problems, research questions, and modeling variables, data from stakeholders can take a variety of forms:

- Data from *environmental* mediators (as developed in Chapter 2) are essential to identify trends that may reveal new product opportunities and problems.
- Data from potential buyers, trade intermediaries, competitors, and other *market* stakeholders (as developed in Chapter 3) are especially important to identify the response to and help refine new product concepts.

- Data from *organizational* members (as discussed in Chapter 4) are pertinent to assessing an organization's propensity to innovate.

Ongoing data collection among major stakeholders helps meet the *interactive* requirement of a new product development process. In the next major section of this chapter, a variety of marketing research approaches that can be used to build an interactive relationship with stakeholders, as well as provide data, are discussed.

Caution should be exercised in collecting data from market stakeholders. Such data are at best *expectations* and must be carefully defined, collected, and analyzed. For example, obtaining *intention-to-buy* data for new product concepts from key market stakeholders may be useful to help make decisions and/or to include in new product decision models. However, simply asking the question of potential buyers without considering conceptualization and measurement issues leads to problems in the interpretation of results. Asking the question in a very narrow context that is not similar to the actual purchase situation, or asking the question too far in advance of the opportunity to purchase, can lead to errors in measurement and, ultimately, in market forecasts. Often, potential buyers (especially those in industrial markets) indicate a strong interest in a new product simply because they are curious to see and try it, but they may have no real intent to purchase it.

Deciding to use the intention-to-buy variable to collect data—or any other psychologically based concept (awareness, perception, preference, and so on)— requires consideration of numerous issues, including defining the concept, operationalizing the measurement approach, selecting a measurement scale, and analyzing and interpreting the results. Because intention to buy is a very important measure in new product forecasting, it is described in greater detail in Chapter 8.

New Product Testing Data

As various forms of the product concept materialize into mockup prototypes, working prototypes, and other versions of early product and process formulations, response from various market stakeholders can be obtained through product testing. If test marketing as a source of data is not feasible, special attention should be given to collecting high-quality data from the various product testing approaches. Testing with end users can also be an important source of data about levels of expected customer satisfaction.

Formalized data collection procedures should be used to retain product testing information for careful analysis and evaluation. These collection procedures can take the form of written forms, questionnaires, observations, videotapes, and/or oral dictations from people who try to use the new product or process. These data should become an integral part of the new product data base. Three forms of product testing provide sources of useful data: alpha-, beta-, and gamma-tests.

Alpha-Testing

Alpha-tests are conducted within the organization. To the extent possible, working prototypes are tried and used by various members of the organization. In effect, the prototype is refined in terms of performance characteristics so that it can be tried by potential buyers. Product modifications at this level are not expected to change the original core product concept. Nevertheless, the need for major changes may dictate re-evaluation of the concept. Manufacturers of new word processing software often test their products internally among their own organizational staff before releasing them for beta-testing.

Beta-Testing

Beta-tests are conducted among potential buyers designated as primary users of the new product. The prototype used by potential buyers helps identify features needing improvement. Data collected from beta-testing of potential buyers can also be used to sharpen estimates made in various forecasts based on the original concept. For example, a beta-test for a new beer product among a panel of users may provide important preference data about the taste of a new product that, when coupled with perceptual data from larger market surveys about beer concepts, enhances prediction of market acceptance in new product models.

Gamma-Testing

Gamma-tests are conducted among stakeholders (other than potential buyers) who are potential influencers of or barriers to new product acceptance. Gamma-tests may be used for obtaining regulatory approval (formal and informal) and/or evaluating usage and acceptance among retail chain buyers, clerks at the retail store level, members of the proposed ad agency account team, and other selected influencers (media, clergy, educators, industry shows, and so on). Subsequent modifications of the new product as a result of gamma-testing may necessitate additional beta-testing, or possibly additional concept evaluation. When an automobile firm introduces a new line of cars, it can get early reaction from major automobile magazine test drivers as data for improvements rather than for promotional purposes. Subsequent testing can be used for promotion.

Test Market Data

With a working prototype of a new product and tentative marketing actions, an organization frequently needs to systematically evaluate market response under conditions that most closely resemble the expected market situation after launch. This evaluation adds considerable information for planning the new product launch. Through *simulated, controlled,* and *conventional* test markets, data can be obtained to assess market response for a variety of decisions. In simulated test markets, purchase laboratories and other convenient settings are used to quickly and inexpensively evaluate market response to new concepts or products. Controlled test markets involve geographically designated regions that are usually equipped with electronic capabilities to measure in-store sales response to the new product, including advertising and special promotions for it. Conventional test markets are designed to provide a setting that is as natural as possible for evaluating market response to the new product.

The selection of one or more test market data sources depends on numerous factors, including the decision to be made, the type and importance of the new product, the amount of uncertainty in the situation, the degree of realism sought, the time available, and cost. Although test market data can improve and update new product forecasting for *go/no-go* decisions, it also provides valuable information for refining the new product and its marketing program to enhance market acceptance. In many new product situations, test marketing provides the first glimpse of implementation difficulties and either paves the way for market entry or leads to a more definitive *no-go, modify,* or *timing* decision. The various approaches for test marketing are discussed in greater detail in Chapter 10.

Planning and Integrating New Product Data Collection

Successful new product projects don't rely on a single method of data collection, but instead incorporate multiple sources of data. In Figure 6.6, the various sources of data are illustrated with respect to evaluating the different levels of product refinement. Clearly, certain sources of data can be used throughout (such as subjective estimates); however, the diagram in the figure illustrates areas of emphasis where certain sources are of the greatest value for evaluating certain formulations of the product. The purpose of Figure 6.6 is not to prescribe a pattern, but to suggest the possibilities among the various data sources and illustrate a data collection plan with which to build a useful data base for the specific new product in question. The process of planning a data base for new product development helps in allocating time, financial, and personnel resources to collect the data, and may lead to more efficient selection of marketing research methods.

MARKETING RESEARCH METHODS

Marketing research methods used to collect and analyze data for new product decision problems and modeling approaches are another major component of a new product decision support system. Figure 6.7 is a brief summary of major topics usually included in marketing research textbooks.[18] The question that must be asked is whether or not the selection of various methods makes a difference for new product decisions, especially for achieving new product sales forecasts. The short answer to the question is "yes."

In a study of new product forecasting methods and data sources among 103 *new* software firms, methods usage was compared among firms that were classified as *more* (less than or equal to 25 percent error) versus *less* accurate

FIGURE 6.6   Planning and integrating data sources into new product development: an illustration.

Data Sources	Level of New Product Refinement				
	Idea ➤	Concept ➤	Prototype ➤	Product ➤	Marketing Program
Subjective estimates (heuristics)	Heavy use of judgment	➤	➤	➤	➤
Analogical product data		Products with similar attributes	➤	➤	➤
Published data sources	Trends, patent search, etc.				
Market stakeholders data	Exploratory focus groups, in-depth interviews	Concept evalution procedures			Ad tests, pricing, distribution
New product testing data			Alpha-tests	Beta-tests, gamma-tests	➤
Simulated test market data				Pre-test marketing of product	
Controlled test market data					
Conventional test market data					Identify launch issues

(greater than 25 percent error) in their first-year new product forecasts.[19] The summary of results in Table 6.1 shows that *personal* data sources tended to be used more by firms that were more accurate in their new product forecasts. Although not widely used, experimental approaches had greater usage among firms with more accurate forecasts. Perhaps the most revealing finding is that firms having more accurate forecasts tended to use more methods and data sources (on average) than less accurate firms. Thus, the kind and number of data sources and methods used can make a difference in the accuracy of new product forecasts.

Determining the number and type of marketing research methods will depend on the specific new product situation, and therefore requires managerial involvement. For example, when time is critical in the development process, certain procedures may be preferable to others. Suppose a firm wants an expe-

FIGURE 6.7   Overview of marketing research methods for new product development.

New product research problem
- ☐ Decision problems
- ☐ Research questions
- ☐ Value of information

Research designs
- ☐ Exploratory (observation, case studies, in-depth interviews, focus groups)
- ☐ Surveys (point-in-time surveys, time-series surveys, panels)
- ☐ Experiments (single-case, controlled experiments, adaptive experimentation)
- ☐ Integrated designs:
     e.g., Exploratory → Survey 1 → Survey 2 → Test market experiment

Sampling
- ☐ Population definition
- ☐ Size
- ☐ Type:
     Non-random (convenience, purposive)
     Random (simple, stratified, cluster)

Data collection
- ☐ Measurement (variables, scales)
- ☐ Research instrument (questionnaire, scanner, protocols, recording sheets)
- ☐ Method (telephone, personal interviews, mail)
- ☐ Integrated procedures:
     e.g., Telephone → Mail → Telephone (TMT)

Data analysis
- ☐ Univariate
- ☐ Bivariate
- ☐ Multivariate

Findings and interpretation
- ☐ Availability and access to data and analyses on data base to answer additional questions
- ☐ Discussions and interpretations of findings
- ☐ Preliminary and final reporting

dient and representative market evaluation of potential buyer response to a new concept for carry-on travel luggage. Alternative conceptions of the proposed luggage can be artistically rendered to show various benefits. A random sample of consumers in the target segment (who meet screening criteria) can be contacted by phone to gain their cooperation and set a time for a subsequent one-hour telephone interview. By overnight delivery services, consumers can be sent a packet that includes the concept descriptions and, if desired, a questionnaire to be returned. The appointed telephone interview can then obtain answers to questions read over the phone from a computer-aided system that allows immediate input and tabulation of responses as they are obtained. Alternatively, a written questionnaire can be returned via overnight delivery for data processing.

TABLE 6.1   Usage of new product forecasting sources and methods.[a]

Rank	New product forecasting data and methods	Total sample ($n = 103$)	Less accurate forecasts ($n = 57$)	More accurate forecasts ($n = 46$)	t-test of differ- ences[b]
	Personal Data Sources				
2	Personal interviews with a few potential buyers	2.93	2.77	3.13	.09[c]
7	Product demonstrations.........................	2.67	2.48	2.89	.08[c]
13	Focus groups.....................................	1.68	1.52	1.88	.08[c]
16	Telephone interviews with a large sample of potential buyers (50 or more).................	1.66	1.60	1.74	.48
18	Personal interviews with a large sample of potential buyers (50 or more).................	1.50	1.32	1.72	.03[c]
	Impersonal Data Sources				
1	Judgment of founder's experience..............	3.35	3.27	3.46	.33
3	Company and product information sources.....	2.75	2.76	2.73	.88
4	Competitive analysis...........................	2.75	2.83	2.65	.40
6	Judgment of industry experts...................	2.68	2.61	2.76	.40
8	Trade publications, journals, periodicals........	2.26	2.29	2.22	.70
9	Trade shows.....................................	2.02	1.95	2.11	.45
10	Trade and professional associations.............	1.96	1.89	2.04	.42
14	Guides and directories..........................	1.85	1.85	1.85	.97
15	Advertising and media sources..................	1.77	1.66	1.91	.16
19	Questionnaire mailed to a large sample of potential buyers (50 or more).................	1.46	1.51	1.40	.56
24	Published government documents..............	1.32	1.22	1.43	.15
25	Government agencies and organizations........	1.27	1.12	1.46	.01[c]
	Research Methods				
5	Beta-test sites...................................	2.69	2.56	2.85	.24
11	New product concept tests......................	1.96	1.89	2.04	.50
12	Quantitative analysis of sales history of similar products..	1.86	1.98	1.72	.23
17	Roll-out research................................	1.56	1.46	1.69	.22
20	Pre-test market models.........................	1.46	1.38	1.55	.35
21	Tradeoff analysis................................	1.44	1.35	1.55	.20
22	Experiments (e.g., Test markets)................	1.41	1.24	1.62	.02[c]
23	Technology diffusion/market penetration curves	1.38	1.35	1.41	.64
26	Cross-impact analysis............................	1.26	1.20	1.33	.29
26	Quantitative simulation based on a model of market..	1.26	1.24	1.28	.74
	Average number of methods used..............	8.29	7.54	9.22	.05[c]
	Weighted usage of forecasting methods........	52.15	50.31	54.44	.06[c]

[a]Scale of forecasting method usage: 1 = did not use, 4 = used extensively.
[b]t-tests are between less and more accurate firms.
[c]Factors significant at $p = .10$ or better.

Source: William B. Gartner and Robert J. Thomas, "Factors Affecting New Product Forecasting Accuracy in New Firms," *Journal of Product Innovation Management,* 10 (January 1993), pp. 35–52.

Although marketing research should not be viewed as a panacea for all new product decision problems, a variety of powerful and creative procedures are available to fit most new product development situations and budgets. However, managerial involvement in the use of such methods is critical if they are to be of any value. Most managers have horror stories to tell about expensive marketing research studies that lie fallow in their desk drawers. Careful examination of these studies would show that during their planning stages there was a wide gulf between the manager who would use the results for decisions and the people who planned and executed the studies. For example, a case study of industry practice involving the regulated need for marketing research to support market demand estimates for a new technology revealed that most studies were poorly designed to answer key managerial questions.[20]

Further, it is commonly believed that the needs of managers and top-level executives to "get close to the customer" and "see real buyers" can be assuaged by allowing these individuals to observe one or two focus groups! Unfortunately, through the various perceptual biases discussed previously, the vivid impressions created by focus groups become strong images of the "market" that often cause managers to eschew findings from broader market surveys. Decisions based on these impressions can be right for the potential buyers in the focus group, but not for those in the "market."

If marketing research is to be of value, people involved in new product decisions must become an integral part of defining the research problems and ensuring that the proposed research design and program of research will lead to information for improved decision making. The purchase of "canned" and custom research services should be executed with care, as should the delegation of research responsibility within the organization. The added cost of time to become involved in designing marketing research that will resolve key new product questions is small in relation to the benefits, especially when the cost of the market research is high. Involvement in the creative and selective design and use of marketing research methods throughout the development process is an important part of the intellectual discipline necessary to build successful new products.

OPTIMIZATION

If consumers have expressed their preferences for new products as defined by five key features, each of which could be set at three different levels, what is the optimal combination of levels on these features to design into a new product? Given the possibility of a segmented market structure, what would be the optimal number of new products to launch into the market and with what features on each? What is the optimal amount of money to spend on the new product's advertising, sales promotion, and sales force to achieve defined goals?

When a decision problem has been formulated into a model relating the decision alternatives with various outcomes, and data have been collected and analyzed to evaluate a model's performance, it remains for the manager to select the best decision—the problem of *optimization*. Whether included formally or otherwise in the new product decision support system, managers will intuitively seek to make the best decision possible with the information available. In the context of a spreadsheet model, this involves conducting multiple "what if" calculations and selecting the decision that yields the best result according to set goals and objectives.

Formalized *programming* procedures have been developing to help managers make optimal decisions. However, many of the assumptions used in such optimization procedures are restrictive when complex marketing behavior is being modeled.[21] For example, optimization through linear programming assumes linearity among the relationships of key variables—an assumption not often met in reality. Nonlinear constrained optimization, geometric programming, and integer programming are a few of the techniques applied to overcome the problem of nonlinearity, but each of these approaches invokes additional assumptions that have precluded their widespread adoption and use for increasingly complex new product decisions.

Although intuitively simple, optimization in practice becomes complicated by the hundreds, thousands, and millions of possible outcomes dictated by the number of decisions and variables included in the decision model. Keeping the number of decisions and variables low may therefore be practical in an optimizing sense (and for other reasons as well); however, it can sacrifice realism. For example, deciding the optimal advertising level from three or four critical variables may yield a problem of reasonable size. However, if the decision requires considering the optimal price, the level of distribution availability, *and* the advertising budget level, the size of the problem and the number of possibilities quickly become large. One project with the goal of designing an optimal product line of cereal, using a sample of 400 consumers and their respective utilities for 12 attributes (each at five levels) of the product, reportedly required 250 hours of computer time to make a complete enumeration of all possible alternatives.[22]

Because of the limiting assumptions of formal models, as well as the complexity of new product decision problems, so-called *heuristic search procedures* have been used to make optimal decisions. These approaches attempt to capture the essence of optimization by defining rules to guide a computerized search among possible decision alternatives to find the best. The rules tend to be *ad hoc*, and can range from simple to complex instructions for most efficiently discovering the best decision. A simple rule would be one that applies successive increments of a decision variable until it reaches the point at which performance improvements are no longer achieved. Another rule would be one that searches for the single largest performance improvement of the decision variable, then the next largest improvement, and so on until no additional improvement is possible.[23]

Optimization has been applied to new product development and forecasting in the selection of design features. Because a product is a multidimensional concept with need-satisfying capabilities, determining the optimal combination of dimensions, attributes, or benefits that defines the core product concept is a central decision problem. In one application, individual measures of choice (multiattribute utilities) from conjoint analysis are used to predict shares of choice in a simulation.[24] A function that relates the product attributes or benefits to the simulation output (share, profitability, and so on), using a response surface methodology, is then optimized according to procedures that vary by whether the product attributes are categorical or continuous. Other applications consider the problems of optimizing a product line and product line extensions.[25]

Managers naturally try to find and make the best decision when confronted with alternatives. The value of formal procedures that help to find optimal decisions depends on managerial willingness to embrace them, especially in situations with numerous alternatives. Managers should be encouraged to participate in the determination of decision alternatives, goals, and constraints, as well as in the selection of logical search procedures and other activities related to optimization. At the minimum, selecting small numbers of decision alternatives on key variables, and using "what if" analyses with spreadsheet models, can enhance understanding and use of optimizing procedures. Meanwhile, research on the development of improved optimization procedures continues in the academic community. As new procedures are developed and as computer processing power continues to increase, the inclusion of optimization in decision support systems promises a way to sharpen new product decisions.

IMPLEMENTING NEW PRODUCT DECISION SUPPORT

Organizations that currently maintain decision support systems (DSS) will have little difficulty incorporating new product decisions into the system. However, for organizations that do not maintain a DSS, the same kind of difficulties that arise in motivating an organization to pursue new product development activities (see Chapter 4) will arise in implementing a new product decision support system. A DSS often represents an innovation for decision making within the organization, and, like any other innovation, it is slow to be accepted. Part of the reason is the familiar new product development paradox: the benefits of a DSS are desired, but managers are often unwilling to change their decision-making approaches to implement it. Probing beneath the surface of organizational life reveals why.

One of the major benefits of a new product DSS is the data base on new products that develops over time. If new product experiences are recorded on a regular basis, valuable learning can result. For example, simply comparing pre-launch estimates (such as surveys of buyer intentions) with actual results and measuring and tracking errors can suggest rules of thumb that may be useful guides in future estimation problems. However, organization members often find it hard to record failures and learn from them. As a general rule, organizations believe failures are best forgotten, despite epithets to the contrary; "we learn from our failures" epithets usually pertain to the intellectual experiences gained by each person involved, not analysis of recorded history. Anything that reminds one of a failure can induce the process of blaming people for it, thus causing managers to be a bit suspicious of such approaches.

Consequently, barriers to implementation of a DSS must be removed and incentives established. Like new product projects, building a DSS is a cross-functional project that requires cooperation among marketing, information systems, and other relevant departments. Further, it requires the leadership and management skills briefly overviewed in Chapter 4: setting direction, aligning people, motivating people, planning and budgeting, organizing and staffing, and controlling and problem solving. Without leadership and management support, the full benefits of a new product DSS may not be realized.

Even without organizational support for a DSS, personal computers contain enough capacity and power to maintain a small-scale DSS for interested managers. Through the use of even basic spreadsheet modeling, a variety of support capabilities can be provided to enhance new product decisions.

SUMMARY

A new product decision support system integrates the managing and forecasting of new product development. Critical managerial new product decision problems require answers to questions based on market response. Determining how much of a new product will be sold in the product's first year depends on the decisions related to its design and marketing program as well as the market's response to them. The modeling, data collection, marketing research methods, and optimizing procedures used to resolve these decision problems are the core of the decision support system—and their quality can make a difference in the outcome of new product decisions.

In this chapter, the major components of a new product decision support system are briefly described. Although the system may at times appear cumbersome, its components represent activities that are intuitively completed by managers whenever new product decisions are made. A growing body of research suggests that formalizing these activities and decisions can make a difference in new product success, as well as in improved forecasting. In a practical sense, even if such a system does not improve new product decision making, at the minimum it maintains a *memory* via its data base and modeling experiences to enhance new product development as a learning process for the organization. For organizations that do not currently maintain a DSS, aggressive leadership and management intervention may be needed to introduce this concept and its benefits.

PART THREE

New Product Development and Forecasting

7 Estimating Market Opportunity for New Products

New product ideas continually surface from a variety of sources within and outside an organization. Sometimes the ideas are unannounced and unexpected, and at other times they are purposely sought to implement a strategy. Whatever ideas emerge, the major question is whether or not they represent viable *market opportunities* as new products. For example, what is the market opportunity for an electric car, a new chain of retail stores, a new lifecare community for the elderly, a new coffee beverage, a new performing arts theater, a new interactive cable television service, or a new frozen dinner entree?

Consider the case of high definition television (HDTV). HDTV represents a major technical innovation in the sending and receiving of television signals.[1] HDTV packs about five times more information in a video screen than traditional television. The anticipated benefit for viewers is the prospect of improved picture quality. Japan led the development of HDTV beginning in 1964. Relying on *analog* signals, the Japanese were able to provide eight hours of HDTV programming daily by late 1991. However, with the initial average cost of a Japanese HDTV set at just over $30,000, adoption was slow.

Although trailing Japan in HDTV development, U.S. firms planned to offer HDTV with *digital* signals. Digital HDTV leap-frogs the analog HDTV developed by Japan because it has more advanced and flexible technology. However, in the United States the advanced digital technology required approval by the Federal Communications Commission (FCC) to select standards and ensure effective delivery of the HDTV signal.

During the early 1990s, five groups were in competition for the license to operate HDTV within the United States. One was the Japanese national broadcasting system (NHK) with an analog signal entry, and the other four were various alliances of organizations offering digital systems. In February 1993, the Japanese system withdrew from competition. Of the four remaining digital systems, two created the picture by scanning every other line, then refilling the missing lines. The other two systems created the picture by successively filling each line. Although slower, the latter systems provided a sharper picture. The FCC required both simulated and field tests as a basis for its decision.

The FCC's selection of an HDTV standard began a more complicated process of enabling households and other potential buyers to acquire television sets with HDTV programming. The necessary HDTV equipment includes the electronics to implement the system at a practical level, new television receivers, and new videocassette recorders (VCRs). Broadcasters must develop new transmission gear, new cameras for HDTV signals, and a variety of studio equipment to send the signal.

If equipment design takes at least two years to deliver, cable operators and broadcasters must decide when to begin programming and sending HDTV signals, and advertisers must decide whether or not to record broadcast messages using HDTV. Attempts to forecast the market opportunity for HDTV must therefore consider the factors and stakeholders in the broader *system* necessary to deliver its potential benefits.

Providers of HDTV signals must make numerous decisions, and so must potential buyers. If the initial price of HDTV receivers is higher than the price of current receivers, as expected, the question arises of how quickly consumers will buy them. Will potential buyers even perceive a difference in picture quality and believe it is worth the cost? Further, who will be among the first to buy the new sets—television enthusiasts, sports programming enthusiasts, restaurants and bars, or upscale consumers who can afford them? These and other questions complicate how and when organizations involved in the television industry will make key new product development decisions. Clarifying and measuring market opportunities for new products such as HDTV can eliminate some of the uncertainty in decisions related to them.

The need to answer the market opportunity question is important to organizations that have made strategic commitments to new product development to improve their performance—for example, Zenith Corporation is among those that have invested heavily in the HDTV project. Estimates of market opportunity provide critical information for deciding whether or not to continue with the development of the project. In this chapter, two central questions representing two crucial types of information about market opportunity forecasting are examined: (1) how to estimate the size and growth of a market opportunity, or its *market potential*, and (2) how to estimate the emergence of the opportunity over time, or *market penetration.*

These are difficult questions at any time during new product development, but they are especially difficult early in the process when little is known about the final shape of the product or who will respond to it. To cope with the unstructured aspects of early new product situations, an approach for market opportunity forecasting is recommended that is more systematic than the one typically associated with *idea screening* for new products. In the next section, a general process to assess market opportunity is presented in the context of HDTV.[2] This process, although comprehensive, is still subject to error, especially in highly uncertain market situations. Consequently, the subsequent section focuses on forecasting market potential with multiple approaches as a way to manage this error. In the final section, the problem of estimating market penetration, or the time-based realization of market potential, is modeled in greater detail.

MARKET OPPORTUNITY FORECASTING

A *market opportunity* for a new product or service is an unfulfilled need among potential buyers (and other stakeholders) that is of sufficient size and attainability to accomplish organizational objectives. Estimates of the size and growth of an opportunity (market potential), and especially its attainability over a planning horizon (market penetration), are important pieces of information for critical *go/no-go* and entry decisions in new product development. However, the shape of a need, the product that might satisfy it, and the number of potential buyers who experience the need may vary over time—like a moving target—thereby challenging the best managerial acuity to forecast the opportunity.

Market potential for a new product is a concept that defines the ceiling number of units that could be purchased at a point in time given a set of assumptions about the environment, the market, the organization and its industry, and the new product marketing program.[3] For most new products and services, however, full market potential is not realized in the first year of the new product's life because many of the assumptions are not met. For example, market potential often assumes 100 percent awareness of the product, but because of market friction, not all potential buyers become aware of the new product during its first year.

Although market potential provides a sense of scope for the new product opportunity, more specific estimates are necessary to support planning. Consequently, estimates of *market penetration* are needed to provide the equivalent of an industry forecast for a designated planning horizon (year 1, year 2, year 3, and so on). The so-called "industry" may simply be the innovating organization's new product, or it can be several innovating firms competing to launch the new product or service during the same year. It can also be an existing industry into which a new product is introduced.

The degree of effort to invest in determining market opportunity should reflect the importance of the project and the uncertainty of the market environment. For example, assume a large computer firm is considering an idea for a new laser printer with several improved features that make it better than its competitors. The strategic aspect of the new product is primarily to sell the printer to the firm's installed base of customers. Although somewhat important, the project does not involve high stakes. This situation should require relatively little effort to determine the market opportunity, because the market situation is fairly well defined with relatively little uncertainty about its size and growth. Although less emphasis can be placed on the market opportunity forecast in this case, considerably more effort might be placed on the *sales forecast* that measures market response to, and helps determine, the new features.

Alternatively, a new technology such as HDTV carries both high stakes and high uncertainty (especially for Zenith), and warrants a fairly systematic approach with committed resources to provide reasonable estimates of market potential. The numerous factors that may complicate the estimation and realization of demand for high stakes/high uncertainty products compel a disciplined approach to the problem of market opportunity forecasting. Because every new product situation is different in its importance and uncertainty, a somewhat comprehensive approach is outlined here to reveal an extensive market opportunity forecasting process. For less intensive projects than HDTV, certain steps and data collection procedures can be omitted.

The approach recommended involves developing a forecasting process to assess the market opportunity by using a variety of tools and data sources, including conceptualization schemes, spreadsheet models, new product scenarios, and other specialized submodels and analytical techniques. The most important feature of the process is that the assumptions are revised over time to include new data and experience collected during the product development process. The emphasis on continual learning about the nature of the market opportunity leads to refined forecasts. The process suggested follows seven major steps that are highlighted in Figure 7.1. Although this process can be used for any new product or service, ones involving new technologies are among the most difficult to forecast. The case of HDTV helps to illustrate some of the pragmatic challenges of market opportunity forecasting. Brief descriptions of each step are followed by an appraisal of the approach.

1. Diagnose and Conceptualize Key Market Factors

New product ideas often arrive with a partial or brief history—sometimes because of their technology, sometimes because they are composites of existing products, and often because they are solutions to the problems of specific consumers. From a combination of experience and initial exploratory investigations of these brief histories, the situational aspects of the new product must be diagnosed. For example, trends on the very broad, less controllable effects of environmental forces (recall Figure 2.1) and their interactions should be considered. Trends and recent behaviors among major stakeholders in the expected market for the new product, especially potential buyers (see Figure 3.1), should also be included. Further, major planned actions by the organization with respect to the new product development process (Chapters 4 and 5) should be considered. From the broad categories, factors should be selected not only for their possible influence on demand for the new product, but also for their effect on each other.

In the case of HDTV, a selected subset of factors is used to illustrate a modeling approach for the market segment defined by potential buying households (as distinct from commercial organizations that might purchase HDTV):

- **Population base.** Any model of market potential requires a population base against which to weight other factors that might limit the size of the opportunity. This variable provides an upper limit on the number of potential buyers. In this case, it could be defined as television-owning house-

FIGURE 7.1   New product forecasting: focus on market opportunity.

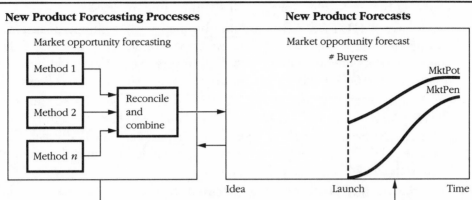

Market Opportunity Forecasting Process

1. **Diagnose and Conceptualize Key Market Factors:** Through a study of market opportunity for the new product, identify and conceptually define the major factors (key variables and stakeholders) in the new product situation hypothesized to influence demand.

2. **Formulate Spreadsheet and Submodels of Major Factors:** Using the identified factors to estimate market size, growth, and penetration, formulate spreadsheet and other submodels to guide data collection.

3. **Collect Data on Key Variables:** Collect data for the various models to develop estimates of the trends or expected directions on the major factors and their interactions over the new product planning horizon.

4. **Analyze Data and Segment Market:** Analyze the data collected, with emphasis on the segmentation structure of the market and possible alternative concepts for segments.

5. **Develop Enhanced New Product Scenarios:** Focusing on a selected segment, create a new product scenario of base case and alternative futures from trends and assumptions about the effects of major factors on the new product.

6. **Estimate Market Potential and Penetration:** In the context of the new product scenario, use the spreadsheet model to develop estimates of market potential and penetration under varying assumptions.

7. **Continually Update Models and Estimates:** Incorporate new data and experience into the new product models and scenarios over the cycle of product development and continually update market opportunity forecasts.

holds. Depending on the characteristics of the television-owning households, trends in major demographic variables defining those households may help estimate growth in this population base.

- **Technology.** This variable defines the probability that the current technology will realize the benefits for potential buyers that were promised at the start of the planning horizon. If the ability of HDTV to perform as promised is uncertain, the probability of realizing the benefits is less than one. For example, there was uncertainty about whether the signal could be received clearly in hilly or metropolitan areas. It is also possible that the equipment that delivers the signal will improve over time, thereby changing the probability that benefits will be fully realized.

- **Awareness of HDTV among potential buyers.** A key assumption in forecasting the size and growth of a market opportunity is awareness of the concept and its benefits among potential buyers. As more people become aware of the HDTV concept, the number of potential buyers will increase.
- **Availability of HDTV programming.** Broadcasters are key stakeholders in the development of HDTV. Because they must purchase the equipment necessary to broadcast HDTV signals, their participation is critical. The amount of HDTV programming they make available may limit the number of households willing to consider HDTV.
- **Intention to buy HDTV among potential buyers.** The proportion of the population that indicates an intention to buy HDTV (assuming certain other factors) helps to qualify the population base. Factored into this estimate are assumptions of complete awareness and availability of HDTV, as well as perceptions among potential buyers of the discriminable quality of HDTV versus current television. If no additional benefits are perceived in viewing quality, or the price of those benefits is too high, the market opportunity could be reduced. Thus, expected price, or a range of expected prices, may influence demand. Also, because price is likely to decline over time, the attractiveness of HDTV to potential buyers may increase.

Numerous other factors might be considered, including segmentation variables that may further refine the definition of potential buyers. Economic conditions, local regulatory restrictions, legal threats, unexpected competitive entrants with new technology, and the developmental capabilities of organizations involved in delivering the new television concept to potential buyers may also be included in the analysis of relevant factors.

2. Formulate Spreadsheet and Submodels of Major Factors

If the limited set of factors identified above are assumed to be the major determinants of HDTV market demand, the relationship among the variables that define market potential and its growth can be considered in the following multiplicative model for market potential over time period t:

$$\mathbf{Pot}_t = (\mathbf{Pop}_t)(\mathbf{Tek}_t)(\mathbf{Awr}_t)(\mathbf{Avl}_t)(\mathbf{Buy}_t) \qquad [7.1]$$

where $\mathbf{Pot}_t$ = market potential at time t (number of potential buyers),

$\mathbf{Pop}_t$ = population base in the selected market segment(s) at time t (maximum number of potential buyers defined by selected demographics),

$\mathbf{Tek}_t$ = technology realization at time t (such as an estimated quality index of HDTV picture),

$\mathbf{Awr}_t$ = awareness of HDTV among potential buyers (percentage aware of HDTV given advertising, word-of-mouth, and so on),

$\textbf{Avl}_t$ = availability of HDTV programming (percentage of HDTV broadcast time to total), and

$\textbf{Buy}_t$ = intention to buy HDTV among potential buyers at time t (index of proportion likely to buy at various prices and assuming best quality picture).

Variables are symbolized by three letters (as above). Another convention used here is to put market-level factors in bold print and organization-level factors in italic print. Thus, **Awr** symbolizes awareness of a new product at the industry level and *Awr* symbolizes awareness for a particular brand of the new product. This distinction also helps to maintain consistency of variable names for sales and financial forecasting in the next two chapters. Figure 7.2 illustrates how a spreadsheet model (using hypothetical data) might be constructed, along with plots of the key estimates over time.

The model in Figure 7.2 suggests that 698,000 potential buyers of HDTV equipment (primarily receivers) may be available in its first year on the market. This number represents less than 1 percent of the estimated 93 million U.S. households. A larger proportion of the total is not estimated to be available because of the market factors identified: (1) limitations in technology to effectively reach all available households, (2) only 25 percent of these households would be aware of HDTV, (3) only half of the available broadcast programming would be available in HDTV format, and (4) given the expected initial $2,000 price level of the receiver, only 12 percent of the households would consider buying it.

The model in Figure 7.2 can be extended to include market potential *volume* by estimating the average number of units purchased per household. Thus, if only one HDTV receiver per household is bought in the first year, the volume is 698,000 units (the same as potential buyers). However, if the estimate of the number of sets purchased per household is more than one, or if it increases over the years, the appropriate number should be factored into the model. By multiplying the volume by the average price per unit, a dollar value estimate of market potential can be obtained. With the stated set of model assumptions, the value of market potential for HDTV receivers in year 1 is just under $1.4 billion (this value is not shown in Figure 7.2).

In Figure 7.2, the market potential model shows growth over the 10-year planning horizon to about 40 percent of total television households (40,685,000 potential buyers). Panels A and B in Figure 7.2 show the market potential growth over time and in relation to the population ceiling of total television households. The three judgmental indices for technology realization, awareness, and programming availability are plotted over time in Panel C.

Also plotted in Panel C of Figure 7.2 is the proportion of the population intending to buy an HDTV receiver over time. Such an estimate is often obtained from a market study of potential buyers who are exposed to a concept of a new product (usually in the form of a scenario) and asked for their response (interest, preference, intention to buy, and so on) at different price levels. This information provides a *response function* of the market to price, which is a different concept than the proportion intending to buy over time. A response

FIGURE 7.2　Market opportunity forecasting: illustrative spreadsheet model for high definition television (HDTV).

Time period t	Market potential	Population base	Technology realization	HDTV Awareness	Program availability	Intention to buy	Average $ price	Analogy market growth	penetration
	(TV households 000)		(Judgmental indices)			(Market survey data)		(Color TV growth)	
Model →	Pot =	Pop ×	Tek ×	Awr ×	Avl ×	Buy	Pri	% of Pot	Pen
Year 1	698	93,000	0.50	0.25	0.50	0.12	2,000	.50	349
Year 2	1,488	93,930	0.55	0.40	0.60	0.12	2,000	.52	774
Year 3	3,287	94,869	0.60	0.55	0.70	0.15	1,800	.48	1,578
Year 4	5,232	95,818	0.70	0.65	0.80	0.15	1,800	.51	2,668
Year 5	10,452	96,776	0.80	0.75	0.90	0.20	1,600	.47	4,912
Year 6	17,281	97,744	0.85	0.80	1.00	0.26	1,400	.48	8,295
Year 7	24,167	98,721	0.90	0.85	1.00	0.32	1,200	.50	12,084
Year 8	27,280	99,709	0.95	0.90	1.00	0.32	1,200	.56	15,277
Year 9	38,268	100,706	1.00	0.95	1.00	0.40	1,000	.54	20,665
Year 10	40,685	101,713	1.00	1.00	1.00	0.40	1,000	.70	28,480

Panel A: Market potential and penetration

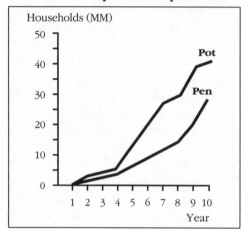

Panel B: Population ceiling

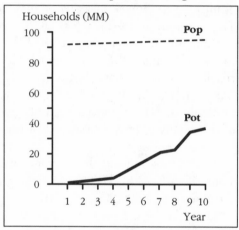

Panel C: Four market factors over time

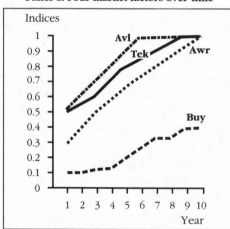

Panel D: Demand curve from survey

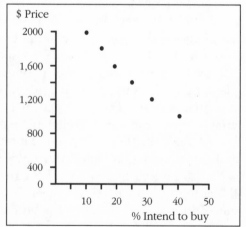

function represents the relationship between a factor over which some control is exerted (such as price, advertising, or distribution) and a response variable (such as awareness, preference, or intention to buy).[4] The goal is to answer the question of how the market is expected to respond to an increase (or decrease) in the level of a controllable factor.

The difference between a time plot and a response function is illustrated in Panels C and D of Figure 7.2. The typical downward-sloping demand curve (response of market to different prices) is shown in Panel D. The link between the proportion intending to buy in Panel C and the response function in Panel D is the price. That is, the expected price for year 1, year 2, and so on determines the proportion intending to buy HDTV in that year. If price is decided by a sole innovating firm, the proportion intending to buy is determined by that decision. However, if competitive forces, costs, investments, and other related factors determine price, they should be included as factors in a more detailed submodel estimating expected market price over time.

In constructing such models and submodels, the variables should be examined for possible interactions among the major factors identified. For example, will increased awareness of HDTV spur broadcasters to switch to HDTV programming more rapidly? If so, trends should be estimated accordingly with an appreciation for the interaction. This can be accomplished as suggested in Chapter 2, Figure 2.4. *Cross-impact analysis* can also be used. It is a more detailed quantitative approach that calls for probability estimates associated with the interactions over a particular time period.[5]

Whatever the value of market potential each year, not all of it may be realized because of various sources of friction in the adoption of new products (see Chapter 3). The learning time, preference formation, trial, and adoption among potential buyers, as well as the behaviors of other market stakeholders, are among the variables that may explain differences in market penetration, the rate at which market potential is reached.

Market penetration is most often estimated by product analogy. For example, the launch of color television might be considered an analogy to the launch of HDTV. Using the historical ratio of annual industry color television sales to the market potential for color television can provide an estimate of HDTV market penetration. This estimate, the last column of the spreadsheet in Figure 7.2, is plotted along with market potential in Panel A of Figure 7.2. Although analogies are expedient, as noted in Chapter 6, there are problems with selecting them without qualification. Consequently, a more comprehensive analogical diffusion modeling approach to estimating market penetration is illustrated in greater detail in a following section.

3. Collect Data on Key Variables

Once the major factors are selected and modeled, data can be collected. As discussed in Chapter 6, a variety of sources may be needed to develop estimates for the major variables included in the model. Possible data sources for the selected variables in the HDTV example follow.

- Population (**Pot**)

    Find statistical sources (print or electronic) on population broken down by selected household demographics over the planning horizon.

- Technology (**Tek**)

    Using judgment from technical experts in a structured decision approach (such as the analytical hierarchy process), estimate quality of signal reception in successive years of operation.

- Awareness (**Awr**)

    Using judgment and measures obtained from the survey of potential buyers, develop estimates of awareness (percentage of population aware of HDTV concept) over the planning period.

- Available Programming (**Avl**)

    Using judgment and interviews with key broadcast executives, estimate percentage of programming available for the HDTV signal over the planning period.

- Intention to Buy (**Buy**)

    Using a survey of potential buyers, estimate intention to buy the new product on the basis of possible prices and picture quality (survey may be conducted in a technical laboratory or consumer clinic in which realistic concepts or prototypes are used as stimuli).

As noted from the examples, some of the data rely on judgment and therefore are ideal applications for the decision calculus and other subjective judgment approaches discussed in Chapter 6.

4. Analyze Data and Segment Market

If time and resources permit, a survey of potential buyers can be used to obtain selected measures (such as intention to buy and awareness) with which to assess market opportunity more carefully. In addition to the more traditional data analyses at the overall market level, one of the major research objectives of the study should be the identification and analysis of relevant market segments. As defined in Chapter 3, market segmentation is a *dynamic decision process* that enables a firm to allocate marketing resources to achieve business objectives.

Segments can be defined on any number of bases, depending on the decision problem. For example, a segment of potential buyers who are *early adopters* may be a desirable target for making decisions about features for a new HDTV product. By using a survey based on *intention to buy* (and similar indicators of early purchase and innovativeness) to define segments, and then using other variables to describe those segments (such as demographics, psychographics, and viewing habits), a firm can pick the one with the greatest likelihood of early purchase as the target market for concept and product development decisions. Alternatively, by including various price levels and other product concept features, a firm can define segments according to buyer needs or preferences. This procedure helps to determine more specific market segment structure and demand estimates for each segment. The segmentation process is illustrated in the next chapter.

5. Develop *Enhanced* New Product Scenarios

A *new product scenario* is an image of the future composed of selected factors that, to varying degrees, can be manipulated for further analysis and understanding of a new product situation. The image can start in the present (built from historical processes) and be projected into alternative futures. These projections can be based on historical trend data for some factors and/or assumptions about trends for other factors (such as the direction of economic factors). If respondents (stakeholders) participate in scenario development, the projections can be idiosyncratic to each respondent; that is, each respondent can forecast an interpretation about the direction of selected factors defining circumstances of the purchase situation (for example, the respondent's views of future economic conditions).

Alternatively, the scenario can start in future time as one or more *ideal* images (for example, when the new product might be available for purchase and use), then be decomposed into component factors back to the present. The idealized visions of the future may or not be based on trends. The point is that if they are new product scenarios to which people respond favorably, they may define the overall system of development necessary to realize the new product. For example, HDTV as a concept may be seen most favorably by a segment of potential buyers as part of an idealized "home theater" scenario. Thus, developing HDTV for this segment may be achieved most effectively by marketing it as a home theater concept, along with complementary products and services to help potential buyers realize the concept within their homes.

Traditionally, scenarios have been used to help define business strategy by focusing primarily on major environmental trends (such as technology, economy, and prices of major supplies).[6] In this context, scenarios are written as narratives or formulated through systematic procedures (such as cross-impact analysis) to depict alternative futures. In the new product development and forecasting context, scenarios should be more enhanced than traditional scenarios to address numerous new product decision problems.

New product scenarios can be *enhanced* in three respects: (1) they can go beyond environmental factors to include relevant market stakeholders (such as potential buyers, trade, and competitors), industry factors, and organizational factors and assumptions about them, (2) their formulation can include the use of creativity and communication technology (such as multimedia and virtual reality) to amplify the imagery surrounding the new product, and (3) they can be adaptive.

New product scenarios can be *adaptive* in two senses. First, they should be continually updated with fresh data and new experiences throughout the development process and again after launch to provide a backdrop for concept development, product design, marketing program decisions, and modifications. Second, scenarios can be designed to allow the interaction of potential buyers to alter aspects of the scenario and/or the new product concept. Such alterations can lead to creative extensions of the new product concept or idealized images of the future that become part of the new product design objectives.

During early new product development, if there are several possible new product market opportunities to evaluate and the new product is a low stakes project in a low uncertainty situation, brief written summaries of the major factors may be adequate to define each scenario. In other cases that are more uncertain and count for higher stakes, more descriptive narratives of possible futures should be incorporated into the data collection process. For example, consumer intentions to buy can be obtained under different scenarios of the new product situation. This effort can improve the overall quality of data collected. Research on intention-to-buy measures has shown that their predictive accuracy improves with the inclusion of contextual aspects of the buying situation.[7]

Creativity and communication technology should also be used to enhance new product scenarios with text, sound, and visual imagery. If possible, the technology and capabilities of one-way and interactive media (such as virtual reality) should be used to simulate what the future may be like for the new product situation. If multimedia capabilities are not available, more standard technologies such as slides, video, artistic renderings, specially equipped rooms or laboratory settings, and consumer clinics should be used to bring to life an image of the future, portraying the new product in its purchase and use. Numerous approaches can be taken to construct new product scenarios, but *environmental simulation* and *information acceleration* are two useful methods that have shown promise in research.

Environmental Simulation

Some new products, especially services, depend on understanding human response to a new physical environment.[8] Prior to major investment in building the environment (for example, a new retail outlet or hotel), it may be possible to simulate it and obtain shopper/buyer reaction to assess market opportunity. The simulation can contain scenarios that are written descriptions, photographs, slides, soundtracks, videotapes, film, or any combination thereof. The key assumption of using environmental simulations is that measures and reactions obtained from imagery created to represent some future reality are very similar to ones that would be obtained in the actual environment. Generally, research supports the contention that there is satisfactory correlation between results from simulated and actual environments.[9] Even so, care should be taken in planning such scenarios to simulate as closely as possible the imagery of the actual environment for a new service or the environment within which a new product might be purchased or used.

Information Acceleration

A new product scenario can include an information accelerator.[10] Information acceleration is a laboratory technique that makes information that might be accessible in the future available to potential buyers (or other stakeholders) today. The purpose of the accelerator is to compress into a few hours a potential buyer's information-search processes that normally take many weeks. Using a multimedia computer, potential buyers can choose freely from any number of pre-programmed information sources, taking as much time as needed. In one application involving the purchase of an automobile (General Motors Buick Division), consumers could access advertising (magazine, newspaper, television), interviews with actual consumers, articles in various consumer and trade publications, and a showroom simulation (including multiple views of the car and its interior spaces, salesperson interactions, price sticker, and brochure).[11]

To make the consumer's decision process in the accelerator more realistic, time budget constraints can be applied, additional information sources about environmental factors can be included, and competitor products can be made available. Confronting potential buyers with various information sources, a new product concept (or even a developed prototype), and potential competitors makes it possible to study a variety of the consumer variables identified in Chapter 3, including the important consumer intention-to-buy measure.

In the reported application, no significant differences were found in purchase intention between consumers who searched for information in the accelerator's showroom and those who visited an actual showroom (although both measures consistently found differences between two competing brands).[12] These findings lend support to the potential value of information acceleration to at least simulate the essence of consumer search processes. The accelerator has also been applied to forecasting market potential for GM's proposed electric vehicle.[13]

Choosing a Scenario

With the capability to build enhanced new product scenarios comes the task of choosing the set of conditions most likely to represent the future for purposes of market opportunity forecasting. If scenarios are based on a sample of independent respondents (such as potential buyers) and the future they believe most likely to occur, a distribution of outcomes is possible. Measures of central tendency (mean, median, mode) then can be used to define a most likely market-level scenario.

Alternatively, the new product development team or suitable panel of independent experts can use a group decision-making process (such as Delphi or the analytic hierarchy process) to review alternative scenarios and choose the most likely one. In this process, it may be helpful to reduce the many possible alternatives to a subset that represents extremes: for example, one scenario with all positive outcomes from the various trends and assumptions and another with all negative outcomes. The reduction process can also proceed through elimination (omitting scenarios that are definitely not possible) or inclusion (selecting those that are definitely possible).

Whatever the process used, the goal should be to conclude with a *base case* scenario and a small number of reasonable scenarios that represent images of the possible future for the new product, then select one for purposes of decision-making. Typically, a base case scenario is defined to depict what might happen if key factors follow their basic trends. Varying the factors provides the capability to generate numerous alternative scenarios. The value of the process is scenario flexibility; that is, as development proceeds and new information about key factors is learned, alternative scenarios can be readily used for further analysis and decision making.

6. Estimate Market Potential and Penetration

Estimating market potential and growth from a spreadsheet model quantifies market opportunity forecasts. As evidenced in the spreadsheet of Figure 7.2, the computations of market potential and penetration for a specific scenario are straightforward. The value of using personal computer spreadsheets to perform these model calculations is the ability to quickly recompute estimates of market opportunity with different scenarios. Once a modeling approach is established, the factors and variables included in the model and the assumptions about them should be challenged throughout the development process.

7. Continually Update Model and Estimates

New product forecasting is a learning process. The greater the accumulation and use of data and experience in the various forecasting models, the greater the reduction in uncertainty about the new product's development and market performance. The use of a managerial spreadsheet model and other submodels in the context of scenarios provides the necessary framework to facilitate managerial learning about the new product over its development cycle.

During the time a new product evolves from an idea to a concept, then to a prototype, and eventually to a refined product, the market opportunity may change. The reason may be external changes or changes in the assumptions used to derive the estimates. For example, discovering during prototype development that the product's costs can be lowered substantially may alter price trends and therefore market potential. Continually evaluating the variables in the model, collecting additional data on the variables, checking assumptions in the scenarios, and updating the forecasts derived from the scenarios provides the most up-to-date information to support decision making about the market opportunity.

At this point, the process of modeling and updating forecasts of market potential and penetration may appear somewhat extensive, and only feasible for the most important projects. Yet detailed market opportunity information appears to be essential to evaluate and screen almost any new product idea, and as research has shown, numerous ideas are often necessary to realize a successful new product. Typically, *idea screening* for new product ideas involves judgmental estimates of a few key market factors or a list of questions or rating scales on several factors, which, when answered, should lead to a decision of whether or not to continue.[14] In practice, each organization (or new product team) tends to develop its own procedure for screening ideas, often including variables relevant to their business situation.

However, when ideas are numerous and sporadic, carefully screening all possiblities may not be easy or cost effective, and the chance of rejecting a good idea or accepting a bad one is high. Ideally, one would like the luxury of an economical *rapid idea-screening* capability that follows a comprehensive market opportunity forecasting process for each idea as described in the seven-step process in this chapter. Though little can substitute for the comprehensive study of each new product idea, the process can be expedited by automating it through *expert systems.*

For example, to cope with the problem of estimating market penetration, it may be possible to accumulate a data base of new product analogies relevant to a particular market. This could be done by defining each new product analogy's situation along a number of factors (as suggested in Figure 6.6), using historical data and expertise. Then, by profiling the new product idea along the factors, a subset of highly similar products can be identified and their growth rates combined for a relatively quick estimation of market penetration.

Using computer software for such a task is reasonable if the data base and rules applied to select the most similar products have proven to be reliable and valid in use. These sorts of problems may best be tackled through the methods and procedures offered by formal expert systems—computer programs that use a *knowledge base* and *inference* procedures to help make decisions on complex problems.[15] The software enables managers to consult the expert system with queries about specific problems.

Though promising, expert systems are relatively new and are only as good as the quality of (1) their knowledge base, or rules about the problem, (2) the data base of facts about the problem, and (3) the built-in reasoning approach that applies knowledge and data to the problem. Issues to be resolved for successful applications include how best to obtain and validate the judgment of experts, how to define who is an expert, and how to develop questions to elicit expert feedback. Also, establishing rules of inference that transform the knowledge base into new information and follow a logic that is acceptable in its conclusions requires further study. Issues in linking data bases, such as product analogies, with the expert system must also be studied further before quick and reliable screening procedures can be developed for large numbers of ideas.

Up-front investment in the development of expert systems can be substantial, but if an organization is committed to new product development as an ongoing process with shared values among its members, the investment will be returned over time. Further, the entire new product development and forecasting process may benefit from the application of expert system methods. However, any attempts at automating the process should commence step by step, perhaps by first tackling small decision problems or subproblems to build confidence in the modeling approach.

The central point of forecast updating and the desire for rapid new product idea screening tools is that the process of forecasting market opportunity is one of learning. At early levels of product definition, little is known about how the product will turn out or how many potential buyers will adopt it. Gaining this knowledge in a systematic way is at the core of new product development.

Appraising Market Opportunity Forecasting Models

Market opportunity forecasting models have several advantages:

- The use of multiple factors in the models and scenarios affords needed flexibility in product design and forecasting, especially at early stages of the development process. The number of scenarios can be narrowed later in the development process.

- The use of traditional scenario analysis is often limited to environmental trends. By incorporating a broader set of major market and organizational factors, more realistic scenarios can be developed.

- Maintaining and refining market opportunity models throughout the development process (which can often last for months or years) provides an additional checkpoint for evaluating alternative formulations of the product.

- The use of various spreadsheet models, specialized submodels, multimedia, and other communication technologies to build scenarios provides a valuable research setting for the continual evaluation of market stakeholder response to evolving levels of product refinement.

Market opportunity forecasting also has certain drawbacks:

- When managers are first exposed to market opportunity forecast models, their reaction is usually: "I can get any numbers out of this I want. What good is it?" The value of such models is more in the disciplined process they bring to relatively unstructured and complex situations than in the outcome of the process. The appropriate emphasis in using such models should be on the quality of their assumptions and the reasonableness (or robustness) of their outcome, not the simple magnitude of the outcome.

- Overreliance on quantitative modeling estimates may imply an exaggerated precision for decisions that might benefit from intuition as much as analysis. This problem may be especially common at early stages in the development process when creativity is crucial. To overcome it, the new product team will have to balance the relative importance of the discipline imparted by a modeling process against the creativity needed to move a project ahead.

- Modeling consumes organizational time and resources, especially if enhanced scenarios are developed. The *value* of information from market opportunity forecasts must be assessed.

Each new product situation should be evaluated with respect to the use and scope of market opportunity forecasting models. Developers of important new products in uncertain environments may want to invest effort and resources to develop and maintain enhanced scenarios and updated modeling estimates of demand throughout the development process to cope with high levels of uncertainty in the project. The opposite may be true for less important new products, which perhaps should rely on simpler models that define the trends of a few important market drivers. However, if market opportunity forecasting is pursued to reduce uncertainty, two important methodological concerns are (1) the estimation of market potential using *multiple methods* and (2) more detailed approaches for estimating market penetration.

ESTIMATING MARKET POTENTIAL
USING MULTIPLE METHODS

For many new products and services, the number representing the potential size of a market can never be really known, even in retrospect. For example, a different launch marketing program (increased promotion or lower price) or a different set of competitive reactions could make a difference in the number of potential buyers. The uncertain effects of environmental and other sources of turbulence on the market opportunity for a new product—which itself may be fuzzily defined as an idea or concept—therefore compel a forecasting approach that can cope with error. Such an approach involves the use of multiple methods.

A multiple-method measurement approach is based on the assumption that weaknesses in a single method will be offset by the counter-balancing strengths of other methods. Implicitly, multiple and independent methods do not share the same weaknesses or potential for bias. The approach is purported to exploit the assets of each method and neutralize the liabilities, thereby averaging out errors.[16] At all levels of new product forecasting—market opportunity, sales, or financial—multiple-method approaches should be used to help manage error.

To implement a multiple-method approach, the first step is to develop at least two independent modeling processes similar to the seven steps discussed in the preceding section to provide two or more forecasts of market opportunity size for a new product idea. The second step is to employ a *reconciling* methodology to explain forecasts that are different, or to ensure that when similar forecasts are obtained, they are acceptable. The third step is to *combine* the independent forecasts into a single forecast to facilitate planning decisions. This process is briefly illustrated in the context of a new electronic mail service.

Electronic Mail Case Study

In this case, the market potential for a new electronic mail service concept was being considered.[17] The new service involved electronic terminal input of a message up to two pages in length, electronic processing (merging) of the message, and hard copy output (stationery and envelope) of at least 200 units, delivered through the U.S. Postal Service. The concern with forecasting market potential was part of a larger concern for estimating year-to-year demand for the new service. Expected demand would provide information for decisions to change product features, price, and promotion. Although managers in the organization supplying the service were the final decision makers, the forecasts were prepared by outside analysts. For purposes of illustration, the analysis focuses on the problem of forecasting market potential for the new service during 1985.

Obtaining Multiple Forecasts of Market Potential Through Different Methods

Three independent forecasts of market potential from three methods illustrate the analysis. Method 1, published in a study by the U.S. Office of Technology Assessment (OTA) in August 1982, involved secondary information sources, expert judgment input, and curve-fitting.[18] Method 2, a primary study (produced in early 1983) of an original formulation of the product concept, was based on a survey. Method 3 also was based on a survey and was conducted in 1983; however, it was conducted by a different sponsor and involved a reformulated product concept (one with different product features).

Table 7.1 includes a description of each method with respect to a selection of factors that defined the potential market opportunity. Each method used a somewhat different operationalization of the concept of market potential for the new product. As indicated in Table 7.1, the three methods generated forecasts of 3.6, 1.4, and 3.0 billion messages, respectively, that could potentially be sent in 1985. The difference of some 2.2 billion messages between the first two methods is substantial. Acceptance of one or the other of these estimates of potential could result in very different views of the size of the market and subsequent 1985 sales forecasts—not to mention investments in plant and equipment to implement the service. The differences compel explanations to reconcile the forecasts and a procedure to adopt one for planning and decision making.

Reconciling the Forecasts

To reconcile different forecasts, a comprehensive review of the methodologies underlying each should be conducted. This step helps reveal whether the differences between methods can account for some of the differences in the estimates. An initial review of the three methods in Table 7.1 suggests major

TABLE 7.1 Three methods of forecasting electronic mail market potential.

Conceptual factors	Method 1 (1982)	Method 2 (1983)	Method 3 (1983)
Environmental factors			
■ Natural resources	□ No assumptions	□ No assumptions	□ No assumptions
■ Population/demographic	□ No assumptions	□ No assumptions	□ No assumptions
■ Cultural	□ No assumptions	□ No assumptions	□ No assumptions
■ Technology	□ Several assumptions	□ No assumptions	□ No assumptions
■ Economic	□ No assumptions	□ No assumptions	□ No assumptions
■ Laws and regulations	□ No assumptions	□ No assumptions	□ No assumptions
Marketing program factors			
■ Product concept definition	□ Electronic input	□ Electronic input	□ Electronic input
	□ Hard copy output	□ Hard copy output	□ Hard copy output
	□ No minimum input	□ Minimum input	□ Minimum input
	□ No minimum output	□ Minimum output	□ No minimum output
■ Price	□ No assumptions	□ Set price/message	□ Set price/message
■ Promotion	□ Buyer knowledge	□ Buyer knowledge	□ Buyer knowledge
■ Distribution	□ Maximum availability	□ Maximum availability	□ Maximum availability
Methodological factors			
■ Sales volume measure	□ Number of messages	□ Number of messages	□ Number of messages
■ Purchase measure	□ Number of messages sent	□ 4-point purchase intention	□ 4-point purchase intention
■ Customer group definition	□ All potential customers	□ Organizations with 20+ employees	□ Organizations (not limited by size)
■ Geographic area	□ United States	□ United States	□ United States
■ Time period of measure	□ 1985	□ 1985	□ 1985
Estimate of market potential	3.6 billion messages	1.4 billion messages	3.0 billion messages

Source: Robert J. Thomas, "Forecasting New Product Market Potential: Combining Multiple Methods," *Journal of Product Innovation Management,* 4 (June 1987), p. 113.

differences on the product concept definition, purchase measures, customer group definition, technological environment, and assumptions about price.

One approach to reconcile (and combine) the results of different forecasts involves the systematic estimation of a judgmental weighting parameter as part of a simple equation for averaging multiple estimates of market potential. More specifically,

$$\mathbf{Pot'} = \sum_{i=1}^{n} (1 + \mathbf{Wtg}_i)(\mathbf{Pot}_i)/(\mathbf{n}) \qquad [7.2]$$

where $\mathbf{Pot'}$ = adjusted market potential forecast for new product,

$\mathbf{Pot}_i$ = market potential forecast from method i, for i = 1 to n methods, and

$\mathbf{Wtg}_i$ = judgmental parameter weighting market potential forecast i, for i = 1 to n methods.

The reference value for the judgmental parameter $\mathbf{Wtg}$ is zero; that is, the full weight of the estimate from a particular method should be counted in the combined forecast. The value of $\mathbf{Wtg}$ can, however, be greater than or less than zero if a review of the method suggests an under- or over-estimation of potential volume for the new product. The judgmental parameter can be expressed as a percentage increase or decrease in market potential. Thus, $\mathbf{Wtg}$ = .20 indicates a 20 percent positive adjustment in the original estimate.

Although numerous judgmental procedures can be used to estimate $\mathbf{Wtg}$, the various conceptual factors defining market potential provide the necessary discipline to formulate this estimate. Each forecast should be systematically evaluated along the conceptual criteria to obtain a $\mathbf{Wtg}_i$ value for each method. More specifically,

$$\mathbf{Wtg}_i = \sum_{j=1}^{k} (\mathbf{Chg}_{ij}) \qquad [7.3]$$

where $\mathbf{Wtg}_i$ = a parameter used to *weight* (judgmentally) market potential forecast i, for i = 1 to n methods, and

$\mathbf{Chg}_{ij}$ = percentage change (increase or decrease) in market potential based on an evaluation of the extent to which the method used to derive each forecast affects market potential on each of j = 1 to k criteria.

As in the case of $\mathbf{Wtg}_i$, $\mathbf{Chg}_{ij}$ can be referenced at a value of zero; that is, zero means the criterion has no appreciable effect on increasing or decreasing market potential. If $\mathbf{Chg}_{ij}$ is assigned a value of, say, $-.20$, it would indicate the effect on market potential of this particular criterion to be a 20 percent decrease. To the extent possible, the same conceptual criteria should be considered in evaluating $\mathbf{Wtg}_i$ for each method.

TABLE 7.2   Market potential adjustments based on conceptual factors.

Conceptual factors	Judgmental estimates of change in market potential due to each factor (Chg_{ij})		
	Method 1	Method 2	Method 3
Environmental factors			
■ Technological[1]	−.20	.00	.00
Marketing program factors			
■ Product concept definition[2]	.00	+.10	+.05
■ Price[3]	−.10	.00	.00
Methodological factors			
■ Purchase measure[4]	.00	.00	.00
■ Customer group definition[5]	.00	+.80	+.05
Net change in market potential (Wtg_i)	−.30	+.90	+.10
Original market potential estimate (Pot_i) in billions of messages	3.6	1.4	3.0
Adjusted market potential estimate in billions of messages (Pot'_i)	2.5	2.7	3.3

Footnoted assumptions

1. Relative to the other methods, Method 1 assumed very optimistic growth rates for personal computers and related technologies, and was therefore adjusted downward by 20 percent.

2. Method 1 made no restrictions about the product concept and was therefore assumed ideal. Method 2 restricted the concept definition with a minimum message size (2 pages) and number of messages per transaction. Method 3 restricted the concept only by message size (also 2 pages). Using survey data, Methods 2 and 3 were therefore adjusted upward to compensate for their restrictions.

3. Methods 2 and 3 included identical assumptions about price, whereas Method 1 included no assumption about price. Because the service would be marketed at a set price, survey data were used to adjust Method 1 downward (by 10 percent).

4. Although different purchase measures were used in the three studies, there was no basis for believing their effects on market potential would differ.

5. Method 1 made no restrictions by market segments or customer groups and was therefore assumed as a true ceiling measure. Method 2 was based on a survey of organizations (not individuals) with more than 20 employees, and Method 3 was based on a survey of organizations of all sizes. Using survey data, each was adjusted upward by the amounts shown to reflect a larger base population.

Source: Based on Robert J. Thomas, "Forecasting New Product Market Potential: Combining Multiple Methods," *Journal of Product Innovation Management,* 4 (June 1987), pp. 109–119.

Table 7.2 illustrates the implementation of equations [7.2] and [7.3] and summarizes judgmental effects of the method differences on the three market potential forecasts. Although *best-* and *worst-*case estimates and various sensitivity analyses were performed, the values in Table 7.2 represent the *most likely* estimates of the Chg_{ij} percentage increase or decrease in forecast potential as defined in equation [7.3]. Note that Table 7.2 includes footnoted assumptions that briefly explain why the specific numerical values were used to adjust each method on the various conceptual factors defining market potential. The assumptions in these footnotes reflect the reconciliation process necessary to compare the methods and estimates. Although not apparent in the summary table, considerable analysis, discussion, and summary judgment underlie each number. Annotating the values with footnotes (or other supporting analyses) establishes a record of the model values for future reference and evaluation.

Combining Multiple Forecasts

At this point, analysts have a variety of options for selecting a forecast of market potential, depending on their decision situation. For example, if the concern is to develop a range of estimates, they could retain the original independent estimates of market potential, from 1.4 to 3.6 billion messages. Alternatively, a single best estimate could be obtained as a simple average of the three forecasts, or a point estimate of 2.7 billion messages [(3.6 + 1.4 + 3.0) = 8.0/3] for the 1985 market potential.

Finally, a judgmentally quantified estimate from the reconciliation analysis (summarized in Table 7.2) uses the weighted model of market potential as proposed in equations [7.2] and [7.3] to combine the three forecasts. The Wtg_i values were computed by using equation [7.3], and these values were used to compute Pot' in equation [7.2]. The weighted forecast of market potential was therefore estimated to be 2.8 billion messages for 1985.

Appraising Multiple-Methods Approaches

A compelling body of research on forecasting strongly supports combining multiple independent estimates to improve accuracy.[19] Research on the number and kinds of forecasts to develop suggests that two to six methods would be satisfactory.[20] Research also supports the notion that benefits will be derived from including different kinds of methods.[21] Further, the simple average of estimates from multiple forecasts has proven to be fairly accurate and easy to use in historical sales forecasting studies.[22]

If a comparative analysis of different methods indicates little or no basis for distinguishing among them, the simple mean of the three estimates might provide a satisfactory measure of market potential. However, when a comparison of methods suggests differences—as in the preceeding case—a reconciliation of methods and a weighted average combining the estimates may prove more beneficial than simple averaging. This reconciliation should be linked to the factors used to define market potential conceptually. As discussed in Chapter 6, decomposing a problem into its components (the conceptual factors) will improve subjective estimation.

The approaches to reconciliation and combining considered here have the limitations of any approach relying, in part, on judgment. Further, there has been little research on *new* product forecasting to validate the benefits of combining. Research has focused predominantly on the accuracy of combining historical sales forecasts. Another possible drawback to combining multiple forecasts is that when the simple averaging approach is used, the range of the ultimate forecast is limited by the low and high forecasts from the available methods. The *true* market potential may be higher than the highest estimate or lower than the lowest estimate.

However, the more systematic—and recommended—approach of weighting the forecasts by the conceptual factors defining market potential could lead to forecasts outside the range of the individual methods used. In the preceding case study, the difference between the mean of 2.7 billion and the weighted estimate of 2.8 billion messages was not substantial, although with the weighted approach the forecast could have been outside the 1.4 to 3.6 billion message range. Focusing on the conceptual factors defining market potential makes possible a broader range than that generated by available forecasts. On balance, for new product situations involving high stakes and high uncertainty, investing in multiple-methods approaches to generate forecasts is desirable.

ESTIMATING MARKET PENETRATION

One of the major problems in market opportunity forecasting during the developmental phases of new products and services is determining the rate at which market potential will be realized over a future planning period after launch—that is, *market penetration*. The estimates are critical input for marketing, production, staffing, financial, and market entry decisions. Managers often rely on experience and their judgment about product analogies to arrive at estimates of market penetration over a reasonable planning period. A more disciplined approach is to use a diffusion modeling methodology in which an innovation introduced to a social system is viewed as part of a communication process.[23] In this section, the electronic mail case study is used to illustrate an *analogical diffusion model* to estimate market penetration.

Diffusion Models

The development and use of diffusion models for a variety of applications, including new products, has been well documented in the literature.[24] The reference point for diffusion modeling is a mathematical model that builds on theory from the innovation diffusion literature.[25] In the model, potential buyers are divided into two major classes: *innovators* and *imitators*. Innovators are viewed as the first buyers to enter a market during a time period. Their purchases are assumed to be motivated by commercial or external sources of communication (such as advertising) over the planning period. Imitators are assumed to purchase on the basis of interpersonal influence processes (such as word-of-mouth communication) within a market.[26]

The diffusion model is formulated as:

$$\mathbf{Adp}_t = \mathbf{Ino}\ (\mathbf{Pot} - \mathbf{Cum}_t) + \mathbf{Imi}\ (\mathbf{Cum}_t / \mathbf{Pot})(\mathbf{Pot} - \mathbf{Cum}_t), \qquad [7.4]$$

where $\mathbf{Adp}_t$ = the number of adopters at time t,

$\quad\quad\quad\ \mathbf{Ino}$ = coefficient of innovation,

$\quad\quad\quad\ \mathbf{Imi}$ = coefficient of imitation,

$\quad\quad\quad\ \mathbf{Pot}$ = market potential, or the number of initial purchases over the product's life, and

$\quad\quad\ \mathbf{Cum}_t$ = the cumulative number of adopters by time t.

The term on the right side of the equation is divided into two parts by the plus (+) sign. The part to the left of the plus sign represents the portion of adopters during time period t designated as innovators, or those whose adoption was influenced by external influences. The part to the right of the plus sign represents the portion of adopters during time period t designated as imitators, or those whose adoption was influenced by interpersonal influence and word-of-mouth. With the formulation in equation [7.4], the relative number of innovators will decline over time as the market potential is absorbed, and the relative number of imitators will rise, then decline. Over time, the value of $\mathbf{Cum}_t$ will take an S-shape (as illustrated in the market penetration curve in Panel A of Figure 7.2).

Typically, these three parameters (**Pot, Ino,** and **Imi**) are estimated with a multiple regression analysis from a product's *historical* sales data, and then used to predict the penetration of market potential.[27] Although this approach can be useful for launched products with several data points (at minimum, three data points are necessary to estimate the three parameters), it does not help for new products yet to be launched. Consequently, an *analogical diffusion model* is recommended.

Analogical Diffusion Modeling

Analogical diffusion models follow the structure of equation [7.4], but the three coefficients (now labeled with a prime symbol)—**Pot′, Ino′,** and **Imi′**—are estimated from historical data of existing product analogies, market studies, published data, expert judgment, test markets, and/or other sources. A four-step procedure that illustrates the use of analogical diffusion models for estimating market penetration is outlined here for the new electronic mail service.

1. Estimate Market Potential (Pot′)

The market potential parameter can be estimated by using the procedure described previously in this chapter, which involves published sources, market studies, and judgment. Note that with this approach, the value of market potential does not have to be fixed over time, but can vary according to the estimates of the conceptual factors defining it.[28] As discussed in the preceding section, studies were available to provide three estimates of market potential for the new electronic mail service (see Figure 7.2).

2. Identify a Set of Candidate Product Analogies

By a procedure similar to that illustrated in Figure 6.5, 16 candidate products were identified as potentially similar to the new electronic mail service on selected features. Such products included overnight package delivery services, electronic funds transfer systems, mailgram-type services, automated teller services, and telecommunication devices (such as modems). These products were hypothesized to have some of the features that satisfy a set of needs related to the new product. Because of time and cost limitations, it was not possible to collect comprehensive data to qualify each analogy; however, the use of experts and secondary information sources proved helpful.

3. Estimate Diffusion Coefficients (*Ino'* and *Imi'*)

Although the coefficients of innovation and imitation can be estimated from meta-analyses of a large number of omnibus products and services,[29] it is preferable to use a selected set of analogies as suggested in the preceding step. This estimation process involves collecting historical sales data for each product analogy and using analytical procedures to derive the coefficients of innovation and imitation for each. Once obtained, the coefficients for one product can be selected (the one most similar to the new product), or the coefficients can be combined for all products to compute the values of *Ino'* and *Imi'* to be used in equation [7.4].

The procedure to combine the various coefficients of innovation and imitation can follow the ones described previously for estimating market potential. A simple average could be computed for each coefficient, or they could be weighted. For example, following the structure of Figure 6.5, an *index of similarity* (comparing each candidate analogy to the new product on various factors) could be estimated and judgmentally quantified. This index could then be used to weight the coefficients for each product analogy, respectively.[30]

To illustrate how *Ino'* and *Imi'* might be computed from coefficients of innovation and imitation, historical data were assumed to be available on four of the 16 candidate product analogies. By regression analysis on these data, the *Ino* and *Imi* diffusion model parameters were estimated for each. The resulting models from these analyses were deemed a satisfactory fit to the data (significant at a 95% confidence level and with values on the multiple correlation coefficients of .8 or better). The estimated coefficients are labeled in Figure 7.3. In this case, the values of *Ino'* and *Imi'* are computed as simple averages of coefficients from the four selected product analogies.

4. Estimate Market Penetration (*Pen_t*) and Number of Adopters (*Adp_t*)

Market penetration for the relevant planning period can be estimated by using the analogical diffusion model represented in equation [7.4]. With the values

FIGURE 7.3 **Illustration of analogical diffusion model for new electronic mail service.**

Diffusion Model Coefficients

Coefficient	Product Analogy 1	Product Analogy 2	Product Analogy 3	Product Analogy 4	Average
Innovation **(Ino)**	0.004	0.014	0.035	0.001	0.014
Imitation **(Imi)**	0.403	0.950	0.428	0.486	0.567

Analogical Diffusion Model Coefficients

Market potential in **(Pot)** $= 2,800,000$
Coefficient of innovation **(Ino$'$)** $= 0.014$
Coefficient of imitation **(Imi$'$)** $= 0.567$

Market Penetration (data in 000)

	Number of Adopters **(Adp)**	Cumulative Adoption **(Pen)**	Market Potential **(Pot)**
Launch	0	0	2,800
Year 1	39	39	2,800
Year 2	61	100	2,800
Year 3	92	192	2,800
Year 4	138	330	2,800
Year 5	200	530	2,800
Year 6	275	805	2,800
Year 7	353	1,158	2,800
Year 8	408	1,566	2,800
Year 9	409	1,975	2,800
Year 10	342	2,317	2,800

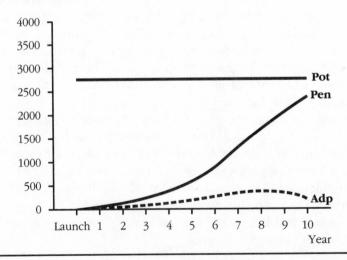

Source: Based on Robert J. Thomas, "Estimating Market Growth For New Products: An Analogical Diffusion Model Approach," *Journal of Product Innovation Management*, 2 (March 1985), pp. 45–55.

of **Ino′** and **Imi′** coefficients and the value for market potential obtained from the multiple-methods estimate (2.8 billion messages), $\mathbf{Adp}_t$ can be calculated over a 10-year planning period. Recall that the value of market potential includes a set of assumptions about environmental and market factors. If these assumptions are varied to accommodate plausible scenarios, alternative market penetration volumes can be estimated. For example, different prices from a buyer intention survey might be used to examine differences in the resulting market opportunities.

To visualize the diffusion process, it is useful to plot the number of adopters ($\mathbf{Adp}_t$) and the cumulative number of adopters, or the market penetration ($\mathbf{Pen}_t$), over the 10-year planning period as shown in Figure 7.3. Once the basic analogical diffusion modeling capability is installed on a spreadsheet, numerous sensitivity analyses can be performed on the various coefficients, and various assumptions can be tested under different scenarios. Further, the model that generates estimates of market potential can be linked to the diffusion model through the market potential variable, and those assumptions can be examined for their effects on market penetration.

Appraising Analogical Diffusion Models

There are several reasons to consider using an analogical diffusion model to estimate market penetration for new products. One is that it provides an intellectually rigorous approach for overcoming the natural bias to overestimate early sales, especially in the critical first and second years of a new product's life.[31] Although parameter estimation departs from normal modeling procedures (by necessity, because no historical data points are available), the diffusion model is a widely accepted and studied model form. Further, the basic model presented here is fairly intuitive to managers, straightforward in assumptions, and amenable to spreadsheet calculations. Managers can interact with the model in a "what-if" fashion by changing parameter values and performing sensitivity analyses.

The model is also flexible. For example, the parameters can be extended to include various assumptions from enhanced scenarios, from numerous factors in the market environment, and from various controllable marketing variables. Price decreases may increase market potential, or increases in advertising expenditures may increase the rate of innovation. Finally, the model is adaptive enough to be continued throughout the development process and into post-launch tracking of performance. As new information and actual data are obtained, model assumptions and performance should be tested to help validate the quality of the model for future use.

Though analogical diffusion models are attractive, and recommended as essential for market opportunity forecasting of new products, caution is recommended in their use. Some research indicates that for certain product classes (such as home appliances) diffusion rates do not appear to be changing significantly over time,[32] but this may not be the case for product analogies in a rapidly changing market environment. Differences in market conditions should be evaluated carefully, as suggested in Figure 6.5. Further, experience has shown that not all data are available to judge the similarity of analogies. For example, marketing strategy and market segmentation data from a 10-year-old product, which might substantially affect a new product's growth rate, are often unobtainable during the early years of a new product—even with only one firm in the market. Also, the resources needed to build analogies may be substantial. The volume and time of data collection and analysis may make the task cumbersome, and the value of the information it might provide should be carefully assessed.

The general form and assumptions of the basic diffusion model can also be limiting.[33] For example, the coefficients of innovation and imitation in the basic model are assumed constant from year to year, but it may be more reasonable to assume that they vary as marketing programs become more effective over time. The value of **Ino'** could be hypothesized to increase and that of **Imi'** to decrease as the market is driven more by external communication sources than by interpersonal ones. In addition, the diffusion model focuses on a single product adoption. For some new products and markets, potential buyers don't simply purchase a single product, but rely on a constellation of products and services to be in place before purchase.[34] Finally, diffusion models do not reflect supply conditions. If sales data from Compaq Corporation's launch of the ProLinea line of competitively priced personal computers were used as an analogy for new computer sales, it would not include demand that was unmet by limited supply, and therefore would provide erroneous diffusion rates.

On balance, the merits of using analogical diffusion models to help forecast market penetration appear to outweigh the concerns. However, tradeoffs should be ascertained in terms of costs and benefits, as in any case where the value of information is an issue. In some new product situations, especially where markets are mature and managers have considerable experience, straightforward managerial judgment of sales growth estimates over a planning period may suffice. However, in other situations, where the new product is important, the market environment is highly uncertain, and managers have little experience in the market, investing in an analogical diffusion modeling approach may prove valuable. In any situation, both judgmental estimation and analogical diffusion model estimation might be used as multiple and independent methods to forecast market penetration of new products.

Ultimately, the learning and investment aspect of the relatively disciplined analogical diffusion modeling process must not be overlooked as a long-term benefit. The process builds managerial experience about market relationships that can translate into improved judgment in future new product situations. The accumulation of analogies in a data base over time will provide a valuable resource for future new product situations in which forecasting market opportunity is an important task.

SUMMARY

Unfortunately, market opportunity forecasts early in a product's development—at the idea and early concept levels—tend to be viewed as low-cost efforts based on back-of-the-envelope calculations or taken from a published study purchased from a commercial research firm. As the product concept becomes more carefully designed at later stages of the development process, more expensive customized studies are often commissioned to assess the new product's market potential and penetration over time. Pressures to move quickly or reduce overall research costs may explain why organizations fail to invest in market opportunity forecasts during early product development—just when reasonably good estimates are needed to make important *go/no-go* decisions.

The cost of developing an ongoing capability for market opportunity forecasting to support new product development may be small in relation to the opportunity costs of making a *go* decision for a loser or a *no-go* decision for a winner. Of course, every organization must carefully assess the strategic role of new product development and the commitment to ongoing processes versus project-oriented development; however, once the commitment is made, a market opportunity forecasting capability is critical to important *go/no-go* decisions.

Suggested guidelines for developing this capability are presented in Figure 7.1 and illustrated throughout the chapter. Estimating market potential and penetration requires a methodical process that includes modeling, data collection, data analysis, scenario building, multiple methods, and carefully reasoned assumptions supported by thoughtful managerial judgment. These procedures represent a disciplined and systematic way of coping with the difficult task of forecasting market opportunity for new products. The next chapter, addresses the challenge of forecasting new product sales to further support decision making.

8 New Product Sales Forecasting

Market opportunity forecasts represent *potentials*—values that are capable of being realized. Sales forecasts represent *expectations*—values that are anticipated outcomes linked to planned actions. Decisions about whether or not to *go* with a particular product concept and marketing program depend in part on the sales forecast; in turn, the sales forecast depends on decisions about which features to include in the concept, its price, its advertising and promotion, its distribution, and other factors. In effect, the development of both new products and their forecasts depends on the response of potential buyers and other major stakeholders; that is why they are described in this book as parallel and interactive processes.

A *sales forecast* for a new product or service therefore measures the value of an organization's effort to meet the unfulfilled needs of a segment of potential buyers and related stakeholders. As illustrated in Figure 8.1, a sales forecast is the product of a process that can be described in seven steps. The next seven sections of the chapter outline each of these steps in the context of a new industrial product, although the process is also appropriate for new consumer products and services. At the core of this process is the measurement of potential buyer values for alternative new product concepts, the segmentation of markets on the basis of those values, and resulting estimates of market share that form the basis for the sales forecast.

1. DIAGNOSE AND CONCEPTUALIZE KEY MARKET RESPONSE FACTORS

To illustrate the seven steps in formulating a sales forecasting model, a case study involving a new product concept for the automated test equipment (ATE) market is used.[1] Firms that manufacture products with electronic com-

FIGURE 8.1   New product sales forecasting.

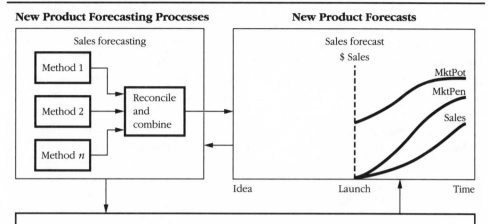

New Product Sales Forecasting Process

1. **Diagnose and Conceptualize Key Market Response Factors:** Based on an understanding of potential buyers and other stakeholders, identify and conceptually define the major factors (stakeholders and key variables) in the situation that hypothetically influence market response to a new product concept.

2. **Formulate Spreadsheet and Submodels of Market Response Factors:** Using selected market response factors, including those that are more and less controllable, formulate spreadsheet and other submodels to guide data collection.

3. **Collect Data on Key Variables:** Collect data for the various models to develop estimates of market response to possible new product concepts and marketing program efforts.

4. **Develop and Evaluate New Product Concepts:** Analyze the data collected, with emphasis on concept development, evaluation, and refinement through market segmentation processes.

5. **Estimate Market Share:** Develop a choice simulation or other approach that will lead to the forecasts of market share, and related estimates.

6. **Estimate Sales:** Link the contexts of the scenarios and models developed for estimating market opportunity by applying the market share estimates to market penetration to obtain forecasts of sales.

7. **Continually Update Models and Estimates:** Incorporate new data and experience into the new product sales forecasting process over the cycle of product development, and continually update and review sales forecasts in the context of changes in the market opportunity forecasts.

ponents may use ATE to execute a series of tests on their products to ensure that they function according to specifications. Prior to 1980, these tests were performed in-house; however, because of rapid changes in electronic technology, buying ATE became more economical than making it, and the market for ATE was born.

The organization that decided to pursue opportunities in this emerging market established a special team made up of individuals with background and expertise in ATE design and development. Their mission was to study the feasibility of developing a new product for the ATE market, as well as to make recommendations about the product's design and whether or not to commit to it financially. The team believed that with the advent of certain new technologies, a relatively *low-cost/high-performing* programmable ATE system could be developed that would be well-received by the market. The basic thrust of their idea was to offer dynamic functional testing, which involved simulating the total electrical environment of a unit according to real-world conditions. A major benefit of this testing approach was reduced programming costs (one-half to one-third of current software development time) and lower initial cost of the product relative to competitors. The team had several concerns about this idea, including the scope of the market opportunity, design features, competitive marketing program needs, and expected sales for the new product. To address these concerns, they formulated more specific research problems that can be framed as the following questions:

- What is the scope of the ATE market, and what factors and trends influence its size and growth?
- What is the response of potential buyers to possible new ATE product concepts, and can potential buyers be segmented according to these responses?
- What is the response of competitors to possible new ATE product concepts, given assumptions about a marketing program necessary to compete and gain a reasonable share?

To consider these questions, a brief review of the market opportunity forecasting process for ATE is outlined to define the situation. Then the major factors involved in market response to a new core product concept for the ATE market are considered.

Market Opportunity Forecasting for ATE

The impact of semiconductors on business and society has been enormous. Their use in a multitude of consumer and industrial electronic products and services has revolutionized the ways by which organizations satisfy the needs of potential buyers. As the need for these end-use products grew, so did the demand for products and services that facilitated the manufacture of products with electronic components. Consequently, the market opportunity for automated test equipment (ATE) was driven by numerous factors, including rapid technology change, price declines, favorable demographics, favorable economic conditions, increasing numbers of end-use applications, changing organizational buying patterns, growing concerns for production quality, segmentation opportunities, and uneven industry barriers. With these factors, and others identified in exploratory research, a market opportunity forecasting process was developed that used multiple methods and provided estimates of market potential and penetration over a 5-year planning horizon. The general process and methods for developing these estimates were similar to those described in Chapter 7, and are not repeated here.

Market Response Factors

Response to a new product concept should be obtained from the major stakeholders defining the relevant market. Major response factors that are the basis for stakeholder interest in the new product should be specified. Among external stakeholders of ATE, potential buying organizations were deemed most critical, followed by competitors and industry media. The responses of others—including the developing organization, sources of capital for the new product, and industry associations—largely depended on the expected responses of the three major stakeholders.

1. **Potential buyers.** On the basis of exploratory research, the following buyer behavior concepts were hypothesized to influence sales response.

   - Potential buyer needs and problems (in their language)
   - Importance of identified purchase criteria
   - Importance of product features
   - Importance of engineering design elements
   - Preferences and intentions to buy in response to alternative ATE new product concepts defined by selected features, including price
   - Perceptions and ratings of major competitors on purchase criteria
   - Current usage of ATE equipment
   - ATE purchasing plans (given the expected business environment)
   - Purchase involvement of different organizational members
   - Involvement of distributors, consultants, and others in the purchase
   - Usage of industry media (such as trade magazines)
   - Response to different types/amounts of advertising and promotions
   - Response to different levels of sales force effort
   - Response to different levels of customer service
   - Response to different modes of dealer support
   - Characteristics of potential buying organizations

2. **Competitors.** An assessment of major competitors along several factors is necessary to develop an understanding of their possible reactions. For example, entrenched competitors that feel threatened might react with dramatic price reductions, retaliatory new products, or product disparagement of any new competitor. In the case of ATE, three major competitors served about half the market, indicating that potential buyer *loyalty* might be a source of market friction that would slow adoption of any new product. The factors considered useful in profiling competitors in the market for ATE included the following.

   - Technological capabilities in ATE, especially technical experts
   - Manufacturing flexibility, cost structure, capacity
   - New product development cycle time, history of product launches, organizational propensity to innovate
   - Financial condition (resources to respond)

- Management resources
- Marketing capabilities
  - Product strengths and weaknesses
  - Brand reputation
  - Sales force, advertising, trade communications
  - Customer service
- Customer loyalty

3. **Industry media.** In industries with rapid change, the media can be influential in helping potential buyers sort through the possibilities and risks. As the market for ATE grew, so did reporting on new ATE products and industry trends, detailed product reviews and evaluations, and so on. Such publications could significantly influence potential buyer response to a new product. Although their primary focus tended to be on new products and technologies offered by competitors in the industry, the media also depended on advertising revenues.

Although these three sets of factors may appear specific to ATE, they are fairly generic and can be applied to any new product or service (see Figure 3.1). Further, they are inclusive of the major marketing program factors (product features, price, media usage, advertising, sales forces, distribution, and so on). Among these factors, however, particular attention is given to consumer preferences and intentions to buy alternative ATE products.

2. FORMULATE SPREADSHEET AND SUBMODELS OF MARKET RESPONSE FACTORS

As in the case of market opportunity forecasting, spreadsheet models that facilitate managerial involvement can be developed for sales forecasting. Typically, a new product sales forecasting model begins with estimates of market opportunity (market size, growth, penetration) as a base from which to estimate sales. Clearly, if the organization's sales are believed to be the entire market (for example, a patented product or process that is unique in fulfilling market needs and for which there are no viable competitors), the market opportunity and sales forecasting models will be the same. In such cases, market penetration estimates can be used to approximate the new product's sales, although more in-depth concept development, evaluation, and market testing are recommended to refine prediction of market response to the new product.

More often, however, organizations need to consider competition, whether in the same or different product classes. By definition, the market penetration estimate includes the volume of all major competitors for the various time periods. Consequently, the penetration estimate can be viewed as a ceiling for the new product, and can be adjusted accordingly by market factors that reflect expected response to the new concept. A sales forecasting model is thus similar in structure to the market opportunity modeling approach, but because of the presence of competitors and the lack of familiarity with the specific new brand and concept, the organization can achieve only a fraction or share of the market opportunity.

For illustration, market response factors selected from those identified in the preceding section are formulated into the following multiplicative model of sales for selected time periods (t):

$$Vol_t = (\mathbf{Adp}_t)(Buy_t)(Awr_t)(Sfc_t)(Use_t) \qquad [8.1]$$

where Vol_t = sales at time t (number of estimated units sold),

$\mathbf{Adp}_t$ = estimated number of adopters in the market at time t (from market opportunity forecast of market penetration),

Buy_t = proportion of adopters estimated to buy the new product concept, given awareness, information about product features, price, and competition (share of market estimated to buy new concept),

Awr_t = awareness (proportion of adopters aware of new brand at time t),

Sfc_t = sales force conversion (proportion of aware adopters converted to buyers through sales force effort), and

Use_t = average number of units per purchase per buyer during time period t (reflects usage rates).

As noted above, the $\mathbf{Adp}_t$ variable represents the number of potential buyers, or adopters, available for the new ATE product during a specified time period. To obtain an estimate of sales, a percentage is applied to $\mathbf{Adp}$ that represents the share of potential buyers that would purchase the new product—the Buy variable in equation [8.1]. This value can be estimated directly through judgment, but obtaining market response estimates for it is highly recommended. Because this is a critical factor in the model, a submodel can be helpful in its determination, as well as the use of multiple methods for estimation purposes.

Generally, a submodel for the Buy variable would indicate that the proportion of organizations buying the new product depends on the new product's features, price, attractiveness relative to competitors, possible competitive reactions, and other relevant factors (or assumptions about them). From a survey of potential buyers, these factors can be measured and used to develop an estimate or range of estimates. Two key assumptions in this approach are that potential buyers interviewed in the survey have 100 percent awareness and that they would buy if aware of the new product. These assumptions are, of course, unrealistic for a new product and a new firm in an industry. Consequently, submodels estimating awareness and sales force effectiveness are important to provide a more realistic estimate of the number of potential buyers for the new product. Response submodels for the key variables in equation [8.1] may take the following general forms.

$Buy = f$ (product features, price, competition, other factors)

$Awr = f$ (advertising, sales force size, publicity, other factors)

$Avl = f$ (number of distributors, size of distributors, other factors)

$Sfc = f$ (compensation plan, effectiveness of sales force, other factors)

This process is focused primarily on the *Buy* submodel here, though consideration is given to other submodels in step 6.

The sales forecasting model presented in equation [8.1] can provide estimates of the number of potential buying organizations, sales volume, and sales revenue. Typically, the most basic model includes the number of potential buying organizations. By including the multiplicative variable of average number of units bought per purchase (*Use*) in the model, unit sales volume (*Vol*) can be obtained. The usage variable can be estimated from a market survey or industry averages. By including the average price per unit in the model as a multiplicative variable, dollar sales volume can be estimated. The price decision is made by the organization, but the price selected should be reflected in the estimation of the submodel for the *Buy* variable.

The sales forecasting model and submodels suggested in equation [8.1] are suitable for durable or less frequently purchased consumer and industrial products and services. For products whose success depends on *repeat* purchases, additional variables are needed for a more realistic depiction of the buying process and formation of sales. Such products and services often have short purchase cycles (bought weekly, biweekly, or monthly), relatively low dollar value per purchase, and low risk (if the product is not liked, little time or money was invested). In these cases, *trial* of the product is an important variable, followed by repeat purchasing if the product is liked. Thus, the proportion of potential buyers forecast to ultimately buy the product on a regular basis depends on the proportion trying the new product and the proportion repeat buying once they have tried.

3. COLLECT DATA ON KEY VARIABLES

Data for numerous spreadsheet models and submodels may be needed to generate estimates of market response to possible product concepts and marketing program efforts. The data will come from a variety of sources, including judgment, published studies, accessible data bases, product analogies, and market research. For most new products, one or more market research studies may be necessary to ascertain product design and to provide measures on the variables hypothesized to be important in the forecasting models.

The market research study in the ATE situation was conducted in two phases. The first was an exploratory phase that carefully diagnosed the managerial and research problems under study—for example, the language of potential buyers, deeper buyer needs and problems not usually identifiable in surveys, and organizational buying processes that may affect adoption of the new product. Exploratory in-depth interviews with key market stakeholders were the central mode of data collection. Though not used in this study, focus group interviews are also productive for early phases of market research.

Generally, first-phase study findings help define the next phase of research. Given the nature of the problems explored in the market for ATE, the decision was made to design a survey to sample 30 *leading-edge* potential buying organizations in three major industries (avionics, communications, and computers). Lengthy interviews would be conducted with each of these organizations on the major variables and measures indentified as important in the purchase process for ATE equipment. In particular, pinpointing the location of major buying influences in the organization was deemed essential, because industry experts revealed that those influences were believed to be shifting.

The questionnaire design followed the general structure of first screening respondents (to identify influencers), then obtaining data on current usage of ATE, ascertaining needs and problems with ATE, measuring perceptions of major competitors on selected ATE purchase criteria, obtaining preferences for ATE on 14 product features and 18 engineering design elements, and finally, determining media usage habits and demographic characteristics of the respondent and the organization. A special feature of the study was the inclusion of a conjoint analysis procedure to help estimate market response to alternative new product concepts.

4. DEVELOP AND EVALUATE NEW PRODUCT CONCEPTS

Developing a core product concept (from an idea to a new product marketing program) involves a combination of creativity, design, and stakeholder analysis. To accomplish this step, the new product team must interact with major stakeholders in an ongoing evolutionary process of concept refinement. The goal is to build a concept that has consistent meaning and integrity among multiple stakeholders.[2] The needs of and benefits sought by potential buyers must be translated into descriptive product features—which in turn must be translated into engineering elements and, ultimately, operational components for assembly.

The major tools and procedures used to develop and evaluate new product concepts are *concept descriptions, intention-to-buy measures, market structure and positioning, preference analysis,* and *segmentation.* Each is illustrated for the new ATE product.

Developing Concept Descriptions

A new product idea that surfaces from initial screening may be worked into a *core product concept*, as described in Chapter 5. This concept is typically a brief description of the major product benefits and the market needs they satisfy. Its initial use is as a communication vehicle to focus organization efforts on the market-driven strategic role of the new product—the link with market needs ensures its *market-driven* nature. It is also the focal point for maintaining the integrity of the new product concept as it wends its way among various organizational functions throughout its development. In the ATE case study, the initial working core concept was simply stated as providing a *low-cost/high-performance programmable ATE product* to potential buying organizations. The concept was expected to vary somewhat; however, its price/performance relationship was seen as its key advantage.

In preparation for research on market response, a more embellished version of the core concept is needed to ensure that the real benefits of the new product can be communicated to potential buyers. Typically, this version provides greater detail than the core concept, including written description, photographs, artistic renderings, computer-animated images, prototypes, or other visually enhanced descriptions. Couching the concept in the context of enhanced new product scenarios is also beneficial in creating a more realistic purchase setting for the measurement of potential purchase. A relatively straightforward written concept was used for the "new ATE" product (or NATE for short). A version of it is presented in Figure 8.2.[3]

Estimating Purchase with Intention-To-Buy Measures

Perhaps the most direct way to obtain estimates of sales response is to use traditional concept-testing procedures. They are usually included in a survey designed to measure the intention to buy one or more (limited to a few) carefully defined concepts. For example, respondents could be shown the concept description in Figure 8.2 and asked to indicate on a rating scale how likely they would be to buy the new product, given current products on the market and assuming it would be available for purchase in one year.

Typically, 5-point rating scales are among the most popular, but scales with 4 to 11 points are often used. The intention-to-buy question can also be formed as a 100- or 101-point (0–100) probability scale, in which the respondent is asked to specify probability of purchase. The probability scale is sometimes used in combination with an intention-to-buy scale (such as the 5-point scale) to obtain more refined estimates.

The framing of each intention-to-buy question is also important to qualify its basic assumptions. The time horizon in the question (intention to buy in next six months, next year, and so on) and the respondent's level of awareness, interest, or preference for the product, as well as its availability, are all factors

FIGURE 8.2   Illustrative concept description.

NATE (New Automated Test Equipment)

NATE is a family of test equipment, configurable for a variety of product testing requirements, including components (especially complex gate arrays), complex boards, and entire systems. NATE will be available both as a production, *quality control* test instrument and as a field service test instrument. Although NATE will be primarily configured as a digital tester, it will have the ability to test analog/digital boards and devices such as analog-to-digital and digital-to-analog converters.

NATE's most unique characteristic will be dynamic functional testing—an ability to simulate the total actual electrical environment that the unit under test would experience in a real world situation. Operating at the speed of the unit under test, NATE will test against the full operating specifications provided by the unit's manufacturer. Because of this approach to testing, NATE is capable of reducing the software programming time by one-half to one-third of the current development time required for software preparation.

NATE is portable (about three feet square) and will consist of a CRT, a special purpose keyboard, a powerful 16-bit microprocessor, a 10-megabyte hard disk and up to 80 digital I/O channels, with a memory depth of 256k bits per channel. A slave chassis may be added containing as many as 160 channels.

The device is capable of testing TTL, CMOS, and ECL devices and boards equipped with these devices. Test generation will be provided for the most part by vendor-supplied utilities based on an algorithmic approach to generating test patterns. Test data can be input in any form, from either an RS-232 or an IEEE-488 interface. User-generated utilities may also be developed using PASCAL, FORTRAN, C, and BASIC.

Depending on its configuration, NATE will range in approximate cost from $250,000 for a 40-channel non-parametric functional tester for field servicing to $750,000 for an 80-channel parametric function product tester.

---

that must either be included in the scenario background for the question or accounted for in some other way. For example, if 100 percent awareness is assumed in the intention-to-buy measure, including awareness as a separate variable in the sales forecast model as in equation [8.1] is recommended.

Once intention-to-buy data are obtained from survey results, they can be used to develop an *intent translation* model of the *Buy* variable in equation [8.1]:[4]

$$Buy = \sum_{i=1}^{k}(Twt_i)(Itb_i) \tag{8.2}$$

where Twt_i = translation weight applied to $i = 1$ to k response categories and

Itb_i = proportion of sample indicating an intention to buy in $i = 1$ to k response categories.

To illustrate this model, assume the following values for *Twt* were judgmentally determined and those for *Itb* were obtained by using a 5-point intention-to-buy measure from the survey sample:

	Twt (%)	Itb (%)	(Twt) (Itb)
Definitely will buy NATE	90	10	9%
Probably will buy NATE	40	20	8%
Might or might not buy NATE	10	20	2%
Probably would not buy NATE	-0-	15	-
Definitely would not buy NATE	-0-	35	-
			19%

Buy = **19%**

Thus, one could estimate that 19 percent of the sample will buy the new product concept. If the sample is representative of the population, or one is willing to make that assumption, the value of 19 percent can be used in equation [8.1] as one way to estimate the proportion of potential adopters who would buy the new concept.

The intent translation model has several benefits. As discussed in Chapter 3, intentions tend to correlate with actual behavior. Further, the intent translation approach is relatively easy to implement, requiring survey data and judgment to estimate the two major variables in the model. The model can also be useful in developing response to marketing variables. For example, the concept can be changed and intention-to-buy measures obtained for each concept. Also, by presenting the concept with different prices to matched samples of potential buyers, a rough estimate of a demand curve can be obtained—that is, the proportion willing to buy at different price levels.

Drawbacks to the model include the implicit assumptions made in its use. In particular, the role of competition for new products is often swept aside to obtain measures of the new concept. Making the competitive situation explicit in the scenario for the concept, or in the actual data collection process, enhances the quality of the estimates. Another concern with the model is the reliance on judgment to establish values for the translation weights (*Twt*). A variety of weights have been used in practice and their selection can be rather arbitrary. For example, in a study comparing estimates from six intention-to-buy weighting schemes with actual purchases for 10 new products (half durable and half nondurable) no particular rating scheme surpassed all others in accuracy.[5] The study revealed that until further research provides improved guidelines, care should be taken in selecting intent translation weights.[6]

Other problems in using intention-to-buy measures include the possibility that they may be subject to the many factors that characterize human behavior—recall the numerous factors used to define purchase behavior in Figure 3.1.—and may also produce bias in respondents. Factors in the perceptions, memories, predispositions, and purchase situations of potential buyers may confound their response to questions about purchase intentions, and even influence their behavior. Consider some of the issues:[7]

- Little is known about how consumers respond to different time dimensions imposed on their purchase intention—will consumers who say they will buy in the next month, the next six months, or the next year actually do so?

- Surprisingly, research supports the proposition that simply measuring intention to buy can change the behavior of respondents toward a particular new product concept. Simply asking the question of respondents may help congeal their attitudes for or against a new product concept.

- Further, individual differences in response to intention-to-buy questions may suggest segmenting the sample to improve forecast accuracy. As noted in Chapter 6, forecasts based on decompositional principles tend to be more accurate than those based on aggregate estimates.

Despite the concerns about using intention-to-buy measures to forecast new product sales, in general they are in widespread use because of their directness in assessing how a potential buyer might respond to a new product. Clearly, care should be taken in using such measures, being sure to specify to the respondent (and to people who use the results) the implicit assumptions. Until additional research provides practical guidelines for their use, accumulated experience and performance tracking of various intention-to-buy modeling approaches and weighting schemes for specific firms and marketing situations may lead to more valid measures.

Market Structure and Positioning

The process of interactively developing a new product concept that is *positioned* to meet potential buyer needs in competitive markets often requires an explicit, even pictorial, understanding of market structure. The various methods and procedures for measuring market structure are beyond the scope of this book and should be pursued elsewhere.[8] However, some very general ideas are briefly reviewed here to highlight the role of understanding market structure in new product development and forecasting.

In many new product situations, the ongoing competitive structure of a market may have an enormous impact on potential buyer reactions to a new concept. Imagine considering a new soft drink concept for a market occupied by such well-known brands as Coca-Cola, Pepsi Cola, and Seven-Up. Understanding how potential buyers perceive such well-entrenched brand names would be of considerable importance in developing and evaluating a new product for this market. Further, information about which brands buyers prefer and for what reasons would help to ascertain the difficulty of positioning a new concept (or of finding a position for a new concept). The basic approach to developing an understanding of market structure for purposes of concept development and evaluation includes the following major steps:

- **Determine key product concept features.** Define the market according to the product features (both physical and psychological) that are linked to the needs of and benefits sought by potential buyers. In-depth exploratory studies are often conducted to discover these features (as discussed in the ATE case).

- **Obtain buyer perceptions of current brands.** From a market survey, obtain potential buyers' perceptions of current brands along key features defining the market. Perceptions can be obtained through rating scales, similarities judgments (between pairs of brands), and other data collection procedures.

- **Develop a perceptual map of the current market on product features.** From analyses of the perceptual data, various *perceptual maps* can be estimated to depict each current brand's positioning in a product *feature space*. These perceptual maps can be so-called *snake plots* that compare the relative positions of the brands on each feature, or two-dimensional maps of the multiple features that show each brand's relative position. The latter approach uses *multidimensional scaling* procedures that conveniently summarize the information in the features into two dimensions for interpretation. Examples of perceptual maps for the ATE market are illustrated in Figure 8.3. The snake plot in Panel A shows competitor 1 (C1) scoring higher in most ratings than C2 and C3. Competitor 3's dominant strength appears to be speed, and it has poor ratings on most other features. Panel B, which represents an analytical summary of the 10 features through *multidimensional scaling*, also shows C1's strong market positioning on a "reliability" dimension and C3's strong position on a "performance" dimension (speed). Generally, the closer the points locating the positionings, the more similar the brands are perceived in the market.

- **Use market structure analysis to position new concept.** It should be evident from Panel B in Figure 8.3 that the upper right quadrant of the map might represent a market opportunity for a new product. If a preliminary new product concept had been developed, it could have been included with the evaluation of existing brands that potential buyers rated during the marketing research study. Plotting the perception of the new brand relative to competitors would provide useful information to determine its competitive position. However, without measures of preference suggesting what potential buyers might want in a new product, it would be difficult to determine whether or not the position is a desirable one and, if it is not, to diagnose what the position should be. For example, the new concept may rate highly, but if it is positioned very close to a strong competitor on all important features, the potential buyer may have little reason to switch to the new concept. Consequently, the use of preference measures to identify features sought by consumers but not yet satisfied by established competitors must augment the perceptual map data.

As noted, market structure analyses can help to identify and/or verify market opportunities. The identification of a current market structure that includes preferences helps to determine whether or not there are positions in the feature space where potential buyers have exhibited preferences, but for which

FIGURE 8.3   Approaches to evaluate market structure and positioning.

**Panel A: Snake plot of major ATE competitors on 10
features, ranked from most to least important**

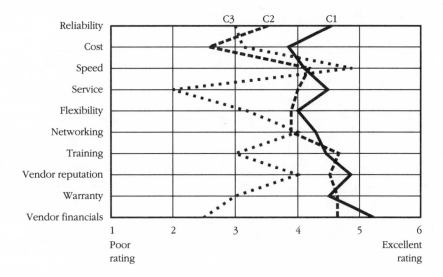

**Panel B: Perceptual map of three ATE competitors in
two-dimensional product features space**

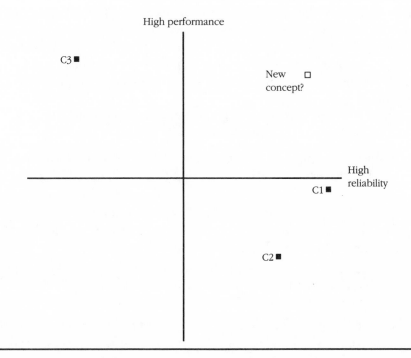

there are no viable competitors. In effect, a *gap* in the market is identified that can indicate a potential market opportunity and prompt the development of a concept to fill the vacant market position.

Preference Analysis

Given a market structure and the desire to develop a position for a new concept that will meet with market success, modeling and forecasting approaches based on preferences are especially important. Typically, these approaches link perceptions of a product (through its features) to potential buyer predispositions (such as preferences and intentions). Predispositions are assumed to reflect the needs of potential buyers.[9] Preference-based approaches include preference regression, expectancy value models, multiattribute value analysis, logit models, and conjoint analysis.[10] For example, a logit model analysis of preference data can help estimate the probability of purchase of a new product concept relative to competitors—a useful way to estimate the *Buy* variable in equation [8.1]. The use of conjoint analysis in the ATE case study illustrates the method's value in concept development and evaluation, and as a way to estimate the *Buy* variable.

Conjoint Analysis

Conjoint analysis originated in the field of psychometrics, or the quantitative analysis of human judgment.[11] Since its introduction to marketing research, its use has grown rapidly and it has become one of the most popular procedures for measuring buyer preferences across a variety of products and industries.[12] The goal of conjoint analysis is to use a potential buyer's evaluations of alternative products to discover the structure of his or her underlying needs and values. From this structure, estimates can be developed about how the buyer might respond to different products designed to address those needs.

The procedure consists of the following steps:

- Product concepts are systematically designed around features (such as price) with various levels (for example, $1, $2, $3) that are believed to make a difference in buyer decisions, given a set of competitors.

- A potential buyer is asked to provide overall evaluations of alternative products; these evaluations can be based on rank orders, rated preferences, intention to buy, or other predispositional measures.

- The evaluations are then mathematically *decomposed* into *utility* scales (based on product features and their levels), which can also be recombined to produce the original evaluations.

- The utility values, which reflect a buyer's underlying needs, can be used to determine the relative importance of a product feature as well as buyer sensitivity to different levels of the feature.

As a simplified example, suppose the two features of a new two-way video telephone that are most important to potential buyers are its price and the clarity of its picture (defined by screen resolution). Further, assume that price could be defined by three different levels ($500, $1,000, and $1,500) and clarity could be defined by three different levels (high, medium, low). Taken together, these two features could define nine different television concepts (concepts A–I) as depicted in the matrix below.

Video-telephone price	Clarity of picture screen		
	High clarity (comparable to a movie screen)	Medium clarity (comparable to current color TV)	Low clarity (comparable to handheld LCD TV)
$500	A	D	G
$1,000	B	E	H
$1,500	C	F	I

How would a potential buyer respond to the task of rank ordering the nine possible video-telephone concepts according to preference or intention to buy? One might expect the most preferred to be the video-telephone with the lowest price and highest clarity (A) and the least preferred to be the one with the highest price and lowest clarity (I). But for potential buyers to complete their evaluation task, they must make *tradeoffs* between the different video-telephone concepts—and in so doing reveal their underlying needs and values. For example, someone whose second choice is concept D (low price and medium clarity) would be expressing a different underlying need structure than someone whose second choice is concept B (medium price and high clarity). The latter indicates a willingness to trade off an additional $500 to maintain a high-clarity screen. Would that potential buyer pay yet another $500 to maintain the high clarity on the next choice?

Once a potential buyer's evaluations are obtained, they can be quantified and further analyzed. To illustrate this process, suppose the rank-order preferences of a potential buyer for various two-way video-telephones are those shown at the top of Figure 8.4. For ease of interpretation, these values are recoded in the second table of Figure 8.4 so that the higher the score, the more the concept is preferred. By computing the simple average of these scores at the row and column margins, the *utility* of each feature's level is obtained. Notice that for this potential buyer, the utility of price declines from 6.3 to 5.3 as price rises from $500 to $1,000. The utility of price drops even further, from 5.3 to 3.3, as the price increases to $1,500. Similarly, as clarity declines from high to medium, its utility drops from 7.3 to 5.7, and then steeply to 2.0 when clarity is low.

FIGURE 8.4   Illustrative conjoint analysis computations.

1. Assume an individual records rank order preferences as follows, where "1" is most preferred:

Video-telephone price	Clarity of picture screen					
	High clarity (comparable to the movie screen)		Medium clarity (comparable to current color TV)		Low clarity (Comparable to handheld LCD TV)	
$500	A	1	D	3	G	7
$1,000	B	2	E	4	H	8
$1,500	C	5	F	6	I	9

2. The preferences are recoded for easier interpretation so that the higher the average utility score, the more the concept is preferred. Note that the rather simplistic averaging process, done for illustrative purposes, violates assumptions about the types of analyses that can be performed on rank-order data. Various conjoint analysis algorithms include the transformations necessary to accommodate assumptions about the data in order to estimate utilities.

Video-telephone price	Clarity of picture screen						Average utility
	High clarity		Medium clarity		Low clarity		
$500	A	9	D	7	G	3	6.3
$1,000	B	8	E	6	H	2	5.3
$1,500	C	5	F	4	I	1	3.3
Average utility	7.3		5.7		2.0		

3. By using the additive utility model, total utility for each video-telephone concept can be estimated:

Concept	Features	Total utility computation	Rank
Concept A:	High clarity/$500	U(A) = 7.3 + 6.3 = 13.6	(1)
Concept B:	High clarity/$1,000	U(B) = 7.3 + 5.3 = 12.6	(2)
Concept C:	High clarity/$1,500	U(C) = 7.3 + 3.3 = 10.6	(5)
Concept D:	Medium clarity/$500	U(D) = 5.7 + 6.3 = 12.0	(3)
Concept E:	Medium clarity/$1,000	U(E) = 5.7 + 5.3 = 11.0	(4)
Concept F:	Medium clarity/$1,500	U(F) = 5.7 + 3.3 = 9.0	(6)
Concept G:	Low clarity/$500	U(G) = 2.0 + 6.3 = 8.3	(7)
Concept H:	Low clarity/$1,000	U(H) = 2.0 + 5.3 = 7.3	(8)
Concept I:	Low clarity/$1,500	U(I) = 2.0 + 3.3 = 5.3	(9)

4. To compute relative importance of each attribute of the product or object, compute the range of highest to lowest utility for each, then divide each by the sum:

Feature	Range	Relative Importance
Clarity	7.3 − 2.0 = 5.3	5.3 / 8.3 = 64%
Price	6.0 − 3.3 = 3.0	3.0 / 8.3 = 36%
Total utility range =	5.3 + 3.0 = 8.3	

The essence of conjoint analysis is found in these utilities. They reveal potential buyer responses and sensitivity to important product design features, as well as price or other aspects of the purchase process that are deemed relevant to include. As shown in the ATE case, these utilities can be plotted to show the *response functions* more graphically. The basic additive utility model behind the estimation procedure is defined as:

$$U(X) = U_1(X_1) + U_2(X_2) + \cdots + U_n(X_n) \qquad [8.3]$$

where $U(X)$ is the total utility for product concept X. It is composed of the sum of the part-worth utilities of the features selected to define each concept. Thus, the value for the estimated parameter U_1 represents the part-worth utility associated with feature (X_1), and so on for n product features. This model assumes that potential buyers evaluate products and services such that the utility of a product concept is equal to the sum of its parts. Further, it assumes that potential buyers make the evaluations in a compensatory manner; that is, high utilities on some features can compensate for low utilities on others. Thus, two concepts can be identical in total utility, but very different in terms of their composition.[13]

The bottom half of Figure 8.4 illustrates the computation of the total utilities for each of the nine concepts and shows the additive and compensatory nature of the model. Note that concepts C and E have similar total utilities (10.6 and 11.0, respectively), but are very different video-telephones. Concept C is a $1,500 phone with high screen clarity, whereas concept E is $1,000 phone with medium screen clarity. Note also in Figure 8.4 that the rank order (highest to lowest) of the total utility scores for the nine concepts is identical to the respondents' original rank orders. The extent to which a conjoint analysis algorithm provides estimates of the decomposed part-worth utilities that lead to a recovery of the original overall judgments is an important criterion for evaluating the integrity of a model.

The bottom part of Figure 8.4 shows how the relative importance of each product feature can be computed from the utilities. Essentially, the range of utility for each is computed and divided by the sum of the ranges for all features. Thus, for this particular potential buyer, clarity (64 percent) is relatively more important than price (36 percent). The valuable aspect of these importance measures is that they are derived from tradeoffs, not from direct importance ratings of each feature. That is, the potential buyer could have been asked to rate price on a 10-point importance scale, then rate clarity on a 10-point importance scale. However, in many cases, respondents may rate both items very high, and hence no insight can be gained about the relative tradeoff between them.

Multiple-Feature Product Concepts

When new product concepts have more than two or three features that make a difference in the market, conjoint analysis procedures can be cumbersome. In the case of ATE, seven product features were identified that were believed to make a difference in potential buyers' choices and in competitive reactions. These seven features and the three levels of each chosen to be studied are shown as step 1 in Figure 8.5. Taken together, these seven features, each at three levels, define some 2,187 possible product concepts! Without even considering the desirability of including more features or levels, one can see that evaluating so many concepts would be an onerous task for any potential buyer.

Fortunately, a major contribution to the development and practical use of conjoint analysis with numerous product features is the use of experimental design procedures.[14] For example, to reduce the number of combinations tested, yet still measure the main effects, so-called *fractional factorial* experimental designs can be used to estimate the part-worth utilities of the 2,187 possible ATE concepts from a subset of 18.[15]

The 18 ATE concepts would first be prepared as stimuli that would be shown to respondents in the survey. These stimuli can be designed as real products, models or mockups, artistic renderings, or concept descriptions. As shown in step 2 of Figure 8.5, in this case they were developed as concept descriptions on cards. Each respondent in the market survey was asked to rank order a randomized deck of 18 cards, and answer other questions in the personal interviews (step 3 in Figure 8.5).[16] By using available conjoint analysis software, the utilities for each potential buyer can be estimated from the rank-order data. Once the quality of each respondent's model is evaluated, the utilities can be used to formulate alternative product concepts, refine concepts by categorizing the sample of potential buyers into segments, and develop choice simulations to estimate market share and sales.

Concept Development

In step 4 of Figure 8.5, a typical respondent's utilities are listed. With individual-level conjoint utilities from potential buyers, one can identify the product concept with the highest total utility, and presumably the one with the greatest likelihood of being purchased (holding all other factors constant). For example, using the data from the illustrative respondent in step 4 of Figure 8.5 and an additive utility model shows the product design with the highest total utility for this respondent to be an ATE that:

- Sells for $250,000,
- Comes in one large box (or equipment housing),
- Has 128 pins,
- Has a pin memory depth of 128k,
- Has a clock rate of 100 MHz,
- Has a timing resolution of 10 ns, and
- Has a voltage set-on accuracy of 1 mV.

This design is determined by selecting the level with the highest utility scores for each feature. These values are in bold type in Figure 8.5.

FIGURE 8.5   Using conjoint analysis for concept development and evaluation.

1. Determine new product concept features and levels:

ATE features	Level 1	Level 2	Level 3
Cost	**$250,000**	$500,000	$750,000
Size	1 box 3'× 5'× 5'	2 boxes 3'× 5'× 5'	**1 box 6'× 20'× 6'**
Pin number	64	**128**	512
Pin memory depth	**128k**	32k	8k
Clock rate	5 megahertz	20 megahertz	**100 megahertz**
Timing resolution	1 nanosecond	**10 nanoseconds**	100 picoseconds
Voltage set on accuracy	**1 millivolt**	10 millivolts	100 millivolts

Note: Cells with bold text define Product Design C stimulus card below.

2. Construct stimuli for alternative product designs:

3. Conduct market research study:

Product Design C

A machine that costs $250,000

Comes in one large box
with dimensions of 6'× 20'× 6'
And has the following specifications:

- Pin number: 128
- Pin memory depth: 128k
- Clock rate: 100 megahertz
- Timing resolution: 10 nanoseconds
- Voltage set on accuracy: 1 millivolt

Within a market research data collection procedure, obtain potential buyer and other stakeholder preferences for alternative new product concepts in the context of purchase scenarios. Select one or more preference measures (rank order, intention-to-buy, or other rating scale) and other variables for analysis.

4. Analyze data with conjoint analysis preference model at individual level to obtain utilities:

5. Segmentation of individual preferences (conjoint utilities) with cluster analysis:

ATE features	Level 1	Level 2	Level 3
Cost	**13.5**	-4.5	-9.0
Size	4.9	-12.1	**7.2**
Pin number	-4.9	**11.2**	-6.3
Pin memory depth	**3.1**	.9	-4.0
Clock rate	-12.1	-4.9	**17.0**
Timing resolution	.5	**4.9**	-5.4
Voltage set on accuracy	**53.4**	-6.7	-46.7

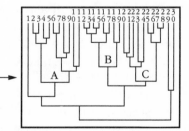

Note: Cells with bold text show highest utility level for each product feature.

By recalling the compensatory assumption about potential buyer choice processes, alternative concepts can be formed. For example, because the respondent in step 4 of Figure 8.5 exhibits such high sensitivity to the voltage set-on accuracy feature, changing pin memory depth or timing resolution in the design would have relatively little effect on total utility. If changing these features would reduce development time or costs, then the research would have produced useful results. Of course, the potential buyer's minimum specifications still must be met for these features.

Possibly the concept with the highest utility cannot be developed within the potential buyer's budget or willingness to pay. In such cases, the new product team can formulate alternative concepts that meet resource constraints and come as close as possible to maximizing the consumer's utility. Figure 8.5 shows the utilities of only a single respondent. Analyzing the utilities of the sample of respondents is necessary to provide further insights for refinement of the new product concept.

Using Segmentation to Refine New Product Concepts

As discussed previously, the process of market segmentation is designed to identify groups of potential buyers who are homogeneous in their response within groups and heterogeneous between groups. Segmenting on the basis of potential buyer response to alternative concepts that include features reflecting buyers' underlying needs is a promising approach to developing new products.[17]

A variety of procedures and tools can be used for segmenting markets, but a practical approach is to select a *basis* (one or more variables) for categorizing potential buyers, then use a cluster analysis of these variables to identify the possible groups, and finally qualify and describe the groups. In the ATE case, the conjoint utilities were selected as a basis for segmentation and submitted to a cluster analysis. A typical hierarchical clustering solution for the sample of 30 potential buyers is illustrated as a tree diagram in step 5 of Figure 8.5. The vertical scale in this diagram represents a *distance* measure of how similar or dissimilar respondents are in their utilities.

To interpret cluster analysis, imagine that all 30 respondents are separate segments. The clustering routine then searches for respondents whose utilities are most similar and joins them together. For example, in step 5 of Figure 8.5, respondents 12 and 13 are very similar in their responses to the product concepts because they are joined together early in the tree diagram with a low distance measure. However, the utilities of respondent 1 are very different from those of the rest of the sample; joining with others does not occur until the distance measure is very high. This joining process continues in hierarchical fashion until all respondents are joined together.

Clearly, any number of segments can be selected. To reduce the arbitrary nature of the process, some of the smaller, more tightly joined groupings of respondents can be described with the segmentation variables (utilities) and the numerous descriptor variables included in the survey (such as usage, perceptions, and demographics). Although programs and analytical approaches are available to facilitate this process, especially for very large sample surveys, judgment plays an important role. In the ATE case, three clusters (labeled A, B, and C) were identified that met criteria of being similar in response within group and dissimilar between groups. Respondents who do not fit well into any of the segments should be treated as a separate group. Only the three major segments are analyzed here.

In Figure 8.6, the utilities for the total sample and for each of the three segments are displayed in the form of plots for the three most important product features. The steeper the plot, the more important the feature; the flatter the plot, the less important the feature. As discussed previously, the average *relative importances* of the features for the total sample and each segment can also be computed. In the ATE case, the pin number feature was most important (34 percent), followed by cost (18 percent), clock rate (13 percent), housing size (10 percent), pin memory depth (9 percent), timing resolution (9 percent), and voltage set on accuracy (7 percent). Examination of the plotted utilities reveals that all segments are sensitive to the pin number feature. The sample clearly finds value in a 512k pin number size.

The segments differ in terms of their response to cost and pin number. Segment A is very cost sensitive relative to the others, and also shows sensitivity to the pin number feature. Segment B is sensitive only to the pin number feature. Segment C is sensitive to the clock rate feature (in addition to pin number).

The segmentation results proved valuable to the new product team. Recall that the initial product concept was to develop a single product for the market with an emphasis on the cost feature. However, cost was of major concern to only one segment constituting about a third of the market. At this point, the new product team revised the original product concept into at least two, possibly three, different products to meet the needs of each segment. The utilities for each segment could be used to estimate response for different product concepts that the team deemed feasible to develop.

Appraising Concept Development and Evaluation via Conjoint Analysis

Using conjoint analysis to develop and evaluate new product concepts has obvious practical benefits, as illustrated in the ATE example and also by the method's widespread application in industry. However, it is not without limitations. Like any measurement approach, it should be carefully applied with respect to its assumptions and estimation procedures.[18]

Experience with the assumed compensatory additive part-worth model of preference (as used in the ATE case study) has been good. Still, the selection of a particular model should be based on the nature of the functional relationship between preference and the feature being measured. For example, if a monotonic linear relationship is assumed (as price declines, preference increases linearly), a vector model may be more appropriate than a part-worth model.

**FIGURE 8.6   Conjoint utilities and importances for selected ATE features:
total sample and by segment.**

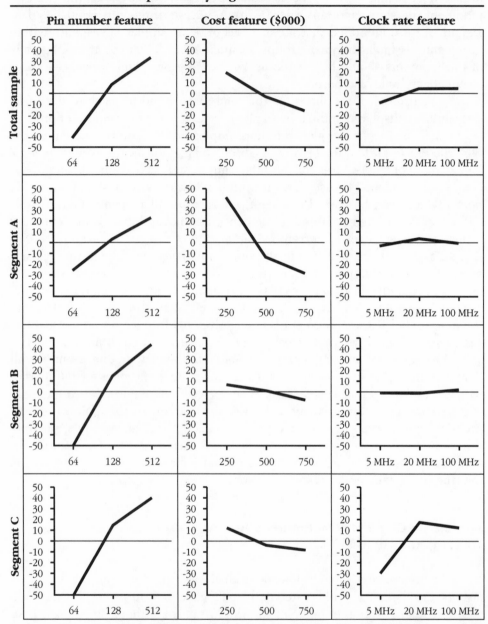

Note: The vertical scale for each graph represents the measure of utility and the horizontal scale measures the level of each product feature. The utility function plotted in each graph associates utility values with the different feature levels. As illustrated by the various plots, the shape of the function can be positive, negative, flat, or peaked in some way. The steeper the slope, the greater the relative importance of a feature. Thus, for the total sample, potential buyers find greater utility with more pin numbers, and that feature is considerably more important than the clock rate or cost.

The full-profile method of data collection, illustrated in the ATE case study, tends to be most popular because it gives respondents a realistic choice task. Obtaining preferences for alternative whole-product concepts defined by features that make a difference can be more realistic than obtaining preferences from lists of pairs of features. However, if a full-profile approach is used, research supports the use of warmup exercises for respondents to familiarize them with data collection tasks that are somewhat different from traditional question-and-answer tasks.[19]

A limitation of the full-profile approach is that concept design may be limited to six or seven features. Additional features and levels increase the number of alternative concepts needed to estimate utilities and may be burdensome for respondents, thereby inducing error. For larger problems, *self-explicated* utilities, *hybrid* conjoint analysis, and *adaptive* conjoint analysis (ACA) are alternative data collection approaches that can reduce respondent information overload.[20]

The stimulus set in conjoint analysis requires care in the selection of specific product features and levels. Omitting important features (and levels) and including redundant features (and levels) can introduce error into the estimation process. This point is especially important when some product features that may be linked to psychological benefits depend on several more tangible engineering elements. Features should be selected that are relatively independent (uncorrelated), but not so independent as to diminish the concept's believablity to the respondent. Care should also be taken in selecting the number and variation of feature levels. For example, if the number of intermediate levels is increased in one feature but held fixed in the others, the importance ratings for that feature will be higher than they would be if fewer levels were used.[21] The use of prior research and judgment is recommended to guide decisions on features and levels.

The product concepts were presented on cards in the ATE case study, but using other media is encouraged. A guiding principle in the presentation of concepts is to make them as realistic as possible within the resource constraints of the development process. An ideal situation would be to use an actual product or service portrayed in the context of an enhanced scenario that describes, as closely as possible, the buying environment (see the discussion of scenarios in Chapter 7).

Conjoint analysis estimation methods depend on the measurement scale of the dependent variable (usually preference or intention to buy). Nonmetric estimation methods (such as MONANOVA) are most appropriate for rank-order scales and metric estimation is best for interval scales (such as ratings), although research has shown that metric methods (regression) used with rank-order data provide results almost equivalent to those of nonmetric methods.[22] The availability of conjoint analysis software with multiple methods suggests that it may be good practice to use them and compare results.[23]

There are other issues related to the reliability and validity of measures obtained from conjoint analysis, but the growing use of the procedure suggests its value in new product development situations. Clearly, additional research on its predictive validity under a variety of circumstances would be helpful. However, using the procedure in a systematic fashion, with a learning orientation, can provide the experience needed to assess its value. For example, tracking the accuracy of market share forecasts from conjoint analysis against actual market response after product launch provides information about the procedure's value.

5. ESTIMATE MARKET SHARE

The concept of market share explicitly introduces competition into new product sales forecasting. Important considerations for estimating market share for a new product include how much sales the product *draws* from competitors and how much it *cannibalizes* from an organization's existing products. In this section, estimating share from potential buyers' preferences through a conjoint analysis *choice simulator* and probabalistic choice procedures is considered. Estimates of market share based on "behavioral" responses from potential buyers in test market settings are considered in Chapter 10.

In its simplest form, a choice simulator hypothesizes that when potential buyers are offered a set of products, they will *choose* one that maximizes their utilities (or adheres to some other choice rule). The total utility for each alternative product is computed from each person's conjoint utility scores. When the choices of all potential buyers in the sample have been recorded, the shares of each product concept can be tallied. By pitting the relevant set of competitors against a particular new product concept, the share of the new concept can be estimated. To the extent that the concept does not generate a satisfactory share of choices, alternative concepts can be tried in a "what-if" fashion to see whether or not share improves.

The first step in a choice simulation requires managers to define each major competitor according to the product features associated with it in the market. This can be accomplished from competitive analyses and also from the perceptions of competitors obtained in a market survey. In the ATE example, assume three major competitors define the market of interest. Their products are profiled on the seven features in step 1 of Figure 8.7, along with two proposed new product concepts.

With the utilities from the illustrative respondent in Figure 8.5, total utilities for each competitor can be computed. They are displayed in the bottom row of the table in step 2 of Figure 8.7. Following the maximum-utility choice rule, the potential buyer would have chosen competitor 2 because that product scored the highest utility. Notably, for this buyer, neither of the proposed new concepts would be attractive. The simulation would then offer the competitive set to the next potential buyer, total utilities would be computed on that buyer's utilities, and again the choice would be recorded. After cycling through the sample, this process will yield a share for each of the competitors.

FIGURE 8.7   Major steps in choice simulator development for estimating market share.

1. Establish profiles of major competitors and alternative new product concepts:

ATE features	Competitor 1	Competitor 2	Competitor 3	New Concept 1	New Concept 2
Cost	$750,000	$500,000	$750,000	$250,000	$500,000
Size	1 large box	1 large box	1 large box	1 large box	1 large box
Pin number	512	128	128	128	512
Pin memory depth	128k	32k	128k	32k	128k
Clock rate	20 MHz	20 MHz	100 MHz	20 MHz	100 MHz
Timing resolution	10 ns	10 ns	100 ps	10 ns	100 ps
Voltage set on accuracy	1 mv	1 mv	10 mv	10 mv	100 mv

Note: Competitors' profiles are based on survey data and judgmental evaluations.

2. Apply individual-level utilities to major product alternatives and use rule to predict choice:

ATE features	Competitor 1	Competitor 2	Competitor 3	New Concept 1	New Concept 2
Cost	–9.0	–4.5	–9.0	13.5	–4.5
Size	7.2	7.2	7.2	7.2	7.2
Pin number	–6.3	11.2	11.2	11.2	–6.3
Pin memory depth	3.1	.9	3.1	.9	3.1
Clock rate	–4.9	–4.9	17.0	–4.9	17.0
Timing resolution	4.9	4.9	–5.4	4.9	–5.4
Voltage set on accuracy	53.4	53.4	–6.7	–6.7	–46.7
Total utility	48.4	68.2	17.4	26.1	–35.6

Note: These utilities are obtained from the individual in Figure 8.5 (step 4) and matched to the product profiles in step 1 above.

3. Accumulate individual choice predictions by product and compute market shares:

Simulation runs	Competitor 1	Competitor 2	Competitor 3	New Concept 1	New Concept 2
1. Current market share for three competitors	45%	35%	20%		
2. Market share with new product concept 1	42%	28%	17%	13%	
3. Market share with new product concept 2	32%	25%	12%		31%
⋮					
Market share with nth new product concept					

Note: Market shares sum to 100% across each row. Simulations with multiple new concepts can also be run.

The summary share of choices for each of the current competitors is shown in step 3 of Figure 8.7. The first simulation shows share estimates of 45, 35, and 20 percent, respectively. The second simulation reveals share changes with concept 1 introduced to the market. The 13 percent share for concept 1 draws largely from competitor 2. Concept 2 draws its 31 percent share from all competitors, but especially from competitor 1. The product features of concept 2 are apparently more attractive to this sample than the features of concept 1.

This simple example shows the value of the choice simulation in facilitating concept development. In addition to trying numerous alternative concepts, it can be used to hypothesize competitive reactions in terms of either a new product launch or the improvement of one or more features (by adjusting the competitive set accordingly). However, estimating competitor reactions is limited to the features selected in the original conjoint analysis and to information known about each competitor. In the absence of a fairly recent and validated competitive response model, trial-and-error simulations with various competitive responses can help prepare for competitor reactions. In any case, the new product concept resulting from the simulation can be incorporated into the spreadsheet forecasting model as an estimate of the *Buy* variable in equation [8.1]. Before this procedure is illustrated, however, several aspects of choice simulators are noted to put their use in perspective.

Defining the Competitive Set

In some market situations, there are numerous small competitors whose product profiles may not be known. These small competitors (especially when their total share is small) can be eliminated in favor of using only the major competitors to define the available market. Alternatively, all of the small competitors can be aggregated into a single *typical* profile for representation in the simulation. In any case, such definitions compromise the validity of the simulation and should be used with care.

Selecting a Choice Rule

In the ATE case study, a choice rule was used that assumed potential buyers would choose the product that maximizes their utility. Alternatives to the *max utility* choice rule based on probabilistic choice have also been used.[24] In these models, a potential buyer's choice probability is estimated as some function of the part-worth utilities computed from the conjoint analysis. For example, the potential buyer's utility for each competing product can be computed, then those utilities can be summed to provide a total utility for all products; dividing each product's utility by the total provides a choice probability for that product. After computation of each potential buyer's choice probability for each product in the competitive set, the results can be averaged. The average choice probability for each product is then assumed to represent that product's market share. Available software packages provide a variety of choice rules from which to select, including ones that incorporate Bayesian procedures. However, because these choice rules include restrictive assumptions, they should be used cautiously.[25]

Segmentation Issues

In the ATE case study, three viable segments based on the utilities were identified. The choice simulation could have been performed for each segment, offering a different new product concept for each and summing the shares across the segments to obtain total market share.[26] Alternatively, multiple new product concepts could have been offered to the entire market and the shares computed. Or different concepts could have been introduced sequentially to the simulated market and the impact (such as cannibalization) of each successive new concept recorded. However, because multiple products can increase costs, the financial implications of each concept must be considered.

Validity Issues

Because any simulation can produce results that may distort reality, every attempt should be made to validate the choice simulator prior to extensive use for decision making. One approach is to evaluate how well market shares of current products (if they are known or estimable) are predicted by the conjoint utilities. It is not surprising that the predictions frequently don't match the actual shares, because product features are only part of the total marketing program offered to consumers. Distribution, customer service, advertising, sales force, and other marketing and promotional efforts may also drive market share.

If product brand names are included as part of the features in the conjoint analysis, some of these marketing and positioning factors may be reflected in buyer choice. In such cases, the choice simulation shares can be adjusted (weighted) to reflect actual market shares before new concepts are considered. If brand names are not included (or even in some cases when they are), the choice simulator shares can be adjusted by estimates of the relative effectiveness of marketing factors for each competitor.

Competitive Response Issues

To develop a submodel of competitive response to a new product would require a comprehensive, dynamic marketing simulation that reliably estimates the reaction of each major competitor to a new product threat. A new entry to the market would set off a chain reaction among competitors, not only to the new product concept, but also to each other. Such models are difficult to build and parameterize, and are outside the scope of this book.[27] However, the use of simulation is encouraged to at least anticipate competitive changes in product features or new product launches. The use of judgment to estimate *relative marketing effectiveness* of competitor advertising, sales force, price, and other marketing variables is also possible. It would necessitate adjusting choice simulation shares through additional multiplicative indicator variables. For example, a variable with an index of 1.0 can mean no relative competitive effect from price changes, and indices greater or less than 1.0 can reflect their respective impact. A case study in Chapter 11 on timing market entry illustrates this type of judgmental adjustment.

Error and Sensitivity Analyses

Conjoint analysis results, like those of most marketing research procedures, are subject to a variety of errors in data collection and from other sources. To improve understanding of the workings of the choice simulator, a recommended practice is to conduct sensitivity analyses. For example, systematically varying the levels of the various features in the proposed new product concept enables one to measure the successive impact on market share. If the sensitivity analyses suggest unusual patterns, more careful examination of individual-level utilities may show the need to consider segmenting the sample results. Until managers accumulate experience with using choice simulators, they can use a variety of sensitivity analyses to gain useful insights about the value of the results for decision making.

Time-Based Market Response

The use of conjoint analysis and a choice simulator is a static set of procedures, and therefore limited in its realism. Measures are taken at a point in time, but used to make decisions for a dynamic environment. Environmental factors, competitors, potential buyers, and other stakeholders can change and diminish the value of the simulated market shares. The part-worth utilities can change (because of environmental effects), as can competitive offerings, and alter the outcomes. Although actions and reactions can be estimated in a sequential sense, such estimates do not truly replicate market response over time. Nevertheless, use of conjoint analysis with a choice simulator provides a structure for beginning to anticipate effects due to the passage of time and to frame the market entry decision.

Unless more sophisticated models are developed, time-based market response can be handled in two ways. First, it can be assumed to be captured by the diffusion process used to estimate market penetration of a new product (or industry) or of a new brand entering an existing market. In this case the conjoint utilities would be held constant over time (the approach used in the ATE case study). The critical assumption is that the organization will implement product changes to keep pace with the market. Alternatively, the utilities can be modeled over time, formally or judgmentally. Will certain ATE features be more or less valued over time? For example, will the utilities for machines with 512 pins decline over time and, if so, can the trend be estimated from analysis of historical preferences or sales? This approach can be implemented by linking the choice simulation results to relevant trends identified in an enhanced scenario of the market opportunity.

Extending the Simulator to New Product Optimizers

An obvious extension of the choice simulation is to develop a search procedure to find the new product concept that provides the greatest market share or profitability. Recall that there were 2,187 possible ATE product concepts (seven features, each at three levels) from which potential buyers might choose. Suppose the goal is to find the concept that generates the highest market share, given the utilities of potential buyers. If all concepts are assumed to be feasible (or infeasible ones are eliminated), simply computing market shares of all 2,187 possible products (under a particular choice rule) and sorting them to find the concept with the highest share is possible on most personal computers. This *complete enumeration* approach to finding the best concept is satisfactory; however, with larger problems (for example, more concepts), more efficient approaches may be needed.[28]

To enhance the value of new product optimizers, the inclusion of cost data associated with the various product features and their levels can facilitate the development of objective functions based on profitability. Thus, if the costs associated with each product concept can be estimated, and presumably price is included as a feature, profit contribution can be estimated for each concept. With a value for the size of a market opportunity, market share can be used to compute the number of units sold, which, when multiplied by the unit contribution, provides a profitability estimate for each concept. A search algorithm can then be used to find the most profitable concept. In their simplest forms, product optimizers are intuitively appealing, attractive to managers, and an aid in new product decision making. However, additional research is needed to make them realistic enough to accommodate multiple stakeholders and multiple factors that affect new product decisions.

6. ESTIMATE SALES

Up to this point, it is apparent that the illustrative sales forecasting model in equation [8.1] depends on the ability of (1) the market opportunity forecasting model to estimate the number of potential buyers (**Adp**) and (2) submodels to estimate the proportion or share of potential buyers (*Buy*) that will respond favorably to the new product, given new product features, various prices, and competitive concerns. The awareness and sales force variables also require submodels, which will involve estimating awareness response functions for decisions on advertising, publicity, and other promotional variables.

In the ATE case (and in many other high-technology markets), industry media can be very influential on purchase decisions. Although it is difficult to develop an estimate of their impact, obtaining their response to the new product throughout development may provide useful information about their eventual published evaluations. A submodel of sales force ability to convert potential buyers to customers should also be developed, considering such factors as sales force compensation plans and effectiveness. As discussed in Chapter 6 and illustrated in Chapter 7 with regard to awareness of a new product at the market level, these response functions are based primarily on managerial judgment, analysis of product analogies, and other market research procedures. From the expected time path of these variables over the 5-year planning horizon, their values can be estimated.

The outcome of the market opportunity and sales forecasting process is summarized in the spreadsheet in Figure 8.8. The market opportunity forecast portion of the spreadsheet is based on the trends in organizational demographics among the certain industries using ATE (the **Pot** variable), a diffusion model of historical ATE sales (the **Pen** and **Adp** variables), and the breakdown of that estimate between new and replacement buyers. The sales forecast portion of the spreadsheet includes the major variables in the sales forecast model of

FIGURE 8.8   Five-year market opportunity and sales forecasts of new ATE concept: spreadsheet model and selected plots.

New Product Forecast Component		Year 1	Year 2	Year 3	Year 4	Year 5
Market Opportunity Forecast[1]						
Market potential	(Pot)	32,000	34,000	35,400	36,900	37,500
Market penetration	(Pen)	18,700	20,600	22,800	25,700	29,100
# Potential buyers	(Adp)	11,250	12,500	14,300	16,250	17,450
New potential buyers	(New)	1,900	2,200	2,900	3,400	2,900
Replacement buyers	(Rpl)	9,350	10,300	11,400	12,850	14,550
Sales Forecast[2]						
Choice simulation share	(Buy)	.31	.31	.31	.31	.31
Proportion aware	(Awr)	.15	.30	.50	.70	.90
Sales force conversion	(Sfc)	.20	.30	.40	.45	.50
Average purchase size (# units)	(Use)	1.5	1.6	1.7	1.7	1.8
Sales volume (units)	(Vol)	157	558	1,507	2,698	4,382
Average price ($000)	(Pri)	500	400	300	250	200
Sales revenue ($000 rounded)	(Rev)	78,500	223,200	452,100	674,500	876,400
Market share of **Adp**	(Shr)	1.4%	4.5%	10.5%	16.6%	25.1%

Notes:
1. Market potential is based on analysis of organizational demographic trends. Market penetration variables are based on a diffusion model of current industry sales.

2. Sales forecast variables are based on choice simulation described in the chapter, and judgmental estimates of awareness and sales force effectiveness.

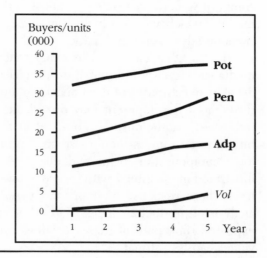

equation [8.1]. For illustration, the 31 percent choice simulation share for new product concept 2 is used. Note that it is assumed constant over time, but its realization depends on the awareness and sales force conversion variables. Although the marketing program components (other than the product and its price) are not explicitly considered here, the modeling approach should reflect their impact through the variables included in the model.

When the selected model factors in Figure 8.8 are multiplied together (following equation [8.1]), annual sales volumes are estimated (*Vol*). When sales volume is multiplied by price, sales revenue forecasts are obtained, which can then be used for the financial forecasts. In the bottom row of the spreadsheet model are the estimated market shares (*Vol*/**Adp**). The difference between the choice simulation share (*Buy*) and market share (*Shr*) shows how the realization of sales depends on factors included in the model other than response to the new product concept.

Once a basic sales forecasting model has been established, it can be improved over time in terms of both changing factors (adding and deleting them) and changing the estimates and assumptions for each factor. With the model computed on a basic spreadsheet, recalculating and updating new product sales forecasts are relatively minor tasks. They are helpful when the forecasts move beyond the first time period and become subject to increasing error as environmental changes occur and as the product concept and other marketing program variables change. As a new product concept moves through various levels of refinement (prototype, product, market entry program), the model structure can be used to incorporate additional research with fresh response data to sharpen the sales estimates.

7. CONTINUALLY UPDATE MODELS AND ESTIMATES

New product sales forecasting should be viewed as an ongoing process that continually requires updated information throughout product development. Changes in product design, marketing program variables, competitor activities, and other factors may be sufficient to warrant the collection of additional information with which to review and possibly revise estimates. For example, if the levels on product features are outside the range of those studied in the conjoint market research study, a subsequent study that includes the relevant ranges may be needed. Or, an unexpected competitive response may necessitate an additional run of the choice simulation with the competitor's product configuration.

In keeping with a decision support system approach as described in Chapter 6, all models and data collected for sales forecasting should be retained in a data base. Estimates quantified with judgment as well as those obtained through research should be included. Such a data base facilitates the update and renewal of sales forecasts for both the current new product and future new products. As a repository of knowledge, the data base not only supports new product decision making, but also becomes part of an organization's *memory* that facilitates organizational learning. Finally, the use of multiple methods to generate the various estimates is encouraged to reduce the ever-present *error* that accompanies new product development and forecasting.

SUMMARY

Whereas market opportunity forecasts are estimates of potential value for which the true magnitude may never be known, sales forecasts are estimates of expected values that can have very real consequences if not achieved. After a new product launch, the notions of error and accuracy (forecast versus actual) become computable measures that have an enormous impact on production, marketing, and financial decisions. Consequently, a process is recommended in this chapter to provide a discipline for developing new product sales forecasts. Although the example used involves an industrial product, the concepts and procedures are applicable to new consumer products and services as well.

At the heart of the sales forecasting process are estimates of market and stakeholder response to the new product and its marketing program. A variety of estimating procedures could be employed, but the use of conjoint analysis as an approach for obtaining market response measures illustrates how new product concepts can be shaped and forecast to generate the most favorable outcome. The utilities of potential buyers can then be used to further refine the product concept through segmentation, as well as input to a choice simulator to estimate market share. Applying these and other factors to the market opportunity forecast in a sales forecasting model provides sales volume forecasts. Although market opportunity and sales forecasts are important measures of a new product's value and potential for strategic success, they must be linked to the financial aspects of a project to guide various new product decisions.

9 New Product Financial Control

New product development encompasses all major business functions in an organization—marketing, R&D, production, accounting—it may even involve the chief financial officer! Unless an organization is committed to an ongoing process of new product development as an intellectual discipline to be shared by all members, people will tend to stay within departmental walls, working contentedly on their individual parts of the project. Occasionally they will venture out to resolve difficulties or get questions answered.

However, nothing brings everyone to the table more quickly than the financial aspects of new product development. If the "numbers" aren't in the ballpark, an entire project could be in jeopardy. Yet some people will argue, "How can you possibly put real numbers on any new product, especially before it becomes a prototype?" And they are quick to add, "The creativity and positive excitement of a new product effort must certainly not be dampened; if the idea is good and executed properly, the numbers will be there." Unfortunately, if some organizational members had their way, they would keep the numbers off the table—and when the facts and figures are seen, they would tend to have an optimistic bias. If others had their way, any new products that could not meet strict financial hurdle rates would be terminated.

In any case, the size of a market opportunity, sales response to it, and the shape of a new product may be seen in a different light when submitted to the careful scrutiny of financial analysis. For the new automated test equipment (NATE) product considered in Chapter 8, will the expected sales of $78 million (see Figure 8.8) in the first year of operations generate adequate cash flow to maintain the project and provide sufficient return on investment to justify continuing it? What will be the profitability of the new product in its first year, and the years thereafter? What will be the return on investment of this project if it continues? Will the *risk* associated with the entire effort be so high as to suggest scrapping the new product?

These financial concerns are among the hardest questions asked in making the *go/modify/timing/no-go* decisions that must be addressed continually throughout new product development. Whatever the attractiveness of a new product, the record of high new product failure rates compels consideration of financial implications sooner or later. Sooner is recommended over later. Concerns about risk, return on investment, and the time value of money must be addressed to gain control of a new product development effort. However, the intent of using financial control measures should not be to stifle creative efforts and risk-taking, but rather to manage them.

Every organization should have a sympathetic ear for creative people, creative new product ideas, and creative problem-solving without fear of financial restrictions. A balance must be struck that provides the flexibility needed to stimulate creativity and problem-solving while maintaining financial integrity. Ideally, a reliable financial control tool will help manage the balance between the costs of development and the promises of revenue opportunities. It defines the boundaries and latitude with which new product development can proceed.

The focus of this chapter is the preparation of a rudimentary new product development *control chart*. The intended use of the control chart is as a flexible forecasting tool with measures that can be used by a new product team early in the development process to set clear financial goals and monitor progress. The chart reinforces a disciplined approach to new product development and integrates with market opportunity and sales forecasting discussed in Chapters 7 and 8. It also requires assessment of investment, costs, risks, and cycle time of development for a new product. The diagram in Figure 9.1 provides an overview of a 7-step process suggested for financial forecasting. Each step is briefly reviewed in the following sections.

1. DIAGNOSE AND CONCEPTUALIZE KEY FINANCIAL FACTORS

The conceptual structure defining new product development presented in Part 1 of the book suggests a variety of factors that drive financial considerations. A few examples are helpful. At the environmental level, slowing economic conditions or improved technology can reduce the costs of new product components; political instability can increase uncertainty and risk associated with forecasts; or regulatory actions can increase costs, investment, and cycle time. At the market level, heightened competitive activity and confused potential buyers can increase the costs of marketing program communications and delay market acceptance. At the industry and organization level, media suppliers can increase advertising costs, raw materials can become scarce and increase production costs, or organizational politics can slow development time.

In effect, most of the factors identified in the market opportunity and sales forecasting processes have the potential to change investment levels, costs, risks, and cycle times of development. Consequently, financial forecasting, which is sensitive to these factors, must systematically account for them. Anticipating costs and time considerations through pro forma analyses and project planning

FIGURE 9.1   New product financial forecasting.

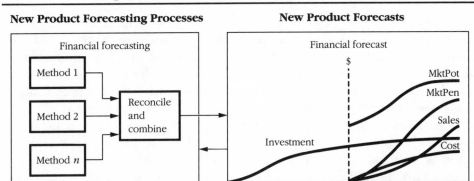

New Product Forecasting Processes   **New Product Forecasts**

Financial Forecasting Process

1. **Diagnose and Conceptualize Key Financial Factors:** Based on an understanding of the environmental, market, and organizational situation, identify and conceptually define the major factors (stakeholders and key variables) that hypothetically influence critical financial indicators.

2. **Formulate Spreadsheet and Submodels of Financial Factors:** Using key financial factors, including risk, formulate spreadsheet and other models to guide data collection.

3. **Collect Data on Key Variables:** Collect data for the various models to develop estimates for key financial factors.

4. **Estimate Investments and Costs:** Prepare pro-forma estimates of cost and investments to measure profitability and return on investment.

5. **Estimate New Product Development Cycle Time:** Using project management and other approaches, prepare estimates of the time to develop the new product.

6. **Estimate Key Financials in a Control Chart:** In the context of a new product control chart, bring together market opportunity, sales, cost, investment, and cycle time estimates to provide key financial measures to support decision making.

7. **Continually Update Models and Estimates:** Incorporate new data and experience into the new product financial forecasting process over the cycle of development, including the continual update and review of market opportunity and sales forecasts.

can help sharpen the quality of profitability and other key financial estimates that might be incorporated into managerial spreadsheet models.

2. FORMULATE SPREADSHEET AND SUBMODELS OF FINANCIAL FACTORS

Establishing a modeling approach to financial forecasting involves three steps: (1) selecting one or more financial measures of return, (2) selecting an approach to assess the risk of the project, and (3) selecting one or more decision rules that provide the financial backbone for a *go/no-go* decision. Each is briefly considered in the following subsections.

Selecting Financial Measures of Expected Return

An organization's new product projects can be viewed as *capital investment* options from which future returns are expected, given cash outlays.[1] Although net income or profit (after taxes) is a useful indicator of a project's performance, *cash flow* (after taxes) is the more critical measure. Whereas net income often includes noncash expenses (such as depreciation), cash flow facilitates comparison of cash investment outlays against cash receipts. Consequently, in Figure 9.2, two financial forecasting models are presented, one based on net profit (equation [9.1]) and the other based on cash flow (equation [9.2]). Thus, by virtue of sales revenues, equations [9.1] and [9.2] link the sales forecasting process with financial forecasting. Also included in Figure 9.2 are standard formulas (equations [9.3]–[9.5]) for estimating three popular measures of expected return from a new product investment: *return on investment, internal rate of return,* and *net present value.*

FIGURE 9.2   Basic financial model and frequently used measures of return for new product projects.[a]

■ Basic profitability financial model

$$PRF_t = REV_t - CST_t \qquad\qquad [9.1]$$

■ Cash flow financial model

$$CSH_t = INF_t - OUT_t \qquad\qquad [9.2]$$

■ Return on investment (ROI)

$$ROI_t = PRF_t / INV_t \qquad\qquad [9.3]$$

■ Internal rate of return (IRR)

$$\sum_{t=0}^{n} (CSH_t / (1 + IRR)^t) = 0 \qquad\qquad [9.4]$$

■ Net present value (NPV)

$$NPV = \sum_{t=0}^{n} (CSH_t) / (1 + RRR)^t \qquad\qquad [9.5]$$

where PRF_t = net profit (after taxes) for time period t
$\quad\quad\quad\;\; REV_t$ = new product sales revenue for time period t
$\quad\quad\quad\;\; CST_t$ = total cost for time period t (including interest and taxes)
$\quad\quad\quad\;\; CSH_t$ = average cash flow (after taxes) for time period t
$\quad\quad\quad\;\; INF_t$ = net cash inflows from product for time period t
$\quad\quad\quad\;\; OUT_t$ = net cash outflows from product for time period t
$\quad\quad\quad\;\; INV_t$ = project investment at time period t
$\quad\quad\quad\;\; RRR$ = required rate of return for the project.

[a]These formulas are typical of those used to calculate measures of return, but the various nuances in their use and computations should be reviewed in basic finance books. These and related formulas are also available in most calculators and personal computer spreadsheet packages.

Return on investment is a simple calculation that uses profit as the performance measure and does not consider the time value of money. The internal rate of return and net present value methods use *discounted cash flow* techniques to include the time value of money in the measure. In evaluating a specific project, these approaches will yield similar results, but care should be taken in evaluating mutually exclusive projects in which only one can be chosen. Organizational practices should also be considered in selecting a particular measure. When in doubt, use multiple measures and reconcile differences.

Estimating Risk of the New Product Project

A decision about an investment project can be reached by using any of the measures of return noted above. In addition, a traditional breakeven analysis can be conducted to determine the level of sales volume needed for zero profit or zero *NPV*. In its simplest form, breakeven is computed as total fixed costs divided by contribution margin (sales price minus variable cost per unit). However, in most new product development projects that are of some importance to an organization, the uncertainty of the situation may raise questions about relying on computations that purport to measure the expected return or cash flow. Further, if two projects have the same return but differ in their uncertainty, the decision maker must view them differently.

As noted throughout the book, the potential for uncertainty raised by environmental, market, and organizational factors motivates a systematic approach to new product development and forecasting processes. Although numerous factors, models, and marketing research methods are identified to help reduce uncertainty and improve the accuracy of sales forecasts, the practical decision maker realizes that there will almost always be some variability in the measures of performance used to evaluate the future outcome of a new product investment project. Some of the uncertainties in a new product project cannot be estimated (such as accidents that might delay a project), but for ones that can, applying the concept of *risk* can improve *go/no-go* decision making.

An approach that includes risk recognizes that not only will there be variability in the outcomes of future cash flow estimates used to make a decision on a specific project, but also that there might be variability in the major factors used to estimate the cash flows.[2] Essentially, whenever a *probability distribution* for outcomes of key variables of interest (such as cash flow, or the factors that determine it) can be identified by the analysts and managers involved, risk analysis is recommended to support decision making. By managerial judgment, the variability (such as standard deviation) of cash flow outcomes can be obtained as a measure of risk.

Typically, the risk analysis approach begins with the identification of key factors involved in the decision process. Figure 9.3 illustrates an application in which managers focused on nine different input factors when deciding whether or not to add a new processing plant. (The logic of this approach can be easily extended to new product projects.)[3] As noted in Figure 9.3, the probability distribution for each factor was obtained from expert managers, who were asked

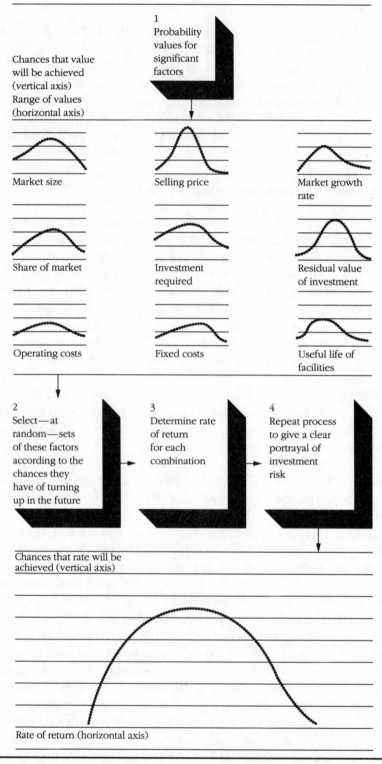

Source: David B. Hertz and Howard Thomas, *Risk Analysis and Its Applications* (New York: John Wiley & Sons, 1983), p. 32. Reprinted by permission of John Wiley & Sons, Ltd.

questions about the likelihood that each factor would take certain values (recall the decision calculus approach discussed in Chapter 6).

Once the probability distributions are obtained, random combinations of the nine factors are used to simulate the outcome measure of interest (such as net present value, or internal rate of return as in Figure 9.3). With this approach, the values of each factor are selected through a random process, then the set of values is used to compute the return measure. This process is repeated numerous times until a distribution of possible return outcomes becomes evident. The plot of these returns (shown at the bottom of Figure 9.3) reveals the risk associated with the particular investment project—in the example, the chances that the internal rate of return will be achieved.

The simulation method of risk assessment just described is most useful for high-stakes, high-uncertainty new product situations. The method requires considerable managerial input on the risk factors defining the situation, as well as estimates of the correlations of these factors. An alternative procedure for assessing risk involves the use of scenario analysis (see Chapter 7). By estimating *NPV* (and *IRR*) for alternative scenarios (which include varying degrees of uncertainty), managers can obtain a distribution of outcomes as a measure of risk. Another extension of the risk assessment approach is to combine it with decision tree analysis. Once the decision tree paths are identified (e.g., national launch versus rollout launch), a distribution of cash flow outcomes for each node on the decision tree can be obtained from managerial estimates. As discussed in the next section, estimated returns that look attractive (on the basis of their expected values) may lead to different decisions when the risk of the project is considered in the decision process.

Selecting Decision Rules

The selection of a financial rule for a new product decision model will depend on the measures selected and whether or not risk has been included in the analysis. The simplest form of decision rule is to compare the financial measure against a *hurdle* rate; the new product project receives a *go* when the hurdle rate is met or exceeded and a *no-go* when the rate is not met. When the net present value (*NPV*) measure is used, the decision rule is to *go* with the project when $NPV > 0$ and *no-go* otherwise. In effect, the required rate of return acts as a hurdle rate in the net present value computation.

In some new product situations or phases of the decision process, a dichotomous *go/no-go* decision may be constraining, and a third decision option may be to *modify* or otherwise revise the project or its *timing.* In these cases, two hurdle rates can be set. The *upper hurdle* defines the rate above which projects are acceptable for continued development (*go*) and the *lower hurdle* defines the rate below which projects are unacceptable for continued development (*no-go*). The zone between the two rates should raise the caution flag, and indicates the need for further evaluation of the project (such as modifying the project or considering timing options). The forms of these rules are summarized below for the internal rate of return (*IRR*) measure (although any measure could be used) and are depicted graphically in the top part of Figure 9.4.

If $IRR_e > IRR_u$, then **go**

If $IRR_e < IRR_l$, then **no-go**

If $IRR_l < IRR_e < IRR_u$, then **modify** or consider **timing** options   [9.6]

where IRR_e = estimated internal rate of return,

IRR_u = upper hurdle internal rate of return, and

IRR_l = lower hurdle internal rate of return.

Although the hurdle rate approach to making the **go/no-go** decision about market entry is fairly direct, it does not account for risk in any formal sense as discussed previously—the specific hurdle rates set reflect a managerial interpretation of risk. More likely, there is a probability distribution of possible returns, as shown in Figure 9.3. In this sense, the magnitude of return from a particular new product project may be offset by the amount of risk associated with it. Projects that have high risk but also high returns may be as attractive as those with lower risk and returns.

A useful way to conceptualize risk and return is the *risk-return chart* shown in the middle of Figure 9.4. As in the case of hurdle rates, it is helpful to conceptualize upper and lower bounds on the relationship between risk and return.[4] If a new product project is above the upper-bound risk-return line, a **go** decision on the project would be appropriate. If a new product project is below the lower-bound risk-return line, a **no-go** decision on the project would be appropriate. The region between the upper and lower bounds is the cautionary zone in which projects require closer examination.

The risk-return lines can reflect management experience with past new product development projects or, alternatively, with all types of investment projects facing the organization in a broader portfolio context.[5] Typically, the upper-bound risk-return line is positively sloping to reflect an organization's experience that projects with higher degrees of risk are acceptable if they are also associated with higher returns. The lower-bound risk-return line can be flat (that is, a hurdle rate) or positively sloping, as shown in Figure 9.4. An organization's experience may also indicate a negatively sloping lower-bound risk-return line, which implies that some projects with higher risk and lower returns can be acceptable, albeit depending on additional information and modification.

If a new product development project (relative to more traditional financial investment alternatives) can be modified by conducting additional research to gain additional information, its risk-return profile can be changed. The bottom part of Figure 9.4 illustrates this more flexible approach to the risk-return chart.[6] In this case, upper- and lower-bound hurdle rates are combined with upper- and lower-bound risk-return lines to define six regions in the risk-return space that can guide decision rules for the **go/no-go** decisions.

Decisions on new product development projects in regions numbered 1 or 6 are clear **go** and **no-go,** decisions, respectively. In this case, no project is

FIGURE 9.4   Use of hurdle rates and risk for go/no-go decisions.

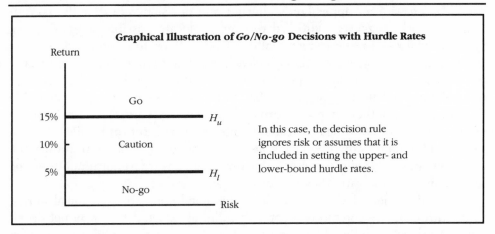

Graphical Illustration of *Go/No-go* Decisions with Hurdle Rates

In this case, the decision rule ignores risk or assumes that it is included in setting the upper- and lower-bound hurdle rates.

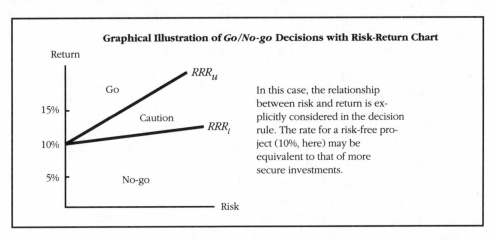

Graphical Illustration of *Go/No-go* Decisions with Risk-Return Chart

In this case, the relationship between risk and return is explicitly considered in the decision rule. The rate for a risk-free project (10%, here) may be equivalent to that of more secure investments.

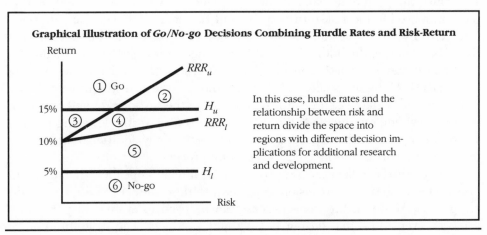

Graphical Illustration of *Go/No-go* Decisions Combining Hurdle Rates and Risk-Return

In this case, hurdle rates and the relationship between risk and return divide the space into regions with different decision implications for additional research and development.

acceptable below the 5 percent lower-bound hurdle rate. Projects in region 2 would be *go* with an upper-bound hurdle rate decision rule, but the consideration of risks suggests additional research to locate possible sources of risk to see if total risk can be reduced (alternatively, efforts to improve returns can be considered). Projects in region 3 clearly meet the risk criterion and would be *go* with respect to the upper-bound risk-return line, but the 15 percent upper-bound hurdle rate suggests that additional research may be advisable to determine whether or not returns can be increased. Projects in region 4 are candidates for additional research to alter their risk-return profiles. Finally, projects in region 5 would be terminated with the lower-bound risk-return line criterion, but because they meet the minimum return requirements of the lower-bound hurdle rate, they can be evaluated further.

The discussion of Figure 9.4 shows that combining strict financial hurdle rates with concerns for the risk-return profile of selected new product development projects implies different decisions, depending on where the project fits in the risk-return space. Additional study and modification can be pursued for any project, but the ones in regions 2 through 5 would benefit from one or more of the following steps to alter the risk-return profile:

- Gather new information (from the environment, market, or organization) to reduce the risk profile of the project.
- Change the product or its marketing program to improve market response and return.
- Lower estimated costs (through product redesign or production changes) to improve expected returns.
- Manage the timing of the investment (accelerate, slow, or hold) to influence its risk profile or improve its returns.
- Engage in strategic alliances to accomplish any of the preceding steps.

Thus, the profile of a specific new product project can be changed and its position moved in the risk-return space, but the decision to conduct additional research raises the question of the cost and value of the additional information. For example, the additional cost to conduct a test market (say, $1 million) to obtain better information may reduce the risk of the outcome by reducing the variance of possible sales estimates. However, the investment costs of the project would be increased by at least the cost of the test market and new competitors may emerge during the test market period, possibly lowering returns. Therefore, assessing the expected value of obtaining any additional information must also be part of the financial forecasting process.[7]

Although the risk-return approach is intuitively appealing, it has limitations. The analysis and decision process just described is limited to a single project. However, the same process can be used to evaluate a portfolio of projects, even those that do not involve new products. The magnitude of the various projects (in terms of size of return) can be plotted as circles in the risk-return space, the size of the circles being proportional to the size of the returns. The resulting diagram facilitates direct comparisons.[8]

The process described is also limited in that it does not explicitly model the risk of the decision maker(s) involved. Decision makers who are risk *averse* may view the organization's risk-return space differently than those with gambling instincts, especially for situations in which multiple projects are above the upper-bound risk-return line. In these cases, estimation of decision-maker utility functions can help to select the best project. When multiple decision makers are involved, the problem of aggregating multiple utility functions can be considered in the context of group decision approaches (see Chapter 6).

Another limitation of the risk-return approach is its emphasis on *financial* return measures. Nonfinancial criteria may also be relevant (such as the enhancement of corporate image). This possibility suggests a broader decision-making process that includes criteria in addition to risk and return. Arguably, many of the other criteria are included in the risk-return approach (enhancing corporate image increases expected returns), depending on the factors included in the sales forecast modeling process to estimate sales response.

In summary, the basic thrust of a financial modeling approach to the *go/no-go* decision is to balance project risks against possible returns, and to decide the value of additional information to move the project's risk-return profile in the direction of a *go* decision. Although it has limitations, it can prove to be an effective conceptual approach to complement market opportunity and sales forecasting in decisions throughout new product development. Using market opportunity, sales, and cost forecasts to generate estimates of return and using risk analysis to measure risk, an organization can locate projects in its risk-return space. If other than a clear *go* or *no-go* decision is apparent, caution should be used in assessing the viability of the new product and additional information can be considered.

3. COLLECT DATA ON KEY VARIABLES

The irony of data collection on financial factors for new product development is that analysts who normally like to work with fairly certain numbers must generate future cost and investment estimates that often depend on market research and judgmental data, which they normally regard with disdain. This irony is especially apparent when analysts are working with new product concepts rather than prototypes. For example, determining the cost of a new ATE product may depend on decisions about product features and their levels obtained from a conjoint analysis study. From these tentative decisions, estimates of costs for raw materials, components, assembly operations, logistics, marketing programs, customer service functions, and other factors must be obtained from a variety of sources within the organization and from experience. Estimates of plant and equipment, additional personnel, incremental R&D expenditures, and other investments necessary to realize the new product also must be obtained.

The need for people responsible for estimating cost, investment, and cycle-time factors to work as members of the new product team from its inception becomes apparent when efforts are made to quantify judgment. The early decisions and assumptions built into the new concept and its process of development will be instrumental in estimating costs. Lack of knowledge about these early decisions and assumptions and the methods used to obtain them will delay the process (while the assumptions are learned) and contribute to errors of interpretation. People involved in cost, investment, and time estimation should even participate in the design of any market research and other data collection methods (see Chapter 6) to ensure that the right questions are asked to return information relevant to understanding the cost structure of the new product. Issues in the estimation of costs, investments, and timing are considered further in the next two sections.

4. ESTIMATE INVESTMENTS AND COSTS

The distinction between new product investments and costs is based primarily on whether they were incurred pre- or post-launch. All costs associated with the development of the project up to the launch date are considered *investment*. For example, in the ATE case, expenditures for market research, consultants, the new product team, prototype development, beta-testing, new plant and equipment for manufacturing, a new sales force, and other marketing costs related to the launch program qualify as cash outlays that define investment.

Expenditures after the launch, including production and ongoing marketing and management outlays to stimulate new product success, are viewed as fixed or variable costs. Of course, any capital costs after launch would be considered investment. Practices and procedures specific to organizations should be satisfactory in helping to discern the differences between investments and costs.

The difficulty of estimating *costs* for new products and services varies substantially according to the specific product under study and the costing practices of organizations. If the new product is one with which a firm has considerable experience (such as a new extension of an existing product), obtaining cost estimates should be rather straightforward. However, if the new product represents a new technology, there may be considerable fuzziness and uncertainty in the estimates. In such cases, using multiple methods (such as analogies and judgment) to prepare estimates is recommended.

Further, estimating costs may be easier for products with predominantly physical features than for ones with aesthetic or emotional features. Emotional and aesthetic features (such as a soft-touch keyboard) often have to be translated into more tangible engineering features with cost elements. In addition to estimating organizational new product costs, estimating the costs of major competitors, various intermediaries, suppliers, and others over a 5-year planning period is important in assessing the strategic response of these stakeholders.

Finally, costs are incurred in different parts of the organization, and they occasionally become the basis for disagreement. Marketing, R&D, and production represent three major cost areas in an organization. For example, members of a new product team may decide that the development process should be extended to further refine the product. Although marketing costs might change little with this decision, R&D costs will increase, and possibly production costs. How these costs are absorbed by the various departments may be a contentious problem unless agreed-upon rules and procedures are established at the outset of the project.

Estimating the time-based costs of an organization and its stakeholders is a daunting task and beyond the scope of this book. Nevertheless, the major aspects of cost that should be considered to complete a new product profitability analysis and forecast are briefly summarized. Of concern are the *types* of costs, the *starting level* of costs, and so-called *experience* effects.

Types of Costs

Every organization has its own basis for defining and allocating costs to products and services. Two approaches to costing can be used in practice, *direct* costing and *absorption* costing. In direct costing, the emphasis is on computing profit contribution by subtracting estimated *variable* costs from sales revenue. Typically, costs that vary with production are classified as variable costs and those that don't vary are classified as *fixed* costs. Costs that vary with production tend to be more identifiable with the new product than fixed costs. In multiproduct firms, costs that are fixed are often associated with overhead, which tends to be difficult to allocate to specific products. Consequently, in many cases (especially in multiproduct firms) it is expedient to use only variable costs to evaluate a new product project. Thus, contribution to overhead and profit can be used in risk-return analyses instead of net profit.

One can argue that a more precise accounting of total costs (fixed and variable) is necessary to really assess the financial impact of specific products.[9] In this view, costs associated with production, distribution, logistics, marketing, sales, information systems, administration, and other categories can be separated and traced to a new product (as well as existing products). For example, in a manufacturing context, this approach requires study of the activities that organizational members perform on various tasks, then costing those activities by the number of people (and their salaries) assigned to them. Next, the activities are associated with an allocation measure (such as annual shipments) and their costs divided by the measure to obtain a unit cost, which is assigned to specific products according to the proportion of activities they require in order to be shipped. The benefits of activity costing—more precise cost information for decision making—must be balanced against its costs.

Starting Level of Costs

When a new product is introduced to a market, it will start at a certain level of unit costs (variable and/or fixed). Usually these costs are expected to decline over time, but where they start may in part influence the rate at which they decline. From a conceptual perspective, the cost levels of a new product or service depend on the resourcefulness with which it is designed for manufacturing and/or designed for servicing. Poor design that allows high tolerances for error will translate to production inefficiencies and higher starting cost levels.

Well-designed products that benefit from fewer components and consideration of assembly or disassembly will generally yield lower starting cost levels.

The starting level of unit costs is therefore a function of *smart design* during the development process, as well as commitment to total quality management (TQM). Dedication by top managers and the new product development team is essential to link the design engineers closely with marketing (to meet buyer needs), financial, and manufacturing people to achieve starting cost-level objectives. The conceptualization of key factors in the environment, market, and within the organization must be revisited. For example, finding new technologies, progressive suppliers, lead users, and expert organization members can lead to ideas for improving design in order to reduce initial unit costs while maintaining or improving sales response. The same resourcefulness can be applied to other costs, including marketing, sales, and customer service. Once estimated, these costs become the starting level for the first time period in the planning horizon.

Experience Effects of Cost

The topic of business strategy has promoted substantial discussion of the experience effects of costs.[10] As observed in a variety of industries, cost declines are associated with cumulative production experience. Figure 9.5 includes

FIGURE 9.5   Hypothetical industry experience curve superimposed on product life cycle.

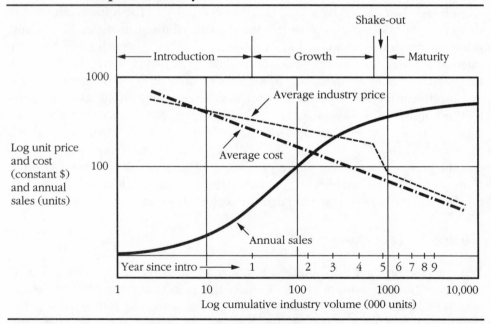

Source: George S. Day and David B. Montgomery, "Diagnosing the Experience Curve," *Journal of Marketing,* 47 (Spring 1983), p. 51. Reprinted by permission of the American Marketing Association.

an illustrative experience curve. If the forecast sales volume over a planning horizon is assumed to be produced, the cumulative volumes associated with the experience curve can be used to arrive at approximate unit costs over a planning period. This estimate (CST) is important for the financial model in equation [9.1].

To estimate an experience curve, industry cost and production data are needed. If the industry is new or no data are available, cost and production data from industry analogies can be selected. Such data can be used to estimate the following standard experience curve model:[11]

$$CST_q = CST_n(Q/N)^{-b}$$

where Q = experience to date (cumulative production),
            N = experience (cumulative production) at an earlier date,
        CST_q = the cost of unit q (adjusted for inflation),
        CST_n = the cost of unit n (adjusted for inflation), and
            b = a constant that depends on the learning rate.

Thus, if the learning constant is estimated from historical analogies, N is the sales forecast in year 1, and CST_n is the starting level of unit cost for year 1, then CST can be estimated for each Q (subsequent-year sales forecasts).

Although the estimated experience curve is an approximation, and possibly based on assumptions about historical analogies, it provides a useful submodel for estimating new product costs over time. However, an important set of assumptions implicit in most experience curves explains why costs might decline with production experience. Cost reductions that come with experience after product launch can be driven by learning through repetition and the resultant opportunities for product and process innovations that lead to lower costs (such as *smart design,* discussed previously). Cost reductions can also be driven by experience associated with traditional *economies of scale,* such as utilizing excess capacity or purchasing in large quantities. Consequently, cost reductions come about through resourceful interventions by management and other personnel—they just don't happen automatically.[12]

The forecast of price is also a critical variable in estimating revenue for the new product concept and often follows the experience effects of costs. In the ATE case study, the effects of price over time were estimated with respect to strategic concerns for the effects on demand, competitive reactions, and profitability. Because the conjoint analysis included price as one of the features, the relationship of price to quantity sold for any given concept could be established. If the conjoint utilities are assumed to measure underlying needs and values, it may be reasonable to assume that the estimated demand curve would prevail over a reasonable period of time. The relationship of unit price and cost over time in the ATE case study is illustrated in step 6.

5. ESTIMATE NEW PRODUCT DEVELOPMENT CYCLE TIME

Forecasting new product development cycle time is in part related to an organization's propensity to innovate (OPI) as discussed in Chapter 4. Cycle time acceleration may be more likely if an organization's process audit reveals a favorable OPI. Recognizing an organization's limitations in this regard helps to improve estimates of time necessary to complete the new product. For example, if major organizational process changes are necessary to put together an effective new product team, development time will lag. These factors must be incorporated into traditional estimates of project time; otherwise, the overly optimistic schedule will quickly become obsolete.

Traditional efforts to measure development cycle time involve the use of scheduling procedures that provide guidelines to estimate *total project time*. Total project time is defined as the time (days, weeks, months, years) between the beginning of the planning period and the date when the first units will be available for sale among potential buyers. Decomposing the time into more discrete activities and tasks and estimating each would allow use of the Program Evaluation and Review Technique (PERT) as a project management tool. The value of PERT for new products is in the probabilistic estimates of the activity times necessary to complete the various discrete activities. The time for each activity is assumed to be a random variable characterized by a beta distribution. Optimistic, most likely, and pessimistic estimates for each activity are obtained from expert judgment and used to calculate the mean and variance of total project time.

The availability of relatively inexpensive personal computer software packages that aid in the step-by-step development of PERT, the critical path method (CPM), and other scheduling approaches obviates the need to describe their operations in detail here. The value of these time-based approaches to project management is that they compel a discipline to consider the variety of tasks involved in a project. The risk is that the project may become such a maze of flow charts and measures that these approaches squelch the development of realistic estimates of its timing. Perhaps the greatest benefit of project management approaches is that the simple listing and estimation of time-based activities facilitates the recognition of opportunities to accelerate (or not accelerate) cycle time.

Knowing the major and critical activities involved in new product development paves the way for managing cycle time. Five basic approaches that organizations have used to accelerate new product development were identified in a literature review: (1) simplify, (2) eliminate delays, (3) eliminate steps, (4) speed operations, and (5) parallel process.[13] Taken together, these approaches can help define an organizational culture or discipline that provides the flexibility necessary to interact with its market environment. Examples of these approaches for the R&D, manufacturing, and marketing functions in new product development are shown in Figure 9.6. At the core of each of these recommendations are the major organizational activities of leadership and management discussed in Chapter 4.

FIGURE 9.6 Approaches for accelerating new product development cycle time.

Acceleration methods	Major organizational functions in new product development			
	Research and development	Manufacturing	Marketing	
Simplify	Generate explicit R&D goals and Link with other groups	Reduce number of vendors and Simplify documentation	Focus product requirements and Minimize user education requirements	
Eliminate delays	Link R&D goals and mfg. capabilities and Provide early product training	Reduce work in process and Maintain equipment	Reduce marketing plan delays and Reduce launch delays	
Eliminate steps	Utilize "lead user" ideas and Reduce number of parts	Reduce assembly steps and Create more reliable products	Minimize formal market testing and Reduce marketing approvals	
Speed up	Use small groups to generate ideas and Initiate computer-aided design	Install on-line product testing and Computer-aided manufacturing	Reduce test market time and Create customer alliances	
Parallel processing	Institute mutually exclusive research and Parallel known applied sciences	Provide collateral and/or Contingency facilities	Concurrent marketing and Plan customer service early	

Source: Murray R. Millson, S. P. Raj, and David Wilemon, "A Survey of Major Approaches for Accelerating New Product Development," *Journal of Product Innovation Management,* 9 (March 1992), pp. 53–59. Reprinted by permission of Elsevier Science Publishing Co., Inc.

245

Unfortunately, not all organizations can benefit from acceleration approaches. For example, parallel processing (often referred to as "concurrent engineering") can induce higher personal stress levels within the organization—perhaps because of the uncertainty of not knowing the outcome of processes that run parallel to each other. Tradeoffs between product quality and rushing to market early can compromise market position and brand image. Failing to properly document the product's development, especially technical and operational factors, can lead to customer service problems after launch. Finally, accelerating new product development can be costly, thereby requiring adequate resources.

Consequently, when new product development is viewed as a specific project, accelerating the process as a "quick fix" may or may not provide the benefits often associated with speed-up actions.[14] Each situation should be diagnosed carefully and specific steps for accelerating the process should be planned and executed with forethought and in concert with the pattern of leadership and management defining the organization. Alternatively, viewing new product development as an ongoing process rather than a single project suggests that the five approaches can become part of an organizationwide discipline based on progressive improvement through organizational change and learning. Increasing an organization's propensity to innovate (OPI) in this fashion can lead to greater flexibility in the cycle-time management of specific projects.

6. ESTIMATE KEY FINANCIALS IN A CONTROL CHART

Financial forecasting brings together all of the critical factors estimated for the new product project at a particular point in time, and provides a "snapshot" or "barometer reading" of its value to the organization. That value may increase over time as more is learned about the new product or it may not increase, in which case the project could be shelved or terminated. Critical estimates of market potential, market penetration, sales, costs, investments, and development time can be assembled into a usable *control chart* to visualize the new product development process and its key measures over time.

An illustrative financial forecast control chart for the ATE case study is provided in Figure 9.7. In one form or another, the basic format of the top part of the chart has been used by various organizations, and it reflects thinking on basic product life cycle theory.[15] Its use has multiple benefits beyond providing information to improve *go/no-go* decisions. For example, as a tool for gauging the progress of a new product project, it integrates the performance of all major organizational functions involved in the development team—marketing, production, R&D, finance, and so on. If the team agrees in advance about target values for the critical measures, and progress is forecast and plotted, differences can be tracked with the chart and corrective actions taken when necessary.

The ATE example in the top "cycle" charts of Figure 9.7 shows investment accumulating from the start of the project (during the development cycle for concept 2). This curve may vary depending on the project's nature. As of the launch date, an estimated $32 million is required to develop and manufacture

FIGURE 9.7 Illustrative financial control chart: new ATE concept 2.

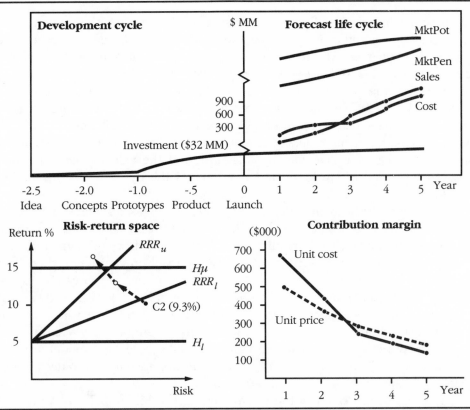

Financial forecasting spreadsheet model							
New Product Forecast Component		**NPD$_I$**	**Year 1**	**Year 2**	**Year 3**	**Year 4**	**Year 5**
Market Opportunity Forecast							
Market potential	**(Pot)**		32,000	34,000	35,400	36,900	37,500
Market penetration	**(Pen)**		18,700	20,600	22,800	25,700	29,100
# Potential buyers	**(Adp)**		11,250	12,500	14,300	16,250	17,450
Sales forecast							
Sales volume	**(Vol)**		157	558	1,507	2,698	4,382
Market share of **Adp**	**(Shr)**		1.4%	4.5%	10.5%	16.6%	25.1%
Average unit price ($000)	**(Pri)**		500	400	300	250	200
Average unit cost ($000)	**(Cst)**		675	425	275	225	185
Financial Forecast							
Sales revenue ($000)	**(Rev)**		78,500	223,200	452,100	674,500	876,400
Cost of goods sold ($000)	**(CGS)**		105,975	237,150	414,425	607,050	810,670
Gross margin (contribution)	**(GM)**		−27,475	−13,950	37,675	67,450	65,730
Overhead ($000)	**(SGA)**		4,000	4,200	4,450	4,600	4,750
Net profit before taxes ($000)			−31,475	−18,150	33,225	62,850	60,980
Net profit after taxes ($000)	**(Prf)**		0	0	23,258	43,995	42,686
Cash flow ($000)	**(Csh)**	−32,000	−31,475	−18,150	23,258	43,995	42,686
Cumulative cash flow ($000)		−32,000	−63,475	−81,625	−58,367	−14,372	28,314
Summary financial measures over the five year planning period for new ATE product concept 2		Average ROI = 67.1%		IRR = 9.3%		NPV(15%) = −9,934 NPV(10%) = −1,442 NPV (5%) = 10,755	

247

the new machines. Specific new product costs begin after the launch date, as do sales. Profitability is shown on the chart as the difference between the sales and cost curves. The data and estimates represented in the cycle charts are taken from the linked spreadsheet models and submodels developed in Chapters 7 through 9 and are summarized in the spreadsheet model at the bottom of Figure 9.7. Although selected forecasts are shown in the figure, they can be customized according to specific organizational needs. The vertical axis ($) in the chart can be scaled in actual dollars or logarithmically, depending on managerial preferences and the magnitude of the values. The horizontal axis can be scaled in any time unit that reflects the dynamics of the market situation.

The chart can also provide specific calendar dates for milestone events during the pre-launch and post-launch phases. Critical dates, such as those for concept evaluation study results, prototype availability, and launch, derive from the development cycle time estimates discussed previously. Further, after launch, the chart will continue to be used for tracking purposes. It can be expanded to include marketing expenditures, awareness levels, trial, repeat purchase, distribution penetration, and other relevant tracking variables. For analytical convenience, plots of the contribution margin (unit costs and prices) over time, the risk-return chart, and an overview spreadsheet model are also summarized in Figure 9.7. Users of such a chart are encouraged to design it to conform to specific organizational requirements.

The risk-return space in the middle left part of Figure 9.7 shows the plot for the new ATE product concept 2 (recall from Chapter 8). The *IRR* value of 9.3 percent raises some concerns about the viability of concept 2, given the various hurdle rates (as is also evident from the *NPV* values). The new concept may support a positive return on the $32 million investment if it survives, but it does not reach payback until about four years and four months after launch (as shown from the accumulated cash flows in the spreadsheet).

The possible path for changing the risk profile and return of the concept is indicated with the dashed line in the risk-return space. In this illustrative case, concept 2 should be re-examined with respect to the given market research data, and possible alternative concepts should be considered by using the choice simulation approach. The value of additional market research and closer scrutiny of cost estimates in early years of production should also be considered. Finally, consideration of other nonfinancial factors may give a different view of the project's viability.

The value of this type of financial forecasting and control chart approach is that once models are developed, establishing a baseline scenario and trying a variety of alternatives is possible—either with explicit assumptions or through sensitivity analyses. Although not shown, more detailed spreadsheets of costs and overhead expenses that are linked to major marketing, R&D, and human resource allocations provide opportunities to try alternative decisions.

Despite the use of a single scenario in Figure 9.7, it is possible to assess the financial effects of different investment levels, alternative concepts, different timing strategies, and so on by using the various models. Because the market opportunity, sales, and financial forecasting spreadsheets and submodels are *linked,* any changes in early assumptions about market size and penetration can also be evaluated rather expediently. Further, different market segment analyses and multiple products can also be developed and included in the basic estimation approach.

7. CONTINUALLY UPDATE MODELS AND ESTIMATES

The inherent value of any modeling approach is the process through which one learns about the phenomenon under study. This is most true for financial forecasts. The financial forecast should not be thought of as a static snapshot, but rather as a dynamic video. It should be framed at the outset of a new product project, and continue to be refined throughout development by the use of new information and multiple methods of estimation where possible. It not only provides a forecasting ability, but also gives clear indications of when revisions are needed. If certain milestones are not met, the cost of accelerating the development process can be estimated and input to the cost submodel to prepare a revised set of estimates. This information will help decide whether or not to accelerate the project.

If a market study shows a shift in potential buyer preferences, the effects on sales response can be estimated. Subsequently, the costs and time of changing the course of the development project to meet new market needs can be evaluated (using the model). In effect, the financial forecasting model is a valuable control tool for evaluating a variety of decisions as they arise during the development process. It also affords a capability to make financially based *go/no-go* decisions throughout the process in order to continually monitor the status of the project and change its direction when necessary.

SUMMARY

Chapters 7 through 9 examine an integrated set of pre-launch new product development and forecasting activities based on market factors identified in the conceptual models of Chapters 2 through 4. In Chapter 7, a process is considered for developing market opportunity forecasts, including estimates of market potential (the size of a market for a new product) and market penetration (period-to-period sales growth). In Chapter 8, a process for sales forecasting is outlined, including estimates of the number of buyers or adopters, unit volume, and sales revenue. In Chapter 9, these two sets of forecasts are brought together with estimates of cost, investment, and new product development cycle time to provide market entry financial forecasts. All of these forecasting processes interact with the new product development process to shape the design of the offering.

The financial forecast is viewed as the primary *control chart* for the entire new product development process. As such, it combines the effects of marketing decisions, design decisions, production decisions, financial decisions, and even human resource decisions. New product teams can use it as a self-evaluation tool to assess their own performance over time, as well as to make changes in the process as necessary to achieve project goals.

The forecasting process described also provides a procedure for making financially based *go/no-go* market entry decisions. A risk-return analysis can be used to compare one or more new product projects to alternative investment projects and as a basis for assessing the value of obtaining additional market information. The collection of forecasting procedures embodied in the financial model are valuable for pre-launch forecasting, but also provide a framework within which to begin to track and diagnose implementation of the new product launch. The forecasts on launch day will furnish a baseline against which to compare actual sales, market shares, financials, and other selected variables.

PART FOUR

Implementing New Product Development

10 Test Marketing New Products

The first step toward implementation of a new product and its marketing program is testing response among potential buyers and other major stakeholders. Will the planned advertising, sales promotion, and sales force efforts generate sufficient awareness and preference for the new product in the targeted market segment? Will buyers experience the benefits and satisfaction planned into the product and its features? Will wholesalers, retailers, and other members in the channels of distribution provide adequate support and service for the new product? Will regulators agree that the new product meets their requirements? Perhaps most importantly, will the sales response support the financial, marketing, and other strategic goals set for the new product? Finding full or partial answers to these questions can confirm the launch marketing program, help fine tune it, or identify the convincing factor that leads to a *no-go* decision.

When a division of American Cyanamid developed Combat, a new insecticide product that uses bait to kill ants and roaches, it decided to conduct a test market to provide additional information relevant to the ultimate launch.[1] Among its concerns was the fact that the new product differed in both form and efficacy from the existing sprays and fogger insecticides on the market. The product was designed as a "cookie" enclosed in a black childproof bait tray. The cockroach eats part of the cookie, takes it back to the nest, and dies a few days after ingestion. Product tests showed Combat to be so effective for roach control that Cyanamid could offer a three-month moneyback guarantee.

Product efficacy aside, whether or not consumers would *believe* that the concept worked, try it, and purchase it again remained to be seen. Two U.S. test markets were selected for their *high* and *average* levels of roach problems—New Orleans and Kansas City, respectively. The equivalent of a full-scale national marketing program was applied to each market for a period of two years. A variety of marketing research measures were taken to monitor market response.

Several lessons were learned from the Combat test market. Initially, the advertising message focused on the efficacy benefit of a three-month guarantee. However, consumers also responded favorably to the "child safety" and "no mess" benefits. Thus, a more balanced message—emphasizing efficacy, aesthetics, and safety—would be used. The company also learned that consumers were still somewhat baffled by the new concept, confusing it with various kinds of roach "traps" that attract and retain roaches with a sticky insecticide. The bait concept required communications that were more educational than persuasive.

Cyanamid also discovered from the test market that repeat purchase was high once consumers tried the product. Consequently, to increase trial, it boosted the value of coupons to levels higher than originally planned. Finally, the role of other relevant stakeholders was discovered to be important. The use of university studies to back efficacy claims, a noted entomologist, and general public interest in the "roach problem" generated a sufficient base of "news" to stimulate publicity related to the new product.

Although a two-year, two-city test marketing program was an important implementation step in the case of Combat, it might not prove as valuable for all new product situations. In some cases, a two-year test market will give competitors sufficient time to prepare a defensive product and/or marketing program; hence, *shorter* and less exposed test marketing would be preferable. In other cases, more detailed information about the appropriate price level, the proper amount of advertising, and which messages to use may be necessary to decide on the best launch program; hence, more *controlled* test marketing would be helpful. In yet other cases, test marketing may not be at all appropriate for the new product, its market entry strategy, or its launch.

In this chapter, *test marketing* is considered as an important first step in the implementation of new product development. The presumption is that the new product or service has passed satisfactory *alpha, beta,* and/or *gamma* use tests (discussed in Chapter 6), though the need for additional product modifications may be learned from test marketing. The types of test marketing, factors to consider in designing a test market, and the analysis process for test markets are discussed, and a summary evaluation of test marketing for different new product situations is provided. Historically, test marketing emerged from the domain of new *consumer* products. However, experience has shown that, if appropriately designed and executed, test marketing is potentially valuable for implementing new services, industrial products, and technologies as well.

TYPES OF TEST MARKETING

Test marketing is learning from the evaluation of *real* market response to *real* new products or services and their marketing programs. At one extreme, the new product may be tested in a *real* market environment with a *real* marketing program (or one or more versions of it). At the other extreme, it may be tested in a simulated market environment (using real potential buyers) with a hypothetical marketing program. Although the focus of this book is on one aspect of a marketing program—the new product and the integrity of its core concept of benefits—a marketing program also includes pricing, distribution, advertising, sales promotion, sales force, customer service, and other related decisions that define the complete *offering* to the market. During early concept development stages, the decisions that define the marketing program are often roughly cut. Typically, the substance of these decisions is reflected in the concept descriptions (especially enhanced scenarios)—the price, the advertising message, the level of availability, the nature of customer service, and so on.

A complete launch marketing program must go beyond the rough-cut aspects of a new product concept and consider more detailed decisions. A typical set of such decisions is illustrated in Figure 10.1. Communication decisions, for example, consist of not just the advertising message or total budget, but the creative approach to message delivery, the budget allocated to various media, the schedule, and the potential market response to the various component decisions of advertising. Clearly, there are many ways to *mix* these decisions, each defining a potentially different strategic approach to marketing. Test marketing can play an important informational and implementational role in refining marketing program decisions on the way to market entry. Although test marketing can take a variety of forms, three popular types used in practice are *simulated, controlled,* and *conventional* test marketing.

Simulated Test Marketing

Simulated test marketing (STM) is a research method that facilitates the measurement of market response to a new product and its marketing program among potential buyers in a pseudo market environment.[2] It can be implemented in a laboratory setting, in the homes or places of business of potential buyers, in shopping malls, or in other places that will simulate the buying process as closely as possible. For new repeat-purchase consumer products, obtaining estimates of trial and repeat purchase intentions can support market entry decisions, and also be used to update estimates in a sales forecasting model. For new durable products, simulating various stages in the buying process (such as information search through shopping and other sources, trying the product, and stated intention to buy) can also improve decision making and sales forecasting.

To see how STM works, consider the following typical research procedure for consumer packaged goods:

- Obtain a sample of potential buyers in the target market segment who may have a need for the new product, then measure their awareness, perceptions, predispositions, and usage behavior for products they currently consider to meet this need, as well as other buyer characteristics deemed

FIGURE 10.1   Selected new product marketing program decisions.[a]

Product decisions (assuming segmentation and positioning strategy)
- Core product concept
- Features/benefits (functional, emotional, aesthetic)
- Engineering/design elements (based on translation of product features)
- Production/operations components (based on engineering/design elements)
- Package (product protection, usage, communication, design, label, decomposition)
- Brand name (corporate name, family brand, new product brand, logo, trademark)
- Product line (styles, features, price points)
- Legal (trade secrets, patents, copyrights, warranties)
- Other

Pricing decisions
- Overall price
- Margins
- Price structure (geography, bundled versus unbundled by features and services, seasonality)
- Price promotions (discounts, allowances, premiums)
- Other

Distribution decisions
- Channel selection (direct, distributors, wholesalers, brokers, agents, retailers)
- Geographic scope (global, regional, national, state, city, community)
- Selectivity (intensive, selective, exclusive)
- Logistics (inventory, warehousing, order processing)
- Other

Communication decisions
- Message goals (awareness, interest, knowledge, preference, intention, action)
- Budgeting (quantity of information, cost of information)
- Scheduling (placement, timing)
- Creativity (emotional, logical, resonance, aesthetic)
- Media
  - Advertising (message goals, creativity, budget, schedule)
  - Sales promotion (message goals, type, creativity, budget, size, schedule)
  - Sales force (message goals, creativity, budget, size, recruitment, training, compensation, motivation, evaluation)
  - Telemarketing (message goals, creativity, budget, schedule)
  - Public relations (message goals, creativity, budget, schedule)
- Effectiveness measures (unaided recall, aided recall, recognition, knowledge, trial, repeat)
- Other

Customer service decisions
- Pre-sale service (financing, trials, planning, education)
- Post-sale service (unpackaging, installation, setup, training, documentation, help lines)
- Relationship building (complaint handling, repairs, replacement policy, extras)
- Other

[a]Because launch marketing programs for new products may vary by product type, organizational practices, and other situational factors, the decisions listed illustrate possible components of a marketing program.

essential (the sample is often obtained through shopping mall intercept interviews in a specially designed research facility).

- Present a new product scenario to the sample—for example, proposed us age situations or advertisements for the new product and its competitors (these can be storyboards depicting the basic message, animated or cartoon-like audio-video storyboards, artistic renderings of a print ad, or actual commercials).

- Give the potential buyer money to shop for and, if desired, purchase the new product in a simulated purchase environment (a laboratory setting, a mock retail store, or an actual retail store in which the new product and its competitors are available).

- Ask those who purchase the product to take it home and use it and, after a suitable usage period (depending on the product):
  — Obtain information from a follow-up survey (telephone or personal interview) on perceptions, predispositions, usage, satisfaction, and other variables with respect to competitors and the new product.
  — Offer the new product to potential buyers for repeat purchase, delivering it either by mail or in person.
  — Offer the product to potential buyers after another suitable usage period (if it is desired) to obtain additional repeat purchase measures.
  — Conduct more in-depth user studies (in a product-testing sense) to determine whether or not product features should be reformulated.

- Those who don't purchase the product can be exit-interviewed to discover their reasons for not buying, and can possibly be targeted for later promotions (such as coupons) or product samples to measure whether or not trial among nonbuyers can be stimulated.

This data collection procedure provides numerous opportunities to measure key variables (suggested in Figure 3.1 of Chapter 3) as indicators of purchase. Although the data collected from STMs are not taken under natural market conditions, in practice they have proven to be useful predictors of behavior when analyzed with pre–test-market models.

The obvious value of STMs and the pre–test-market models used to evaluate them is their relatively low cost, speed of execution, and secrecy from competitors. In many cases they are used to decide whether or not it is feasible to conduct a test market, and in other cases they are used to bypass test markets altogether and move directly to launch. Several commercial marketing research firms offer STMs as part of their new product services. If designed appropriately, they can be used to enhance new product decision making, as well as update the sales forecasting model.

A short case study using the BASES new product testing service illustrates the value of simulated test marketing.[3] A leading butter and margarine manufacturer sought to launch a new product that was a mixture of butter and margarine. The manufacturer faced several decision problems: (1) how would the new product perform in the market, (2) to what extent would the new product cannibalize the company's existing butter and margarine products, and (3) which of two different brand names should be used—a totally new brand name, or the current brand name of the manufacturer's other butter and margarine products?

To test the two different brand names, two separate analyses were conducted. A sample of some 900 respondents was split between the two brand name cells to be tested. Respondents were female consumers, 18 years of age and older. After being exposed to the new product concept, they were asked a series of standardized questions related to key measures used in the forecast model. A series of replacement/substitution questions were also asked to assess the competitive environment for the product and to assess cannibalization. Of the 900 consumers, 560 (62.2 percent) indicated a favorable response to the new concept (those who would *definitely* or *probably* buy), and they were then asked if they would take the new product home to use for two weeks.

A telephone callback survey was conducted among the respondents who used the new product. The questions asked were similar to those of the earlier phase, but additional sets of questions were asked about the product's perfor-

TABLE 10.1   Response to new product concepts: old versus new name

Concept responses		
Purchase intent	New name (N = 450)	Old name (N = 450)
Definitely would buy	20%	22%
Probably would buy	41	38
Might or might not buy	14	13
Probably would not buy	15	18
Definitely would not buy	10	9
Average hedonic (6 points)	4.7	4.7
Average price value (5 points)	3.9	4.0

After-use responses		
	New name (N = 201)	Old name (N = 210)
Definitely would buy	53%	50%
Probably would buy	28	30
Might or might not buy	11	12
Probably would not buy	4	6
Definitely would not buy	4	2
Average hedonic (6 points)	4.8	4.8
Average price value (5 points)	4.1	4.1

Source: Lynn Y. S. Lin, Alain Pioche, and Patrick Standen, "Estimating Sales Volume Potential for New Innovative Products With Case Histories," paper presented at the 39th ESOMAR Congress, Monte Carlo, September 1986; "Anticipation and Decision Making: The Need for Information." Reprinted by permission of the European Society for Opinion and Marketing Research, ESOMAR.

TABLE 10.2   Summary estimates versus actual in-market results

	Estimates	Actual
Year 1 trial rate	14.5%	14.0%
Average trial units (packs)	1.04	1.05
Measured repeat rate	54%	58%
Average purchase cycle (weeks)	4.6	4.1
Average repeat units (packs)	1.15	1.10
Year 1 consumer sales volume (index)	95	100

Source: Lynn Y. S. Lin, Alain Pioche, and Patrick Standen, "Estimating Sales Volume Potential for New Innovative Products With Case Histories," paper presented at the 39th ESOMAR Congress, Monte Carlo, September 1986; "Anticipation and Decision Making: The Need for Information." Reprinted by permission of the European Society for Opinion and Marketing Research, ESOMAR.

mance relative to expectations and about desired product improvements. The major consumer responses to the new product before and after usage are reported in Table 10.1. The data show little difference in response between the new and the old name.

Using a proprietary estimating procedure to forecast sales, the company found that the volume difference favored the old brand name by less than 3 percent. However, data from an analysis of potential sources of the new product's volume under the different brand name conditions suggested that using the manufacturer's existing brand name would result in a cannibalization rate about two and a half times that of the new brand name. Using the BASES analyses, the company launched the new product under the new brand name. The estimated trial and repeat rates from the model are plotted in Figure 10.2, and a summary of model estimates versus actual results is provided in Table 10.2.

Controlled Test Marketing

One of the growing sources of data for new product test marketing is the so-called controlled or *electronic* test markets that provide *single-source* data.[4] Typically, these are commercial services that have *wired* selected cities for test marketing. Selected retail outlets in these cities are equipped with electronic checkout scanners to record sales. A recruited panel of customers agrees to shop in these stores, and the individual order and a special identification card are scanned every time a panel member makes a purchase. Each card code is associated with a profile of a customer kept in a data base (demographics, psychographics, preferences, and so on).

Further, the homes of the same panel customers are wired with cable television such that the commercials they receive can be monitored and controlled. Thus, certain homes can be targeted with advertising messages or appeals that are different from those broadcast to the other homes. Magazine and newspapers are also coordinated in these markets to allow special ad and coupon

**FIGURE 10.2   Simulated test marketing results: plot of trial and repeat
rates for new dairy products.**

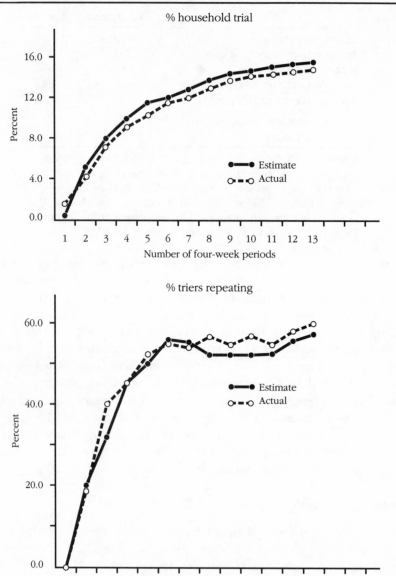

Source: Lynn Y. S. Lin, Alain Pioche, and Patrick Standen, "Estimating Sales Volume Potential for New Innovative Products With Case Histories," paper presented at the 39th ESOMAR Congress. Monte Carlo, September 1986; "Anticipation and Decision Making: The Need for Information." Reprinted by permission of the European Society for Opinion and Marketing Research, ESOMAR.

inserts. Bringing these data sources together on a weekly (or even daily) basis can provide a powerful and highly controlled testing environment.

When Campbell Soup was developing its Chunky Soup line in shelf-stable microwavable containers, it first decided to use a nine-month electronic test market in Pittsfield, Massachusetts, and Merion, Ohio.[5] The company was the second to enter the market after Hormel's successful Lunch Bucket meals and soups. As in most test marketing situations, the major concerns were sales response, especially cannibalization from the regular Chunky Soup line, and consumer response to advertising (awareness) and coupons. Finding an acceptable 10 percent cannibalization rate, and a 50 percent repeat rate, Campbell proceeded to an in-market test in Milwaukee. From this controlled test marketing experience, it learned about consumer usage (50 percent of the consumers used the product away from home), which helped better define the entry positioning strategy. It also learned that price should be lowered upon entry.

The real value of controlled test marketing is the opportunity to evaluate different marketing program strategies in a market environment that is much closer to actual market conditions than simulated test marketing. In the area of consumer packaged goods, the commercial firms that offer controlled test marketing services typically arrange *forced distribution*. The client pays for shelf space to ensure adequate availability to evaluate the effects of the price, promotion, and product features aspects of the marketing program. Consequently, controlled test marketing is not helpful if a company needs to know how effectively the sales force can *sell in* the new product to the trade and gain distribution.

Conventional Test Marketing

Conventional test marketing provides an opportunity to understand market response to the new product and its proposed marketing program in a more realistic market environment than is possible in simulated and controlled test marketing. It is especially useful for measuring response to the product from a broader set of stakeholders, including competitors, the trade, media, regulators, and others. It is also very helpful for discovering organizational and other in-market problems in implementing the new product program. The real benefits to conventional test marketing are the learning and subsequent adjustments that help ensure a successful launch—especially for new product situations with high stakes and high environmental and market uncertainty. However, these benefits must often be traded off against cost and demands to speed market entry.

New products considered for conventional test marketing tend to have unresolved concerns about certain aspects of their development or the launch program. For example, further reaction from potential buyers about the product and how they use it may be necessary and may result in product reformulation. When Procter & Gamble used conventional test marketing of a new disposable diaper, it was concerned with determining how the absorbency and fit-to-the-body features of the new product worked with parents and their children under a variety of different usage situations (such as children asleep, at play, or traveling). It was also concerned with the usual tracking of repeat purchase patterns and response over time. The data to resolve these concerns can best be gathered under normal use conditions—hence the real value of conventional test marketing.

Suspicions that retailers may be slow to stock or promote a particular new product can also be studied in a conventional test market situation. Recall the case of Holly Farms roasted chicken that was a hit with consumers, but not well-received by supermarkets. Conventional test markets may also be useful for new products that are based on new technologies, production processes, or operations that require a *shakedown* period before they reach their intended level of performance. Even under pilot plant conditions, gains in learning about assembly and subassembly processes, packing, shipping, unpacking, setup, and, when necessary, shelving can lead to a launch process that is smoother and more efficient than one without the test market experience.

TEST MARKETING DESIGN ISSUES

For test marketing to be helpful in refining the implementation of a launch marketing program and market entry decisions, care should be taken in its design and execution. Test marketing as the first step in the implementation of a new product marketing program and as a form of marketing research can be one of the more costly procedures in new product development. Among the major issues in test marketing, whether simulated, controlled, or conventional, are the test marketing problem, the research design needed to resolve the basic test marketing problem, the test units selected, the types of data and measures, and the length of the test.

Test Marketing Problem Definition

As revealed in examples of its three general types, test marketing can be used for a variety of new product issues and decisions, such as those described in Figure 6.2 of Chapter 6. However, certain problems can be resolved only with certain types of test marketing. For example, issues involved in identifying competitor reactions and other stakeholder responses to a comprehensive new product marketing program can best be addressed with conventional test marketing. Leaving the product in the market for a period of time—as in the case of Combat—may be the only way to assess problems related to the education of consumers, the role of external stakeholders (such as the media), or competitor response.

Other issues may center on the best mix of marketing decision variables for a new product. In this case, controlled test marketing may be most appropriate (as in the Campbell Soup situation) to establish the best levels of advertising, sales promotion, or price. In other cases, the issue may be speed to market. The use of simulated test marketing may provide sufficient information for deciding whether to use a conventional test market or to launch without it. In any case, carefully diagnosing the new product situation and clarifying the major questions to be answered is an important first step in deciding the type and value of test marketing and whether or not to use it.

Type of Research Design

Depending on the types of expected launch problems, test market research designs can range from *single-case* designs to more complex *experimental* designs. In a single-case design, one test market unit is selected for careful study and serves as its own control.[6] The performance of various launch program elements is assessed continuously over time. If desired, varying the launch program elements of greatest concern can create a change in performance that follows a change in program elements and helps to rule out other factors that might explain the changes. In practice, the single-case test market tends to be an evaluation of a planned launch marketing program and a source of estimates for trial, repeat, and usage behavior.

For example, during 1992 GTE began a 15-month test market of wireless pocket phones in the Tampa Bay area of Florida.[7] Whereas cellular phones are designed to be used in rapidly moving vehicles across wide areas, pocket phones are for use in pedestrian areas, are less expensive, and operate on a different communication system than cellular phones. Although the test is being run on GTE's cellular network, it is invisible to the potential buyer. The purpose of the test is to focus on how people will use the phones. The 3,000 people selected to receive the phones had to pay a refundable amount of $175. Usage rates (not conversations) are monitored through computerized switching devices in the communication system. Consumer reaction will be obtained from focus groups and survey questionnaires. Such designs require careful measurement and control of numerous factors, not unlike those that would be used in actual launch tracking for the new product.

Test markets based on multiple-unit experimental designs with a built-in *control* feature can provide more precise information about market response to various program alternatives. Suppose a manufacturer of a new bar soap with cleaning, moisturizing, and deodorant features would like to know whether to launch it at a price 10 percent higher than that of the competitors, as well as whether or not the advertising program should tout the features of the soap, as competitors do, or utilize a new humorous creative approach with an emotional appeal that highlights the brand's new name. A fairly straightforward 2×2 factorial experimental design could be employed. The layout for this design follows.

	New product advertising appeal	
New product price	**Traditional functional features appeal**	**New humorous appeal**
Competitive price	**Test unit 1 (control):** Competitive price Functional appeal	**Test unit 2:** Competitive price Humorous appeal
Priced 10% higher	**Test unit 3:** 10% higher price Functional appeal	**Test unit 4:** 10% higher price Humorous appeal

In this case, test unit 1 is designated the *control* unit and the others are called *treatment* units (in the sense that they are *treated* with different programs). The control unit provides the base from which reasonable comparisons can be made to evaluate the effects of a higher price and a very different creative approach for the competitive environment.

With a number of cities (or other test units) randomly assigned to each of the four test units and with the appropriate measures and data collection, the design can provide information about the *effects* of different program elements. The main effects of a 10 percent higher price versus a competitive price, the main effects of the new humorous appeal versus a more traditional appeal, and the *interaction* effect of both price and appeal on the performance of the new product can be estimated. When appropriate data are collected for each test unit, they can be analyzed with traditional analysis of variance techniques to test the main and interaction effects of these launch program elements. This technique tests for statistically significant differences between and among the various test units.

If the effects of additional launch program elements are of interest, more complicated experimental designs can be used to accommodate them. However, as the number of test units increases to measure these effects, costs and other difficulties arise. For example, external events may occur in one test unit but not another, leading to differences attributable to the event, not the program elements. As in the single-case study, it is useful to include measures on numerous other factors that may influence market response, track these measures, and through statistical analysis remove their effects on performance (using, for example, analysis of covariance). Nevertheless, as in any type of market research, the value of information gained from such designs must be weighed against the costs of poor decisions.[8]

Test Unit Selection

Test units should be defined and selected to be as representative as possible of the ultimate market or market segment that is being targeted with the new product. Moving away from this *representativeness* ideal reduces the ability to make valid projections about trial, repeat, and other measures from the test unit to the target market. When multiple units are used in an experimental setting to test alternative programs, those units should be matched as closely as possible. Typically, for convenience they are defined in terms of the same geographic units that define the target market—cities, regions, and countries (or other geographically based statistical and media units).

In the bar soap example, if all U.S. households define the market opportunity, a sample of cities should be selected for the test market, each of which would represent a cross-section of the United States. Theoretically, that may not be possible, but statistically and with some assumptions, cities can be identified that resemble the United States (or other definition of the target market). Data must be collected on the characteristics of each test unit and compared to identify those that are most similar in profile.[9] Occasionally, the use of weighting or adjustment factors can help to make different units more comparable. Test units can also be defined in terms of trade intermediaries (such as retail outlets, shopping centers, and industrial distributors), especially if they are consistent with the definition of the target market.

Type and Source of Data Collected

The type of data collected from a test market should reflect anticipated launch marketing problems. For example, if sales forecasting is of paramount concern, data on sales volume, market share, consumer trial, repeat purchase, depth of repeat purchase, usage, purchase cycle, brand awareness, brand image, and other factors will help develop estimates that can be projected to the target market. To the extent desired, further refinement of estimates of market response to different product features (via interviews with various types of users), advertising budgets and appeals, pricing, and other factors can be assessed. In effect, the test market should be viewed as a more realistic and information-rich environment in which to answer questions that have been difficult to resolve throughout the development process. Thus, reviewing the factors in the conceptual models defining market opportunity and sales forecasting can help define factors for which measures can be obtained in a test market.

The data collection sources for test markets can be as creative as necessary to answer the research questions. For example, consumer panels can help measure trial, repeat usage, and other questionnaire items; bar code electronic checkout scanners can provide detailed breakdowns of sales; store audits can be used to measure distribution levels achieved and displays used; surveys can measure awareness and brand positioning; focus groups and in-depth personal interviews can measure specific reactions to the product; and so on.

Duration of Test

Test marketing should last long enough to cover at least one purchase cycle when it is important to measure repeat purchasing, and preferably more than one. Opportunity for seasonal, climatic, and other sources of variation should also be considered—primarily factors that are related to product demand. The duration should also be sufficient to identify any suspected implementation problems in manufacturing, distribution, promotion, customer service, or other processes important to the product's eventual performance. Typical test markets run 6 to 12 months; however, for high stakes, high uncertainty new products, two-year test markets are plausible.

For example, Lever Brothers Co. launched its Lever 2000 bar after a two-year test market in Atlanta, Georgia. The product effectively combined deodorant and moisturizer in one bar soap that appealed to multiple members of the family—for example, a husband and wife who share the same bathroom could be happy with the same soap. The two-year test market time paid off; the product gained slightly more than the predicted 8 percent market share after its first year on the market, which put it in the top three brands. Although speed to market is critical, for some product and market situations, getting the launch program bugs worked out in a comprehensive, long-term single-case test market may be the best way to proceed.

ANALYSIS AND MODELING FOR TEST MARKETING

The value of any test marketing effort can be realized only from the information derived from analyses of data that have been collected to resolve the decision problems for which the effort was originally implemented. In addition to being analyzed with traditional marketing research methods (univariate, bivariate, and multivariate analyses) to learn about implementation issues and improve decision making for the new product, such test marketing data can be included in the new product forecasting models. These models are considered first for test marketing in general, and then for *simulated test marketing,* where the markets and marketing program implementation are less realistic and more assumptions are necessary to arrive at estimates.

Revisiting the Forecasting Models

Numerous forecasting models have been developed and evaluated for various types of test marketing.[10] Though these models typically focus on improved sales forecasting, data from test marketing should be used to update all three forecasting models discussed in Part 3 of the book: market opportunity, sales, and financial forecasting. All major assumptions should be challenged by the new information and key factors added (or deleted) in the models to better reflect understanding of the new product situation.

Reconsidering the sales forecasting model in Chapter 8 illustrates this procedure. Assume the new product depends on repeat purchase for its success (like the Combat roach and ant insecticide discussed previously). Repeat purchasing can denote a level of satisfaction that is a strong indicator of success. Of course, multiple repeat-purchases are even stronger indicators. The following multiplicative model of sales for selected time periods t provides a useful approach for organizing test marketing data for repeat-purchase products or services:

$$Vol_t = (\mathbf{Adp}_t)(Awr_t)(Try_t)(Rpt_t)(Avl_t) \qquad [10.1]$$

where Vol_t = sales at time t (number of estimated units sold),

$\mathbf{Adp}_t$ = estimated number of potential buyers (adopters) in the market at time t (from market opportunity forecast of market penetration),

Awr_t = awareness (proportion of potential buyers aware of new brand at time t),

Try_t = trial (proportion of aware potential buyers trying the new brand at time t),

Rpt_t = repeat purchase (proportion of trying potential buyers who repeat purchase new brand at time t), and

Avl_t = availability of new product through distributors (proportion of potential buyers for which product is available at time t).

Note that a major difference between this model and equation [8.1] (which was used for a new industrial product) is that separate trial and repeat variables replace the *Buy* variable (the proportion intending to buy the new product).

Just as in the approaches discussed in Chapter 8, each of the variables in the model can be estimated with submodels related to marketing program elements. For example, the awareness variable could be linked to advertising decisions. The trial variable could be linked to sales promotion devices (such as coupons, free samples, and special offers). Repeat purchase could be linked to satisfaction with various product features and price. Presumably, the test marketing data can be useful to update earlier model estimates obtained from judgment or surveys of buyer intentions. Other variables (not shown) that might be learned from the test market or hypothesized to be important in the purchase situation—such as the publicity variable discovered in the Combat case—can also be added to the model.

Using sales forecasting models throughout test marketing helps sharpen a sense of control of the new product's future financial performance by updating assumptions on the control chart of Figure 9.7. Decision making related to the financial aspects of the project can be based on market experience with the product, real or simulated. Learning more about appropriate levels of advertising, promotion, sales force, and distribution helps refine the estimates of costs necessary for new product success. In the Combat case, more expensive sales promotion coupons to encourage trial would increase program costs, but possibly increase revenue estimates. Further, learning about pricing can alter sales revenue estimates. Lowering price to be competitive in a particular situation may not build volume, thereby lowering revenue and profitability.

Even the market opportunity forecasting model should be revisited to check assumptions in the scenario defining the market opportunity. Are there reasons to believe that lifestyle, technology, or economic assumptions made in defining the opportunity may no longer be valid? Are there potentially new competitors on the horizon that might revise the expected market penetration rates? Careful analysis of test marketing data not only provides feedback on response to early implementation issues, but also helps maintain and update the linked new product forecasting models to support decision making.

Pre–Test-Marketing Models

The need for cost effective forms of marketing research that can provide the information necessary to reduce new product risk and alter the risk-return profile has spawned the development of a special class of models most useful in repeat-purchase consumer product situations. These *pre–test-market* models used in conjunction with STMs can help to decide whether or not a test market is worth conducting and, in many cases, whether or not to bypass a test market entirely to gain rapid market entry.

Pre–test-market models are focused versions of the general sales forecasting model in equation [10.1]. They are used to model data collected in STMs and tend to concentrate on a three-variable buying process:

Awareness $\longrightarrow$ *Trial* $\longrightarrow$ *Repeat purchase*

The models generally assume that of all potential buyers in a given time period, only those who are aware of the new product could potentially try it (trial), and only those who try it could potentially buy it again (repeat). Applying measures of these variables (for example, as probabilities or proportions) to the market opportunity facilitates estimation of market share and sales.

Pre–test-market models also include assumptions about the new product marketing program. The magnitude of planned distribution and promotion expenditures (advertising, sales promotions, sales force, and so on) can affect initial trial of the brand. Once trial is achieved, repeat purchases depend on how well the product meets consumer needs, as well as on continuing advertising and promotional efforts. The models can also be used to evaluate response to a proposed advertising approach. For example, if real or mock ads are shown in the STM data-collection process, direct consumer evaluation of them can be obtained via questionnaires.

There are a variety of ways to creatively use and model STM data, as evidenced by the numerous pre–test-market models available from commercial market research firms. These models have gained widespread use among consumer products manufacturers and are therefore worth a brief review to improve understanding of their general structure.[11] Because of the availability of published details on the early form of the models, an overview of the ASSESSOR modeling approach and its submodel equation is presented in Figure 10.3.

As revealed in the diagram of ASSESSOR in Figure 10.3, two models are included in the procedure: a preference model and a trial and repeat model.[12] Both are designed to predict brand shares, but rely on different measurement approaches. Recall the discussion of the value of multiple methods and approaches in Chapter 7. If the ASSESSOR model estimates converge, one has greater confidence in the results; however, differences require managers and analysts to reconcile outputs to arrive at share predictions.

From the trial and repeat model equations in Figure 10.3, it is evident that *long-run* market share depends on estimates of the trial rate and the repeat rate.[13] Note that all of these estimates assume a long-run equilibrium market share. The model does not reflect share growth from year to year. Thus, it generally corresponds to a manager's interest in knowing whether or not the product will ever make it in the market as it is now defined. However, it does not allow for share-building strategies over time (increased promotional efforts, product line extensions, price declines, and so on).

The trial rate in the model depends on two components: (1) FKD—the probability of long-run trial (with unlimited awareness and distribution) mul-

FIGURE 10.3 Overview of ASSESSOR pre–test-market model.[a]

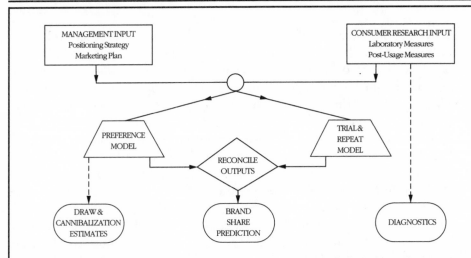

Preference model

Market share model

$$M(t) = \left(E(t) \sum_{i=1}^{N} L_i(t) \right) / N$$

where:

$M(t)$ = expected market share for the new brand t

t = index for the new brand

$E(t)$ = proportion of consumers who include new brand t in their relevant set of alternatives

$L_i(t)$ = predicted probablility of purchase of new brand t by consumer i, $i = 1$ to N consumers

Purchase probability model (after exposure to new brand)

$$L_i(t) = [A_i(t)]^\beta / \left([A_i(t)]^\beta + \sum_{k=1}^{m_i} [A_i(k)]^\beta \right)$$

where:

$L_i(t)$ = probability that consumer i chooses the new brand t after having tried it

k = index for m established brands in consumers' relevant set of alternatives

$A_i(t)$ = estimated preference of consumer i for the new brand t after having tried it

$A_i(k)$ = estimated preference of consumer i for established brand k after having tried the new brand

β = a parameter to be estimated from preference data for established brands prior to the new brand, and assumed stable after trial of the new brand

Purchase probability model (pre-exposure to new brand)

$$P_i(j) = [V_i(j)]^\beta / \left(\sum_{k=1}^{m_i} [V_i(k)]^\beta \right)$$

where:

$P_i(j)$ = probability that consumer i chooses brand j

$V_i(j)$ = estimated preference of consumer i for brand j

$V_i(k)$ = estimated preference of consumer i for established brand k

Trial & repeat model

Market share model

$$M(t) = TS$$

where:

T = ultimate cumulative trial for the new brand, t

S = ultimate repeat purchase rate for the new brand, t

Trial model

$$T = FKD + CU - (FKD)(CU)$$

where:

F = long-run probability of a consumer making a first purchase of the new brand given awareness and availability of it

D = long-run probability that the new brand is available to a consumer

K = long-run probability that a consumer becomes aware of the new brand

C = probability that a consumer will receive a sample of the new brand

U = probability that a consumer who receives a sample of the new brand will use it, and the term $[(FKD) - (CU)]$ represents an adjustment to avoid double counting

Repeat model

$$S = R(k, t) / (1 + R(k, t) - R(t, t))$$

where:

$R(k, t)$ = probability that a consumer who last purchased *any* of the established brands (k) will switch to the new brand (t) on the next buying occasion

$R(t, t)$ = probability that a consumer who last purchased the new brand will repurchase it on the next buying occasion

---

[a]Note that the equations and variable names presented here are based on the original presentation of the model by Alvin J. Silk and Glen L. Urban, "Pre–Test-Market Evaluation of New Packaged Goods: A Model and Measurement Methodology," *Journal of Marketing Research*, 15 (May 1978), pp. 171–191. Reprinted by permission of the American Marketing Association.

tiplied by the probabilities of awareness and distribution, respectively, *and* (2) CU—the probability of consumers receiving the new brand as a sample multiplied by the probability that those who receive the sample will use it. The variable F can be estimated from the initial proportion of purchases in the STM; K can be estimated from advertising variables (budget, copy, media, and so on) that might be used to build awareness; D can be estimated from promotions, sales force, and other efforts to sell-in the new product to the trade; C can be estimated from the proportion of samples sent out to the total market segment; and U can be estimated from historical rates of sample usage.

As shown in Figure 10.3, the probability of repeat purchase is modeled as the equilibrium share of a first-order, two-state Markov process and depends on estimates of switching and repeat purchase probabilities. These transition probability estimates can be obtained from the STM questionnaire data. Note that a combination of data from the STM and judgment is required to estimate the trial model parameters. However, the repeat model parameters, which reflect estimates of long-term purchase behavior, depend on questionnaire data, not behavior.

The preference model in ASSESSOR is a logit-type probability model. It estimates individual consumer probabilities of purchasing the new brand from measures of brand preference taken before and after use. These individual measures are then aggregated to estimate market share for the new brand amid the set of competing brands. By measuring preferences for a respondent's evoked set of brands (for example, in a task of allocating a fixed number of points to each brand) at the outset of the STM, relative preference ratings are obtained. After the new product has been tried, the same allocation task can be performed, but including the new brand. Comparing the market shares obtained from these two sets of preference measures makes it possible to estimate which brands gave up share to the new brand (its *draw*); if one of the existing brands was marketed by the firm developing the new product, share lost to the new brand can be estimated as well (*cannibalization*).

Once the pre–test-market model has been estimated, the results can be used in a spreadsheet format to try alternative levels of advertising, distribution, sampling, or other parameters in a "what-if" fashion to assess their impact on market share estimates. The ASSESSOR model (and those like it, such as the BASES model, discussed previously) has been applied to numerous consumer packaged goods categories, and reported forecast accuracy and user reaction to the model appear to be satisfactory.[14] However, to date, no major studies have comprehensively compared these commercial models, some of which have variations in assumptions, variables used, and data collection procedures.

EVALUATION OF TEST MARKETING

A summary comparison of the three major types of test marketing is provided in Figure 10.4. These generalizations should be used only as guidelines to develop a more specific set of criteria for each new product situation. A review of this chart suggests that STM is most useful when speed, cost, and secur-

FIGURE 10.4 Summary comparison of three major types of test marketing.[a]

Criteria	Simulated Test Marketing	Controlled Test Marketing	Conventional Test Marketing
Cost	Least expensive	Moderate to very expensive, depending on design and scope	Very expensive, unless creatively designed or incorporated as part of rollout launch strategy
Control of test units	Moderate control because of reliance on sampling to define test units	Greatest control of test units (for example, distribution outlets, cable TV advertising)	Moderate control (can control selection of different test units, but limited control within test units)
Ability to test selected marketing program variables	Limited, but can be improved with multiple STMs	Excellent for advertising, promotions, price, and product features	Moderate to excellent, depending on scope of design and controls; can assess entire program performance
Effectiveness in revealing implementation problems	Least effective, because no implementation occurs	Moderately effective, because some implementation problems will be evident	Most effective, especially when treated as testing launch marketing programs
Security (for example, from competitors)	Good to excellent	Moderate	Poor to moderate, because it's a public event
Speed of execution	Excellent (about three months)	Moderate to good, depending on design and purpose	Poor, can take months to years in some cases
Captures buyer behavior	Least effective (because of nature of STM data collection process)	Good, because of control and measurement of market response	Moderate to good, but can be excellent with appropriate data collection techniques (for example, panels, scanner data)
Captures trade behavior	Least effective, because trade behavior is not included in STM design	Limited, because trade cooperation is obtained in advance	Excellent if marketing program to trade is used over obtaining advanced cooperation of stores
Captures other stakeholder behavior	Least effective, because not included in STM design	Limited, unless special efforts to include stakeholders in test communities obtained	Moderate to good, especially with broad regional test markets
Captures environmental forces	Least effective, because not included in STM design	Moderate, but limited to test communities	Moderate to good, especially with broad regional test markets
Captures organizational resistance to change	Limited, because design of STM does not often call for broad organizational involvement to implement	Moderate to good, because organizational efforts are necessary to complete product and develop launch programs	Excellent, because most organizational functions are tasked to perform, especially sales force
Helps forecast new product costs	Limited, unless different STMs selected to test alternative product formulations	Moderate, helps to estimate certain marketing costs (for example, ad budget, promotions)	Good to excellent, depending on design of test market
Other			

[a]The judgments shown are generalizations. Depending on extent of use, each organization should develop its own criteria and record its experience with each data source to better support market entry decisions.

ity are important determinants of the new product situation. An STM can be conducted in about three months, will cost between $50,000 and $100,000 (relative to $1 million+ for test markets), and can be completed in relative seclusion from competitors. Further, its results have been satisfactory in forecasting market share of a test market.[15] In cases where this is the major criterion for new product launch and deciding whether or not to invest in a test market, an STM can provide value to its users.

The downside of STM is the difficulty of capturing realistic implementation problems in preparing for market entry. For example, it would be difficult to capture trade behavior, long-term buyer behavior, regulatory reaction, environmental trends, or organizational problems in realizing the new product or service. Observing such behaviors is difficult when the focus is limited to consumer choice in a laboratory or some other simulated setting. These testing procedures are also done within the confines of current consumer experience, which can lead to the rejection of really new products that are not consistent with it. Breakthrough products may require time for potential buyers to recognize their real product benefits.

As shown in Figure 10.4, the criteria that favor controlled or conventional test marketing are almost the reverse of those for STM. The more realistic approaches provide greater diagnostic flexibility for testing specific decisions; they better capture long-term behaviors of a variety of new product stakeholders; and, perhaps most importantly, they help identify implementation problems prior to market entry. But these benefits come at the expense of higher costs, longer time, and loss of competitive secrecy. As for most difficult decisions, whether or not to use one or more of these test marketing approaches depends on situational factors, such as the nature of the new product or service, its importance to the firm, and the degree of uncertainty in its market environment.

Most applications of all forms of test marketing appear to be for repeat-purchase consumer packaged goods. Durable consumer and industrial products and services are often difficult to offer to consumers until they have gone through a complete purchase, use, and satisfaction cycle. For example, consider a new credit card that places a portion of every purchase in the user's retirement account; the potential buyer may have a difficult time envisioning the benefits of this product because they accrue slowly over time. Consumers may buy the card, but will they use it often? Or will they use the card from which they receive travel bonus points?

Nevertheless, creative attempts to utilize the various test marketing techniques for durable new products and services have been undertaken and are encouraged.[16] Recall GTE's test of its new wireless pocket phones in Tampa. Sensormatic Corp. reported the use of conventional test marketing to discover implementation problems with its SensorGate electronic tag security system marketed to retailers concerned with pilferage of high-priced products.[17] In 1991, United Parcel Service of America, Inc. selected five cities to test market a new second-day letter delivery service priced at $5.00.[18] Finally, direct marketers have also used test marketing effectively—for example, trying different catalog themes in test markets to determine which are the most effective. The ability of direct marketers to manipulate mailing lists and target circulation affords considerable control in testing various combinations of offerings.

The situational aspect of a new product in terms of its importance and the uncertainty in its market environment also provides guidelines for thinking about how to use the various types of test marketing. The table below may help to provoke thinking about the use of the different approaches according to various product/market situations.

Degree of new product importance	Degree of environmental, market, and organizational uncertainty	
	High uncertainty	**Low uncertainty**
High stakes	Simulated TM Controlled TM Conventional TM Launch and track	Controlled TM Conventional TM Launch and track
Low stakes	Simulated TM Launch and track	Launch and track

The logic of the table should be apparent. Assume the decision maker is risk averse (as is common in new product situations where resistance to change tends to be high). When stakes and market uncertainty are high, a full array of test marketing approaches might be used to ensure successful entry. At the other extreme, with little to lose in rather stable market circumstances, even the risk-averse manager might launch and track the new product without any form of test marketing.

When uncertainty is high and stakes are low, a rather inexpensive simulated test market can be used to decide whether or not to launch the new product. When stakes are high but uncertainty is low, more carefully controlled test marketing followed by conventional test marketing may eliminate any defects in what should be a smooth market entry. The high stakes justify the investment in more expensive approaches. Finally, all of these entry programs are subject to the other criteria listed in Figure 10.4. For example, on the issue of timing, if accelerated development is necessary, controlled and conventional test marketing can be omitted altogether. If the decision makers are willing to take the risk, the new product can be launched without any test marketing— but those in charge must be prepared to track and monitor the launch very closely and make adjustments as needed. Various market entry strategies and launch and tracking capabilities are discussed in Chapters 11 and 12.

SUMMARY

Test marketing represents the first real chance to implement the new product marketing program and evaluate market response to it. The emphasis is clearly on *learning* what should be changed prior to a full-scale launch of the new product—even the new product itself is subject to modification. Depending on managerial concerns about the new product, test marketing can be conducted in simulated, controlled, or conventional market environments.

Determining the type of test marketing to use, and whether or not to use it, requires careful consideration of the problems to be addressed and decisions to be made, the research design principles for resolving the problems, and the expected analyses and modeling of data collected from test marketing. Fitting these concerns with the nature of the new product, its importance to the organization, and the amount of uncertainty in the market environment helps to resolve the question of how best to use test marketing as a first step in marketing program implementation and as a basis for challenging and updating the various new product forecasts. It can also provide valuable input for deciding on the best market entry strategy.

11 Market Entry Decisions

The everyday pressures in organizational life to generate a continuous stream of profitable new products can blind managers to the possibility of terminating a new product project—the *no-go* decision. Once a new product idea surfaces, and a product champion overcomes inertia to get the project off the ground with a new product team, natural pride in the new product creates a momentum that makes it difficult to say "no." This pride is reinforced when the information from market opportunity and sales forecasts is interpreted in a favorable light—the bias of optimism. The momentum for the new product continues to build, and the decision to *go*—whether implicit or explicit—becomes a decision to *go now!* Lost in the rush to get the new product on the market quickly are the strategic aspects of the market entry decision.

The market entry decision is at the heart of several interrelated new product development problems. What will be the financial outcomes if a new product is launched early, on time, or late? If resources could be invested to accelerate the product development cycle, what difference would the competitive time advantage make in terms of financial and other returns? What is lost (or gained) if entry is delayed to meet competitors or market needs with improved product quality? Should market entry proceed quietly in selected geographic markets with subsequent national or global rollout or should it proceed globally with considerable fanfare and hype?

Unfortunately, there are few rules to help executives make these difficult market entry decisions. Market entry tends to be a highly situation-specific decision. The dynamics of the environment, the market, the organization, and its new product development process must be assessed by the decision maker. Although rules are lacking, some guidelines might help to make a sound decision: (1) recognize the situational aspects of market entry, (2) clarify the strategic importance of the market entry decision, and (3) formulate the market entry decision problem. These guidelines are considered in the three major sections of this chapter. The last section includes a comprehensive case study that illustrates many of the concepts and forecasting processes used throughout this book.

THE SITUATIONAL NATURE
OF MARKET ENTRY DECISIONS

Research on market entry has been perplexing. Some studies have shown that being a market pioneer has considerable benefits, whereas others have shown that being a follower pays off handsomely. For example, one study revealed that organizations entering the market an average of 13 years after the pioneer eventually became the market leaders.[1] Clearly, numerous factors—other than just being the first to enter a market—are at work in determining long-run strategic success. As has been emphasized throughout this book, new product development is highly situational, and therefore involves consideration of a variety of factors that might drive long-run market success. The following brief case studies highlight some of the situational aspects of market entry.

Entry Decisions Are Crucial in *High-Stakes* Markets

In May 1992, Kimberly-Clark Co. launched a new disposable diaper that was 50 percent thinner than its regular Huggies brand, but had the same absorbency.[2] It offered consumers a snugger fit with a felt-like lining. The company beat its arch rival Procter & Gamble into the $4 billion market with the new superabsorbent product. Two weeks later, in reprisal, P&G announced it too would launch a new version of a superabsorbent disposable diaper through its Pampers and Luvs brands by October of the same year. That would put P&G only three months behind Kimberly-Clark. Apparently, its product would not be as thin as the Huggies new diaper, but would be more absorbent. These products were high stakes to both organizations—they represented some 16 percent of P&G's sales revenue and some 24 percent of Kimberly-Clark's sales revenue. Together, the two firms accounted for about 80 percent of the disposable diaper market.

However, by October 1992, it became clear that P&G was not ready to launch its promised new product. It announced a test market in Eugene, Oregon, during December 1992. Stock analysts were reportedly concerned because P&G appeared to be at least six months behind Kimberly-Clark. By November, Kimberly-Clark had achieved 80 percent distribution and was poised to take share from P&G. To combat the new product, P&G resorted to price cuts of its current line, thereby reducing profit margins.

Could P&G have launched its new product as planned in October instead of opting for further development? Perhaps after seeing Kimberly-Clark's new product, it decided that it could compete more effectively by developing even better diaper features. Why else would it conduct a test market for a product that would not match the thinness feature of Huggies? Of course, these are speculative questions, but this case shows that market entry in high-stakes new product situations has important consequences for a variety of stakeholders and requires consideration of numerous market factors.

Entry Decisions Are Crucial in *Uncertain* Markets

In the 1960s, AT&T top management approved the development of Picture-phone,[3] a device that would enable callers to see each other on small screens while talking. Picturephone was launched in 1969, and sales volume projections showed annual sales growth to $1 billion by 1980. Unfortunately, after considerable investment, the service was removed from the market. A favorable market response failed to materialize. Undaunted, AT&T relaunched Picturephone in 1981 as the Picturephone Meeting Service to provide televised meetings between executives in different cities. Positioning the service in a more well-defined business market may have motivated the re-entry. However, in early 1985, this service also was removed from the market because of insufficient sales. The market remained elusive and uncertain.

Nevertheless, hope springs eternal for the basic technology. Two small firms, Compression Labs and PictureTel, survived by offering their services to an apparently small market for video conferencing. As technology improved and prices dropped, they anticipated a growing market. In fact, in 1992, using Compression Labs' technology, AT&T announced another re-entry into the market with a $1,500 videophone. By the end of 1992, AT&T dropped the price by $500 in hopes of getting an edge on competitors. Then MCI announced it would soon be entering the market with a $750 videophone. Would the market be ready for this new videophone, or would as many uncertainties surround this latest version as surrounded earlier ones? Improved technology, the emergence of competitors, and declining prices may signal a reduction of some of the uncertainty in the market for potential buyers—still, there may be additional hurdles to overcome before the market begins to grow and videophones succeed.

The lesson to be learned from these new product situations is that market entry depends on numerous factors brought about by environmental, market, and organizational conditions. The uncertainty of technology, cost, buyer acceptance, and other factors drove the "when" and "how" of market entry for videophones. The importance of the disposable diaper market, coupled with intense competitive pressure and fickle consumers, drove P&G's response of cutting prices on its existing product and refining its new product and marketing program through test marketing rather than rushing to market with an inferior new product. Clearly, in both cases, a strategic view of market entry was needed to put the immediate business pressures into a long-term perspective for competitive advantage and market success.

STRATEGIC ASPECTS OF MARKET ENTRY

The launch marketing program at market entry represents the point of execution of a business strategy. It contains all the information defining a new product's role in an organization's business strategy. Thus, market entry for a new product includes its launch marketing program to a target market segment, preferably refined through a test marketing experience; a *timing* decision (when to enter); a *launch scale* decision (how to enter); and a *resonance* decision (the level of intensity with which to enter). These strategic aspects of market entry are illustrated with Intel Corp.'s Pentium line of microprocessor products.[4]

Intel has continually faced the problem of balancing its successive generations of microprocessor chips with market dynamics in order to fashion a strategic approach to its market entry. The successful line of 8086, 80286, 80386, and 80486 chips reflects market entry decisions that involved when to enter, what features to include on each new generation, what price to set, and what other marketing and promotion efforts to use with the new launch. The market included both software and hardware manufacturers of personal computers whose new product plans interacted with Intel's market entry decisions. In addition, Intel focused on end users with a broadcast and print campaign that featured the message "Intel Inside," an otherwise hidden quality in personal computers.

Recognizing the growing importance of its market entry decisions, Intel approached its next-generation chip with a different strategy. This shift may have been the result of taking into account numerous changes in the key factors defining the market environment. The company was facing additional competition from successfully cloned chips (Advanced Micro Devices and Cyrix Corp.), as well as various legal battles over patent rights. Workstation manufacturers were lowering prices on their machines, bringing them closer in value to the more powerful personal computers. Anticipated new software from Microsoft Corporation (Windows NT) held the promise of power and flexibility that might enable personal computers with *their* next-generation chip to compete in the workstation market. Finally, when the new chip became ready for the market, the 80486 chip was still very successful. Introducing the new chip prematurely could cannibalize sales of the older one.

These and other factors led to a change in Intel's market entry strategy. The new chip would not be given the obvious numerical extension (80586), but rather the name "Pentium." It would be priced low enough to enable early-adopting personal computer manufacturers to sell their initial machines at a price that might be competitive with the declining price of high-powered workstations, yet higher than the price of machines with the 80486 chip. Moreover, an advertising and promotion campaign for the new Pentium product would position it toward a "power users" segment of the market, downplaying its role as the next-generation upgrade chip and suggesting that only a few computer users would really need its power. The product was launched in May 1993, when Intel's 80486 chip was just becoming the market leader. The market entry was significant, but subdued in contrast to the traditional highly resonating launches of new products in the personal computer business.

The Intel case illustrates the use of a different market entry approach to change the momentum of an existing business strategy. Timing the launch well before the existing 80486 chip matured made clear to personal computer manufacturers that Pentium was not meant to be a replacement product. The launch scale was modest by past standards, with the product rolled out in limited quantities to a segment of "power users" who would likely be the first to adopt. Further, the market entry was intended to be relatively *low key*—without the normal hype and hoopla that can cause an entry strategy to resonate in its impact (although it was of more than passing interest to the business press because of Intel's stock market performance). Intel faced an uphill battle in changing the traditional market momentum, but its new market entry approach illustrates how the use of launch timing, scale, and resonance can help shape a new product's role in business strategy.

Market Entry *Timing*

The time of market entry anticipates the formal starting point for the implementation of a new product strategy, and depends not only on the organization's cycle time to development, but also on anticipated environmental turbulence and market friction. How long it takes to get to the starting point depends largely on an organization's propensity to innovate (discussed in Chapter 4) and the forecast of development time. However, whether or not potential buyers and other stakeholders are ready to buy the new product, and how many will buy it as developed, will also determine entry time. Thus, market entry timing is highly situational and, for important projects, requires analytical support for decision making.[5]

Managing and planning the activities to determine the best time (or at least the best range of time) to enter a market not only forces the consideration of potential post-launch implementation problems, but may also provide unexpected strategic leverage for establishing or defending long-run competitive advantage. Potential advantages that might accumulate because of early entry can dissipate unless critical program and market factors are carefully managed.[6] To illustrate the link between market entry timing and long-run competitive advantage, three general time-based actions are considered: *early* entry, *parity* entry, and *delayed* entry.[7]

Early Entry Timing Strategy

There is some evidence, though not definitive proof, that early market entry timing can provide competitive advantage.[8] The general reason is that the first mover in a market has the opportunity to build *barriers* to entry to defend against competitors. The early entrant's new product and launch marketing program should provide a significantly satisfying and sustainable competitive advantage among potential buyers. If the new product was developed to satisfy an unmet need, potential buyers should be highly receptive to information about the new product and be quick to try it and develop loyalty if it clearly satisfies the need. Building an early and loyal base of customers, who might also favorably influence other potential buyers, is a critical step in building a strong market position.

Whether the new product and the need it satisfies are based on price (lower costs) or other distinctive features (and the technologies they reflect, proprietary or otherwise), opportunities for building barriers are possible with an early entry. These barriers can be based on economies of scale, experience effect, marketing program changes after launch (lower price, increased communication, intensified distribution, etc.), continual improvements in product, production, and technology, and increasingly effective and efficient resource allocations in other areas.

The carpet deodorizer market provides an example of the advantages of early entry.[9] After a two-year product development cycle and an investment of $15 million, Airwick Industries, Inc. launched Carpet Fresh in 1978. The product was a first—when sprinkled on a carpet and vacuumed, the powder deodorized the carpet and the air in the room. Families with pets and smokers responded positively to the new concept. However, just six months after Airwick's successful introduction, Lehn & Fink entered with an identical product (Love My Carpet). The market grew into a $100 million business in two years. Despite increased competition, at the two-year mark Airwick still maintained a leadership position, with a 60 percent market share. For Airwick, pioneering paid off; but Lehn & Fink's quick response may have helped that company to benefit as well, depending on the investment required to enter the market so soon.

Parity Entry Timing Strategy

Parity entry timing involves introducing the new product at, or very near, the time a significant competitor is expected to enter. The *parity entry time zone* is one within which being first does not make a difference to the market and other stakeholders. The underlying market behavior that supports the logic of parity entry is that before potential buyers have a chance to understand a new brand, try it, and develop a preference, a second new entry shares the attention, thereby bringing the market back to competitive equilibrium. Recall the competitive situation in the disposable diaper market. A two- to three-month-late market entry by P&G may not have had a significant impact on its business; however, a six-month delay may have put it at a competitive disadvantage. The length of the parity entry time zone may vary by product and market situation; needless to say, its length is important to ascertain in highly competitive and turbulent market situations.

Parity entry can be useful in markets characterized by a proliferation of brands and when information and estimates about the product development plans of major competitors are available or discoverable. Parity entry timing tends to be defensive to offset potential advantages that might be created by competitive product development efforts. It can also be used as an offensive strategy in a multi-product market situation. Knowing that a competitor is a quick imitative follower can be used to advantage in smaller markets to draw attention away from the competitor in more important markets.

For example, in the highly competitive beer market, Anheuser-Busch introduced its low alcohol brand (LA) after one month of test marketing. LA was introduced to 65 percent of the United States by early June 1984 and became available nationwide by fall of the same year. In a parity move, Miller Brewing Co. introduced its low alcohol entry (Sharp's LA) into the market by the end of August 1984 and it was available nationwide by fall, thereby precluding any substantial early share-building by Anheuser-Busch because of potential time leverage. Miller clearly showed quick defensive maneuvering in this situation. However, an offensive interpretation of this sequence of events could be Anheuser-Busch's desire to draw attention away from Miller's strong position in the light beer market while pushing its own Bud Lite marketing efforts against Miller Lite.

Delayed Entry Timing Strategy

Delayed entry timing involves *postponing* the launch date for a new product to accomplish long-run competitive advantage. Given the apparent benefits of early entry, why delay entry?[10] A major advantage of delaying entry is waiting for a market opportunity to grow to an attractive size. For example, after an investment of some $25 million, Time Inc. shelved plans to enter the teletext market in 1984 because of uncertainties about market size.

Delayed entry may also allow a competitor to be a first mover. The major advantage of following a competitor is the possibility of *learning* from the early entrant's market experience. Capturing and capitalizing on this information can influence almost every aspect of the new product development process. The learning can translate to lower costs of innovation, design, marketing research, and production. Perhaps most importantly, buyer preferences will be revealed and can be used to improve product features and market positioning approaches for the late entrant's launch. Learning can also translate to lower risk—simply knowing the mistakes of others can reduce the number of problematic decision alternatives, or the size of a decision tree with all of its possible outcomes.

As an example of successful delayed entry, consider the automated teller machine (ATM) market pioneered by Docutel in 1970. In the early and mid-1970s, while Docutel dominated the market, Diebold Inc. was developing its entry. When Diebold finally entered in late 1975, its product had improved competitive features and managed to obtain a steadily increasing market share. By 1982, Diebold had achieved a 47 percent market share, followed by IBM with 25 percent and Docutel with 19 percent.

Market Entry *Scale*

Market entry scale recognizes that the execution of a new product launch can be either on a full-scale basis to the target market segment or on a smaller scale. It combines the number or type of subsegment schemes with a rollout sequence to best meet the goals of the business strategy. Typically, a new product marketing program is based on the selection of one or more target market segments. These segments can often be broken down further into units or subsegments that may afford more efficient allocation of resources for market entry. Typical subsegments include those defined by new product adoption categories, geography, distribution channel, sales force, advertising media, or some other useful variable. The targeted segment can be reached through any of these subsegments, but the entry approach can be executed as a sequential rollout or full-scale launch to augment some aspect of the basic business strategy.

For example, new products that depend on word-of-mouth influence for success would benefit from a rollout market entry that focuses initially on the subsegment of *innovators*. Recall from discussions in Chapter 3 that if these influential buyers are persuaded to buy early, they can speed the diffusion process for the new product—and presumably help achieve cash flow and related financial and marketing goals—through their influence on *imitators*. For other products, market subsegments based on geographic location may be the best basis for market entry. Some firms first enter segments that are geographically local and then expand to regional, national, and eventually global levels.

Market entry can also proceed through a segmentation rollout across different distribution channels. For example, a new *perfume* product targeted to women for use during the evening might first be distributed to expensive department stores and specialty retail stores. It may then be rolled out to other department stores and drugstores, and finally to mass merchandisers and discount stores. Similarly, marketing programs can be rolled out to subsegments through specific media vehicles (broadcast versus print) or sales forces (for firms that have segmented their sales force). Finally, a full-scale launch into the entire market segment is always an option.

Rollout market entry through segmentation can be helpful in situations with high stakes and high uncertainty about market response. Launching a new product in a subsegment under carefully controlled conditions can provide valuable early market response information to identify necessary adjustments. What is learned from the first subsegment can be transferred to the second, and so on, until sufficient information is available for a comprehensive launch. If adequate lead time is available, sequential market entry can even obviate the need for additional pre-launch market research. The logic is to get the product into a market as soon as possible, to make adjustments, and to continue rollout until the desired product development and launch marketing program decisions are reached.

Market Entry *Resonance*

The concept of *resonance* has been used to describe the echoing or doubleness within an advertisement that gives it a distinctive style or appeal.[11] With some modification of meaning, the idea of resonance is applicable to marketing programs in general and to new product launch programs in particular. Resonance might be viewed on a continuum from high to low. In a physical sense, resonance is the intensification and enrichment of a tone. In the context of a launch program, it could mean the configuration of communicative elements or symbols (product features, price, ads, promotions, displays, and so on) to echo each other, thus giving the program an impact upon entry that would resonate in the market.

For a high-resonance launch, the goal would be to create a marketing program targeted to relevant stakeholders that generates a doubleness of message, almost a vibration, that carries with the stakeholders to accelerate the diffusion of information about the new product. In a new product context, the tool to achieve this has been called "marketing hype"—the prelaunch activities leading to the creation of a marketing environment conducive to the acceptance of a new product.[12] A marketing hype program for a new product launch should:

- Target segments of relevant stakeholders.
- Have substantial magnitude and impact.
- Be timed correctly (long enough to be effective but not so long as to frustrate).
- Convey a consistent message to stakeholders, yet one that differentiates the firm from competitors.

Although they are intuitively appealing, highly resonant launch programs can create expectations for the new product that can't be met, or otherwise cause unanticipated consequences—for example, signaling competitors too early, failing to meet a real or implied launch date, or generating inadvertent negative publicity prior to launch, especially if double meanings embedded in communications to create resonance are misconstrued.

At the other extreme are market entry launch programs that are low in resonance—in effect, a *stealth* market entry. The objective is to enter the market as quietly as possible, without fanfare or communications that echo in any way. Firms launching multiple new products that are based on a strategically segmented market may want to enter each segment quietly without signaling their overall strategy. Firms launching products in highly sensitive markets also may opt for a low resonance entry. For example, a bank marketing a new asset management service to private clients with net worth of $20 million or more may choose a quiet approach to market entry. So may a firm entering markets with products that are culturally taboo, yet needed by certain potential buyers.

The level of entry resonance can be anywhere between the two extremes. Perhaps the primary benefit of considering entry resonance is that, to decide on the appropriate level, new product launch goals must be carefully specified. Often new product objectives, goals, and launch criteria for *go/no-go* decisions are set with little attention to the kinds of effects desired for the launch program among the various stakeholders. Setting the level of resonance requires an understanding of the major sources of market friction that may delay new product acceptance, and may require models and methods that more specifically assess market response to the new product.

FORMULATING MARKET ENTRY DECISIONS

As developed in Chapter 6, the key *go/no-go* new product decision consists of four major sets of alternatives:

1. *Go*—Proceed to launch (market entry timing, scale, and resonance).
2. *Modify*—Revise the new product and/or its marketing program.
3. *Timing*—Accelerate, slow, or hold the development process.
4. *No-go*—Re-examine prior steps or terminate the project.

The *go* decision is the gateway to market entry. It should be continually appraised throughout the development process. It includes decisions on market entry timing (early, parity, delay), launch scale (limited rollout, full scale), and resonance (low to high). The approach used to decide on the various options may depend on organizational preferences and practices. Some organizations may prefer the decision to be informal and based largely on judgment or intuition. Others may prefer more formal procedures involving systematic processes that assess the risk and return of the project in comparison to other investment projects. The recommendation throughout this book is to use managerial models that encourage a combination of data and judgment focused on the decisions at hand. In the case study that follows, a managerial model illustrates how several of the concepts and procedures presented in this book can be employed to help make the market entry timing decision.

In Figure 11.1, an approach for evaluating the market entry timing decision is outlined. The basic logic of the approach is consistent with the preceding chapters: use an understanding of the major conceptual factors defining the business situation to formulate forecasting models and submodels that will provide input for the market entry decision. In the decision process outlined in Figure 11.1, market opportunity, sales, and financial forecasts are used to compare performance estimates under different entry timing and competitive assumptions. Also, by changing various model assumptions, sensitivities and contingencies can be evaluated.

FIGURE 11.1   An approach for market entry timing decisions.

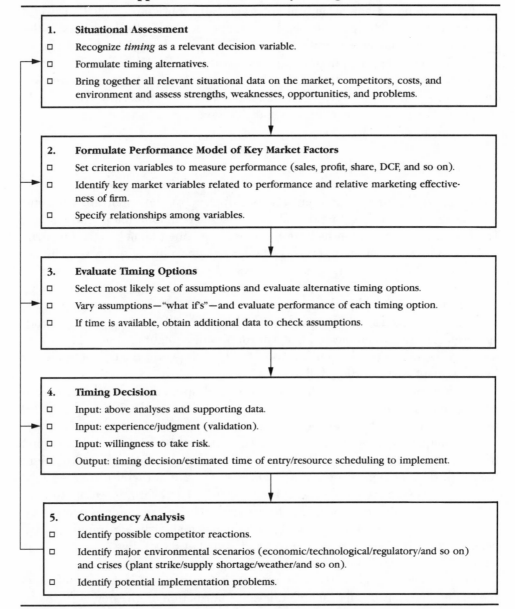

1.   Situational Assessment

□   Recognize *timing* as a relevant decision variable.

□   Formulate timing alternatives.

□   Bring together all relevant situational data on the market, competitors, costs, and environment and assess strengths, weaknesses, opportunities, and problems.

2.   Formulate Performance Model of Key Market Factors

□   Set criterion variables to measure performance (sales, profit, share, DCF, and so on).

□   Identify key market variables related to performance and relative marketing effectiveness of firm.

□   Specify relationships among variables.

3.   Evaluate Timing Options

□   Select most likely set of assumptions and evaluate alternative timing options.

□   Vary assumptions—"what if's"—and evaluate performance of each timing option.

□   If time is available, obtain additional data to check assumptions.

4.   Timing Decision

□   Input: above analyses and supporting data.

□   Input: experience/judgment (validation).

□   Input: willingness to take risk.

□   Output: timing decision/estimated time of entry/resource scheduling to implement.

5.   Contingency Analysis

□   Identify possible competitor reactions.

□   Identify major environmental scenarios (economic/technological/regulatory/and so on) and crises (plant strike/supply shortage/weather/and so on).

□   Identify potential implementation problems.

Source: Robert J. Thomas, "Timing—The Key to Market Entry," *Journal of Consumer Marketing*, 2 (Summer 1985), pp. 77–87.

The case study described here involves the early development of the mobile telephone industry.[13] Cellular mobile telephone combines microwave technology, solid-state electronic switching, and computerization to provide an improved mobile telephone service to users. It overcame problems of existing mobile telephone services by substantially improving voice transmission quality and increasing user and usage capacity in the system.

As developed in the mid-1980s, cellular telephone technology was operationalized through a honeycomb of geographically contiguous cells that would facilitate rapid switching of signals. It theoretically enabled subscribers of the service to place and receive calls anywhere in the world without being tied to a wire. To encourage competition and efficiency in the provision of this new mobile telephone service, the FCC ruled that one firm (designated a *nonwireline* carrier) would be selected in a comparative hearing process to be the sole competitor to a *wireline* carrier in a specified geographic area.

1. Situational Assessment

A leading firm in the telecommunications industry won the opportunity to compete against the wireline carrier in the new cellular mobile telephone market. The firm was about 18 months from the initially planned launch date of its marketing program for the new service, when, through industry sources, it discovered that the major wireline competitor was also planning to enter the market at about the same time. Because the product was initially targeted to commercial users, some value was placed on getting early account subscribers. Consequently, *time* was recognized as a key variable in the situation. Discussions with the product development team indicated that a *crash* program might enable market entry within six months—resulting in 12 months of lead time over the competition—at a cost of about a half-million dollars.

Unfortunately, there was little consensus of opinion among the key managers about whether or not to make the investment to buy the 12 months of lead time. Consequently, they decided to approach the problem in a systematic way, with particular concern about the financial impact of the various options. First they recognized three general strategic market entry alternatives: (1) implement the crash development program and enter with 12 months of estimated lead time, (2) proceed on schedule and enter on a parity basis with the competitor, or (3) delay entry until after the competitor enters. The last option was considered because one manager felt the market would not materialize as rapidly as expected. Once the competitor entered and revealed its strategy, counteracting adjustments could be made.

The managers recognized that a number of situational factors could affect the timing decision, so all available relevant information on the new service was assembled next. Fortunately, demand and market studies had been conducted, as well as initial situation analyses in preparation for the strategic planning of the new service. Anticipated strengths, weaknesses, opportunities, and problems with the new service had been identified and reviewed. A two-week time period was set as the maximum allowable time to conduct a formal analysis and to decide on the timing of entry. Thus, as summarized in Figure 11.1, the timing of entry was recognized as a key decision, three broad strategic alternatives were formulated, and situational data were collected and evaluated.

2. Formulate Decision Model of Key Market Factors

From the analysis of situational factors, several variables were identified that were hypothesized to play a role in the timing decision. Expected sales volume, share, profitability, and cash flow over a five-year planning period were designated as key measures of performance to compare against the effects of alternative timing strategies. Other important variables were the market potential over the planning period (number of subscribers to the new service), market penetration (how much market potential would be realized from year to year), price dynamics (in part because of experience effects over the planning period), and relative marketing effectiveness of the firm with respect to the anticipated competitor.

In the simplest spreadsheet form of the decision model, sales is expressed as a function of market potential, market penetration, the price of the service, and the relative marketing effectiveness of the firm. Profitability is based on estimated sales and costs. By developing estimates for the key variables in this basic decision model (through the market studies and judgment), the managers could assess the relative effectiveness of each timing option.

Market Potential

Market potential was defined as the number of persons expected to subscribe to the new service at a specific price if it were available. As described in Chapter 7, market potential was modeled to reflect several market factors hypothesized to affect the total number of possible subscribers. For example, because organizations and individuals with particular demographic characteristics were targeted as the market for the new service, the expected annual growth of this demographic group was factored into the market potential estimate.

Market Penetration

As discussed in Chapter 7, it is difficult to estimate the expected market penetration or annual growth in demand for a new service. An analogical diffusion modeling approach was used whereby mobile paging services provided a case history to help estimate the growth rate of the new service. This growth rate was then applied to develop annual estimates of market volume. Judgment was used to estimate slow, moderate, and rapid growth rates.

Price Dynamics

The managers and engineers involved felt that future price declines would occur because of cost-related experience effects and competition. They subjectively estimated the most likely patterns of experience effects and translated them into expected prices over the five-year planning period. They estimated three price scenarios: slow, moderate, and rapid declines in price, expressed as average monthly operating costs for users. Their estimates were aided by surveys designed in part to measure intention to subscribe to the new service at alternative prices and average usage rates. These price dynamics are illustrated in Figure 11.2.

Relative Marketing Effectiveness

Expected sales were hypothesized to be affected not only by market size and growth rate, but also by the marketing efforts of the major competitor. Relative marketing effectiveness was therefore used as a composite indicator of how well the firm could perform competitively on such marketing variables as advertising, sales force, distribution, specific product features, and corporate image. The managers agreed that a simplistic aggregate index of relative marketing effectiveness would serve their purposes for the timing decision.

The relative marketing index specified a value of 1.0 to indicate comparable competitive marketing efforts (in terms of dollar expenditures); that is, neither competitor had a marketing advantage. This meant that with all other factors held constant, if the competitors expended approximately equal marketing resources, they would gain equal market shares. Relying primarily on subjective estimates and some of the preliminary market study results, the managers felt that the worst they could do against the competitor was to be 70 percent as effective, and the best they could do was to be 30 percent more effective. Thus, they assumed the relative marketing index would range from .7 to 1.3—recognizing that near (and beyond) these points, diminishing effects of their expenditures on market share would occur. They also estimated the approximate dollar costs (in advertising, sales promotion, sales force, and distribution) of attaining these levels.

Although numerous other factors were considered, taken together, these variables provided a parsimonious set that managers felt comfortable using for their timing decision. There was sufficient opportunity for testing a variety of assumptions related to timing.

3. Evaluate Strategic Timing Options

To evaluate the strategic timing options, certain assumptions about the entry timing of the firm and its major competitors must be established. Of particular importance is the selection of the time unit of analysis. Should sales be measured by days, weeks, months, years, or some other unit? The selection of the time unit should be based on the most meaningful sales interval relevant to the new product introduction. In the application described here, 12-month intervals were satisfactory. Also, the analyses were conducted on a discrete rather than a continuous basis.

Three timing options were developed. The first involved a 12-month early entry advantage for the firm. Under this option, the firm gained all available industry subscribers in year 1, while the competitor gained none; in year 2, the firm was assumed to keep its year 1 subscriber base, but its importance was

FIGURE 11.2 An approach for market entry timing decisions.

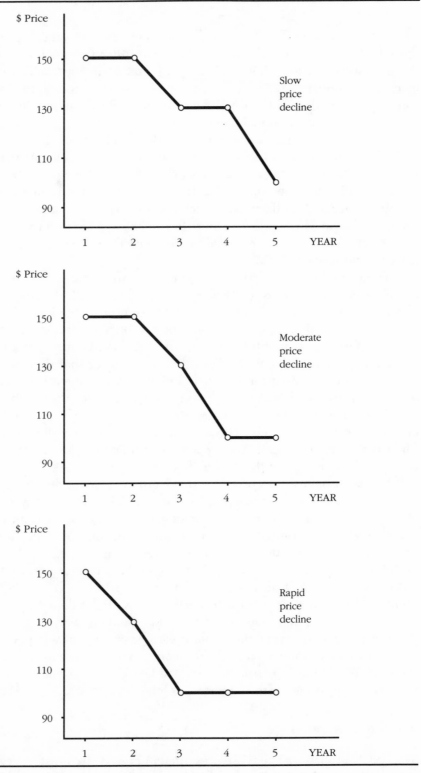

Source: Robert J. Thomas, "Timing—The Key to Market Entry," *Journal of Consumer Marketing,* 2 (Summer 1985), pp. 77–87.

factored into year 2 sales. This was accomplished by estimating a proportion of the year 1 base that would favorably *influence* other potential buyers to adopt the new service (using the coefficient of imitation in the analogical diffusion model). The remaining potential buyers were then available to the firm and its competitor according to their relative marketing effectiveness. This assumption was used to obtain the remaining estimates.

To illustrate, if there were an estimated 400 subscribers in year 1, the firm would obtain all of them. In year 2, the firm would get 30 percent (assuming this to be the estimated influence factor) of the 400, or 120 new subscribers of the available 515 subscribers in year 2. It would then compete for the remaining 395. If the marketing effectiveness factor were 1.0 (equal marketing effort), the firm would have 318 new subscribers $[(.3 \times 400) + (395/2)]$ in year 2 plus 400 subscribers from year 1, or a total of 718 subscribers. The competitor would have 198 subscribers (395/2).

The preceding assumptions suggest some advantage for the early entrant in the form of early sales and the influence effect. In this case the influence effect was found to be important. However, in other situations, the influence factor may be minimal; the advantage to early entry is therefore only the sales gained before the competitor enters. As noted, the influence effect is based on the theory of diffusion of innovations, but it is a factor that in many cases may not be easy to estimate prior to launch. Judgment and the mathematical analysis of the sales history of analogous products are sources for these estimates.

The timing option of equal entry is straightforward. The competitive shares of the industry are assumed to be a function of relative marketing effectiveness. The timing option of late entry (12 months in this case) follows the same logic as the early entry option described above.

Figure 11.3 illustrates results of the decision model under the three timing options over the five-year planning period. Included are the key market situational assumptions and annual estimates of sales and profit from the performance model. By varying some of the market situation and timing assumptions in a "what-if" fashion, the managers were able to get a feel for the sensitivity of the results to different factors. These numerous analyses are not presented, but each "what-if" option was profiled as in Figure 11.3. Also not shown are a number of best- and worst-case scenarios that were developed.

In some cases, decision model and timing option analyses may reveal the need for additional information about the various assumptions. If time is available, additional data can be collected and incorporated into the analyses. In effect, the value of additional information—which takes time to collect—should be assessed carefully in light of the importance of the timing decision to overall strategy.

4. Timing Decision

The results of analyses like those presented in Figure 11.3 must be reviewed and evaluated as input to the timing decision—however, they should not be accepted at face value or allowed to be the sole determinant in the decision. Unless the decision model has been validated and proven to generate results that exec-

FIGURE 11.3   Illustrative market situation and performance model results.

MARKET SITUATION (Scenario)

■ Price dynamics . . . . . . Moderate price decline
■ Market growth rate . . . Moderate growth rate
■ Market potential

Year	Potential number of subscribers	Market price per mo.	Estimated number of new subscribers	Cumulative subscribers
1	16,000	$150	400	400
2	16,400	150	515	915
3	25,215	125	876	1791
4	43,076	100	1559	3350
5	44,152	100	1969	5319

ESTIMATED MARKET PERFORMANCE

■ Relative marketing effectiveness. . . . . Parity

1. Early entry assumption: 12-month head start

Year	Estimated number of new subscribers	Cumulative subscribers	Sales revenue (000)	Profit (000)
1	400	400	$ 720.0	$ 144.0
2	318	718	1,292.4	232.6
3	516	1234	1,851.0	296.2
4	881	2115	2,538.0	355.3
5	1116	3231	3,877.2	581.6
5-year sum			$10,278.6	$1,609.7

2. Equal entry assumption: equal start

Year	Estimated number of new subscribers	Cumulative subscribers	Sales revenue (000)	Profit (000)
1	200	200	$ 360.0	$ 72.0
2	258	458	824.4	148.4
3	438	896	1,344.0	215.0
4	780	1676	2,011.2	281.6
5	984	2660	3,192.0	478.8
5-year sum			$7,731.6	$1,195.8

3. Delayed entry assumption: 12-month late start

Year	Estimated number of new subscribers	Cumulative subscribers	Sales revenue (000)	Profit (000)
1	0	0	$ 0.0	$ 0.0
2	197	197	354.6	63.8
3	360	557	835.5	133.7
4	678	1235	1,482.0	207.5
5	853	2088	2,505.6	375.8
5-year sum			$5,177.7	$780.8

Source: Robert J. Thomas, "Timing—The Key to Market Entry," *Journal of Consumer Marketing,* 2 (Summer 1985), pp. 77–87.

utives can trust, the results should be tempered by experience and judgment. This is not to say that such an approach should not be used if validation is not possible; rather, it is important to recognize that for any decision model it is desirable to question the face value of the results.

In its simplest form, the validation could include the judgment of an experienced executive not involved in the model formulation aspects of the approach, or a separate group of managers who develop an independent set of estimates. For example, in the application described here, the financial, marketing, and R&D executives were involved in the development of the first three steps of the approach. The president was purposely held out of all but information-gathering discussions until the final timing decision sessions. At these sessions, he was given the various results and asked to correlate them with his experience and judgment. This procedure proved invaluable in that it resulted in the re-examination of certain assumptions. For example, the president provided some compelling logic that changed certain assumptions about how prices for the new service would decline over the five years.

The importance of strategy—developing a basis for establishing long-run competitive advantage—became evident in the analysis. The analysis suggested that parity entry would yield slightly better financial results than early entry. As illustrated in Figure 11.3, the five-year profitability of early entry was $1.6 million compared to $1.2 million for parity entry. Adding $.5 million in crash development costs for early entry erased its profit advantages. Even with a very high relative marketing effectiveness, parity was slightly better than early entry in terms of profitability because of the added cost of the marketing effort needed to gain the relative advantage.

However, examining the market share of subscribers in a long-run strategic perspective showed that the firm would be better off with early entry (some 60 percent share) than parity entry (50 percent share). The managers in this particular situation placed considerable value on building a share advantage. For example, with a strong subscriber base, future add-on services would be very profitable. Further, because the costs of a customer switching to a competitor after subscribing were estimated to be high, regaining lost subscribers would be difficult.

Through additional "what-if" analyses, the managers determined that with a relative marketing effectiveness factor of 1.2, they could obtain approximately the same market share with parity entry as with early entry; however, the five-year profitability would drop to just below $1 million (because of higher marketing costs). The $1.6 million five-year profit under early entry was therefore somewhat more attractive, even with the $.5 million crash development cost.

The element of risk was also considered in the analysis. For example, risk was associated with realizing the 12-month early entry advantage through the crash development program. Risk was also associated with realizing the 1.2 marketing effectiveness factor. An evaluation of these and other risks in the context of the various analyses was leading the managers to a tentative decision in favor of the early entry strategy, but the details of implementation and contingencies had to be considered. Consequently, a calendar-specific entry date was targeted, and a resource schedule was specified to accomplish entry on the targeted date. The activities and events necessary to execute the schedule were also identified and planned.

5. Contingency Analysis

The final step in the approach was to identify major unanticipated events that might affect the tentative market entry timing decision and planning schedule. These events included possible competitive reactions, technology changes, regulatory actions (the FCC in this case), economic changes, and other environmental changes or crises. The effects of these events on the decision model and timing assumptions were hypothesized and used to determine how the decision might be changed if and when these events occurred.

Contingency analysis, often considered as an afterthought, ought to be routinely and rigorously included in decision making. The point is driven home by a hindsight example of a contingency in the cellular telephone industry.[14] Fear that mobile telephones might be associated with brain cancer arose after the appearance on television talk shows of a person who claimed his wife had died of brain cancer after frequent use of a cellular telephone. Publicity escalated, stock prices fell, and sales of mobile telephones abated. As a consequence, the Cellular Telecommunications Industry Association responded by commissioning health studies to determine the scientific basis for the claimed association. In the six months after the health scare, although no studies had yet been published, sales and stock prices of the cellular phone companies resumed their growth.

In addition to contingency factors, problems in implementing the timing decision were assessed. For example, the likelihood that the crash development program would take 12 months to complete, rather than the planned six months, was considered. This extension would not have changed the decision to enter early, but it would have resulted in increased marketing expenditures and somewhat lower profitability over the planning period. One of the major benefits of the systematic approach recommended here is the ability to quickly perform such contingency analyses on a personal computer.

After analyzing the possible contingency factors for the tentative early entry timing decision, the managers reached a consensus decision to aggressively pursue the early entry strategy and to enter 12 months before competitors. This meant investing the half-million dollars in the crash development program. On the basis of the strategic importance of entry timing to future market share, the various analyses performed with the available situational data, and managerial judgment, the benefits from the crash development program were assessed to outweigh the costs. The managers had different views at the outset of the decision process but were generally pleased, if not surprised, with the degree of resolve and commitment in the final decision.

Appraisal of Formalizing the Market Entry Timing Decision

If asked, most managers would agree that time and timing are key factors in business success in the context of the market entry of a new product or service.

Typically, timing decisions are implicitly biased toward speeding development and launching as soon as the product is available.[15] However, launch timing decisions should not be left to the whims of the sometimes roller-coaster patterns of organizational processes. Rather, they are decisions with top-level business strategy implications, requiring the best managerial thought.

A systematic approach to launch timing decisions has all the benefits associated with developing decision models with managerial involvement. Structuring the decision model identifies variables and issues that are sometimes overlooked. The costs of developing such a decision model are relatively low if market opportunity, sales, and market entry forecasting have paralleled the development process. The data and models generated from these processes will generally be adequate to support the timing decision model. The focus on launch timing also enhances the value of understanding organizational processes to implement product development and launch activities.

The downside of building a launch timing model is the possibility of delays because of the modeling process. Further, as with any such modeling process, the assumptions made can be erroneous and lead to faulty conclusions. However, on balance, if a firm anticipates the use of a timing decision model early in the development process, collects data relevant to it, and objectively approaches the decision process with the new product team, such models can prove valuable at or very near the time when implementation becomes crucial.

The decision model just described emphasizes the timing aspects of market entry. However, the scale and resonance of market entry are also critical dimensions for strategic success. Their effectiveness depends more on *implementation* than modeling—a key topic in the next chapter.

SUMMARY

If a new product passes critical market tests and its forecasts reveal favorable results, the market entry decision is often taken for granted. In this chapter, market entry is viewed as an important step toward implementation, with decisions that can have major repercussions for competitive strategy. Although being the first to enter a market is often presumed to have long-lasting advantages, research and case studies do not support such a conclusion. Market entry decisions are therefore highly situational and should be evaluated accordingly.

The timing, scale, and resonance of a new product launch marketing program are three important strategic aspects of market entry. Timing alternatives include early, parity, and delayed entry; scale alternatives include full-scale and limited-scale segment rollout; and resonance alternatives range from low- to high-intensity launch marketing programs. To cope with the situational aspects of market entry, a managerial modeling approach is illustrated with a case study of the market entry timing decision. It demonstrates the convergence of many of the concepts and methods discussed throughout the book and sets the stage for launching and tracking a new product.

12 Launching and Tracking New Product Programs

There is never really an end to new product development. Setting the date and launching a new product program merely marks a point on the calendar of a continuous development process. Monitoring, experimenting, learning, and otherwise constantly improving the new product and how it meets the needs of potential buyers give a product its life. In fact, in some new product situations, a commitment to continual improvement may dictate launching and tracking the new product without substantial test marketing.

When launch day arrives, the stakes of the project may not change, but a new dimension of realism is introduced—feedback information begins to reduce some of the uncertainty of the project, for better or worse. Real-time sales and cost data can be compared to plan, and the discrepancies become warning signals for change. Tracking the new product program has begun.

In this chapter, a case study that exposes many of the challenges of launching new products is considered. It is especially interesting because it reveals the important link between new product development and forecasting in support of market entry. Also included in this chapter is a discussion of the process of *launch implementation*—the execution of planned actions that make things happen. Subsequently, the value of *tracking* a new product launch is reviewed; here it becomes clear why new product development really never ends. The same models and methods that provided estimates for a new product's expected performance are used to keep it on track, or understand why it is veering off course in order to make corrections. The chapter concludes with a 12-step summary of recommendations for new product development based on the 12 chapters in the book.

THE CHALLENGE OF LAUNCHING NEW PRODUCTS

The case of WordPerfect Corporation helps illustrate some of the issues involved in launching new products.[1] During the 1980s, WordPerfect was the clear leader in word processing software for IBM PC and compatible computers, which largely ran under Microsoft Corporation's DOS operating system. In 1985, Microsoft launched a different operating environment called Windows. Windows offered a *graphical user interface* (GUI) that, for a segment of users, represented a friendlier and easier-to-use working environment than DOS, although DOS was still required to run Windows. This type of graphical user interface was developed by Xerox Corporation's Palo Alto Research Center (PARC) and was popularized with the Apple MacIntosh computer, launched in 1984.

Adoption of Microsoft's Windows operating environment was relatively slow until May 1990, when its Version 3.0 was released with major new features and extensive marketing. Sales of Windows grew rapidly. Unfortunately, WordPerfect's software was based on DOS and could not benefit from the Windows operating environment. WordPerfect users who wanted the benefits of Windows could not readily switch over to the new system without giving up WordPerfect.

Microsoft, which bet on the success of Windows, had a competitive word processing software program readily available (Word for Windows, launched in 1989). In fact, Microsoft's DOS-based product, Word, had developed a good reputation and became a challenging competitor for WordPerfect for DOS during the 1980s. Microsoft's Word for Windows was clearly a desirable alternative for the segment of WordPerfect users who wanted to use Windows—and a threat to WordPerfect's market dominance if Windows' success continued.

As one might expect, WordPerfect was not just watching from the sidelines. It was developing a version of WordPerfect for Windows. However, the product was not shipped by the announced date of first quarter 1991 because it was still under development. Faithful WordPerfect users clearly had a dilemma—switch to the new, appealing Windows operating system and leave WordPerfect for a competitor, or wait for WordPerfect to eventually launch its new product? Even potential buyers new to personal computing had to decide whether to go with the market leader on a DOS system or switch to the new Windows system and a different word processor.

The problem for WordPerfect would not have been so bad if the Windows 3.0 system had not been so attractive. Microsoft's heavy marketing efforts and the availability of numerous software applications for Windows (which had been encouraged by Microsoft over the years) gave buyers numerous ways to satisfy their needs. Perhaps more importantly, highly favorable software industry reviews and forecasts that Windows would become the future operating environment of choice propelled market adoption.

To compete, WordPerfect had to get its product on the market as soon as development would allow, yet without jeopardizing performance. A software program full of bugs would create poor first impressions and leave WordPerfect in a vulnerable competitive position. Further, the company had to help current WordPerfect users manage their dilemma of whether or not to move to Windows. Its response was to develop an innovative launch marketing program that created a sales forecasting contest for the new WordPerfect for Windows, even though it was not yet available on the market. The program was introduced in April 1991 as a series of print advertisements in popular computer trade magazines. The headline and text of the first print ad appear below:

WordPerfect for Windows promises to be a sure thing, but sales projections are anyone's guess.*

In a short time, WordPerfect for Windows will debut on dealer shelves throughout the English-speaking world. This new word processor combines the powerful features of our world-famous WordPerfect for DOS with the ease of use of a graphical interface.

While we're confident WordPerfect for Windows will live up to our standards as the industry leader, we are much less confident about our sales projections. Our Vice President of Product Marketing, Clive Winn, is having trouble predicting how many copies we need to produce for our first month's orders.

Here are some questions he must consider. Of the more than 150,000 people who will purchase a WordPerfect for DOS each month, how many will prefer a Windows product? Of the more than six million WordPerfect for DOS users worldwide, how many will take advantage of our $125 trade-up to WordPerfect for Windows in the first month? Of the 40,000 people who purchase a Windows word processor each month, how many will prefer WordPerfect for Windows instead of the products they are now buying? And of two million or so Windows owners who have not purchased a word processor, how many are waiting for WordPerfect?

The more we look at all the variables, the more we think we need your help. So we're going to do what we do best: listen to what you, our current and potential customers, have to say. We'd like you to call us at (800) 526-5069 between the hours of 9:00 a.m. and 5:00 p.m. MST on or before April 30, and make a projection of the public's demand for WordPerfect for Windows during its first month on the market.

Historically, we have received orders from eager customers before the product is officially available for purchase. Therefore, you will need to include these advance orders of WordPerfect for Windows as part of your estimate of the total number of orders placed during the first 30 days after the product officially becomes available. We will use your estimate to help us project an appropriate number of units to meet our first month's demand.

Give us your best guess and we'll make it worth your while. We will reward the person whose estimate comes closest to the actual number of copies ordered during the specific time period with $25,000 cash. So get out your calculator, some paper and pencils, and possibly your algebra book, and call us with your estimate.

The ad also included 13 official rules that specified conditions for the contest. They indicated that the winner would be announced on or before

*©1991 WordPerfect Corporation. Used with permission.

October 31, 1991. During May 1991, WordPerfect ran a follow-up ad that described the public response with the following headline: "WordPerfect for Windows is just around the corner, but sales projections are all over the map." Sales forecasts ranged from zero to 910,620,044 units for first-month orders! The mean forecast was 640,955 units and the median 261,381.

Launch Marketing Programs Should Be Linked to New Product Development and Forecasting Processes

In the WordPerfect case, the market opportunity was largely defined by the rapidly growing Windows program, which, in turn, depended on numerous other factors that drove the growth of personal computing. The size of the market opportunity would affect the magnitude of the WordPerfect for Windows sales forecast, but the sales forecast also depended on a host of other influences: factors related to customer behavior, competition, and the response of these and other stakeholders to WordPerfect's marketing program.

Would WordPerfect customers wait, especially given the contest and the advertising campaign? Would potential buyers just entering the word processing market bypass WordPerfect and the DOS operating system and go directly to Microsoft's Word for Windows? Would the trade begin to lose confidence in WordPerfect and shift allegiance and shelf space to competing products? Perhaps most importantly, would all of these stakeholders begin to perceive that WordPerfect's leadership in word processing software was slipping and lose confidence in its ability to offer state-of-the-art products?

What truly characterizes a *programmatic* approach to new product launch is the organization's dedicated and continuous commitment to a sequence of actions that culminate in the desired outcome. It is not enough to conceive a launch program as a one-shot marketing effort that announces the new product, then trails off. For example, in August 1991, WordPerfect ran another ad with the following headline: "Those of you waiting for WordPerfect for Windows are about to receive a sign." The ad featured a photograph of a road with a sign that read "END CONSTRUCTION, Thank you for your patience."

Although the product was still not available, the ad was intensifying WordPerfect's promise that it would be available soon. In addition to describing salient features of the new product, the August ad offered potential buyers the opportunity to trade-up to WordPerfect 5.1 DOS software for $150, and then get WordPerfect for Windows for $59 when it became available. Note that this promotion, which might have had an effect on orders, took place after the contest entrants had submitted their forecasts.

The response of potential buyers, competitors, the trade, and other stakeholders (such as computer industry media) to the features of the new product and WordPerfect's launch marketing effort would drive performance. Competitors could offer comparable price promotions, computer consultants might recommend that their clients switch to Windows and Microsoft Word for Windows, and so on. Of course, the time of product availability (and hence the month of the forecast) had still not been specified in the August ads. Clearly, the timing accuracy of a forecast depends on an organization's time-based product development capability.

The Rest of the Story

The benefits of a carefully executed launch marketing program are evident in the conclusion of the WordPerfect story. The new WordPerfect for Windows product was launched in November 1991 with an extensive advertising and promotion campaign. The ads in this high-resonance launch played on WordPerfect's strengths as a word processing platform across multiple operating systems, including DOS and Windows. The new product received favorable reviews, indicating that perhaps the thorough testing procedure to produce a quality product was justified. It would be a major contender in the Windows software application market.

Then, in January 1992, the winner of the forecasting contest was announced. Recall that the *average* forecast of all entries was 640,955 units. The actual number of units ordered during the product's first 30 days on the market was 369,693 packages. The winner came within 40 units of the actual number. The methodology the winner had used was also reported in the ad: *the winner's age, followed by the four digits of her home address!*[2]

LAUNCH IMPLEMENTATION

In the preceding example, and for new product situations in general, it is one thing to decide on an entry time for a new product or service, but another to execute the launch program for success. Once the timing decision is made and the market entry program drawn up, targeted efforts are needed to make key events happen as planned. Even under delayed market entry, emphasis on tracking the implementation of competitive actions in the market provides vital information. Experience gained from any early entrant is a key advantage for the later entrant.

The process of implementation has been a topic of the management literature for years—how to get things done with people—and every organization may have evolved processes for getting things done. The goal here is not necessarily to change those processes (unless they need change), but rather to identify factors that should be considered to implement new product development and launch processes.

New product development should retain its integrity as an ongoing intellectual process for the organization, but resource allocations may vary considerably throughout this process. Resource allocations often take on *project* status. For example, determining the state-of-the-art in display screens for a new portable computer can be viewed as a project, measuring potential buyer preferences for alternative new product concepts as input to product design can be viewed as a project, and so on. In reality, new product development involves a series of interrelated projects and teams to get things done.

In a study based on the project management literature, a 10-factor process model has been developed to heighten attention to the strategic and tactical aspects of implementation.[3] This process model is presented in Figure 12.1 and briefly considered here. Many of these topics are discussed in Chapter 4 and relate to an organization's propensity to innovate—however, their focus here is on accomplishing specific projects. The first three factors are viewed as strategic, the next four factors as tactical or executional, and the last three as key organizational processes that facilitate project flow.

- **Project mission:** The objective and goals of the project should be clearly defined and agreed upon at the outset of a project.

FIGURE 12.1   Ten-factor process model of implementation.

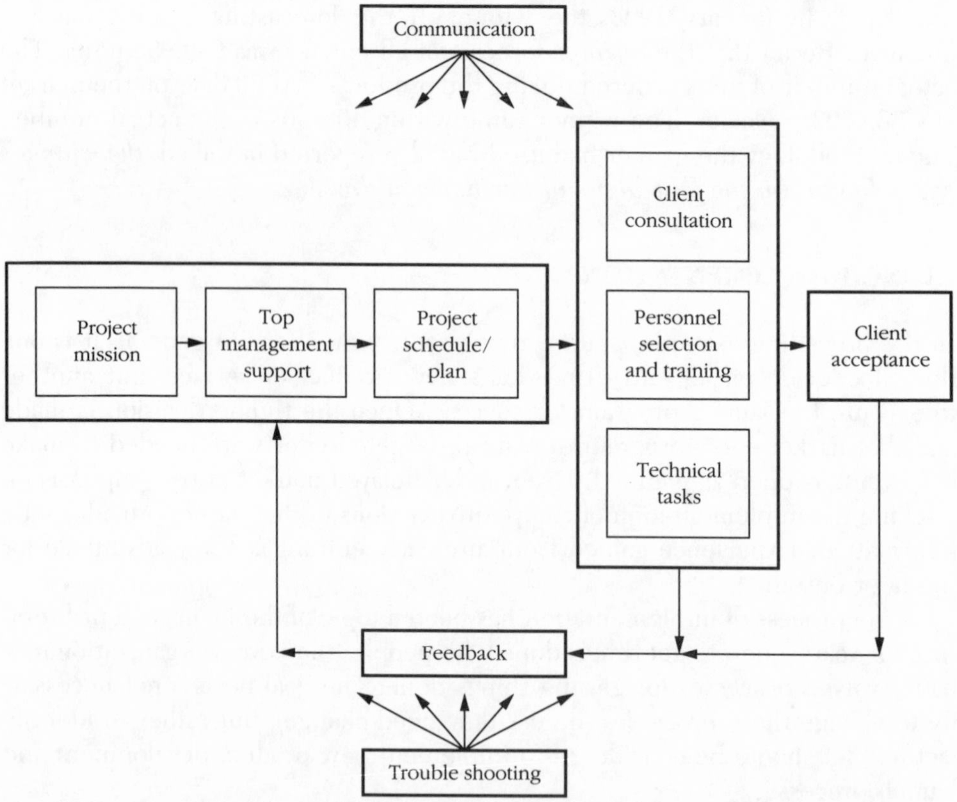

Source: Randall L. Shultz, Dennis P. Slevin, and Jeffrey K. Pinto, "Strategy and Tactics in a Process Model of Implementation," *Interfaces,* 17 (May–June 1987), p. 41. Reprinted by permission of The Institute of Management Sciences, 290 Westminster Street, Providence, RI 02903.

- **Top management support:** To the extent that the new product champion (team leader) is not part of top management, it is critical for this person to have the support and resource commitment of top management in pursuing the project. This commitment must be communicated clearly to all participants in the project.

- **Project schedule or plan:** The use of the critical path method (CPM) or program evaluation and review technique (PERT) is strongly recommended to help develop a detailed plan of the steps and resources needed to implement the project.

- **Client consultation:** The project is assumed to be required by someone inside or outside the organization. In most cases, the clients will include the core new product development team, although projects may evolve hierarchically or in other ways such that clients may vary. The central point is that client needs should be carefully defined in order to properly specify the people and tasks necessary to get the job done.

- **Personnel:** As in forming an initial new product development team, several project teams may be needed to fulfill various projects. Recruitment, selection, and training of personnel for each team are necessary for technical and logistical support of the project.

- **Technical tasks:** Most projects require a portfolio of tasks to achieve project goals. Specifying these tasks and matching personnel with the expertise to achieve them is critical to project implementation.

- **Client acceptance:** Project completion depends on the client's decision that the project mission has been acceptably met. This is not always an accept/reject decision, but rather one that may involve negotiation, personal selling, and further discussion. Initial goals, task mis-specification, changing circumstances, and other contingencies may need to be discussed before project acceptance.

- **Monitoring and feedback:** As project implementation proceeds, tracking information about how project performance compares to the plan provides a signaling mechanism for revisions.

- **Communications:** As noted in Chapter 4, communication processes are central to all organizational activities. They are particularly important to project implementation in complex new product development situations because of the interdependence of most project tasks. Because new product development and launch are characterized by interlocking sets of teams tackling a variety of interrelated projects, communication within and across teams is essential for success.

- **Troubleshooting:** Problems spotted throughout implementation should be identified through communication and feedback, but a troubleshooting capability should be set up to cope with problems at different levels. Problems left unresolved will only fester and plague the entire project at some future date. The troubleshooting capability should have a degree of built-in decentralization to allow team members to resolve certain local problems to expedite matters. It should also include a mechanism to bring more comprehensive interproject and interactive problems to the attention of various team leaders so they can coordinate problem resolution.

The 10 factors and their arrows of directionality in Figure 12.1 should not be thought of as a tight process to follow for project implementation, but rather as a way to begin thinking about what commitment must be done—even as a simple checklist. Organizations tend to have current implementation processes that should be matched with the implementation problems at hand to decide whether or not they need revision. The 10 factors, which should be thought of as interdependent, suggest a set of process guidelines that may be helpful in implementing both development and launch activities.

A focus on implementation can be particularly beneficial when time is an important competitive factor and current processes must be accelerated. However, as noted in Chapter 9, accelerating development processes can be achieved by thinking smarter as well as faster. In particular, simplifying a project, eliminating steps, removing delays, and parallel processing are ways of accelerating projects besides simply speeding up the process. In the same way, conceptualizing implementation projects more systematically, as suggested in Figure 12.1, may induce smarter ways of thinking about successful project completion.

The drawback of an overemphasis on the planning of implementation processes is that one is essentially *planning how to plan the execution of the launch plan!* In large organizations, such recommendations are welcomed as important new organizational work, and another (often undesirable) layer of the so-called "planning community" is instituted in an already overly complex structure. Clearly, a balance must be drawn between planning and action. Organizations with either a bias for action or a bias for planning should review their implementation processes to ensure key activities and projects are being completed in efficient and economic ways.

TRACKING THE LAUNCH

Tracking a new product launch brings the same kind of *control* to post-launch time periods as tracking development brings to pre-launch periods. Tracking a new product launch involves developing a capability to compare plans and forecasts against actual results, and then being able to take action if it is deemed necessary. At the heart of tracking is the diagnostic process of identifying error and searching for factors that explain it. Before a 6-step process for launch tracking is described, it is useful to consider the kinds of factors that have been generally associated with new product forecasting accuracy.

A study of 103 new computer software firms provides some insight about the types of factors that can explain differences between pre-launch forecasts and post-launch results.[4] In the study, which used a survey design, founders and key managers in the sampled firms provided first-year new product forecasts prior to launch and actual first-year results. The differences defined forecast error. In addition, numerous questions on a variety of environmental, market, and organizational factors were included to identify ones that might explain differences. Notably, error measures ranged from −2900 percent to +1500 percent. The average percentage error was −46.9 percent but was heavily weighted by 10 firms with errors greater than −100 percent. For comparison, the 46 firms with ±25 percent error measures were defined as *more* accurate, and the 57 firms outside that range were defined as *less* accurate in new products forecasts.

The study revealed significant differences between firms classified on both pre-launch and post-launch factors. Firms *more* accurate in their forecasting tended to have founders with 2.8 years more marketing experience on average; spent more on marketing research ($46,421 versus $26,093); used more methods, especially those that reach potential buyers (personal interviews and product demonstrations); introduced products into less volatile markets (entered their market later and faced larger numbers of competitors) and into markets with more focused applications (government markets); and attributed a significantly lower proportion of sales effects to buyer behavior than *less* accurate firms.

Although these are aggregate findings for a sample of 103 firms in a specific industry, they show that *controllable* factors are viewed as important in explaining differences, and environmental and market factors that are *less controllable* also explain differences. Thus, any tracking system must be capable of monitoring both through new product launch. The 6-step process briefly reviewed next provides an approach for launch tracking that can be modified for different types of products, market situations, and data availability.

1. Select Tracking Factors

For some new products and services where markets are very small and potential buyers are well defined and few in number, tracking may be a relatively easy task involving direct communication with buyers and other key market stakeholders. However, as markets grow in size and geographic scope, the need for more systematic tracking becomes evident. The first step in this process is to define the key factors that will be monitored over the post-launch period. At first glance, it would seem desirable to track measures for all key conceptual factors identified in Chapters 2 through 4 that were selected to develop the forecasting models of Chapters 7 through 9. If the stakes are high for the new product, the benefits of gathering and analyzing the data for numerous tracking variables may outweigh the costs. Otherwise, the value of the information to be tracked should be carefully considered.

The general selection of factors should begin with the more obvious performance measures: sales, costs, and profits. The next factors selected should have *diagnostic* capability and depend on the situational aspects of the new product and the problem areas discovered throughout the development process. For example, a truly innovative product may require diagnostic information on potential buyer response factors, which will most likely be more important than competitor and other variables. For a new product introduced to an existing market structure, competitor factors (especially sales, to compute share and other competitive actions) will be of interest. For high-technology health care products, continued monitoring of technology, regulatory, medical, social, and political trends may be desirable. For frequently purchased consumer products, trial use, repeat purchases, awareness, preference, and level of distribution achieved may be important sources of diagnostic information. Prioritizing key factors that are necessary tracking measures to assess performance, followed by diagnostic factors to explain deviation from the forecast, is the important first step in the tracking process.

2. Select Error Measures

Several types of error measures can be used for tracking. With the symbol A denoting the actual result and the symbol F denoting the forecast, some useful single-period measures are summarized next, along with examples where $A = 8,000$ units sold and $F = 10,000$ units forecast:[5]

Directional error	$= (A - F)$	$=$	$-2,000$ units (under forecast)
Directional error %	$= (A - F)/A$	$=$	-25.0% error
Absolute error	$= \lvert A - F \rvert$	$=$	$2,000$ units error
Absolute error %	$= \lvert A - F \rvert /A$	$=$	25.0% error
Error ratio %	$= (A/F)(100\%)$	$=$	80.0% of forecast achieved

These measures can be used for daily, weekly, monthly, or annual (or any other time period) analysis. Because post-launch new product data will be arriving sequentially, it may be feasible for some factors to cumulate data over time as well as maintain their time-period integrity. For example, cumulating number of subscribers, or number of units sold, and computing error measures provides a different perspective than computing the number of new units each time period.

In other situations, when a sufficient number of time periods have been recorded, computing average error measures may be useful. For example, assume monthly scanning data are collected for a new consumer frozen food product. Monthly error measures can be averaged over the first 12 months (summing and dividing by 12). This procedure may be useful for comparing first-year results with error measures of other related products. There are other measures (such as squaring the errors), but selecting one or more depends on the product/market situation, organizational practices, and, most importantly, what managers find to be an easily understood way to track differences between forecast and actual results.

3. Select Data Collection Procedures

Data on the various factors and measures used in the forecasting models must be collected continuously after launch. Depending on the new product, various commercial sources may be retained to monitor these measures. They can be complemented by in-house data base development, although it is often surprisingly difficult to obtain timely sales information through company information systems. After the orders are taken, filled, and shipped, and returns are accounted for, several months may elapse before the accounting department releases actual sales information. New product managers often find themselves working with rough information (orders entered) or using commercial marketing research services.

For example, for consumer packaged goods, retaining a scanner service to report brand sales, competitor sales, price, coupon redemption, and related measures provides one source of useful information. Ongoing national panels of consumers can be used to survey measures of awareness, preference, trial, usage, and satisfaction. Specialized services that provide information on in-store retail display and shelf location and facings can help formulate distribution estimates. Other services track advertising placement of the new brand and relevant competitors, as well as each brand's share of advertising expenditures.

Similar research approaches can be used for more durable consumer and industrial products and services. However, the types of commercial services available vary by industry. In industries without commercially available services, firms may have to design primary marketing research studies to collect the needed data. In addition, for any type of product or service, surveys of potential buyers, ongoing panels of customers, competitors, and other stakeholders are effective ways to recover diagnostic response information to explain error. Focus groups and other exploratory research procedures can also be used to get more specific responses among targeted stakeholders.

Collecting real-time data necessitates a data base, preferably in the context of a decision support system (see Chapter 6). The data base design should be flexible enough to incorporate scanning sales data, internal financial and cost results, survey data, economic indicators, and other needed data to provide information on factors that might explain forecast error.

4. Select Problem Detection Signals

How large should an error be to signal that a problem exists and that remedial action is necessary? Few reliable guidelines are available. Several studies suggest that a ±25 percent directional error range is satisfactory for many new product situations. However, this is clearly a statistical average and may not be relevant to a particular new product situation. The new product team should establish guidelines based on their experience and any industry information they believe may be relevant to their situation. In some cases, a 10 percent error is unacceptable, particularly if a firm suspects that other market factors may not be moving in a favorable direction. For example, sales may be acceptable, but awareness may not be building.

However, as more factors are added to the list, the costs of gathering and analyzing the tracking data must be balanced against the benefits. One useful approach is to define error ranges, such that if a measure is within a pre-defined range, it signals that performance is tracking as expected. The assumption is that when the measure is within the upper and lower bounds of this range, troubles elsewhere are unlikely. If an error measure is outside the range, it signals a cautionary approach; a potentially serious problem may be at hand. Here a decision must be made on whether or not to study the problem in depth. For high-stakes products in uncertain markets, this may be an easy decision. However, for other situations, a wait-and-see attitude may postpone data collection in favor of additional feedback.

Finally, care must be taken when an error measure is outside an acceptable range. Unfortunately, managers have a bias for action in these situations and rather than trying to isolate the causes of the discrepancy through systematic inquiry, they may attempt to increase advertising, drop another coupon, issue another round of samples, lower price, or offer retailers a free case for every 10 bought to revive flagging sales. Whether special studies are conducted, new commercial data collection services are added, or experimentation prevails, the problem must be diagnosed further.

5. Diagnose Problems

Performance outside the error range calls for diagnostic attention. Diagnosis recognizes that error measures in selected factors are indicators of problems elsewhere in the system. These other factors must be found and, if possible, changed; if they can't be changed, then the subfactors that drive them must be identified and, if possible, changed; and so on. Diagnosis often leads to chains of complex problems and for most managers turns out to be a painstaking and frustrating process. It's no wonder there is a bias for action; changing things that are accessible (controllable marketing variables) is much easier than finding the things that really need to be changed and developing a program to change them. However, without a sense of the underlying market-based problems, trying different remedies can be expensive and can lead to a rapid decline in profits and perhaps a premature top management decision to terminate the new product.

For experienced managers, the pain of doing unanticipated diagnosis is why a variety of diagnostic factors are tracked along with performance measures on a regular basis. Studies of awareness, brand image, preference, trial, repeat usage, satisfaction, distribution, and other factors are ordered by launch day. As an illustration of the diagnostic process, consider a new frozen diet dinner product for which sales data were collected on a monthly basis after launch. Further, assume that the pre-launch tracking process for market entry forecasting presented in Chapter 9 has been followed and will continue to be used by the new product development team for post-launch tracking.

In Figure 12.2, the first 12 months of actual and forecast sales for the United States are plotted. The top panel provides ample evidence that after the sixth month, sales were not meeting forecast. Only two of the six months were within the lower bound of the ±20 percent error range. Without any additional information, several lines of diagnostic reasoning are possible.

- **High trial/low repeat.** The differences could be explained by modest to high trial rates among consumers, but low repeat purchases. This pattern might signal that the product is not meeting taste or value expectations relative to competitors. It could also mean that competitors are saturating the market with high-discount coupons to offset the new entry.

- **Low trial/high repeat.** The differences could also be explained by low trial and high repeat purchases. This pattern might signal that once tried, the product is well-liked. Low trial may mean that consumers are not able to buy the product through stores (low levels of availability), or that not enough potential customers are aware of or informed of the new product's benefits. The latter possibility might suggest an increase in advertising spending. However, if awareness were high, it could mean that only a very small segment of consumers are responding to the creative appeal in the advertising, and it is turning off other potential buyers. This possibility would call for a change in the advertising's creative approach, not increased spending. Of course, the competitive factor cannot be overlooked here, either.

- **Modest trial/modest repeat.** This situation might indicate that advertising and the product are somewhat mediocre in generating enthusiastic response, and/or that competitors are also dropping coupons or launching their own new products. Other factors at work could be weak economic conditions, uneven distribution, or seasonality (consumers are notoriously diet-conscious after year-end holidays and in anticipation of heading to the beach during the summer).

Clearly, any number of alternative corrective marketing actions can be taken, but which ones? If one were armed with forecasts from test marketing results and post-launch tracking data, the various possibilities could be diagnosed until the problem is discovered.

For example, the bottom two panels of Figure 12.2 show the test marketing forecasts of trial and repeat purchasing of the new product, respectively. Note that trial purchases appear to be within the error range—though with a tendency to be underforecast. However, repeat purchase tracks well for the first seven months, then begins to trail off precipitously. This diagnostic reveals the need for additional analysis to find out why consumers are not repeating their purchases. The analysis could involve examining other tracking

FIGURE 12.2   New product post-launch tracking with diagnostics.

Sales forecast (000 units) with ±20% error range; Note: Actual total sales begin to sag after the eighth month.

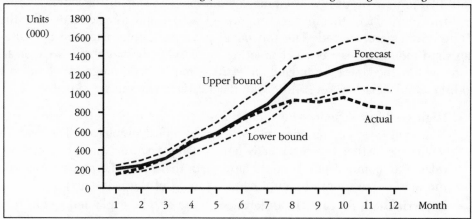

Trial forecast (000 units) diagnostic with ±20% error range; Note: Trial of the new product is satisfactory.

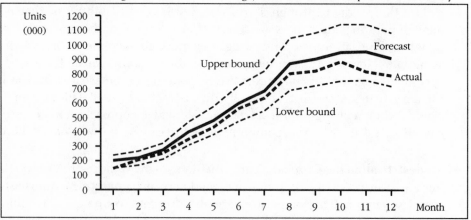

Repeat forecast (000 units) diagnostic with ±20% error range; Note: Repeat purchases are declining rapidly, suggesting the need for diagnosis to discover the problems.

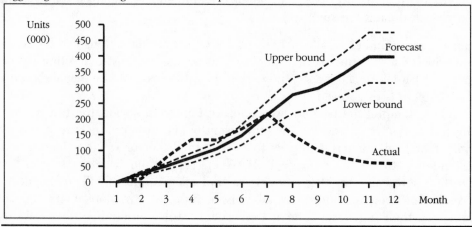

measures if data have been collected and conducting marketing research among consumers who have discontinued purchasing.

The process would be very similar for durable consumer and industrial products, as well as services, though post-launch factors and tracking data would differ. For example, assume a new laser-printing fax machine for office use has generated very high intention-to-buy scores, and the diffusion model based on product analogies has indicated rapid market penetration. However, post-launch results reveal a performance 50 percent below forecast during the first year on the market.

A follow-up diagnostic study discovers that intention-to-buy measures are still high, but decisions to purchase are being postponed because little reason is seen to discard a perfectly functional existing machine, despite the benefits of the laser-printing fax. Because replacement rates were not factored into the diffusion model growth rates, forecasts were higher than should have been expected. To accelerate the replacement process, various marketing program efforts could be tried on an experimental basis, such as high trade-in values for existing fax machines and a new price discount program for volume purchases. With one year of diagnostic data, the diffusion model parameters can be re-estimated to provide updated forecasts to evaluate whether or not they are more in line with current experience.

6. Implement Program Changes

Once problems are diagnosed, the hope is that program changes will become clear. Then the process of implementation should be straightforward. However, what usually happens is that several possibilities can be ruled out, but doubt lingers about which of two or three program elements to change in order to improve performance. If repeat purchase is a problem area, the decision may be between changing product features (such as adding more food to the frozen dinner entree) and lowering price to increase the perception of value. If trial is a problem, the decision may be between increasing advertising and dropping high-discount coupons.

In high-stakes situations, if resources are available, both options can be tried. If time is available, further data collection and analysis can help determine the best decision—for example, a conjoint analysis using the real product (instead of concepts) in the decision between changing product features and lowering price. Alternatively, various types of adaptive experimentation can be employed in market.[6] For example, in the case of the trial problem, this approach might involve selecting four regions and trying different levels of advertising in two and different levels of couponing in two, and then comparing the results with those from regions that received the usual program. Firms may even decide to use this approach for market entry without any market research or test marketing—especially for low-stakes, low-uncertainty products.

Of course, a logical extension of program changes through the tracking process is the development of the next-generation product. The very process of learning why the first product worked, or did not work so well, may logically lead to the next new product. It can be an extension of the same brand name, but with a new and improved version of the product, or it can be an entirely different brand name. Personal computer software manufacturers have managed this process of continual product improvement very effectively, offering version 1.0, version 2.0, version 5.0, version 5.1, and so on. The basic idea of new product extensions is to leverage any accumulating equity, whether it is market-based value in the brand name or organizational sweat-equity in gaining know-how in manufacturing, process, and new product development capabilities.[7]

Appraisal of Tracking Processes

On the surface, the tracking process appears to be a pragmatic approach to maintaining control of a new product after launch. Conceptually, it is a self-correcting process that may prevent premature product abandonment decisions. It can also lead to new product opportunities from the learning process invested in the original new product. But why is it not as widely practiced in a formal way as, say, simulated test marketing?

Part of the reason is the cost/benefit aspect of obtaining reasonably good post-launch diagnostics. High-stakes products may get considerable attention and resources when they are launched. However, the majority of new products are launched in well-known markets and are often line extensions of existing products. These products may not be worth the effort of conducting extensive post-launch diagnostics. It may cost less in time and management effort to simply move to the next new version than to correct the most recent release. Further, the information generated from diagnostics is not always conclusive about the source of a problem, additionally reducing the value of post-launch diagnosis.

Organizational issues may also explain why post-launch diagnostics are not pursued with rigor on most new products. When a new product does not achieve its forecast, a certain stigma associated with being a *loser* causes managers to distance themselves from the situation. Rather than diagnosing and therefore belaboring the problem, they would rather move to the next opportunity and can justify doing so because of the costs of diagnosis and contingency planning. Finally, new product development is generally seen as a high-energy championing process. Why submit the new product to post-launch scrutiny that may foster a hypercritical environment that can be a letdown for the new product team?

If an organization sees relatively low information value in diagnostics, it may overlook an underlying market problem. For example, few people would fault manufacturers of household cleaning products for downsizing their plastic containers to hold more concentrated versions of liquid detergent. Although consumers might complain about learning a new measurement system, they and other stakeholders generally prefer products that put less waste into the environment. However, do these "new" products address the real underlying concerns of society and the consumers of tomorrow in terms of the ecological issues associated with the chemical contents of the product and their effects on water supplies and other aspects of the environment?

To probe these issues would require a very different view of new product development than many organizations now hold. Digging deeper into the market, even for mundane products like detergent, and interacting closely with consumers to better diagnose their needs and create new products to satisfy them yields a different kind of learning. It is a learning that may break the pattern of extending what has been done in the past and establish a new one that discovers new insights and opportunities for satisfying consumers of today and tomorrow. On balance, a properly conducted process of post-launch tracking and diagnosis can lead to benefits beyond the immediate product situation and evolve into a continuous process of development and renewal that becomes part of the intellectual fabric of the organization.

TWELVE SUMMARY STEPS FOR NEW PRODUCT DEVELOPMENT

The 12 chapters in this book cover topics central to developing a conceptual, yet practical view of new product development. Part 1 presents an integrated conceptual orientation to new products, Part 2 provides an overview of tools and methods to manage new product development processes, Part 3 addresses the more practical aspects of integrating the development process with forecasting, and Part 4 covers major implementation activities.

The goal of the book is to develop an intellectual process for managing new product development in complex and rapidly changing environments. How one *thinks* about new product development defines how one will *behave* in response to market opportunities and problems. The topic of each chapter is a fundamental aspect of new product development that forms one's thinking about the problem. The factors, frameworks, and approaches presented are designed to provide a reference point to react to a variety of emerging issues. The following steps briefly summarize the major dimensions of new product development.

1. Clarify the Organization's Goals and the Strategic Role of New Product Development for Competitive Advantage

New product development can play a variety of roles in defining corporate strategy to gain competitive advantage. This variability makes the process of new product development subject to the emerging organizational issues of the day. In general, a long-run, focused, and ongoing strategic commitment to attractive market opportunities should define the role of new product development. New product development should be integrated into an organization's strategy and significantly contribute to its perpetual renewal. Achieving this integration requires the dedication of intellectual resources at all organizational levels. This intellectual process begins with a responsiveness to the business environment.

2. Build Flexibility to Cope with and Mediate Environmental Turbulence

Turbulent global business environments are the source of new product opportunities and problems for an organization. Consequently, the critical factors defining the organization's market environment for new products must be scanned on a regular basis. In particular, the effects of technology that reduce the life cycles of a firm's products and services must be carefully monitored. For example, the effects of changing *information* technology will continue to alter the way organizations innovate, design, manufacture, and market new products, as well as the way consumers and other stakeholders respond to those products. They may even redefine markets from traditional channel-dependent institutions to direct, interactive exchanges between buyers and sellers. Consumers may dial up a manufacturer's electronic catalog, send in specifications, and receive a customized product (from flexible manufacturing processes) through an express delivery service in days.

The increasing role of governments in global business may also change the opportunities for new product development. For example, government support of alliances and industry-based consortia may alter patterns of competitiveness. Strategic alliances are a logical response to rapidly changing business environments—to the point that organizations join forces in new product development to capitalize on a relatively short-lived market opportunity. After the opportunity is realized, the alliance dissolves or moves to the next opportunity.

3. Anticipate Market Acceptance of New Products

The crux of new product development is identifying the unmet needs of potential buyers and other key market stakeholders as the basis for defining market opportunities and translating them into *core new product concepts*. Potential buyers who are affected by turbulent global environments respond largely to their own needs and problems. Identifying the needs of potential buyers and segmenting markets according to those needs is a challenging prospect, but one that enhances new product acceptance. It requires a variety of research approaches that should bring the innovating organization as close to potential buyers as possible. In fact, for many situations, new product development should be viewed as an *interactive* relationship between the innovating organization and potential buyers (and other key stakeholders) to jointly define and develop the new product. The best way to anticipate market response for a new product is to jointly create it with potential buyers, then estimate *when* and *how many* consumers might enter the market to buy.

4. Prepare the Organization for the Change Needed to Develop New Products on a Regular Basis

The *new product development paradox* suggests that organizations respond to the demands of a new product in ways that often create organizational resistance and slow development time. To overcome this resistance, strong leadership, good management, cross-functional teams, and new product champions are crucial. Although the prescription for success may be clear, implementation can be difficult. How does the interruption of organizational processes by new products affect individual career patterns? What are the incentive systems that will motivate highly qualified individuals to join high-risk new product development teams? Where in the organization should the new product development team be located—internally or externally?

Resolving organizational issues related to new product development requires an understanding of critical organizational processes such as strategic choice, influence, communication, decision making, resource allocation, and implementation. Studying and profiling these processes in terms of an *organization's propensity to innovate* will help (1) identify areas needing change, and (2) if processes cannot be changed in a reasonable time, estimate response time to innovate. The outcome of this process will be realistic estimates of development cycle time. The process will also help focus educational efforts among employees to bring about an enlightened view of new product development and its role in the future of the organization and their own careers.

5. Operationalize an Ongoing Process of New Product Development

How the organization decides to respond to environmental forces, organizational resistance, and market stakeholder needs defines its new product development process. This process has been observed to be sequential, overlapping, holistic, or chaotic. However, because business situations vary, each organization should craft a process that enables it to (1) maintain a *strategic* focus, (2) remain *flexible* to cope with varying degrees of environmental turbulence, (3) *interact* with the market to anticipate and/or overcome friction in formulating the new product, (4) *integrate* organizational efforts and resource commitments to motivate the process through cross-functional new product development teams, and (5) commit to new product development as an *ongoing* process of organizational renewal. The process should encompass different levels of product concept refinement (ideas, concepts, prototypes, products, and launch programs) and critical management activities (diagnosis, search, design, evaluation, decision making, implementation, and monitoring).

6. Build a New Product Decision Support System

Viewing new product development as an ongoing organizational process requires a *decision support system* to provide timely information. Key elements are identifying new product *decision problems, modeling* those problems, establishing a *data base* of the important variables and relations in the model, collecting and analyzing the data through *marketing research methods,* and using *optimization procedures* to find the best decision. The design and implementation of *new product* decision support systems should be linked to an organizationwide system to build a useful historical data base, yet provide a capability for off-line analysis to support rapid retrieval and manipulation of data. Further, the role of decision-maker judgment in data collection and modeling activities should be integrated into the new product decision support system, albeit with care and scrutiny in order to continually learn from its use.

7. Estimate the New Product Market Opportunity

The objective of *market opportunity forecasting* is to clarify the nature of a market opportunity and to estimate its market potential and market penetration. To accomplish this objective, a model of critical factors that drive the new product opportunity should be formulated, data should be collected to operationalize the model, and the resulting forecasts should be updated throughout development. Estimates of year-to-year growth, possibly obtained from a data base of analogical diffusion models, are critical for rapidly deciding the value of a new product idea. Unfortunately, the procedures for quickly screening new product ideas with such information rely heavily on judgment. Future research on *expert systems* and industry-based product analogy data bases may help to improve the speed and reliability of market opportunity forecasting. In addition, the use of enhanced scenarios employing advanced multimedia technology to further define a core concept in the context of rapidly shifting environments is a promising way to better understand the possible evolution of and response to new products.

8. Formulate a Sales Forecasting Process that Captures Market Response to New Product Alternatives

In developing models for any of the forecasting processes, but especially sales forecasting, several guidelines should be considered:

- Develop a system of conceptual models that includes relevant variables.
- Develop a managerial decision model that is simple, intuitive, and logical; if after very careful study it is not understood, revise it or don't use it.

- To the extent possible, develop rigorous submodels of selected variables in the spreadsheet model to improve estimation and link decisions to market response.
- Use a variety of data sources (market studies, expert judgment, secondary data) and methods (such as perceptual mapping, positioning, conjoint analysis of preferences and simulations) to operationalize the models and submodels.
- Submit the model to sensitivity tests with different values and check for robustness (for example, using the "what-if" tool on computer spreadsheets).
- Check assumptions carefully.
- Use multiple, different, and independent approaches and reconcile estimates when they are divergent.
- Formulate alternative scenarios using variation in the values and assumptions of the model—and consider contingencies.

9. Establish a Financial Forecasting Capability that Provides a New Product Control Chart

Combining market opportunity and sales forecasts with estimates of new product costs, investments, risks, and development cycle time provides a financial control capability that can be summarized in a *control chart*. The format of this control chart should be agreed upon by the new product team at the outset of the project and followed thereafter. It should include the key measures of performance that guide the pre-launch development and post-launch tracking of the new product. Continual updating of all major forecasting processes to reflect changes in the shape of the new product and in the organization and market environment is the basis for realizing a capacity for *control* throughout new product development.

10. Consider Test Marketing as a First Step to Implementation

Prior to launching a new product, it is strongly recommended that a market entry strategy and launch marketing program be orchestrated and tested. This process should involve the use of *simulated, controlled,* and/or *conventional* test marketing to evaluate, decide, and refine the product and its launch program. Designing and implementing test marketing approaches should consider the nature of the implementation problems, the new product, its importance to the organization, and the amount of uncertainty in the market environment. In some cases, test marketing can be bypassed in favor of immediate market entry. This approach can succeed with careful attention to tracking the new product launch and modifying accordingly.

11. Develop a Market Entry Approach that Capitalizes on the Current Market Situation and Complements the Strategic Role of the New Product

Market entry for new products is highly situational—being first does not always pay. The market entry approach should reflect environmental, organizational, and market factors (potential buyers, competitors, trade, stakeholders) that define the situation. A market entry approach should be based on the *timing, scale,* and *resonance* of the launch marketing program. Using market opportunity, sales, and financial forecasts can provide input to an approach for modeling market entry decisions. In particular, launch timing is critical when cycle time and/or competitive factors can make a difference in performance. Recognizing time as a key variable, and making it the focus of a special decision model, may be the best way to handle this market entry decision.

12. Launch and Track New Product Programs to Implement Needed Modifications for Success

Once a new product is launched, the use of various data collection procedures and forecasting models to track performance, modify, and otherwise control the new product can lead to product and program improvements or to a comfortable decision to terminate the product. One issue related to how much effort an organization is willing to invest in post-launch tracking is problem diagnosis. Quick fixes and program changes that are based on impressions of market problems rather than diagnosis can lead to a product's early demise or the extension of mediocre performance. Finding early launch marketing problems may lead not only to quick modifications, but also to the next-generation new product.

Experience has shown that although it will not be used often, diagnosis can be helpful in all pre- and post-launch circumstances, even in a postmortem sense. The ultimate value of new product development may be the learning it makes possible—learning how to adjust the marketing program to consumer needs; learning how to educate the potential buyer on the benefits of the new product; learning why the product won't succeed in the market and why it should be abandoned now; learning that complete withdrawal is not necessary, but that a next-generation product can overcome the diagnosed difficulties; and, perhaps most importantly, learning to have the patience to learn.

SUMMARY

Above all else, new product development represents an intellectual process that must be shared by the members of an organization to respond to rapidly changing and uncertain business environments. Communicating this intellectual process is the responsibility of the organization's leadership and management. The process should align with an organization's competitive strategy and the two should be mutually reinforcing. The process should be ongoing, and capable of flexibility to manage multiple projects in the face of fast-moving business conditions.

Resources should be committed to the process in proportion to the importance of new products to the organization's future. Multifunctional organizational teams will be essential to complete the variety of needed interdisciplinary tasks. These teams should have incentives, strong leaders—product champions—and committed followers to achieve project success. The use of a three-level modeling approach—conceptual models, managerial spreadsheet models, and specialized submodels—is the focal point of the intellectual process. The conceptual models are used to drive data collection as a basis for developing and evaluating a new product core concept. Market opportunity, sales, and financial forecasting help to monetize and control the intellectual process.

The new product launch does not mark the end of the process, but merely a calendar point in the process of continuous development. After launch, however, sales, costs, and other data represent real market transactions—or the absence of them. When performance does not materialize as forecast (as will often be the case), data collection and diagnosis are essential to make product and program changes. The diagnostic element of tracking provides strong feedback to the new product development process in the form of learning. This continual process of learning carries the product through its life cycle, including extensions and spinoffs, or into another new product development process to capitalize on the previous learning and perpetuate a strong ethic of organizational renewal.

Notes

Chapter 1
Why New Product Development?

1. The discussion of Compaq Computer Corp. in this chapter is based upon: Michael Allen, "Developing New Line of Low-Priced PCs Shakes Up Compaq," *The Wall Street Journal* (June 15, 1992): pp. A1+; Catherine Arnst and Stephanie A. Forest, "Compaq: How It Made Its Impressive Move Out of the Doldrums," *BusinessWeek* (November 2, 1992): pp. 146–151; Kyle Pope, "Compaq Can't Cope With Demand for ProLinea PCs," *The Wall Street Journal* (July 10, 1992): pp. B1+; and Kyle Pope, "Compaq Remains Unable to Meet Demand for New ProLinea Line," *The Wall Street Journal* (September 1, 1992): p. B2.

2. Alan M. Webber, "Consensus, Continuity, and Common Sense: An Interview with Compaq's Rod Canion," *Harvard Business Review* 68 (July–August 1990): pp. 115–123; the quote is taken from page 122.

3. Webber, op. cit., p. 116.

4. For more comprehensive descriptions of business and marketing strategy, see David A. Aaker, *Strategic Market Management*, 2nd ed. (New York: John Wiley & Sons, 1988); Roger A. Kerin, Vijay Mahajan, and P. Rajan Varadarajan, *Contemporary Perspectives on Strategic Market Planning* (Boston: Allyn and Bacon, 1990); Michael E. Porter, *Competitive Strategy* (New York: The Free Press, 1980); and George S. Yip, *Total Global Strategy* (Englewood Cliffs, NJ: Prentice-Hall, 1992).

5. A more extensive discussion of the meaning of a new product is provided in Chapter 5.

6. For a discussion and model of the defensive (and therefore offensive) aspects of marketing strategy against new product entry, see John R. Hauser and Steven M. Shugan, "Defensive Marketing Strategies," *Marketing Science* 2 (Fall 1983): pp. 319–360.

7. See Eric von Hippel, "Lead Users: A Source of Novel Product Concepts," *Management Science* 32 (July 1986): pp. 791–805.

8. Laurence Hooper, "Xerox Tries to Shed Its Has-Been Image With Big New Machine," *The Wall Street Journal* (September 20, 1990): pp. A1+; and Todd Vogel, "At Xerox, They're Shouting 'Once More Into the Breach'," *BusinessWeek* (July 23, 1990): pp. 62+.

9. Dean Foust with Mark Maremont, "The Baggage Weighing Marriott Down," *BusinessWeek* (January 29, 1990): pp. 64+.

10. "Estimating Volume is Critical for Both Goods and Services," *Marketing News* (January 2, 1987): pp. 45+.

11. An approach to quantify these tradeoffs (conjoint analysis) is discussed further in Chapter 8.

12. See Gregory Witcher "Slow Start for Upjohn's Baldness Drug," *The Wall Street Journal* (April 5, 1989): p. B1; and David Woodruff "For Rogaine, No Miracle Cure—Yet," *BusinessWeek* (June 4, 1990): p. 100.

13. Bradley Johnson, "It's Service in a Box from Hewlett-Packard," *Advertising Age* (May 10, 1993): p. 6.

14. David A. Aaker, *Managing Brand Equity* (New York: Free Press, 1991).

15. G. Pascal Zachary, "Apple Computer to Fire 10% of Its Staff In Restructuring Bid to Cut Expenses," *The Wall Street Journal* (May 21, 1991): p. B4.

16. Aaker, *Strategic Market Management*.

17. For a review of several forecasts that have not been realized, see Steven P. Schnaars, *Megamistakes* (New York: The Free Press, 1989).

18. The data in this paragraph are drawn from C. Merle Crawford, *New Products Management*, 3rd ed. (Homewood, IL: Irwin, 1991).

19. For example, see: Robert G. Cooper, *Winning at New Products* (Reading, MA: Addison-Wesley Publishing Company, 1986); C. Merle Crawford, *New Products Management*, 3rd ed. (Homewood, IL: Irwin, 1991); Robert J. Dolan, *Managing the New Product Development Process: Cases and Notes* (Reading, MA: Addison-Wesley, 1993); Walter Henry, Michael Menasco, and Hirokazu Takada, Eds. *New-Product Development and Testing* (Lexington, MA: Lexington Books, 1989); Thomas D. Kuczmarski, *Managing New Products* (Englewood Cliffs, NJ: Prentice-Hall, 1992); Edgar A. Pessemier, *Product Management*, 2nd ed. (New York: John Wiley & Sons, 1982); Eberhard E. Scheuing, *New Product Management* (Columbus, OH: Merrill Publishing Company, 1989); William E. Souder, *Managing New Product Innovations* (Lexington, MA: Lexington Books, 1987); Glen L. Urban and John R. Hauser, *Design and Marketing of New Products* (Englewood Cliffs, NJ: Prentice-Hall, 1980); Steven C. Wheelwright and Kim B. Clark, *Revolutionizing Product Development* (New York: Free Press, 1992); and Yoram Wind, *Product Policy* (Reading, MA: Addison-Wesley, 1982).

20. The philosophy of managerial self-determination has been effectively stated in Russell L. Ackoff, *Creating the Corporate Future* (New York: John Wiley & Sons, 1981).

21. See William B. Gartner and Robert J. Thomas, "Factors Affecting New Product Forecasting Accuracy in New Firms," *Journal of Product Innovation Management* 10 (January 1993): pp. 35–52.

22. For a discussion of ethical issues in marketing, and related case studies, see N. Craig Smith and John A. Quelch, *Ethics in Marketing* (Homewood, IL: Irwin, 1993).

Chapter 2
Mediating Turbulent Business Environments

1. See David Taylor, "Micromotor," *Highlife* (March 1985): pp. 88+; and "Sinclair Halts C5 Output to Fix Defect in Vehicle," *The Wall Street Journal* (April 1, 1985).

2. Discussion of the electric vehicle case study in this chapter is based upon numerous sources, including the following articles: Neal Templin, "Auto Makers Strive to Get Up to Speed on Clean Cars for the California Market," *The Wall Street Journal* (March 26, 1991): pp. B1+; Joseph B. White, "GM Shelves Program to Make Its Own Electric Car and Joins Ford, Chrysler," *The Wall Street Journal* (December 14, 1992): p. A3; Madilee Wnek, "Cars for the New Millennium," *AAA World* (May/June 1991): pp. 2b+; David Woodruff, "GM: All Charged Up Over the Electric Car," *BusinessWeek* (October 21, 1991): pp. 106+; and David Woodruff, et al., "GM Drives the Electric Car Closer to Reality," *BusinessWeek* (May 14, 1990): pp. 60+.

3. The discussion of the ecology of natural resources in this section is based upon W. Jackson Davis, *The Seventh Year* (New York: Norton, 1979).

4. See Thomas C. Schelling, "Global Environmental Forces," *Technological Forecasting and Social Change* 38 (1990): pp. 257–264.

5. The formal study of populations, or demography, involves the internal and external dynamics of populations. For further discussion, see Charles B. Nam, "The Progress of Demography as a Scientific Discipline," *Demography* 16 (November 1979): pp. 485–492; and Louis G. Pol, "Demographic Contributions to Marketing: An Assessment," *Journal of the Academy of Marketing Science* 19 (Winter 1991): pp. 53–59.

6. See Valarie A. Zeithaml, "The New Demographics and Market Fragmentation," *Journal of Marketing* 49 (Summer 1985): pp. 64–75.

7. This definition is based on a discussion presented in James F. Engel and Roger D. Blackwell, *Consumer Behavior*, 4th ed. (New York: Dryden Press, 1982): pp. 72–79.

8. See William Echikson, "Electrolux's Brand of European Unity," *The Wall Street Journal* (August 20, 1990): p. B4B.

9. See Peter Waldman, "Federal Express Faces Problems Overseas," *The Wall Street Journal* (July 20, 1990): p. A4; Daniel Pearl, "Federal Express Finds its Pioneering Formula Falls Flat Overseas," *The Wall Street Journal* (April 15, 1991): pp. 1+; and Daniel Pearl, "Federal Express Mulls Options to Stem Losses," *The Wall Street Journal* (February 12, 1992): p. A3.

10. The definition of technology is discussed in greater detail in Joseph P. Martino, *Technological Forecasting for Decision Making*, 2nd ed. (New York: Elsevier Science Publishing, 1983).

11. Personal communication from Simon Stern and Bernard A. Amsterdam, National Fisheries, Inc.; Miami, Florida.

12. See G. Pascal Zachary, "Industry Finds Growth of Digital Electronics Brings in Competitors," *The Wall Street Journal* (February 23, 1992): pp. 1+.

13. Neal Templin, "Nissan Says Its Electric Car Reduces Battery-Recharge Time to 15 Minutes," *The Wall Street Journal* (August 27, 1991): p. B4.

14. "Space Age Technology for the Family Car," *BusinessWeek* (June 18, 1984): pp. 82+.

15. See Laurence Hooper and Jacob M. Schlesinger, "Precise Navigation Points to New Worlds," *The Wall Street Journal* (March 4, 1991): pp. B1+.

16. For more comprehensive reviews and analyses of the role of the U.S. government in laws and regulations that affect business and marketing decisions, see George S. Dominguez, *Marketing in a Regulated Environment* (New York: John Wiley & Sons, 1977); Louis W. Stern and Thomas L. Eovaldi, *Legal Aspects of Marketing Strategy* (Englewood Cliffs, NJ: Prentice-Hall, 1984); and Ray O. Werner, *Legal and Economic Regulation in Marketing* (New York: Quorum Books, 1989).

17. Bob Davis and Rose Gutfeld, "New EPA Rules on Air Pollution Blocked by Bush," *The Wall Street Journal* (January 31, 1992): p. A3.

18. Jeffrey Taylor, "Global Market in Pollution Rights Proposed by U.N.," *The Wall Street Journal* (January 31, 1992): p. C12.

19. See *Certain Personal Computers and Components Thereof*, Investigation No. 337-TA-140, USITC Publication 1504, Washington, DC, March 1984.

20. For a description of this study, including countries and industries most affected by the regulations, see Robert J. Thomas, "Patent Infringement of Innovations by Foreign Competitors: The Role of the International Trade Commission," *Journal of Marketing* 53 (October 1989): pp. 63–75.

21. For an overview of possible relations between mass media and their audiences, see John E. Merriam, "Clues in the Media," *American Demographics* (February, 1991): pp. 39+.

22. Joanne Lippman, "ABC to Relax Longstanding Guidelines for Ad Content," *The Wall Street Journal* (September 5, 1991): p. B1; and Joanne Lippman, "ABC Retreats on Bid to Relax Ad Guidelines," *The Wall Street Journal* (March 13, 1992): p. B1.

23. For greater detail on the cases mentioned in this paragraph, see Joanne Lippman, "Hurt by Ad Downturn, More Magazines Use Favorable Articles to Woo Sponsors," *The Wall Street Journal* (July 30, 1991): pp. B1+; and Neal Templin, "Car Magazine Signals End to Auto Makers' Freebies," *The Wall Street Journal* (February 5, 1991): pp. B1+.

24. See Joanne Lippman, "CNN to Offer a World-Wide Ad Package," *The Wall Street Journal* (May 23, 1991): p. B6.

25. For a description of the emergence of research and development consortia, as well as a profile of 137 consortia registered under the National Cooperative Research Act, see William M. Evan and Paul Olk, "R&D Consortia: A New U.S. Organizational Form," *Sloan Management Review* 31 (Spring 1990): pp. 37–46. The material in both this paragraph and the next are based on this article.

26. See Bruce Ingersoll, "Irradiation Foes Plan Media Blitz to Block Plant," *The Wall Street Journal* (June 26, 1991): p. B1.

27. Ira Teinowitz and Steven W. Colford, "Targeting Woes in PowerMaster Wake," *Advertising Age* (July 8, 1981): p. 35.

28. For discussions of the more traditional views on environmental scanning as used in strategic planning, see F. J. Aguilar, *Scanning the Business Environment* (New York: MacMillan, 1967); and Roland Calori, "Designing a Business Scanning System," *Long Range Planning* 22 (February 1989): pp. 69–82.

Chapter 3
Anticipating Market Acceptance of New Products

1. Discussion of the Goldman, Sachs & Co. situation is based upon Randall Smith, "How Goldman Scored With a 'Vulture Fund' Yet Decided to Kill It," *The Wall Street Journal* (June 4, 1991): pp. A1+.

2. See, "Will Coffee Perk Up a Flat Soda Market?" *The Wall Street Journal* (February 13, 1991): p. B6.

3. The study of buyer behavior continues to be the subject of extensive academic inquiry. More comprehensive descriptions of consumer behavior can be found in: James R. Bettman, *An Information Processing Theory of Consumer Choice* (Reading, MA: Addison-Wesley, 1979); James F. Engel and Roger D. Blackwell, *Consumer Behavior*, 4th ed. (New York: Dryden Press, 1982); John A. Howard and Jagdish N. Sheth, *The Theory of Buyer Behavior* (New York: John Wiley & Sons, 1969); William L. Wilkie, *Consumer Behavior*, 2nd ed. (New York: John Wiley & Sons, 1990). Organizational buying behavior is described in Frederick E. Webster, Jr. and Yoram Wind, *Organizational Buying Behavior* (Englewood Cliffs, NJ: Prentice-Hall, 1972). Fundamental views of consumer behavior in the context of innovations and new product situations can be found in Thomas S. Robertson, *Innovative Behavior and Communication* (New York: Holt, Rinehart and Winston 1971) and Everett M. Rogers, *Diffusion of Innovations*, 3rd ed. (New York: The Free Press, 1983).

4. Characteristics of needs as a way to organize thinking about the relationship between them and new product development is outlined in John B. Stewart, "Product Development," in *Science in Marketing*, ed. George Schwartz (New York: John Wiley & Sons, 1965).

5. Numerous theorists have developed classification systems that have been used to better understand consumer needs. For a classification based on a need hierarchy (biological, security, social, self-esteem, self-actualization), see Abraham H. Maslow, *Motivation and Personality*, 2nd ed. (New York: Harper & Row, 1970). A list of some 20 instrumental human needs is suggested by H. A. Murray, *Explorations in Personality* (New York: Oxford University Press, 1938).

6. Attempts to develop and test comprehensive theories of buyer behavior have met with limited success. Nevertheless, they helped to define the complexities of the process and are useful to review. For an example of a comprehensive theory, see Howard and Sheth, op. cit.

7. For an overview of organizational buying behavior, see Webster and Wind, op. cit. The role of interpersonal influence in organizational buying processes is considered in Ajay Kohli, "Determinants of Influence in Organizational Buying," *Journal of Marketing* 53 (July 1989): pp. 50–65 and Robert J. Thomas, "Correlates of Interpersonal Purchase Influence in Organizations," *Journal of Consumer Research* 9 (September 1982): pp. 171–182. For an overview of family buying behavior, see Harry L. Davis, "Decision Making Within the Household," in *Selected Aspects of Consumer Behavior*, ed. R. Ferber (Washington, DC: U.S. Government Printing Office, National Science Foundation, 1977).

8. Consumer choice as a comprehensive information processing approach is developed by James R. Bettman, *An Information Processing Theory of Consumer Choice* (Reading, MA: Addison-Wesley, 1979). He views the consumer as a processor of information that is "characterized as interacting with his or her choice environment, seeking and taking information from various sources, processing this information, and then making a selection from among some alternatives" (p. 1).

9. Various choice heuristics and their evaluation processes with respect to alternatives, including affect referral, linear compensatory, information integration, conjunctive, disjunctive, lexicographic, sequential elimination, elimination by aspects, lexicographic semiorder, additive difference, and phased strategies are discussed in Bettman, op. cit.

10. The view that objects of individual evaluation can be defined in terms of their attributes gained momentum in works on economics and psychology, respectively, by Kelvin Lancaster, *Consumer Demand: A New Approach* (New York: Columbia University Press, 1971); and Martin Fishbein and Icek Ajzen, *Belief, Attitude, Intention, and Behavior: An Introduction to Theory and Research* (Reading, MA: Addison-Wesley, 1975). Marketers embraced this theoretical work to define products, including new ones, in terms of consumer perceptions of multiattribute objects.

11. Cognitive dissonance, employed as a useful concept by marketing managers to direct communication to recent purchasers of new products to reduce the dissonance, was formulated by Leon Festinger, *A Theory of Cognitive Dissonance* (Stanford, CA: Stanford University Press, 1957).

12. Research on attitudes versus intentions as predictors of behavior reveal the latter to be more accurate; see Fishbein and Ajzen, op. cit.; and Blair H. Sheppard, Jon Hartwick, and Paul Warshaw, "The Theory of Reasoned Action: A Meta-Analysis of Past Research with Recommendations for Modifications and Future Research," *Journal of Consumer Research* 15 (December 1988): pp. 325–343.

13. For a comprehensive review of consumer satisfaction, see Youjae Yi, "A Critical Review of Consumer Satisfaction," in *Review of Marketing*, ed. V. Zeithaml (Chicago: American Marketing Association, 1990): pp. 68–123.

14. A broad conceptualization of *trying* behavior in the context of achieving specific goals is presented by Richard P. Bagozzi and Paul R. Warshaw, "Trying to Consume," *Journal of Consumer Research* 17 (September 1990): pp. 127–140. Trying to lose weight, to stop smoking, to become a more effective manager, represents goal-directed consumer behavior that involves the purchase of numerous kinds of products and services to achieve.

15. Robertson, op. cit.

16. Examples of approaches that incorporate a variety of concepts and measures to model consumer response to new products or services include Richard P. Bagozzi, "A Holistic Methodology for Modeling Consumer Response to Innovation," *Operations Research* 31 (January–February 1983): pp. 128–176; and John R. Hauser and Glen L. Urban, "A Normative Methodology for Modeling Consumer Response to Innovation," *Operations Research* 25 (1977): pp. 579–619.

17. For discussions of the methods and issues involved in segmentation processes, see Ronald E. Frank, William F. Massy, and Yoram Wind, *Market Segmentation* (Englewood Cliffs, NJ: Prentice-Hall, 1972); Yoram Wind, "Issues and Advances in Segmentation Research," *Journal of Marketing Research* 15 (August 1978): pp. 317–337; and Yoram Wind and Robert J. Thomas, "Segmenting Industrial Markets," in *Advances in Business Marketing*, Vol. 6, ed. A. Woodside (Greenwich, CT: JAI Press, 1993), forthcoming.

18. These techniques will be more fully illustrated in actual examples in Part III of the book.

19. For more detailed discussion and analysis of competitive effects, see David A. Aaker, *Strategic Market Management*, 2nd ed. (New York: John Wiley & Sons., 1988); Michael E. Porter, *Competitive Strategy* (New York: The Free Press, 1980); John E. Prescott and John H. Grant, "A Manager's Guide for Evaluating Competitive Analysis Techniques," *Interfaces* 18 (May–June 1988): pp. 10–22; and Alan E. Singer and Roderick J. Brodie, "Forecasting Competitors' Actions: An Evaluation of Alternative Ways of Analyzing Business Competition," *International Journal of Forecasting* 6 (1990): pp. 75–88.

20. For an exception, see the conceptual model and its subsequent empirical test in Thomas S. Robertson and Hubert Gatignon, "Competitive Effects on Technology Diffusion," *Journal of Marketing* 50 (July 1986): pp. 1–12; and Hubert Gatignon and Thomas S. Robertson, "Technology Diffusion: An Empirical Test of Competitive Effects," *Journal of Marketing* 53 (January 1989): pp. 35–49. See also Oliver P. Heil and Rockney G. Walters, "Explaining Competitive Reactions to New Products: An Empirical Signaling Study," *Journal of Product Innovation Management* 10 (January 1993): pp. 53–65.

21. See Robert Dolan, "Models of Competition: A Review of Theory and Empirical Evidence," in *Review of Marketing*, ed. B. Enis and K. Roering (Chicago: American Marketing Association, 1981): pp. 224–234.

22. See Hubert Gatignon, Erin Anderson, and Kristiaan Helsen, "Competitive Reactions to Market Entry: Explaining Interfirm Differences," *Journal of Marketing Research* 26 (February 1989): pp. 44–55.

23. Based on Joseph Weber, "A Big Company that Works," *BusinessWeek* (May 4, 1992): pp. 124+.

24. For discussion of distribution factors listed in the Appendix and others, see Louis W. Stern and Adel I. El-Ansary, *Marketing Channels*, 3rd ed. (Englewood Cliffs, NJ: Prentice-Hall, 1988).

25. Arthur Buckler, "Holly Farms' Marketing Error: The Chicken That Laid an Egg," *The Wall Street Journal* (February 9, 1988): p. 44.

26. Valerie Reitman, "Kimberly-Clark to Introduce Thinner Diaper," *The Wall Street Journal* (May 22, 1992): pp. B1+.

27. For a presentation of the original diffusion model, see Frank M. Bass, "A New Product Growth Model for Consumer Durables," *Management Science* 15 (January 1969): pp. 215–227. For a comprehensive review of new product diffusion models, see Vijay Mahajan, Eitan Muller, and Frank M. Bass, "New Product Diffusion Models in Marketing: A Review and Directions for Research," *Journal of Marketing* 43 (January 1990): pp. 1–26.

28. See Jagdish N. Sheth and S. Ram, *Bringing Innovation to Market* (New York: John Wiley & Sons, 1987).

Chapter 4
Preparing the Organization for New Product Development

1. Discussions of Motorola in this chapter are based upon Stephen K. Yoder, "Motorola Loses Edge in Microprocessors by Delaying New Chips," *The Wall Street Journal* (March 4, 1991): pp. 1+.

2. For example, see the widely cited study of new products by Booz-Allen & Hamilton, *New Products Management for the 1980's* (New York: Booz-Allen & Hamilton, 1982).

3. Alecia Swasy, "How Innovation at P&G Restored Luster To Washed-Up Pert and Made it No. 1," *The Wall Street Journal* (December 6, 1990): pp. B1+.

4. Michael J. McCarthy, "Frito-Lay Bets Big With Multigrain Chips," *The Wall Street Journal* (February 28, 1991): pp. B1+.

5. This story was adopted from Elting Morrison, *Men, Machines, and Modern Times* (Cambridge, MA: MIT Press, 1966); and Donald A. Schon, *Beyond the Stable State* (New York: W. W. Norton & Company, Inc., 1971).

6. For further discussion and development of issues related to resistance to change within organizations, see Schon; and Danny Miller and Peter H. Friesen, "Momentum and Revolution in Organizational Adaptation," *Academy of Management Journal* 23 (December 1980): pp. 591–614; and Michael T. Hannan and John Freeman, *Organizational Ecology* (Cambridge, MA: Harvard University Press, 1989).

7. See the review of research by Walter R. Nord and Sharon Tucker, *Implementing Routine and Radical Innovations* (Lexington, MA: Lexington Books, 1987).

8. For a discussion of the organization as a "psychic prison," and other metaphorical explanations of organizational behavior, see Gareth Morgan, *Images of Organizations* (Beverly Hills, CA: Sage Publications, 1986).

9. For a discussion of the impact of organizational histories on resistance to change, see Hannan and Freeman, op. cit.

10. This example is described in Richard N. Foster, *Innovation* (New York: Summit Books, 1986).

11. For a comprehensive discussion of the role of power in organizations, see Jeffrey Pfeffer, *Managing with Power* (Boston, MA: Harvard Business School Press, 1992).

12. See Volney Stefflre, "Organizational Obstacles to Innovations: A Formulation of the Problem," *Journal of Product Innovation Management* 2 (March 1985): pp. 3–11.

13. See Walter Kiechel III, "The Politics of Innovation," *Fortune* (April 11, 1988): pp. 131–132.

14. See Andrew M. Pettigrew, *The Politics of Organizational Decision-making* (London: Tavistock, 1973).

15. Stefflre, op. cit.

16. This study is described in detail in Pettigrew, op. cit.

17. Gary L. Lilien, "20/30 Hindsight: If the President Likes a New Product Program a Model Won't Kill It," *Interfaces* 13 (June 1983): pp. 54–58.

18. For example, see Michael L. Tushman and Ralph Katz, "External Communication and Project Performance: An Investigation Into the Role of Gatekeepers," *Management Science* 26 (November 1980): pp. 1071–1085; Yar M. Ebadi and James M. Utterback, "The Effects of Communication on Technological Innovation," *Management Science* 30 (May 1984): pp. 572–585; Ashkok K. Gupta, S. P. Raj, and David L. Wilemon, "R&D and Marketing Dialogue in High-Tech Firms," *Industrial Marketing Management* 14 (November 1985): pp. 289–300; Mary Beth Pinto and Jeffrey K. Pinto, "Project Team Communication and Cross-Functional Cooperation in New Program Development," *Journal of Product Innovation Management* 7 (September 1990): pp. 200–212.

19. See Richard M. Cyert and James G. March, *A Behavioral Theory of the Firm*, (Englewood Cliffs, NJ: Prentice-Hall, 1963); and L. J. Bourgeois III, "On the Measurement of Organizational Slack," *Academy of Management Review* 6 (1981): pp. 29–39.

20. See Nord and Tucker, op. cit.

21. For organizations trying to develop successful innovations, this is referred to as "the expertise barrier" by Jagdish N. Sheth and S. Ram, *Bringing Innovation to Market* (New York: John Wiley & Sons, 1987).

22. For a more complete review of the S-curve phenomena, see Foster, op. cit.

23. Paul B. Carroll, "IBM Bends Its Rules to Make a Laptop; New Process Slashes Development Time," *The Wall Street Journal* (April 15, 1991): p. B4.

24. For the original article by Brown and the letters to the editor, see John Seely Brown, "Research That Reinvents the Corporation," *Harvard Business Review* 69 (January–February 1991): pp. 102–111 and "Can Research Reinvent the Corporation?" *Harvard Business Review* 69 (March–April 1991): pp. 164–165.

25. See the work by Charles B. Perrow, "A Framework for the Comparative Analysis of Organizations," *American Sociological Review* (April 1967): pp. 194–208; and Arthur G. Bedeian, *Organizations: Theory and Analysis,* 2nd ed. (Chicago: Dryden, 1984).

26. This section on leadership and management is based largely on the ideas of John P. Kotter, "What Leaders Really Do," *Harvard Business Review* 68 (May–June 1990): pp. 103–111.

27. See Abraham Zaleznik, "Managers and Leaders: Are They Different?" *Harvard Business Review* 55 (May–June 1977): pp. 67–78.

28. For example, see Kurt Lewin, *Field Theory in Social Science* (New York: Harper & Row, 1951); Peter A. Clark, *Action Research and Organizational Change* (New York: Harper & Row, 1972); John P. Kotter and Leonard S. Schlesinger, "Choosing Strategies for Change," *Harvard Business Review* 57 (March–April 1979): pp. 106–114; and Noel M. Tichy and David O. Ulrich, "The Leadership Challenge—A Call for the Transformational Leader," *Sloan Management Review* 25 (Fall 1984): pp. 59–68.

29. See Kotter, op. cit.

30. See Karen N. Gaertner, "Winning and Losing: Understanding Managers' Reactions to Strategic Change," *Human Relations* 42 (1989): pp. 527–546.

31. See: Rosabeth Moss Kanter, *The Change Masters* (New York: Simon and Schuster, 1983); James Kouzes and Barry Posner, *The Leadership Challenge* (San Francisco: Jossey-Bass, 1987); Edward F. McDonough, III and Richard P. Leifer, "Effective Control of New Product Projects: The Interaction of Organization Culture and Project Leadership," *Journal of Product Innovation Management* 3 (September 1986): pp. 149–157; and Gloria Barczak and David Wilemon, "Leadership Differences in New Product Development Teams," *Journal of Product Innovation Management* 6 (December 1989): pp. 259–267.

32. See Kotter, op. cit., p. 107.

33. See Kotter, op. cit.

34. See Erik W. Larson and David H. Gobeli, "Organizing for Product Development Projects," *Journal of Product Innovation Management* 5 (September 1988): pp. 180–190.

Chapter 5
The Ongoing Process of New Product Development

1. The Gavilan case materials used throughout this chapter were adopted from: Corey Sandler, "A Textbook Case: The Rise and Fall of Gavilan Computer," *PC Week* (May 14, 1985): pp. 135+; and "Two Lessons in Failure from Silicon Valley," *BusinessWeek* (September 10, 1984): pp. 78+.

2. Several authors refer to a core product concept as a *product concept,* a *core product,* or a *core benefit proposition.* See Kim B. Clark and Takahiro Fujimoto, "The Power of Product Integrity," *Harvard Business Review* 68 (November–December 1990): pp. 107–118; Philip Kotler, *Marketing Management,* 7th ed. (Englewood Cliffs, NJ: Prentice-Hall, 1991); and Glen L. Urban and John R. Hauser, *Design and Marketing of New Products* (Englewood Cliffs, NJ: Prentice-Hall, 1980).

3. For a more comprehensive description of this case study, see Clark and Fujimoto, op. cit.

4. For additional information on the relationship between product design and manufacturability, see James W. Dean and Gerald I. Sussman, "Organizing for Manufacturable Design," *Harvard Business Review* 67 (January–February 1989): pp. 28–36+; and Daniel E. Whitney, "Manufacturing by Design," *Harvard Business Review* 66 (July–August 1988): pp. 83–91. However, as noted in the following article, care should be taken in evaluating the tradeoff between

lower costs and longer cycle time in design for manufacturing: Karl Ulrich, David Sartorius, Scott Pearson, and Mark Jakiela, "Including the Value of Time in Design-for-Manufacturing Decision Making," *Management Science* 39 (April 1993): pp. 429–447. For a review of the broader issues and underlying concept of manufacturing *flexibility,* see Donald Gerwin, "Manufacturing Flexibility: A Strategic Perspective," *Management Science* 39 (April 1993): pp. 395–410.

5. For a more comprehensive description of the *sequential* new product development process, see the booklet *New Product Management for the 1980's* (New York: Booz-Allen & Hamilton Inc., 1982).

6. The description of QFD and the house of quality in this section are based on the excellent presentation provided in John R. Hauser and Don Clausing, "The House of Quality," *Harvard Business Review* 66 (May–June 1988): pp. 63–73. For a discussion of consumer measurement techniques used in this approach, see Abbie Griffin and John R. Hauser, "The Voice of the Customer," *Marketing Science* 12 (Winter 1993): pp. 1–27.

7. For detailed results of this study, see Abbie Griffin, "Evaluating QFD's Use in U.S. Firms as a Process for Developing Products," *Journal of Product Innovation Management* 9 (September 1992): pp. 171–187.

8. The idea of *holistic* new product development is presented in Hirotaka Takeuchi and Ikujiro Nonaka, "The New New Product Development Game," *Harvard Business Review* 64 (January–February 1986): pp. 137–146.

9. Takeuchi and Nonaka, op. cit.

10. This case study is based on G. Pascal Zachary, "Theocracy of Hackers' Rules Autodesk Inc., A Strangely Run Firm," *The Wall Street Journal* (May 28, 1992): pp. A1+.

11. For a highly readable overview of chaos, see James Gleick, *Chaos: Making a New Science* (New York: Viking Penguin, Inc., 1987).

12. For a discussion of the effectiveness of teams for new product development and for alternate organizational concepts involving teams and clusters to improve effectiveness, see, respectively, Steven C. Wheelwright and Kim B. Clark, *Revolutionizing Product Development* (New York: Free Press, 1992) and D. Quinn Mills, *Rebirth of the Corporation* (New York: John Wiley & Sons, 1991).

13. Reported in the pamphlet *New Product Management for the 1980's* (New York: Booz-Allen & Hamilton Inc., 1982).

14. This study is reported in detail in Eric von Hippel, *The Sources of Innovation* (Oxford: Oxford University Press, 1988).

15. See Leonard J. Parsons, "Product Design," in W. Henry, M. Menasco and H. Takada, eds., *New Product Development and Testing* (Lexington, MA: Lexington Books, 1989), pp. 51–75.

16. For a review of creativity issues in business, see John J. Kao, *Managing Creativity* (Englewood Cliffs, NJ: Prentice-Hall, 1991).

17. The material in this paragraph on NCR Corporation's approach to design is provided in the pamphlet *The Search for Design Excellence* (Dayton, OH: NCR Corporation Industrial Design Center, 1992).

18. Based on the following report by Georgetown MBA students: Jennifer Givens and James Kyle Lynch, "MCI Friends and Family: A New Product Success Story" (Washington, DC: Georgetown University, 1992).

Chapter 6
Building a New Product Decision Support System

1. The short case study of Beecham Product's Delicare draws from the following sources: Matt Rothman, "A Case of Malpractice—in Marketing Research?" *BusinessWeek* (August 10, 1987): pp. 28+; Jack Honomichl, "How Beecham Suit Affects Contracts," *Advertising Age* (August 17, 1987): pp. 23+; Annetta Miller and Dody Tsiantar, "A Test for Market Research," *Newsweek* (December

28, 1987): pp. 32–33; and Judann Dagnoli, "Beecham, Yankelovich Settle Lawsuit Centering on Research for Delicare," *Advertising Age* (August 29, 1988): p. 63.

2. For a conceptualization of marketing decision support systems and the importance of market response, see John D. C. Little, "Decision Support Systems for Marketing Managers," *Journal of Marketing* 43 (Summer 1979): pp. 9–26. For an overview of decision support systems in general, see Peter G. W. Keen and Michael S. Scott Morton, *Decision Support Systems: An Organizational Perspective* (Reading, MA: Addison-Wesley, 1978).

3. Vijay Mahajan and Jerry Wind, "New Product Models: Practice, Shortcomings, and Desired Improvements," *Journal of Product Innovation Management* 9 (June 1992): pp. 128–139.

4. William B. Gartner and Robert J. Thomas, "Factors Affecting New Product Forecasting Accuracy in New Firms," *Journal of Product Innovation Management* 10 (January 1993): pp. 35–52.

5. The decision calculus approach discussed here is described by John D. C. Little, "Models and Managers: The Concept of a Decision Calculus," *Management Science* 16 (April 1970): pp. B466-B485. For a review of applications, see Leonard M. Lodish, "Experience with Decision-Calculus Models and Decision Support Systems," in R. L. Schultz and A. A. Zoltners, eds., *Marketing Decision Models* (New York: North Holland, 1981), pp. 165–182. For a review and description of more traditional new product models, see Yoram Wind, Vijay Mahajan, and Richard N. Cardozo, eds., *New Product Forecasting* (Lexington, MA: Lexington Books, 1981).

6. The definition and criteria are drawn from Little, op. cit.

7. For excellent coverage of a variety of marketing models, see Gary L. Lilien, Philip Kotler, and K. Sridhar Moorthy, *Marketing Models* (Englewood Cliffs, NJ: Prentice-Hall, 1992).

8. For additional examples of the complexities of new product decision problems associated with breakthrough products, see Shelby H. McIntyre, "Market Adaptation as a Process in the Product Life Cycle of Radical Innovations and High Technology Products," *Journal of Product Innovation Management* 5 (June 1988): pp. 140–149.

9. This example draws from Judann Dagnoli, "How Stouffer's Right Course Veered Off Course," *Advertising Age* (May 6, 1991): p. 34.

10. This discussion of the benefits of decomposition in forecasting draws from Scott Armstrong, *Long-Range Forecasting: From Crystal Ball to Computer,* 2nd ed. (New York: John Wiley, 1985), pp. 57–61.

11. Hal R. Arkes and Kenneth R. Hammond, eds., *Judgment and Decision Making: An Interdisciplinary Reader* (Cambridge, England: Cambridge University Press, 1986), pp. 1–10.

12. Little, op. cit.

13. Criticism of the decision calculus approach revolves around the use of judgment: Dipankar Chakravarti, Andrew Mitchell, and Richard Staelin, "Judgment Based Marketing Decisions Models: Problems and Possible Solutions," *Journal of Marketing* 45 (Fall 1981): pp. 13–23. A defense of this approach and its use are provided by John D. C. Little and Leonard M. Lodish, "Commentary on Judgment Based Marketing Decision Models," *Journal of Marketing* 45 (Fall 1981): pp. 24–29. Both papers are recommended reading to develop a balanced perspective on this type of modeling. See also, Shelby H. McIntyre and Imran S. Currim, "Evaluating Judgment-Based Marketing Models: Multiple Measures, Comparisons, and Findings," in A. Zoltners, *Marketing Planning Models* (New York: North Holland, 1982), pp. 185–207; as well as the following book: Randall L. Schultz and Andris A. Zoltners, eds., *Marketing Decision Models* (New York: North Holland, 1981).

14. For a brief review of the Delphi method, see Joseph P. Martino, *Technological Forecasting for Decision Making* (New York: North-Holland, 1983), Chapter 2. For additional views and applications, see Harold A. Linstone and Murray Turoff, eds., *The Delphi Method: Techniques and Applications* (Reading, MA: Addison-Wesley, 1975).

15. This section and the example are based on Yoram Wind and Thomas L. Saaty, "Marketing Applications of the Analytical Hierarchy Process," *Management Science* 26 (July 1980): pp. 641–658.

16. See Robin M. Hogarth and Spyros Makridakis, "Forecasting and Planning: An Evaluation," *Management Science* 27 (February 1981): pp. 115–138; and Tyzoon T. Tyebjee, "Behavioral Biases in New Product Forecasting," *International Journal of Forecasting* 3 (1987): pp. 393–404.

17. Dedre Gentner, "Structure Mapping: A Theoretical Framework for Analogy," *Cognitive Science* 7 (2, 1983): pp. 155–170.

18. For discussions and examples of various marketing research methods, see Paul E. Green and Donald S. Tull, *Research for Marketing Decisions*, 3rd ed. (Englewood Cliffs, NJ: Prentice-Hall, 1978); or Donald R. Lehmann, *Marketing Research and Analysis*, 3rd ed. (Homewood, IL: Irwin, 1989). For a brief overview of marketing research topics and issues, see Vincent P. Barabba, "The Market Research Encyclopedia," *Harvard Business Review* 68 (January–February 1990): pp. 105–116.

19. Gartner and Thomas, op. cit.

20. For an in-depth discussion of this case study, see Robert J. Thomas, "Problems in Demand Estimation for a New Technology," *Journal of Product Innovation Management* 2 (September 1985): pp. 145–157.

21. See Andris A. Zoltners, "Normative Marketing Models," in *Marketing Decision Models*, R. Schultz and A. Zoltners, eds. (New York: North Holland, 1981), pp. 55–76.

22. See Rajeev Kohli and R. Sukumar, "Heuristics for Product-Line Design Using Conjoint Analysis," *Management Science* 36 (December 1990): pp. 1464–1478.

23. For brief descriptions of other useful heuristics, see Zoltners, op. cit.

24. For a discussion of one approach to optimizing product design, see Paul E. Green, J. Douglas Carroll, and Stephen M. Goldberg, "A General Approach to Product Design Optimization Via Conjoint Analysis," *Journal of Marketing* 45 (Summer 1981): pp. 17–37.

25. See Kohli and Sukumar; and Paul E. Green and Abba M. Krieger, "A Consumer-Based Approach to Designing Product Line Extensions," *Journal of Product Innovation Management* 4 (March 1987): pp. 21–32.

Chapter 7
Estimating Market Opportunity for New Products

1. The discussion of HDTV in this chapter is based upon numerous sources, including: Otis Port et al., "Super Television," *BusinessWeek* (January 30, 1989): pp. 56+; Richard Ernsberger, Jr. et al., "The Race for HDTV," *BusinessWeek* (December 16, 1991): pp. 66–67; Bob Davis, "FCC's Proposal for HDTV May Restrict Broadcasters," *The Wall Street Journal* (April 10, 1992): pp. B1+; Mark Lewyn et al., "HDTV Homes In On the Ultimate Test: The Market," *BusinessWeek* (April 27, 1992): pp. 108–109; Robert L. Rose, "How U.S. Firms Passed Japan in Race to Create Advanced Television," *The Wall Street Journal* (July 20, 1992): pp. A1+; Gary McWilliams, "This HDTV Pioneer Sees a Better Way," *BusinessWeek* (August 31, 1992): pp. 62+; Robert L. Rose, "Zenith Faces Liquidity Crunch in Wake of Price Wars," *The Wall Street Journal* (November 11, 1992): p. B4; Jeffrey A. Trachtenberg, "High-Definition TV Has Networks, Outlets Worried About Costs," *The Wall Street Journal* (November 11, 1992): pp. A1+; and Mark Lewyn and Lois Therrien, "Sweating Out the HDTV Contest," *BusinessWeek* (February 22, 1993): pp. 92+.

2. For an excellent overview of HDTV and an evaluation of demand forecasts using a diffusion modeling methodology, see Barry L. Bayus, "High Definition Television: Assessing Demand Forecasts for a Next Generation Consumer Durable," *Management Science*, forthcoming, 1993.

3. For an overview of various concepts of market demand, see Philip Kotler, *Marketing Management: Analysis, Planning, Implementation, and Control* (Englewood Cliffs, NJ: Prentice-Hall, 7th ed., 1991), Chapter 9. See also: William R. King, "Estimating Market Potential," in *Handbook of Marketing Research*, ed. R. Ferber (New York: McGraw Hill, 1974), pp. 4.3–4.16; and Brian C. Twiss, "Forecasting Market Size and Market Growth Rate for New Products," *Journal of Product Innovation Management* 1 (January 1984): pp. 19–29.

4. Although it is possible and often important to consider the relationship between multiple controllable variables and multiple response variables, for purposes of illustration, bivariate response functions are considered here.

5. For an early application that illustrates cross-impact analysis, see T. J. Gordon and H. Hayward, "Initial Experiments with the Cross Impact Matrix Method of Forecasting," *Futures* 1 (December 1968): pp. 100–116.

6. For a readable overview of traditional scenario analysis, including numerous references, see Steven P. Schnaars, "How to Develop and Use Scenarios," *Long Range Forecasting* 20 (February 1987): pp. 105–114.

7. See Paul R. Warshaw, "Predicting Purchase and Other Behaviors from General and Contextually Specific Intentions," *Journal of Marketing Research* 17 (February 1980): pp. 26–33.

8. For an overview of environmental simulations, see John E. G. Bateson and Michael K. Hui, "The Ecological Validity of Photographic Slides and Videotapes in Simulating the Service Setting," *Journal of Consumer Research* 19 (September 1992): pp. 271–281.

9. See Bateson and Hui, op. cit. and Peter Bosselmann and Kenneth H. Craik, "Perceptual Simulations of Environments," in *Methods in Environmental and Behavioral Research* eds. R. Bechtel, et al. (New York: Van Nostrand Reinhold, 1987), pp. 162–190.

10. Information acceleration is described in John R. Hauser, Glen L. Urban, and Bruce Weinberg, "Time Flies When You're Having Fun: How Consumers Allocate Their Time When Evaluating Products," (Cambridge, MA: Massachusetts Institute of Technology, Working Paper #68-92, International Center for Research on The Management of Technology, 1992).

11. Hauser, Urban, and Weinberg, op. cit.

12. Hauser, Urban, and Weinberg, op. cit.

13. See Raymond Serafin, "How To Plug Electric Cars," *Advertising Age* (January 11, 1993): p. 12.

14. For various approaches and viewpoints on idea screening, see: Kenneth G. Baker and Gerald S. Albaum, "Modeling New Product Screening Decisions," *Journal of Product Innovation Management* 3 (March 1986): pp. 32–39; Ulrike D. Brentani, "Do Firms Need a Custom-Designed New Product Screening Model," *Journal of Product Innovation Management* 3 (June 1986): pp. 108–119; and Robert G. Cooper, "Selecting Winning New Product Projects: Using the NewProd System," *Journal of Product Innovation Management* 2 (March 1985): pp. 34–44.

15. For a brief readable overview of expert systems, see Kenneth Fordyce, Peter Norden, and Gerald Sullivan, "Review of Expert Systems for the Management Science Practitioner," *Interfaces* 17 (March–April 1987): pp. 64–77. For the description of a specific application to new product idea screening, see Sundaresan Ram and Sudha Ram, "Expert Systems: An Emerging Technology for Selecting New Product Winners," *Journal of Product Innovation Management* 6 (June 1989): pp. 89–98. For an application to advertising and an overview of key issues on expert systems, see Raymond R. Burke, Arvind Rangaswamy, Jerry Wind, and Jehoshua Eliashberg, "A Knowledge-Based System for Advertising Design," *Marketing Science* 9 (Summer 1990): pp. 212–229.

16. See Todd D. Jick, "Mixing Quantitative and Qualitative Methods: Triangulation in Action," *Administrative Science Quarterly* 24 (December 1979): pp. 602–611.

17. This case study and the illustration of a multiple methods approach are described in greater detail in Robert J. Thomas, "Forecasting New Product Market Potential," *Journal of Product Innovation Management* 4 (June 1987): pp. 109–119.

18. See *Implications of Electronic Mail and Message Systems for the U.S. Postal Service* (Washington, DC: Office of Technology Assessment, 1982).

19. For a review of the literature on combining forecasts, see Robert T. Clemen, "Combining Forecasts: A Review and Annotated Bibliography," *International Journal of Forecasting* 5 (1989): pp. 559–583.

20. In the following study of sales forecasting with historical data, gains in accuracy after five to six methods began to decline rapidly: Spyros Makridakis and Robert L. Winkler, "Averages of Forecasts: Some Empirical Results," *Management Science* 29 (September 1983): pp. 987–996. The following study involving judgmental methods (widely used in new product forecasting) found satisfactory accuracy in combining two and three forecasts: Alison H. Ashton and Robert H. Ashton, "Aggregating Subjective Forecasts: Some Empirical Results," *Management Science* 31 (December 1985): pp. 1499–1508.

21. See Anthony E. Bopp, "On Combining Forecasts: Some Extensions and Results," *Management Science* 31 (December 1985): pp. 1492–1498; and Murphy A. Sewall, "Relative Information Contributions of Consumer Purchase Intentions and Management Judgement as Explanators of Sales," *Journal of Marketing Research* 18 (May 1981): pp. 249–253.

22. Clemen, op. cit.

23. See Frank M. Bass, "A New Product Growth Model for Consumer Durables," *Management Science* 15 (January 1969): pp. 215–227; and Everett M. Rogers, *Diffusion of Innovations* (New York: The Free Press, 1983).

24. Excellent reviews of diffusion literature are provided by the following: Vijay Mahajan, Eitan Muller, and Frank M. Bass, "New Product Diffusion Models in Marketing: A Review and Directions for Research," *Journal of Marketing* 43 (January 1990): pp. 1–26; Vijay Mahajan and Robert A. Peterson, *Models for Innovation Diffusion* (Beverly Hills, CA: Sage Publications, Inc., 1985); and Vijay Mahajan and Eitan Muller, "Innovation Diffusion and New Product Growth Models in Marketing," *Journal of Marketing* 43 (Fall 1979): pp. 55–68. For an important study of methodological considerations in using the diffusion model, see Roger M. Heeler and Thomas P. Hustad, "Problems in Predicting New Product Growth for Consumer Durables," *Management Science* 26 (October 1980): pp. 1007–1020.

25. Bass, op. cit. The model combined the separate innovative and imitative effects of two earlier models, respectively: Louis A. Fourt and Joseph W. Woodlock, "Early Prediction of Market Success for New Grocery Products," *Journal of Marketing* 24 (October 1960): pp. 31–38; and Edwin Mansfield, "Technical Change and the Rate of Imitation," *Econometrica* 29 (October 1961): pp. 741–765.

26. See James S. Coleman, Elihu Katz, and Herbert Menzel, *Medical Innovation: A Diffusion Study* (Indianapolis: Bobbs-Merrill, 1966).

27. Equation [7.4] can be restated as a second-degree polynomial with respect to Cum_t, and by using historical data and ordinary least squares regression, the parameters **Pot**, **Ino**, and **Imi** can be estimated. For a more in-depth evaluation of ordinary least squares as an estimation procedure (versus nonlinear estimation and so on), see Vijay Mahajan, Charlotte H. Mason, and V. Srinivasan, "An Evaluation of Estimation Procedures for New Product Diffusion Models," in *Innovation Diffusion Models of New Product Acceptance*, eds. V. Mahajan and Y. Wind (Cambridge, MA: Ballinger, 1986), pp. 203–232.

28. For additional discussion of using a dynamic interpretation of market potential in the diffusion model, see Vijay Mahajan and Robert A. Peterson, "Innovation Diffusion in a Dynamic Potential Adopter Population," *Management Science* 24 (November 1978): pp. 1589–1597; and Shlomo Kalish, "A New Product Adoption Model With Pricing, Advertising, and Uncertainty," *Management Science* 31 (December 1985): pp. 1569–1585.

29. See Fareena Sultan, John U. Farley, and Donald R. Lehmann, "A Meta-Analysis of Applications of Diffusion Models," *Journal of Marketing Research* 27 (February 1990): pp. 70–77. In this study, a meta-analysis of coefficients from some 213 applications of diffusion models to a variety of products and services produced an average value of $Ino' = .03$ and $Imi' = .38$. With no other basis for establishing these values, they represent a starting point for an analogical diffusion model. However, care should be taken in blindly accepting these specific values, because the research showed that differences in the coefficients across culture, by type of innovation, and by estimation method can be significant.

30. Note that if it is believed that certain factors are relatively more important than others, they can be weighted accordingly. Further, *potential buyer* evaluations of similarity can also be developed. See Robert J. Thomas, "Estimating Market Growth for New Products: An Analogical Diffusion Model Approach," *Journal of Product Innovation Management* 2 (March 1985): pp. 45–55. For additional research on using product analogies, see Bayus, op. cit. and Christopher J. Easingwood, "An Analogical Approach to the Long Term Forecasting of Major New Product Sales," *International Journal of Forecasting* 5 (1989), pp. 69–82.

31. See William B. Gartner and Robert J. Thomas, "Factors Affecting New Product Forecasting Accuracy in New Firms," *Journal of Product Innovation Management* 10 (January 1993): pp. 35–52.

32. For an overview of research on these issues and an empirical study, see Barry L. Bayus, "Have Diffusion Rates Been Accelerating Over Time?" *Marketing Letters* 3 (July 1992): pp. 215–226.

33. For a more comprehensive review of the issues related to diffusion models in general, see Mahajan, Muller, and Bass, op. cit.

34. See Barry L. Bayus, "Forecasting Sales of New Contingent Products: An Application of the Compact Disc Market," *Journal of Product Innovation Management* 4 (December 1987): pp. 243–255.

Chapter 8
New Product Sales Forecasting

1. This case study is based upon an actual situation in the early 1980s. Though much of the data is disguised, it does not detract from presenting the basic process involved in sales forecasting and new product development.

2. See the discussion in Chapter 5 on the importance of core product concept *integrity* throughout the development process.

3. For some practical insights into the development of new product concepts, see David Schwartz, *Concept Testing* (New York: Amacom, 1987).

4. The intent translation and weighting models used here are based on Glen L. Urban and John R. Hauser, *Design and Marketing of New Products* (Englewood Cliffs, NJ: Prentice-Hall, 1980); and Linda F. Jamieson and Frank M. Bass, "Adjusting Stated Intention Measures to Predict Trial Purchase of New Products: A Comparison of Models and Methods," *Journal of Marketing Research* 26 (August 1989): pp. 336–345.

5. Jamieson and Bass, op. cit.

6. The development of models that hypothesize a relationship between *true* and *stated* intention to buy with assumptions about the distributions of these variables has been promising, but they require actual purchase data (or experience with similar products) to parameterize. See, for example, Donald G. Morrison, "Purchase Intentions and Purchase Behavior," *Journal of Marketing* 43 (Spring 1979): pp. 65–74; Manohar U. Kalwani and Alvin J. Silk, "On the Reliability and Predictive Validity of Purchase Intention Measures," *Marketing Science* 1 (Summer 1982): pp. 243–286; and Jamieson and Bass, op. cit.

7. For further consideration of the issues raised in this section, see the program of research represented in the following papers: Vicki G. Morwitz and David Schmittlein, "Using Segmentation to Improve Sales Forecasts Based on Purchase Intent: Which 'Intenders' Actually Buy?" *Journal of Marketing Research* 29 (November 1992): pp. 391–405; Vicki G. Morwitz, Eric Johnson, and David Schmittlein, "Does Measuring Intent Change Behavior?" *Journal of Consumer Research* 20 (June 1993): pp. 46–61; and Vicki G. Morwitz, "The Predictive Validity of Timed Intent Measures: When Will I Buy My Next Car?" (New York University, Stern School of Business Working Paper #MARK-92-13), July 1992. For a discussion of risk in using intention-to-buy scales for decision making, see Haim Levy and Chezy Ofir, "New Product Screening Via the Intention-To-Buy Scale," *Decision Sciences* 17 (1986): pp. 65–78.

8. In addition to marketing research textbooks, for a valuable guide to multidimensional scaling procedures for evaluating market structure, see Paul E. Green, Frank J. Carmone, Jr., and Scott M. Smith, *Multidimensional Scaling* (Boston: Allyn and Bacon, 1989). A variety of approaches to construct perceptual maps (like the one illustrated in Figure 8.3) are reviewed, along with guidelines for their interpretation and use.

9. The individual level variables defining potential buyer behavior were reviewed in Chapter 3 and conceptually summarized in Figure 3.1.

10. For a review of these approaches, see Glen L. Urban and John R. Hauser, *Design and Marketing of New Products* (Englewood Cliffs, NJ: Prentice-Hall, 1980), Chapter 10. Early influential papers in this area include Paul E. Green and Vithala R. Rao, "Conjoint Measurement for Quantifying Judgmental Data," *Journal of Marketing Research* 8 (August 1971): pp. 355–363; and Allan D. Shocker and V. Srinivasan, "A Consumer-Based Methodology for the Identification of New Product Ideas," *Management Science* 20 (February 1974): pp. 921–937. For a review of the multiattribute value analysis procedure, also applied to automated test equipment, see Ralph L. Keeney and Gary L. Lilien, "New Industrial Product Design and Evaluation Using Multiattribute Value Analysis," *Journal of Product Innovation Management* 4 (September 1987): pp. 185–198.

11. See R. Duncan Luce and John W. Tukey, "Simultaneous Conjoint Measurement: A New Type of Fundamental Measurement," *Journal of Mathematical Psychology* 1 (February 1964): pp. 1–27.

12. Conjoint analysis was introduced to marketing research by Green and Rao, op. cit. For a managerial overview, see Paul E. Green and Yoram Wind, "New Ways to Measure Consumers' Judgments," *Harvard Business Review* 53 (July–August 1975): pp. 107–117. For a study that shows the extensive use of conjoint analysis, see Dick R. Wittink and Philippe Cattin, "Commercial Use of Conjoint Analysis: An Update," *Journal of Marketing* 53 (July 1989): pp. 91–96.

13. For a review of alternative models of utility, see Paul E. Green and Yoram Wind, *Multiattribute Decisions in Marketing* (Hinsdale, IL: Dryden Press, 1973).

14. The use of experimental procedures in defining conjoint product concepts can be found in Paul E. Green, "On the Design of Choice Experiments Involving Multifactor Alternatives," *Journal of Consumer Research* 1 (September 1974): pp. 61–68.

15. Most personal computer software packages that perform conjoint analyses typically include a module that assists in the determination of fractional factorial designs.

16. It is customary to include one or more *holdout* concept descriptions to ascertain whether or not their original evaluation can be predicted from the conjoint analysis results. If a large proportion of these holdout concepts can be predicted, then one has greater confidence in the results.

17. See Paul E. Green and Abba M. Krieger, "Segmenting Markets With Conjoint Analysis," *Journal of Marketing* 55 (October 1991): pp. 20–31; and Arch G. Woodside and William G. Pearce, "Testing Market Segment Acceptance of New Designs of Industrial Services," *Journal of Product Innovation Management* 6 (September 1989): pp. 185–201.

18. The major issues raised in this section are based on: Paul E. Green and V. Srinivasan, "Conjoint Analysis in Consumer Research: Issues and Outlook," *Journal of Consumer Research* 5 (September 1978): pp. 103–123; and Paul E. Green and V. Srinivasan, "Conjoint Analysis in Marketing: New Developments With Implications for Research and Practice," *Journal of Marketing* 54 (October 1990): pp. 3–19.

19. See Joel Huber, Dick R. Wittink, John A. Fiedler, and Richard Miller, "The Effectiveness of Alternative Preference Elicitation Procedures in Predicting Choice," *Journal of Marketing Research* 30 (February 1993): pp. 105–114.

20. For a review of hybrid conjoint models, see Paul E. Green, "Hybrid Models for Conjoint Analysis: An Expository Review," *Journal of Marketing Research* 21 (May 1984): pp. 155–169. For a description of adaptive conjoint analysis, see Richard M. Johnson, "Adaptive Conjoint Analysis,"

in *Sawtooth Conference on Perceptual Mapping, Conjoint Analysis, and Computer Interviewing* (Ketchum, Idaho: Sawtooth Software, 1987), pp. 253–265.

21. See Dick R. Wittink, Lakshman Krishnamurthi, and David J. Reibstein, "The Effect of Differences in the Number of Attribute Levels on Conjoint Results," *Marketing Letters* 1 (June 1990): pp. 113–123.

22. See Green and Srinivasan, op. cit.

23. For reviews of Bretton-Clark's personal computer conjoint software, see Paul E. Green, "Conjoint Analyzer," *Journal of Marketing Research* 24 (August 1987): pp. 327–329; and Gerald Albaum and Frank Carmone, "Conjoint Linmap," *Journal of Marketing Research* 28 (February 1991): pp. 117–119. See also Paul E. Green, "CONSURV: Conjoint Analysis Software," *Journal of Marketing Research* 29 (August 1992): pp. 387–390.

24. For a more formal presentation of the various choice rules discussed in this section, especially the choice rules based on max-utility, BTL choice probabilities, and logit choice probabilities, see Green and Krieger, op. cit.

25. Another approach to resolve the choice rule problem is to develop an algorithm that evaluates a variety of choice rules (and their parameters) according to some criterion (for example, actual market shares of competitive products in the choice set). For a description of this approach, see Paul E. Green and Abba M. Krieger, "Product Design Strategies for Target-Market Positioning," *Journal of Product Innovation Management* 8 (September 1991): pp. 189–202.

26. For a more complete discussion of market segmentation with conjoint results, see Green and Krieger, op. cit.

27. "Marketers have handled competitive behavior in three ways: (1) by ignoring it, (2) through the judgmental-model approach, and (3) through the reaction matrix approach." The source of this quote and an overview of how competition has been modeled can be found in Gary L. Lilien, Philip Kotler, and K. Sridhar Moorthy, *Marketing Models* (Englewood Cliffs, NJ: Prentice-Hall, 1992), pp. 538–542.

28. For a variety of different applications of product optimization (and optimizing algorithms), see Paul E. Green, J. Douglas Carroll, and Stephen M. Goldberg, "A General Approach to Product Design Optimization Via Conjoint Analysis," *Journal of Marketing* 45 (Summer 1981): pp. 17–37; Rajeev Kohli and Ramesh Krishnamurti, "A Heuristic Approach to Product Design," *Management Science* 33 (December 1987): 1523–1533; D. Sudharshan, Jerrold H. May, and Allan D. Shocker, "A Simulation Comparison of Methods for New Product Location," *Marketing Science* 6 (Spring 1987): pp. 182–207; and Fred S. Zufryden, "A Conjoint Measurement-Based Approach for Optimal New Product Design and Market Segmentation," in *Analytic Approaches to Product and Market Planning*, ed. A. Shocker (Cambridge, MA: Marketing Science Institute, 1977), pp. 100–114.

Chapter 9
New Product Financial Control

1. For further development of the financial concepts discussed in this section, see Stephen A. Ross, Randolph W. Westerfield, and Jeffrey Jaffe, *Corporate Finance*, 3rd ed. (Homewood, IL: Irwin, 1993).

2. For an overview of the inclusion of risk in complex decisions, see David B. Hertz and Howard Thomas, *Risk Analysis and its Applications* (New York: John Wiley & Sons, 1983).

3. This example is developed in Hertz and Thomas, ibid.

4. See Philip Kotler, *Marketing Decision Making: A Model Building Approach* (New York: Holt, Rinehart, and Winston, 1971), chapter 10; and Glen L. Urban and John R. Hauser, *Design and Marketing of New Products* (Englewood Cliffs, NJ: Prentice-Hall, 1980), chapter 15.

5. Although not developed here, this type of *go/no-go* decision making can also be recast in the traditional capital-asset pricing model discussed in Ross, Westerfield, and Jaffe, op. cit.

Because other criteria can also drive new product development decisions, comparing new product projects and securities in their markets may not be feasible, although the information from such a comparison may be helpful to put the new product project in perspective with a firm's total asset portfolio.

6. Variations on the risk-return chart, along with examples, are discussed in: Kotler, op. cit.; Urban and Hauser, op. cit.; and Richard N. Cardozo and Jerry Wind, "Risk Return Approach to Product Portfolio Strategy," *Long Range Planning* 18 (April 1985): pp. 77–85.

7. Discussions of estimating the value of information can be found in most basic marketing research textbooks.

8. For a broader discussion of product and strategic business unit portfolios, see Yoram Wind and Vijay Mahajan, "Designing Product and Business Portfolios," *Harvard Business Review* 59 (January–February 1981): pp. 155–165.

9. The idea of activity-based costing discussed in this paragraph is based on Robin Cooper and Robert S. Kaplan, "Measure Costs Right: Make the Right Decisions," *Harvard Business Review* 66 (September–October 1988): pp. 96–103. See also Robert S. Kaplan and H. Thomas Johnson, *Relevance Lost: The Rise and Fall of Management Accounting* (Boston: Harvard Business School Press, 1987).

10. See Derek F. Abell and John S. Hammond, *Strategic Market Planning* (Englewood Cliffs, NJ: Prentice-Hall 1979); William W. Alberts, "The Experience Curve Doctrine Reconsidered," *Journal of Marketing* 53 (July 1989): pp. 36–49; and Louis E. Yelle, "The Learning Curve: Historical Review and Comprehensive Survey," *Decision Sciences* 10 (April 1979): pp. 302–328.

11. Abell and Hammond, op. cit.

12. Alberts, op. cit.

13. See Murray R. Millson, S. P. Raj, and David Wilemon, "A Survey of Major Approaches for Accelerating New Product Development," *Journal of Product Innovation Management* 9 (March 1992): pp. 53–69; Vincent A. Mabert, John F. Muth, and Roger W. Schmenner, "Collapsing New Product Development Times: Six Case Studies," *Journal of Product Innovation Management* 9 (September 1992): pp. 200–212; Milton D. Rosenau, Jr., "Faster New Product Development," *Journal of Product Innovation Management* 5 (June 1988): pp. 150–153; and Necmi Karagozoglu and Warren B. Brown, "Time-Based Management of the New Product Development Process," *Journal of Product Innovation Management* 10 (June 1993): pp. 204–215.

14. The importance of diagnosing the need to accelerate new product development in an organization, aside from the numerous prescriptions to do so, is evident in the point and counter-point interplay of the following articles: Joseph L. Bower and Thomas M. Hout, "Fast Cycle Capability for Competitive Power," *Harvard Business Review* 66 (November–December 1988): pp. 100–118; and C. Merle Crawford, "The Hidden Costs of New Product Development," *Journal of Product Innovation Management* 9 (September 1992): pp. 188–199.

15. Original ideas about product life cycles were provided by Joel Dean, "Pricing Policies for New Products," *Harvard Business Review* (November–December 1950): pp. 45–53. Hypothetical curves (sales, profit, and so on) of the pre- and post-launch life cycles of new products are illustrated by Chester R. Wasson, *Dynamic Competitive Strategy and Product Life Cycles*, rev. ed. (St. Charles: Challenge Books, 1974). The practical use of product/project life cycle measures at Hewlett-Packard is described by Charles H. House and Raymond L. Price, "The Return Map: Tracking Product Teams," *Harvard Business Review* 69 (January–February 1991): pp. 92–100. Also, see: Milton D. Rosenau, Jr., *Innovation* (Belmont, CA: Lifetime Learning Publications, 1984).

Chapter 10
Test Marketing New Products

1. This short case study is based on "How Cyanamid Prepared for Combat," *Sales and Marketing Management* (March 11, 1985): pp. 92+.

2. The development of simulated test markets was derived from early laboratory studies of consumer response to price and other marketing variables. For example, see Cycil C. Herrmann and John B. Stewart, "The Experimental Game," *Journal of Marketing* 21 (July 1957): pp. 12–30; John R. Nevin, "Laboratory Experiments for Estimating Customer Demand: A Validation Study," *Journal of Marketing Research* 11 (August 1974): pp. 261–268; Edgar A. Pessemier, "An Experimental Method for Estimating Demand," *Journal of Business* 33 (October 1960): pp. 373–383; Alan G. Sawyer, Parker M. Worthing, and Paul E. Sendak, "The Role of Laboratory Experiments to Test Marketing Strategies," *Journal of Marketing* 43 (Summer 1979): pp. 60–67.

3. This example using BASES, acronym for the Booz-Allen Sales Estimating System, is derived from Lynn Y. S. Lin, Alain Pioche, and Patrick Standen, "Estimating Sales Volume Potential for New Innovative Products With Case Histories," paper presented at the 39th ESOMAR Congress, Monte Carlo, September, 1986.

4. See Richard Kreisman, "Buy the Numbers," *INC.* (March 1985): pp. 104+.

5. This example from Campbell Soup is based on Leslie Brennan, "Meeting the Test," *Sales and Marketing Management* (March 1990): pp. 57+. For additional examples of Campbell Soup's test marketing activities, see Ed Russell, Jr., Anthony J. Adams, and Bill Boundy, "High-Tech Marketing at Campbell Soup Company," *The Journal of Consumer Marketing* 3 (Winter 1986): pp. 71–80.

6. See Alan E. Kazdin and A. Hussain Tuma, eds., *Single-Case Research Designs* (San Francisco: Jossey-Bass, Inc. 1982).

7. See John J. Keller, "GTE Sets Big Test of Pocket Phones in Tampa Bay Area," *The Wall Street Journal* (August 26, 1992): p. B2.

8. For expanded discussions of experimental research designs for test marketing, see Seymour Banks, *Experimentation in Marketing* (New York: McGraw-Hill Book Company, 1965).

9. For example, see Paul E. Green, Ronald E. Frank, and Patrick J. Robinson, "Cluster Analysis in Test Market Selection," *Management Science* 13 (April 1967): pp. B387–B400.

10. For a review of major test marketing models, see Chakravarthi Narasimhan and Subrata K. Sen, "New Product Models for Test Market Data," *Journal of Marketing* 47 (Winter 1983): pp. 11–24.

11. For selective reviews of pre–test-market models, see Vijay Mahajan and Yoram Wind, "New Product Forecasting Models: Directions for Research and Implementation," *International Journal of Forecasting* 4 (1988): pp. 341–358; and Allan D. Shocker and William G. Hall, "Pretest Market Models: A Critical Evaluation," *Journal of Product Innovation Management* 3 (June 1986): pp. 86–107.

12. As of 1993, the ASSESSOR service was called MACRO Assessor and owned by MACRO Strategies, Inc., a M/A/R/C Group Company. The estimation procedure now includes three different methods, adding *attitudinal measures of appeal* to the trial and repeat and preference models.

13. For detailed description of this model with an application, see Alvin J. Silk and Glen L. Urban, "Pre-Test-Market Evaluation of New Packaged Goods: A Model and Measurement Methodology," *Journal of Marketing Research* 15 (May 1978): pp. 171–191.

14. For discussions of model validation and user comments, respectively, see Glen L. Urban and Gerald M. Katz, "Pre-Test-Market Models: Validation and Managerial Implications," *Journal of Marketing Research* 20 (August 1983): pp. 221–234; and Glen L. Urban, Gerald M. Katz, Thomas E. Hatch, and Alvin J. Silk, "The ASSESSOR Pre-Test Market Evaluation System," *Interfaces* 13 (December 1983): pp. 38–59.

15. Urban and Katz, op. cit.

16. For a review of the difficulties of prelaunch forecasting of durables, and a model, see Glen L. Urban, John R. Hauser, and John H. Roberts, "Prelaunch Forecasting of New Automobiles," *Management Science* 36 (April 1990): pp. 401–421.

17. "The Urge to Test Market," *Sales and Marketing Management* (March 12, 1984): pp. 82+.

18. See Daniel Pearl, "UPS Plans Test of Second-Day Delivery of Documents," *The Wall Street Journal* (May 16, 1991): pp. B1+.

Chapter 11
Market Entry Decisions

1. See Peter N. Golder and Gerard J. Tellis, "Pioneer Advantage: Marketing Logic or Marketing Legend?" *Journal of Marketing Research* 30 (May 1993): pp. 158–170.

2. This short case is based on "P&G to Offer a Superabsorbent Diaper to Challenge Thinner Entry of Rival," *The Wall Street Journal* (June 9, 1992): p. B4; and Valerie Reitman, "P&G Delays Introduction of New Diaper, Giving Kimberly-Clark an Advantage," *The Wall Street Journal* (October 28, 1992): p. B10.

3. The material in this case study is based on the following references, listed by date: "Behind AT&T's Change at the Top," *BusinessWeek* (November 6, 1978): pp. 115+; "AT&T Plans to Revive Picturephone Service By Shifting Suppliers," *The Wall Street Journal* (October 10, 1983): p. 26; "Videoconferencing: No Longer Just a Sideshow," *BusinessWeek* (November 12, 1984): pp. 116+; Dennis Kneale, "AT&T Ends Televised-Meeting Service in 6 Cities, Despite '81 Plans to Expand," *The Wall Street Journal* (January 4, 1985): p. 2; Diane Lynn Kastiel, "Videoconference Vendors Tout New Solutions Orientation," *Business Marketing* (June 1986): pp. 84+; Paul B. Carroll, "Video Phones: Picture Looks Brighter at Last," *The Wall Street Journal* (August 13, 1990): pp. B1+; William M. Bulkeley, "The Videophone Era May Finally Be Near, Bringing Big Changes," *The Wall Street Journal* (March 10, 1992): pp. A1+; and John J. Keller, "AT&T Picturing Sales Increase, Cuts Price on Videophone," *The Wall Street Journal* (January 6, 1993): p. B6.

4. The discussion of Intel in this chapter is based on Robert D. Hof, "Inside Intel," *BusinessWeek* (June 1, 1992): pp. 86+; Stephanie A. Forest and Richard Brandt, "The Upstart Chip Designer That's Chipping Away at Intel," *BusinessWeek* (September 14, 1992): pp. 62+; Bradley Johnson, "Intel Puts Pentium Chip on a Pedestal," *Advertising Age*, (May 10, 1993): pp. 3+; and Kyle Pope and Stephen K. Yoder, "Computers with New Intel Chip to Make Debut Without Fanfare," *The Wall Street Journal* (May 14, 1993): pp. B1+.

5. See Robert J. Thomas, "Timing: The Key to Marketing Entry," *Journal of Consumer Marketing* 2 (Summer 1985): pp. 77–87; Gary L. Lilien and Eunsang Yoon, "The Timing of Competitive Market Entry: An Exploratory Study of New Industrial Products," *Management Science* 36 (May 1990): pp. 568–585; and William P. Putsis, Jr., "Why Put Off Until Tomorrow What You Can Do Today: Incentives and the Timing of New Product Introduction," *Journal of Product Innovation Management* 10 (June 1993): pp. 195–203.

6. This point has been effectively argued in Chaim Fershtman, Vijay Mahajan, and Eitan Muller, "Market Share Pioneering Advantage: A Theoretical Approach," *Management Science* 36 (August 1990): pp. 900–918.

7. These strategies are based on Thomas, op. cit.

8. For a review of selected studies on first-mover advantages, see Roger A. Kerin, P. Rajan Varadarajan, and Robert A. Peterson, "First-Mover Advantage: A Synthesis, Conceptual Framework, and Research Propositions," *Journal of Marketing* 56 (October 1992): pp. 33–52. Although the studies reviewed tend to support early entry advantages, the reviewers conclude that "they do not provide unequivocal evidence."

9. This material is based on the following: Robert Levy, "Innovate or Replicate?" *Dun's Review* (June 1980): pp. 87+; and "Airwick's Discovery of New Markets Pays Off," *BusinessWeek* (June 16, 1980): pp. 139+.

10. For a more complete discussion of the advantages of late market entry, see George S. Yip, "Gateways to Entry," *Harvard Business Review* 60 (September–October 1982): pp. 85–99; Marvin B. Lieberman and David B. Montgomery, "First-Mover Advantages," *Strategic Management Journal* (Summer 1988): pp. 41–58; and Golder and Tellis, op. cit.

11. See Edward F. McQuarrie, "Advertising Resonance: A Semiological Perspective," in *Interpretive Consumer Research*, ed. E. Hirschman (Provo, UT: Association for Consumer Research, 1989), pp. 97–114.

12. This discussion of marketing hype is based on Jerry Wind and Vijay Mahajan, "Marketing Hype: A New Perspective for New Product Research and Introduction," *Journal of Product Innovation Management* 4 (March 1987): pp. 43–49.

13. The situation and data presented here are disguised. The situation is described further in Robert J. Thomas, "Timing: The Key to Market Entry," *Journal of Consumer Marketing* 2 (Summer 1985): pp. 77–87.

14. See John J. Keller, "Cellular Industry Group Acts to Avert Crisis by Research Into Phones' Safety," *The Wall Street Journal* (February 1, 1993): p. B7; Bart Ziegler, "The Cellular Cancer Risk: How Real Is It?" *BusinessWeek* (February 8, 1993): pp. 94+; and Bart Ziegler, "Remember the Cellular Phone Scare?" *Business Week* (July 19, 1993): p. 83.

15. For example, see Joseph L. Bower and Thomas M. Hout, "Fast-Cycle Capability for Competitive Power," *Harvard Business Review* 88 (November–December 1988): pp. 110–118; and Preston G. Smith and Donald G. Reinertsen, *Developing Products in Half the Time* (New York: Van Nostrand Reinhold, 1991).

Chapter 12
Launching and Tracking New Product Programs

1. The case of WordPerfect® software sales forecasting is based upon their advertising campaign. WordPerfect is a registered trademark of WordPerfect Corporation. Copy from the ads is used with permission of WordPerfect Corporation. See also, G. Pascal Zachary, "WordPerfect Ships Windows Version of Software, Heating Up Competition," *The Wall Street Journal* (November 11, 1991): p. B3.

2. It is suspected that the *average* forecast may have come closer to the actual if a *trimmed* mean was used. That is, the outlier forecasts that are not possible (for example, zero and 910,620,044 units) or in which one is confident that they will not occur should be eliminated from the computation of the *average* forecast.

3. This discussion of implementation is based on Randall L. Schultz, Dennis P. Slevin, and Jeffrey K. Pinto, "Strategy and Tactics in a Process Model of Implementation," *Interfaces* 17 (May–June 1987): pp. 34–46.

4. See William B. Gartner and Robert J. Thomas, "Factors Affecting New Product Forecasting Accuracy in New Firms," *Journal of Product Innovation Management* 10 (January 1993): pp. 35–52.

5. For a detailed review of forecast accuracy measures for a time series, see J. Scott Armstrong, *Long-Range Forecasting* (New York: John Wiley & Sons, 1985).

6. For discussions of adaptive control and experimentation, see John D. C. Little, "A Model of Adaptive Control of Promotional Spending," *Operations Research* 14 (November–December 1966): pp. 1075–1098; and Yoram Wind, *Product Policy* (Reading, MA: Addison-Wesley, 1982).

7. See David A. Aaker, *Managing Brand Equity* (New York: Free Press, 1991).

Company/Brand Name Index

Name Index

Subject Index